Ecological experiments

CAMBRIDGE STUDIES IN ECOLOGY

EDITORS:

R. S. K. Barnes *University of Cambridge*
H. J. B. Birks *University of Bergen*
E. F. Connor *University of Virginia*
J. L. Harper *University College of North Wales*
R. T. Paine *University of Washington, Seattle*

ALSO IN THE SERIES

Ecological experiments

Purpose, design, and execution

NELSON G. HAIRSTON, SR.

Department of Biology
The University of North Carolina at Chapel Hill

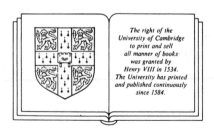

The right of the
University of Cambridge
to print and sell
all manner of books
was granted by
Henry VIII in 1534.
The University has printed
and published continuously
since 1584.

CAMBRIDGE UNIVERSITY PRESS
Cambridge
New York   Port Chester   Melbourne   Sydney

Published by the Press Syndicate of the University of Cambridge
The Pitt Building, Trumpington Street, Cambridge CB2 1RP
40 West 20th Street, New York, NY 10011, USA
10 Stamford Road, Oakleigh, Melbourne 3166, Australia

First published 1989
Reprinted 1990

Printed in the United States of America

Library of Congress Cataloging-in-Publication Data

Hairston, Nelson G.
Ecological experiments: Purpose, design, and execution / Nelson G.
Hairston.
    p.   cm.
Bibliography: p.
Includes indexes.
ISBN 0-521-34596-0. – ISBN 0-521-34692-4 (pbk.)
1. Ecology – Experiments.   I. Title.
QH541.24.H35   1989
574.5'0724 – dc19   89–979

British Library Cataloguing-in-Publication Data

Hairston, Nelson G. (Nelson George), 1917–
Ecological experiments: Purpose, design, and execution
1. Ecology, Field studies. Techniques
1. Title
574.5'0723

ISBN 0-521-34596-0 hardback
ISBN 0-521-34692-4 paperback

To the loving memory of my parents,
Peter Wilson Hairston and
Margaret Elmer George Hairston,
in grateful appreciation for their patient understanding
of my fascination with nature.

Contents

vii

Preface

The presidential address of G. C. Varley to the British Ecological Society in 1957 was entitled "Ecology as an Experimental Science." Though delivered in January, it was published in November and thus was not known to me in June, when I made a plea for ecological field experiments at the Cold Spring Harbor Symposium on Quantitative Biology. It is an irony of history that Hutchinson's "Concluding Remarks" at the symposium set off an extremely popular movement in ecology that was almost the antithesis of experimentation. Despite the widely acclaimed experiments of Connell and Paine, the method attracted few practitioners for at least fifteen years, while the ecological world stood bemused by mathematical theory as a way of explaining observations made in the field. The wave of enthusiasm was most pronounced in the United States, but it affected, and still affects, ecologists in all parts of the world, as a perusal of the journals will show.

Some of the observations did not confirm the theories, but were nevertheless claimed to do so (Roth 1981; Simberloff & Boecklen 1981). During that period, few authors considered alternative explanations for their observations, and in addition there was the danger that the confirmatory evidence was known in advance of the construction of theory. Such a sequence involves circularity, with its obvious flaws as a method of scientific procedure. Explaining data, whether verbally or through mathematics, is a legitimate method of stating hypotheses, but they remain just that until put to an a priori test.

Conducting an experiment implies testing an idea, whether the idea was stated as a conclusion or as a hypothesis, and it remains the most convincing method of preventing the test from being made after the outcome is known. True predictions constitute equally valid tests, but frequently they are "predictions" only in that they were stated to be. I am not alone in having committed this scientific sin. [See the description of Hairston (1964) in the Introduction to Chapter 1.] The pleas of 1957 were not heeded for fifteen years. I have made a survey of the journal *Ecology*, with the following results: in 1959, 3 of 90 consecutive papers (3.3%) concerned field experiments; in 1969, there were 2 of 90 (2.2%). By 1979, the figure had risen to 11 of 66 (16.7%). In the most recent complete year (1987), there were 67 papers reporting field experiments out of 190 full-length papers (35.3%). The trend has been evident across the Atlantic. For the same years, *The Journal of Animal Ecology* had the following: 1 of 25 (4%) in 1959, 3 of 41 (6.2%) in 1969, 7 of 63 (9.6%) in 1979, and 16 of 50 (32%) in 1987. The trend is not confined to animal ecologists. *The Journal of Ecology*, though less regular, showed the following: for 1959, 5 of 36 (13.9%), for 1969, 3 of 56 (5.3%), for 1979, 4 of 51 (7.8%), for 1987, 17 of 76 (22.4%). This increasing emphasis on experiments is gratifying, if belated.

It is clear that not all experimenters have paid attention to the requirements of experimental design and analysis, as was provocatively shown by Hurlbert (1984). For a number of years, I have offered courses emphasizing the appropriate ways in which to test hypotheses and have described for my students many field experiments, commenting on examples of good and poor experimental design. I have not made a quantitative analysis, but I have the subjective impression that the quality of experiments has improved greatly over the past fifteen years. It is routine now to see accounts of randomized block designs and other refinements that were virtually unknown in the ecological literature a relatively short time ago. Ecologists are now concerned over pseudoreplication, and there is even a debate about the universal application of the rules to which Hurlbert called attention. The rules are much easier to follow in laboratory experiments than in the field, and I have included discussions of only a few laboratory experiments. These involve mostly cases for which field experiments have not been devised or cases in which the results of field experiments have proved inadequate for understanding. An example is the work on decomposers described in Chapters 4 and 5. At the other extreme, there are quasi-experiments involving the results of human activity, but carried out with a nonexperimental intent. These can be revealing about ecological mechanisms. An example is provided by Edmondson's successful efforts to restore Lake Washington to its condition before the effects of sewage input were apparent (Lehman 1986). Despite their interest, it would stretch the purpose and definition of an experiment too far for them to be included.

I have used three criteria in selecting experiments to be described. I chose them to be representative of all levels of quality, as far as meeting the requirements of experimental design was concerned; I chose experiments that I felt covered interactions important to understanding the operation of the community under investigation; and I chose experiments of historical interest, in the hope of showing my readers what the original authors really did, rather than what some other reviewers said they did. I hope to persuade ecologists to read more than the abstracts of the papers they cite. Most authors meet their obligation to give a sufficient description of their methods and techniques, but abstracts are where they present their conclusions, which are rarely to their disadvantage.

A word on names is in order. Scientific names are changed frequently enough to make it impossible to keep those in this book current, covering as they do plants and animals of a great array of taxa. Even though I know some of the current names, I have retained those used by the authors of the original papers that are described here.

This book grew out of my lecture notes. Its purpose is to instruct researchers in the good and poor points in experiments that have been carried out. As I searched for representative experiments, it became clear to me that the best organization for the book, for both pedagogical and scientific reasons, was to arrange the descriptions according to the general kinds of environments in which the experiments were conducted. Anyone preparing to begin an experiment can find representative examples from most of the habitats in which work is planned, can see the problems that others have encountered, and, I hope, can avoid their mistakes.

A more cogent reason for separate chapters on the experiments in different environments is a clear message from the results. A much better and more precise understanding of ecological processes is to be obtained by confining interpretations to a single environment. No matter how we arrange the experiments (e.g., by the effect of physicochemical factors, by competition, predation, or other kind of interaction, or by trophic level), the ecological phenomena within an environment make good sense in most cases; whereas if we combine environments, the interpretation becomes much weaker. This discovery should allow us to reduce some of the complexity of ecology into manageable parts. If it means that a hypothetical "general theory of ecology" must be postponed indefinitely, so be it.

The introductory section of this book contains three chapters of a general nature, with some comments on ecological problems, the history of a few hypotheses, and the difficulties encountered by ecologists in meeting the requirements of experimental design. The second and third sections contain chapters on five distinct kinds of environments. These sections will irritate at least three classes of ecologists: those whose papers are not described, many of those whose papers are described and criticized, and those whose favorite environments have not been treated adequately. (For example, natural grasslands, savannas, and tropical forests are omitted).

Of course, the whole book will irritate ecologists who adhere to the claim that direct observations of what are sometimes called "natural experiments" are sufficient to draw conclusions about ecological phenomena. Although these observations are necessary for the construction of hypotheses, they should not be claimed to justify conclusions until the hypotheses have been put to scientifically satisfactory tests.

Because I hope that this book will contribute to the improvement of our field, I have found it necessary to be frank about the shortcomings of many experiments. The authors can be assured that nothing personal is intended, for practically all of the experiments have advanced our understanding better than could purely observational studies, many of which should have come to the conclusion that "unfortunately, the biological significance, if indeed there is any, of these results remains obscure" (Pianka 1971, p. 1028).

The last section of this book consists of a single chapter in which I use the experiments in each kind of environment to draw conclusions about the kind and strength of ecological phenomena that have been demonstrated there. A final part of the chapter suggests specific kinds of experiments for the improvement of our understanding. More experiments are needed in all of the environments covered in this book, and doubtless even more are needed in the environments that have not been covered.

Acknowledgments

I have had the benefit of perceptive comments from a number of people. John Birks and Bob Paine have helped with all chapters as they were completed. John's comments and suggestions for the passages on plant ecology are much appreciated. They educated me and forced me to consider that work more carefully than I ever had before. Besides other parts of the book, Bob helped especially with Chapter 8, which covers experiments in marine environments – locations where I have not worked. Without always suggesting changes, he wrote fascinating little essays in the margins of the manuscript. In a similar vein, Nelson Hairston, Jr. straightened things out for experiments in fresh water (Chapter 7). He, Alan Stiven, Jim Petranka, and Tommy Edmundson commented on several other chapters, much to their improvement. Alan was especially gracious about my criticism of one of his experiments. Henry Wilbur's help with the correct and incorrect application of rules concerning pseudoreplication is greatly appreciated.

Frances O'Halloran and Susan Whitfield redrew many of the illustrations. Those of lesser quality are my own. The cover illustration is the result of collaboration between Susan and me. As with the graphs, the better part is hers. Frances also drew the cover illustration for my first book, which contribution was not acknowledged there.

Along with the authors who freely gave permission to copy their figures and tables, I thank the editors and publishers of the various publications in which they originally appeared, especially the Ecological Society of America for graciously waiving their fee for the numerous figures and tables reproduced here.

1

Ecological problems and how they are approached

Introduction

Much of ecology consists in making observations and then devising plausible explanations for the observations. Because alternative explanations of the observed phenomena frequently are available, the process by which the conclusions have been reached is known as "weak inference." It is not that the conclusions are necessarily wrong; the problem is that there is little assurance that they are right, and the widespread use of the approach has led to severe criticism, from both outside and inside the field.

In principle, manipulative experiments provide a preferable alternative, because their planning requires at least an implied prediction of the outcome, and making predictions is an integral part of science. The after-the-fact explanations mentioned earlier are sometimes called "predictions" by their promulgators, but there is no assurance that the information was not available before the prediction was made. There is no implication of dishonesty. The danger is as follows: All workers in ecology have a lot of factual information about the real world, and assuming that they are interested in understanding nature, they think about how things work. It is virtually impossible to separate known facts from the thought process. The knowledge is, perhaps unconsciously, taken into account in formulating hypotheses about how nature works. Thus, when a "test" is proposed, the prior knowledge is used, and the outcome is known in advance. Such a confirmation is, of course, spurious. I have selected an example from one of my own publications (Hairston 1964). In a consideration of the relationship between species abundance distributions and trophic level, I predicted that there should be a greater variance among the abundances of terrestrial carnivores than among the abundances of the coexisting herbivores. The reasoning was that the carnivores should be affected more by competitive interactions, which would be expected to be stable and hence would lead to large differences in abundance. Herbivores, on the basis of the arguments in Hairston, Smith, and Slobodkin (1960),

1

should be affected by their respective intrinsic rates of increase, which should vary irregularly with weather conditions, involving frequent reversals. Thus, the herbivores would have less chance for long-continued trends in their respective abundances, and they were predicted to show less variance in abundance. After a tenuous series of assumptions and calculations, I presented evidence that confirmed the predictions for soil arthropods. It must be pointed out that my graduate students and I had carried out research on those organisms irregularly for thirteen years (Hairston & Byers 1954; Hairston 1959; Engelmann 1961), and much of the relevant information must have been in my mind, at least subconsciously, at the time that I made the predictions. Such lapses of rigor were common at the time, and remained largely unchallenged until the current controversy over hypothesis testing in ecology. [See the papers in Strong et al. (1984b), for example.]

Appeals are sometimes made to the complexity of nature, apparently in the hope of avoiding the rigorous thought that is required to formulate clear hypotheses, and to avoid devising proper tests to permit choices among competing hypotheses. The process of formulating clear hypotheses and devising acceptable tests, called "strong inference," was clearly described and vigorously promoted two decades ago in a famous paper by Platt (1964). An integral part of the process is planning experiments that will yield answers to the questions that are asked about nature. Some ecological questions are posed on such a broad scale and are of such complexity that satisfactory experiments have not yet been devised to answer them. Nevertheless, successful completion of many field experiments over the past twenty-five years has shown that some problems that once were considered unapproachable by experimentation have been attacked and solved.

Before considering the ecological problems that remain to be solved, we may as well admit that one person's solution is another's challenge. That is because ecologists are not in full agreement as to what is acceptable as "proof." There are some who regard at least one of the following questions as having been answered, and probably there are some who do not agree that these questions are important.

Ecological questions amenable to experimentation

All of the questions that follow have been attacked through field experiments, but few ecologists would argue that they have been answered fully. In later chapters there are descriptions and critiques of a number of these experiments. The experiments are arranged according to the various habitats in which ecologists have worked, rather than the kind of questions that follow. The reason for categorizing experiments by habitat is the hope that the arrangement will encourage an understanding of the ecological processes in each kind of setting, rather than trying to generalize over all settings. The field has not advanced to the stage where we even know if such generalizing is possible in principle.

What determines the abundance of species in nature?

This question continues to vex ecologists, despite much work on the subject since 1957, the date of the Cold Spring Harbor Symposium at which the proponents of various views vigorously aired their opinions. The stimulus for the symposium was the debate over density dependence versus density independence. One of its unfortunate aspects was that the protagonists never agreed on the terms of the debate. Both groups conceded the accuracy of the observations of the other. It was the relevance of the observations that was at stake. On the one hand, there were the plain correlations of abundance and population changes with aspects of weather (Davidson & Andrewartha 1948a,b), or the determination of the intrinsic rate of natural increase by laboratory-controlled temperature and moisture (Birch 1953). On the other hand, there were many laboratory populations showing a reasonably good fit to the logistic (the most density-dependent) model, long-term field studies showing fluctuations around a fairly constant mean, and the logical and mathematical argument that without density dependence, populations would fluctuate with increasing amplitude, eventually either going extinct or reaching completely unrealistic numbers. After the symposium, the debate was not so much settled as exhausted, and except for the exchange between Smith (1961,1963a) and Andrewartha (1963), most ecologists simply turned to other interests.

The dichotomy has been shown to be false, in that unexpected effects have been found. For example, it had been more or less assumed that the limitation of a population by its food supply automatically meant that the population was under density-dependent control. Yet Wise (1975) showed that spiders were food-limited, without their abundance being able to affect the supply of food, and Juliano (1986) reported a similar finding for scavenging carabid beetles. Filter-feeding sessile organisms in large bodies of water must frequently be in the same kind of situation.

As a result of work in the last three decades, the question is now posed in a more sophisticated manner, and we are concerned with whether density-dependent factors operate continuously or are interrupted by stochastic disturbances. Some ecologists are arguing that the disturbance itself is necessary for the stability of some ecosystems (Lewin 1986). If that is the case, we need to know the frequency of the disturbance, and especially the environmental factor that constitutes the disturbance. The dispersal phase in the life cycle seems to be especially sensitive to density-independent influences, especially when the dispersers are numerous and small and are carried passively by wind or water. Their success or failure in reaching a particular habitat has been known to determine the outcome of carefully executed experiments. For example, Paine's famous demonstration that a predatory starfish determined the composition of the community of sessile invertebrates (Paine 1966, 1974) could not be confirmed by his student Dayton (1971) because the mussels, which were the competitive dominant, failed to settle in large numbers during his study (Underwood & Denley 1984).

How important are interactions between species?

Ecological field experiments have established beyond question the fact that interspecific competition, predation, and mutualism are not rare in nature. What has not been settled is whether or not any of them, especially competition, is sufficiently pervasive to have an important effect on the dynamics and structure of assemblages of coexisting species. In two surveys of the literature that appeared almost simultaneously, Schoener (1983) and Connell (1983) reached different conclusions about the prevalence of interspecific competition, as shown by field experiments. The difference was only partly due to Connell's more restricted set of journals and years. Interpretation was more important. Connell was more rigorous in what he accepted as a satisfactory experiment, but he omitted from his analysis experiments involving an effect on one species at one time and place. As might be expected, he found interspecific competition less common than Schoener did. Schoener (1985) has reviewed the differences between the analyses, and it seems clear to me that the difference is largely related to the prior mind-sets of the two authors, Connell (1975, 1980) having moved away from an initial partiality toward the frequent occurrences of competition, and Schoener (1974, 1982) arguing strongly for their importance in ecological systems.

Mathematically derived community theory relies heavily on the assumption that interspecific competition is the primary negative interaction among species. Therefore, the question debated by Connell and Schoener is vitally important to our understanding of the sets of coexisting species that we call guilds. The term "community" is here used in its original sense to mean all organisms in an area – the living part of an ecosystem. Thus, the application of theory really applies almost exclusively to guilds, as restricted from the original proposal of Root (1967), to include by usage, if not by formal agreement, a group of taxonomically related species that presumably are competing for a common resource. The critical word here is "presumably," because even in cases where competition has been conclusively demonstrated by satisfactory experimentation, the finding is nearly always confined to fewer species than a prior choice of guild membership would dictate (Hairston 1984). Schoener (1986) has discussed the usages and defended the restrictions. I refrain from quoting his preferred term, and continue to use "guild" in the restricted sense. In no example is guild membership based on demonstrated interspecific competition among all necessary combinations of the proposed members. The existence of ecological or morphological differences has been used to justify the assumption that guilds are structured by competition among the members. But that leads to the circularity that the differences arose because competition was the force selecting for the development of the differences. Noncircular identification of guilds based on interspecific competition would be difficult; there has been no successful attempt in that direction.

Given this unsatisfactory state of affairs, our recourse must be to conduct the complete set of experiments necessary to test the postulated composition of a guild. Some authors accept the assumption that competition in the past was responsible for the differences and that therefore competition is no longer detectable. They ignore the fact that prevailing theory does not require the elimination of competition, only that it be reduced in intensity to the point where coexistence is possible. The experiments in which competition has been demonstrated have shown that it could still be detected. There have been relatively few examples in which even an approximately complete set of experiments has been carried out on all members of a proposed guild.

When predation is a relevant interaction, either with or without competition, the term "food web" is satisfactory; unlike "community," it is a term that has carried the same meaning for many years. A theory of food webs is being developed (Cohen 1978; Pimm 1982), but there is serious question that it will provide predictions of the outcomes of experiments, for a number of reasons explained by Paine (1988). It is true that both predation and competition have been demonstrated experimentally in some associations of species, but those phenomena were looked for independent of each other and independent of any unifying theory. One problem with current food-web theory is that it does not provide for competition at the lowest trophic level – an obvious shortcoming in most terrestrial ecosystems. Quantification of food-web relationships is a need that has caused difficulties in the construction of theory and has forced theoreticians to use qualitative relationships. The difficulty should be overcome by properly designed experiments.

Parasites constitute a different category, but one that is overlapping with predators. Mathematical models of their populations and those of their hosts have produced a variety of results. In some models, very regular cycles are predicted, a prediction that has been verified for some human viral diseases (Anderson & May 1979). Other kinds of parasites, with life cycles differing from those of viruses, carry quite different predictions (May 1985; Toft 1986). The rarity with which populations fluctuate cyclically in nature suggests either that they are unaffected by their parasites or that the important parasites of natural populations have some of the complex properties discussed by Toft (1986) or by Holmes and Price (1980). One example of an experimental test of the influence of a metazoan parasite on the population of its host is provided by the red grouse, *Lagopus lagopus scoticus*, and its nematode parasite *Trichostrongylus tenuis*. The parasite has been implicated in the long-term cycle of its host (A. Dobson, pers. commun.).

The natural history of mutualistic relationships has always fascinated ecologists. Only recently has mutualism been investigated quantitatively [see Addicott (1986) for a review]; its consequences for the structure and dynamics of guilds and communities are largely unknown (Schoener 1986). I predict that experimentation with mutualists will prove to be more difficult than has experimentation with competitors, whereas predator–prey systems will be intermediate in difficulty.

How important are competition, predation, and mutualism?

This question cannot be answered at present because of the uneven attention that has been paid historically to the three kinds of interaction. Competition has received the most attention, probably because of its central position in community theory. Sih et al. (1985) attempted to address this question, but their analysis misinterpreted the experiments, as far as the hypotheses of Hairston et al. (1960) are concerned, and the result is unsatisfactory. As already stated, mutualism lags far behind as a subject of experimentation.

Progress will be made in studying the relative importance of the different kinds of interaction only when experiments are planned to answer the specific question. My experiments on the salamander genus *Desmognathus* show that it is possible to obtain results in systems in which both predation and competition are operating (Hairston 1986), and the earlier work of Paine (1966, 1974) and Menge (1972) had done the same for the rocky intertidal habitat.

Do interspecific interactions affect larger ecological units than guilds?

Guilds are defined in such a way that competition is all-important within them, and although it is possible to imagine competition affecting communities of a variety of taxonomic groups, predation will be the interaction of interest where more than one trophic level is involved. Experiments have been conducted in the rocky intertidal, where it is difficult to confine the definition of a guild, a difficulty that appears to be due to the nature of the limiting resource: space on a solid substrate. The papers by Yodzis (1986) and Roughgarden (1986) analyze this situation. In terrestrial assemblages larger than guilds, there have been no attempts to separate the interspecific interactions discussed earlier from what are called "ecosystem processes" – production, consumption, and decomposition. Freshwater habitats, in contrast, have yielded important results on the interactions within entire communities. The experiments of Neill (1981, 1984), Neill and Peacock (1980), Schindler (1974), Hall, Cooper, and Werner (1970), and others are described in Chapter 7.

Do interspecific interactions determine the composition of multispecies associations, or do these mostly reflect adaptations of individual species?

This question asks whether guilds and communities are "real" or are the products of our imagination. A negative answer to the former question, or a positive answer to the latter does not necessarily imply that species interactions are of trivial importance in ecology. That would mean that we would have no a priori means of estimating what array of species would have detectable interactions. Thus, a guild would be defined as a group of species among which competition has been demonstrated. There would be no means by which we could choose a set of species before the necessary experiments were conducted. Thus, sophisticated theories could be constructed to explain the mechanisms by which such guilds function and the abundances of the species involved, but it would not be possible to predict anything about guilds not yet identified. Community ecology would be in the position it has long occupied, that of writing theory to explain what is already known. The composition of many groups "of taxonomically related species that presumably are competing for a common resource" would be at least partly determined not by the strength of interactions among them but by the adaptations of the individual species to the physical environment.

What is the expected effect of any of these ecological forces in determining the direction of natural selection?

It is frequently stated that evolutionary questions are not approachable by field experiments, despite the fact that such experiments have been carried out. It is true that it is necessary to grant a basic assumption before accepting the result of such an experiment. That assumption is that the current ecological conditions will continue to provide the selective pressures that presumably led to adaptive differences between related populations. If the differences relate to the physical environment, physiological experiments will suffice to confirm adaptive differences. Where interspecific interactions are involved, it is much more difficult to meet the necessary conditions than it is where the physical environment provides the selective pressure, because proper experiments are a prerequisite for demonstrating the existence of the interactions. The whole question of demonstrating natural selection under field conditions has recently been treated at length by Endler (1986), and it should be noted that one experiment, described in less than a page of text, constitutes his treatment of field experiments.

How would the effects of these forces differ?

The answer to this question is likely to be highly specific to the individual situation. Theoretical work in both population biology and evolutionary ecology on the effects of competition and predation (Roughgarden 1979) has given fairly straightforward distinctions of the expected differences, but Dayton (1973) showed how interpretation could change when observations were followed by experimental analysis, and my experiments with *Desmognathus* showed that what had been interpreted as the result of competition was largely the result of predation (Hairston 1986). The topic is in need of much more critical work before any generalizations can be made.

A discussion of the ways proposed to solve the problems

The questions posed earlier are much the same as those posed throughout the history of ecology. It is true that the relative emphasis placed on the different questions has shifted over the years, with recent work concentrating on interspecific interactions. There have been dramatic changes in the methods used to attack the problems. During the past decade, the use of field experiments has increased exponentially (Schoener 1983), and a longer period beginning in the mid–1960s saw the dominance of mathematical models, including the introduction of at least two new journals to handle the flood of papers (Simberloff 1983). A review of the recent literature shows that all of the methods to be discussed next are actively used at present. There is, of course, variation in emphasis among ecological journals, depending on editorial policies and the tastes of contributors.

Field observations

Ecological problems are recognized through observations made in the field, and therefore such observations are vital to the science. To become preoccupied with theory or with methodology to the exclusion of looking at nature is surely to lose contact with the world that we are trying to understand. Such preoccupation always leads to oversimplification and thus to a limited vision of how nature works. It is true, of course, that some simplification is involved in any explanation of a natural phenomenon, and if we do not seek explanations, we can scarcely be said to have a science. Therefore, most publications of ecological observations are accompanied by interpretations. The emphasis in this book is to question the extent to which natural situations can be used to interpret the processes that brought them about. Interpretations of natural situations may be correct, but frequently they have been shown to be incorrect on subsequent experimentation. Despite the popularity of direct interpretation of ecological observations throughout the history of ecology and its advocacy by prominent ecologists, there are strong theoretical objections to this use of weak inference (Peters 1976); consequently, ecological experiments have become popular, even though they are "labor intensive, time-consuming and expensive" (Rosenzweig et al. 1985, p.194).

The members of one subset of direct observations have been called "natural experiments," and their importance in interpreting ecological processes has been defended vigorously by Diamond (1986). I argue that to label natural events experiments evades the issue of why manipulative experiments are conducted, which is first to test the validity of a specific idea, and second to avoid the charge of a posteriori reasoning.

There is no question that some situations and events in nature are especially favorable for constructing hypotheses about how the compositions of certain communities were determined and about how they function. This is especially true when a significant spontaneous event occurs after the start of a study, providing the very important initial conditions: those existing before the "experiment" began. Such a phenomenon provided the basis for the size-selective predation hypothesis of Brooks and Dodson (1965). After observations had been made on the plankton community in a small lake in Connecticut, it was colonized by a planktivorous fish, *Alosa pseudoharengus*. The subsequent difference in species composition among the planktonic crustaceans stimulated Brooks and Dodson to propose their hypothesis. Even though such events increase the likelihood that their interpretations are correct, that does stretch the concept of an experiment, and it exaggerates their significance to give them that name. Nature has no stake in being understood by us, and the so-called natural experiments universally lack important elements of experimental design, topics deferred to Chapter 2.

Mathematically derived theory

Direct interpretations of nature have been bolstered in recent decades by the application of mathematics, thus giving the appearance of scientific rigor to what in principle is a more sophisticated version of the same process of explaining what has been observed. The approach has been to think how nature might work and to formulate a mathematical model of the process. This has the merit of requiring specific hypotheses and has the potential of making precise predictions. Models force their creators and users to think clearly. They also contain two inherent weaknesses. The first is that mentioned earlier: explaining what is already known. The second is their incorporation of assumptions that frequently are unjustified. This point has been made repeatedly, especially with respect to the most widely used ecological model, the logistic equation [see discussions by Smith (1952) and Andrewartha & Birch (1954)]. It should be appreciated that much subsequent mathematical theory, such as the Lotka–Volterra competition equations, the community matrix (Levins 1968) and niche partitioning theory (MacArthur & Levins 1967; Roughgarden, 1976), is based on the same assumptions contained in the logistic equation. We should not be surprised if experiments have falsified various parts of these theories. The example of Dayton (1973) has already been cited. What are falsified usually are the assumptions on which the theory is based. Deliberate verification of the assumptions has been attempted in laboratory experiments, such as those of Gause (1934), Crombie (1945), and Vandermeer (1969), but nearly all field experiments involve conditions that are too daunting for more than an overall result. For example, my experiments on interspecific competition in the salamander genus *Plethodon* (Hairston 1980a) revealed that mutual negative influences were involved, but the assumptions on which the calculations of the coefficients of competition were based were not verified.

An even more invidious aspect of mathematical models is that unacceptable assumptions can be contained within the mathematics, as opposed to those made in constructing the theory. Those made in constructing the model usually can be identified, with sufficient effort, by nonmathematical ecologists, but the assumptions buried within the mathematics require the attention of other mathematical ecologists. The best-known case is one involving the mathematically derived conclusion of May and MacArthur (1972) and May (1973) that the original form of the MacArthur–Levins (1967) approach to limiting similarity was robust to a considerable amount of stochastic variability. That apparently got rid of a most restrictive assumption in the original model, namely, that abundances in the community are completely determined by the coefficients of competition. Relaxation of that assumption yielded important implications about overlap in resource use and the sizes of carrying capacities of competing species that permitted coexistence of competitors. Unfortunately for this apparently encouraging development, Turelli (1978) found that some assumptions implicit in May's mathematical treatment imposed very restrictive conditions on the form of the model. That discovery severely limits the applicability of May's conclusion. The message for all ecologists, whether mathematically inclined or not, is to insist on clear, well-informed statements of the assumptions behind any theoretical models of how natural communities work.

Planned experiments

Experiments are conducted for the purpose of answering specific questions about nature. These questions ordinarily are stated as hypotheses, which are statements about how someone thinks nature works. In other words, they contain implied predictions, and confirmation of those predictions is the most powerful means available to demonstrate the accuracy of our understanding of the world around us. In the foregoing sections of this chapter, I have stated my reservations about other approaches to understanding ecological processes. Experimentation must come under the same kind of scrutiny. How does it propose to test hypotheses?

Laboratory experiments. Experimentation is most easily repeatable, and gives the most convincing results, when all the variables are under the control of the investigator. Then, one of the variables is manipulated in a systematic way in order to answer a specific question, such as this:

> What is the effect of temperature on the intrinsic rate of increase of this species?

In conducting such an experiment, one should minimize variations in such factors as the duration and intensity of periods of light and the amount of moisture available, or else incorporate them in the experimental design. The ability to hold all such conditions constant, or to vary them in a systematic way, requires that the experiment be undertaken in the laboratory. In subsequent chapters, some illuminating laboratory experiments will be described. With sufficient care, laboratory experiments should, in principle, be repeatable – a hallmark of a convincing scientific test. Even a rigorous ecological experiment in the laboratory is accompanied by the unsettling question of its applicability in nature, and controversies on this point have been severe (see the discussions of the papers by Nicholson, Birch, and Andrewartha in the Cold Spring Harbor Symposium on Quantitative Biology, 1958).

Field experiments. Under field conditions, it is not possible to exercise control over most variables. Usually, the variable of interest is manipulated in a predetermined way, and the remaining variables fluctuate independent of the experiment. Occasionally, more than one variable can be manipulated, but the number is severely limited. The questions asked in field experiments tend to be less precise than those asked in the laboratory:

> Do these two species compete in nature, or, more properly for most such experiments, do they affect each other adversely?

With good luck, one can go one step further and ask this:

> Under which of these conditions do the two species compete more strongly?

It is assumed that the naturally varying factors affect all experimental treatments equally, or at least randomly. The assumption introduces an element of uncertainty into the interpretation of the outcome, and reduces the assurance of being able to repeat the result. An example from execptionally well-designed experiments is the work of Morin (1983a), Wilbur, Morin, and Harris (1983), and Morin, Wilbur, and Harris (1983). Those experiments were conducted out-of-doors under conditions that can be called seminatural or semilaboratory, depending on one's point of view, because the experimenters had control over many aspects of the conditions in the cattle tanks where the experiments took place. That fact makes the example especially pertinent. Morin conducted experiments on the effects of different levels of predation by the newt *Notophthalmus viridescens* on competitive communities of frog tadpoles of six species. The competitive dominant, *Scaphiopus holbrooki*, was also a favored food of the newt, and its relative abundance decreased with increased predation. In a similar but more elaborate experiment by Wilbur et al. (1983) and Morin et al. (1983) with four species of frog tadpoles, three of them the same as those used by Morin (1983a), *Scaphiopus* failed to dominate the communities without predatory newts. The reason was an unexpected bloom of filamentous green algae that appeared because a spring drought held back the breeding of some of the species of frogs, leading to a change in the conditions in the tanks. The filamentous algae were shown experimentally to be unsuitable as food for *Scaphiopus*. Thus, the intrusion of an uncontrolled environmental factor prevented the original result from being repeated.

Some well-known ecological hypotheses and their origins

Anyone who has any curiosity is likely to have ideas about the processes going on in nature. These ideas come from having a sufficient amount of factual information, plus, especially, having the ability to visualize a problem that requires a solution. The solution of any ecological problem should begin with the formulation of one or more hypotheses about how nature works. Only rarely do authors call their own thoughts hypotheses. More frequently, they call them theories, models, conclusions, or even proofs. The appelation "hypothesis" is given by other, more skeptical ecologists.

This section describes three famous (or infamous, depending on one's point of view) hypotheses. The descriptions include the basis, factual and logical, of each hypothesis.

Santa Rosalia

The first hypothesis we shall consider is contained in G. E. Hutchinson's well-known presidential address to the American Society of Naturalists (Hutchinson 1959): "Homage to Santa Rosalia *or* Why are there so many kinds of animals?" Imaginative perception was required to see that that was an interesting problem – one for which the solution would reveal a great deal about ecological processes.

Hutchinson's reasoning is as follows: There are as many as 10 million species of animals on earth, and yet as far as the physicochemical environment is concerned, the number of different sets of conditions to which species can be adapted is fairly limited, especially when we consider the range of conditions that most ordinary species are able to tolerate. His next possible candidate to account for diversity is food chains. Energy considerations will limit the number of links, because the efficiency of conversion of energy from one link to the next higher link is less than 0.2, and because predators (he assumes) are, on the average, twice the mass of their prey. That will mean that after five links, the population of the fifth link will be 10^{-4} that of the first, and after fifty links, 10^{-49}. Even starting with algal cells at the first link, and at a density of 10^6 per milliliter, the volume needed to hold one individual of the fiftieth link would be much greater than all of the oceans combined. From this approach, the limit in total species is small compared with the millions being sought. Hutchinson considers whether or not there are enough different food chains, at five links each. He points out that many herbivore species are selective in their food plants, and hence each plant species theoretically could support a food chain. With 200,000 species of terrestrial producers, a large number of animal species can be accounted for. This ignores the fact that predators are not selective, and there would be much overlap between food chains. But to proceed with the reasoning: Why are there so many species of plants? He suggests that the same principles apply as to animals. The following principles are then enunciated:

1. Diversity enhances stability. This is stated to be intuitively satisfying. In support of the statement, Hutchinson first cites prominent ecologists, such as Elton, and then claims that there is formal proof by MacArthur (1955).

2. Diversity enhances stability, because when species are added to a community, that involves taking over part of the niche of a species already present. That reduces fluctuations in the population of the latter and keeps it from "being underrepresented to a dangerous degree" (Hutchinson 1959, p. 150). No evidence is given that fluctuations are less dangerous for small populations. To the contrary, small populations are vulnerable to practically all hazards, including especially fluctuations, which can carry a small population to extinction. Niche partitioning, the means whereby diversification is achieved, depends on the hypothesis that by sharing overlapping niches, the average population is reduced, and *therefore* fluctuations are reduced.

The cornerstone of the reasoning is an appeal to "modern ecological theory," which claims that communities of many species persist better than those containing fewer, less diversified organisms. The theory, supplied by MacArthur's paper, was a popular one that appealed to the intuitive desire for a reason for preserving diversity in the face of habitat destruction and monoculture. MacArthur's paper itself, however, points out that the model is based on several unrealistic simplifications, some of which are unrealistic enough to matter (Hairston et al. 1968). There is, for example, the implicit circularity that both diversity and stability depend ultimately on the number of species present, and there is the possibility, now generally accepted, that cause and effect are reversed. Stability enhances diversity. Subsequently, May (1972) showed that interactions among a large number of species would tend to decrease the stability of the system, but it would, of course, be unfair to expect Hutchinson to anticipate that result.

Having stated the basis for his hypothesis, Hutchinson considers the limits to which the proposed process can go. There is a "problem as to how much difference between two species at the same level is needed to prevent them from occupying the same niche" (Hutchinson 1959, p. 152). He suggests that this difference can be measured by size, and he gives some data supporting a ratio of about 1.3 in a linear dimension of feeding structures as being sufficient to permit coexistence. Community composition was thus firmly based on the adaptation of the species to competitive relationships among them.

It would be difficult to exaggerate the influence of Hutchinson's paper. It stimulated a large number of papers showing confirmations of the ratio and the existence of other regular ecological differences among coexisting species [see the references in Roth (1981) and Simberloff & Boecklen (1981)]; it also provided the theoretical basis for most of the theory of interspecific relationships during the next fifteen years, as seen in the work of MacArthur (1960, 1962, 1968, 1969, 1970), MacArthur and Levins (1967), Levins (1968), Levins and Culver (1971), May (1973), May and MacArthur (1972), May and Leonard (1975), Roughgarden (1972, 1974, 1976), and Schoener (1974, 1976). There was a great desire for coherent and precise theory among ecologists at the time, and Hutchinson and his intellectual companions and descendants supplied it. Small wonder that most of the tests of the hypothesis were actually searches for confirmatory evidence.

It was some time before weaknesses in the original hypothesis and in the theoretical edifice built on it were appreciated. Eventually, the importance of predation became apparent, following the experiments of Paine (1966, 1974), Connell (1970, 1975) and others, and an increasingly skeptical attitude (Simberloff 1970, 1974, 1980, 1983; Simberloff & Connor 1981; Connor & Simberloff 1978, 1979) has led to a situation where a rethinking of much ecological theory is needed.

Hairston, Smith, and Slobodkin (HSS)

The second hypothesis to be considered has been controversial for several reasons. It was published shortly after Hutchinson's paper, and the authors were not aware of that publication. Hairston, Smith, and Slobodkin (1960) originally submitted their paper to the editor of *Ecology* in May 1959. Its rejection and subsequent submission to another journal caused a year's delay in its publication. The background for the paper was the debate over density dependence, and the paper originated in an argument among the authors about the evidence favoring competition for resources. There was agreement that "food not consumed by herbivores or carnivores is ultimately used by reducers . . . and that in any balanced state, such as we assume communities to be, the food is completely consumed by some species or other" (Hairston 1959, p. 414). We thus believed that there was good evidence for density-dependent resource limitiation among the decomposers, and hence competition between the species of bacteria and fungi.

The vexing situation, as far as we were concerned, was the following: Inasmuch as nearly all of terrestrial primary production falls to the ground uneaten, it is difficult to visualize how there can be any competition for it, either intraspecifically or interspecifically. That was a point that L. C. Birch had made forcefully; yet we could not accept his explanation, which was that weather was severe often enough to keep the populations of terrestrial herbivores well below the level set by their food supply. The solution to the dilemma came when we started to consider exceptions to the observation that only a small proportion of green plant production is consumed by herbivores. The most frequent exceptions are outbreaks of introduced species that, though less clearly adapted to the local climate than native species, manage to become numerous enough to defoliate the vegetation. The explanation at which we arrived was that the introduced species had left a large number of their predators and parasites behind, and from that we concluded that the natural state of affairs is for terrestrial herbivores as a group to be preyed on at a sufficiently high rate that their numbers never reach a level where they consume much of the dominant vegetation.

It followed from that explanation that terrestrial predators (including parasites) as a group are limited in abundance by the supply of herbivores, because the latter constitute most of their food (some, of course, prey on each other). The full set of HSS hypotheses was as follows (Hairston et al. 1960). After the first one, the others were stated to apply to terrestrial situations, and we specifically excluded successional stages, as well as aquatic systems.

1. Decomposers as a group must be food-limited. (p. 421)
2. Producers are neither herbivore-limited nor catastrophe-limited and must therefore be limited by their own exhaustion of a resource. (p. 422)
3. The usual condition is for populations of herbivores *not* to be limited by their food supply. (p. 422)
4. Although rigorous proof that herbivores are generally controlled by predation is lacking, supporting evidence is available. (p. 423)
5. The predators and parasites, in controlling the populations of herbivores, must thereby limit their own resources, and as a group they must be food-limited. (p. 423)
6. Therefore, interspecific competition for resources exists among producers, among carnivores, and among decomposers. (p. 423)

The paper has been controversial. It is opposed, for example, by advocates of density independence (Ehrlich & Birch 1967), advocates of the universality of competition in structuring communities (Gill 1981), advocates of the ecological importance of herbivore-resisting compounds (Murdoch 1966, Janzen 1969), and advocates of selection for ecosystemwide traits [Patten and Odum (1981) do not specifically cite our paper, but they argue strongly for group selection among ecosystems, and they object to hypotheses that require only Darwinian selection]. In addition to those objections, Murdoch (1966) claimed that the hypotheses were untestable and therefore unscientific. In our response (Slobodkin, Smith, & Hairston 1967), we listed means whereby each hypothesis could be falsified.

Despite the widespread opposition, the interrelated set of hypotheses appeals to enough different ecologists for discussion to continue; see, for example, Fretwell (1977, 1987), Strong (1982), Strong, Lawton, and Southwood (1984a), Menge et al. (1986a), and especially Oksanen (1988). Both Schoener (1983) and Connell (1983) included analyses of the frequency with which individual experiments did or did not confirm the existence of competition among herbivores. Such a "majority vote" was specifically excluded in our clarification (Slobodkin et al. 1967): "We were not making statements about most herbivores, or most carnivores, but about these trophic levels as wholes. Our statements, then, apply to the quantitatively dominant species but not necessarily to the numerical majority of species in any ecosystem"

(p. 109). The analyses of the literature could not not have falsified the hypothesis, but could have provided incidental support, as was the case with Schoener's analysis. That was the commonest misinterpretation, a second one being a failure to note our exclusion of all "herbivores" except those that consume the foliage or sap. Specifically, the hypothesis does not apply to seed eaters, nectar feeders, or pollen feeders.

The HSS hypotheses have recently aroused some interest; their eventual influence cannot be predicted. Perhaps, when the workings of different kinds of ecosystems are considered separately, terrestrial ecology will be shown to have been influenced.

The broken stick

The final hypothesis to be considered is an example of one that has shown extraordinary viability in the face of negative evidence regarding its validity. The background of the "broken stick" model is in the large amount of data on the relative abundances of species and in attempts to interpret the observation that when comprehensive collections of any taxonomic group of organisms are made in a specified area, a common pattern of relative abundances is revealed: A few species are quite abundant, and many species are rare, and that pattern is found in nearly all groups for which adequate data exist (Fig. 1.1). The first attempts to interpret this relationship involved trying to fit the relative abundance distributions to mathematically defined statistical formulae. The aim was to find a common formula, so that the diversities of different communities could be compared (Fisher, Corbet & Williams 1943; Preston 1948). It was hoped that an "index of diversity" would allow investigators to assess the relationship between the number of species and the number of individuals for different situations, specifying the relative "richness" of the fauna. The match of Fisher's logarithmic series to the data is shown in Figure 1.1; Preston's lognormal match of the same data is shown in Figure 1.2.

In 1957, MacArthur took a different and intuitively more satisfying approach to the regularity that the data showed. His idea was to consider how the community might be organized in several different ways, construct a mathematical model for each of the imaginary organizations, and compare them to real data to permit a choice among the models. Imagine that the total number of individuals has some correspondence to the total available niche space. The species can be

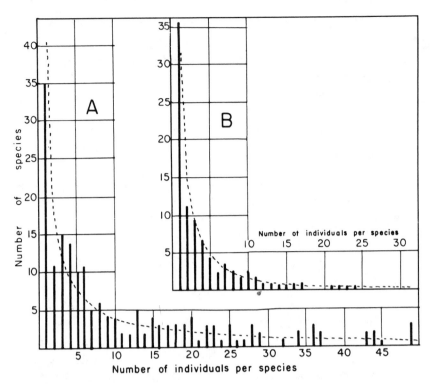

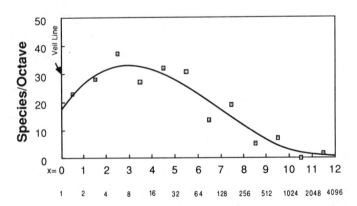

Figure 1.1. Species abundance distributions of Lepidoptera caught in a light trap at Rothamsted, England. The graphs show the number of species represented by different numbers of individuals. The broken lines were calculated from Fisher's logarithmic series. (From Fisher, Corbet, & Williams 1943.)

Figure 1.2. The same data as in Figure 1.1, with the abscissa on a scale of logarithms to the base 2, the successive intervals of which are called octaves. The line was calculated from Preston's lognormal distribution. (From Preston 1948.)

thought of as dividing up the niche space in several different ways. First, suppose that they divide the niche space in a nonoverlapping way and that the relative sizes of the different niches are determined by so many factors that the result is a random array of abundances. Such a nonoverlapping arrangement would be arrived at through competitive interactions among the species, each acquiring its part of the niche space by being superior there. MacArthur's image was of a line on which points are thrown at random until the number of segments between points is equal to the number of species involved. A second model, in which the abundances were allowed to overlap by throwing pairs of points at the line, was claimed to represent some common overlapping use of niche space by the different species, and a third model assumed independently acquired abundances. MacArthur (1957, 1960) found some data on birds that fit his first model and suggested that a commonly observed form of the relative abundance data, in which common species are too common and there are too many rare species, was due to the pooling of data from heterogeneous sources. That was shown not to be the case (Hairston 1959, 1964, 1969), as pooling data brings about a closer fit to the first model. The second model was incorrect mathematically (Pielou & Arnason 1966; Vandermeer & MacArthur 1966) and the third was never mentioned after the original paper.

The first model continues to fascinate some ecologists, despite the demonstration by Cohen (1968) that the mathematical formula could be derived from premises other than the original competition-based premises of MacArthur, and despite MacArthur's own public abandonment of the whole approach (MacArthur 1966). Perhaps it is the universal regularity of the numerical relationships of the abundances of coexisting species that is so fascinating, but it is more likely that the original approach of MacArthur in starting from biological relationships, rather than the statistical distribution, that continues to hold the attention. Some ecologists continue to cling to the model, ignoring its obvious failures (De Vita 1979; Sugihara 1980; Bush & Holmes 1983; May 1986).

Synthesis

This introductory chapter is intended to place ecological experimentation into the broader context of the whole field, including such issues as why we need experiments, what sorts of questions can be answered by good experiments, how the questions have been asked in the past, and how hypotheses have been formulated in proposing answers to some of the questions.

The remainder of this book consists of a discussion of scientific requirements in ecological research, some of the special problems that ecologists face in meeting the requirements, and critiques of a number of ecological experiments in each of the environments in which they have been conducted. This is not an attempt to discuss all ecological experiments, a task that would require an encyclopedia. The experiments selected for treatment were chosen for many reasons: because they can be used to illustrate difficulties in the implementation of experiments in the field, because they illustrate failures to follow acceptable design, because they illustrate outstanding scientific procedure, because they illustrate especially important ecological phenomena, or because they are necessary to an understanding of the habitat in which they were performed.

2

Minimal requirements of experimental design in ecology

Introduction

Ecological experiments come in many forms, and at all levels of sophistication. At the simplest, they involve an ecologist thinking that something interesting is happening, and deciding to change the system to find out more about possible causes. If the change is followed by a dramatic "result," the curious ecologist may decide that the case is proved, and write the experiment up for publication. The change in the system would be classified as an experiment, but there would be problems in accepting the conclusion, unless certain precautions had been observed. There is the question whether or not a rare or even unique event has been observed. Can the result be repeated? Very few ecological field experiments have been repeated, but the use of a satisfactory experimental design can remove at least some of the uncertainty. Our ecologist is faced with a choice, either to carry out a simple manipulation to satisfy a perhaps uncritical curiosity or to invest more work and conduct an experiment that will convince the array of scientific colleagues.

It might seem superfluous to describe the requirements of experimental design, but they have been violated regularly enough in published works that all should be warned of errors. It is possible to do anything badly, even something as desirable as an experimental approach to ecology. One of the features that distinguish science from other approaches to understanding the world is the set of rules by which scientists operate. As best they can, the rules prevent scientists from yielding to temptation, and it is generally accepted that, in principle, our colleagues will catch us if we do not follow the rules. The most formal and widely accepted of the rules are those contained in the requirements of experimental design. The more complex the experiment, the more complex the requirements, but the minimum requirements are a knowledge of the initial conditions, adequate controls, and replication. These are explained next, and the explanation is followed

23

by two examples of good experiments. Finally, an example of an experiment in which all of the rules were violated is presented.

Initial conditions

Experiments should be designed to test hypotheses, and a satisfactory hypothesis must, at the very least, contain one or more overt or implied predictions, the role of which has been mentioned in Chapter 1. Our curious ecologist would not perform the simplest manipulation if there were no expectation of some result, however nebulous, and that expectation constitutes an implied prediction.

A prediction requires a clear statement of the conditions that must exist for it to be confirmed. Therefore, to carry out a satisfactory experiment, one must have full knowledge of the conditions existing before the experiment is begun. Otherwise, there is a limited assurance that the hypothesis is being tested properly. This would not appear to be a difficult requirement to meet in ecological research, as it is the natural situation that leads to the hypothesis. The commonest failing in this regard is inadequate description, a problem that can be avoided by a sufficient period of taking baseline data – following populations in locations to be used for controls and experimentals before any manipulations are begun. As one example of the use to which such preliminary information can be put, I have selected the work of Hurlbert and Mulla (1981). They planned to test the effect of the mosquitofish, *Gambusia affinis*, on the plankton community in small artificial ponds. Even though the ponds had been specially constructed as replicates, the baseline data of Hurlbert and Mulla showed that the variability in population densities was great. They used that information to assign ponds to treatments so that each treatment received the full range of densities, thus avoiding chance assignment of high densities to one treatment and low densities to another. The choice between random assignment (the hypothetical ideal) and deliberate stratification is one that is not easily settled (Hurlbert 1984).

In the process of making observations on initial conditions, it is inevitable that variation will be encountered. This variation imposes a decision on what part of the environment will actually be used in the proposed experiment. There is a trade-off between including a wide range of conditions, so as to make any conclusions general, and using a restricted set of conditions, to avoid so much variability that analysis of the results yields no conclusions, or at best weak conclusions. The principle to be followed is not to become so enmeshed in experimental design that common sense cannot dictate the choice. A knowledge of the natural history of the organisms involved is absolutely essential in making the choice.

The requirement of adequate knowledge of initial conditions has important implications for the validity of so-called natural experiments. Inasmuch as those "experiments" are recognized only when they are completed, or in progress at the earliest, it is impossible to be certain of the conditions that existed before such an experiment began. It then becomes necessary to make assumptions about those conditions, and any conclusions reached on the basis of "natural experiments" are thereby weakened to the point of being hypotheses, and they should be stated as such.

Controls

The necessity for controls is obvious, but there are examples in the ecological literature of experiments without them, and there are more examples of inadequate controls. In ecological experiments, there are so many factors that must be allowed to fluctuate naturally that it is essential to know what would have happened if the experimental manipulation had not been performed. A simple example will demonstrate the necessity. The example is of my own experiment testing for the existence and strength of interspecific competition between two species of terrestrial salamanders in the Great Smoky Mountains (Hairston 1980a). On the basis of the altitudinal distributions of *Plethodon jordani* and *P. glutinosus* it was originally postulated that they were in strong competition (Hairston 1951), and experiments were subsequently proposed to test the hypothesis. These experiments would involve the removal of each species (from separate plots), with the expectation that the other would respond favorably (Hairston 1973). The expectation was met, the population of *P. jordani* increasing on the experimental plots during the first three years after the start of the removal of *P. glutinosus* (Fig. 2.1). The population on the control plots, however, showed an almost identical increase during the same three years. The elementary message is that without the controls, a positive result on the density of *P. jordani* might mistakenly have been claimed. As an aside, the means constitute temporal pseudoreplication, as discussed later. That is, they imply more independent observations than were available. In the statistical analysis of this experi-

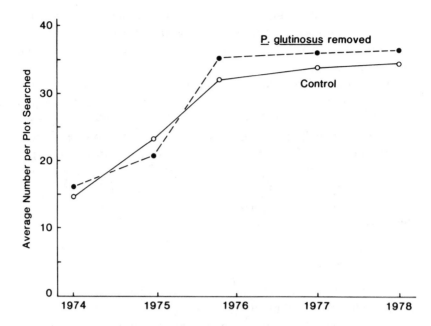

Figure 2.1. Annual average numbers of *Plethodon jordani* per plot search on plots from which *P. glutinosus* were removed (broken line) and on control plots (solid line). Data from the experiment in the Great Smoky Mountains.

ment, the problem was resolved by a procedure that avoids the issue (Hairston 1980a,b).

It is obvious that control areas should be as much like experimental areas as is possible. This usually can be established by preliminary study, such as repeated sampling of all areas to be included in the experiment. The analysis of these samples will also permit estimation of the number of replicates that may be needed, as discussed later. The inability to obtain this information in "natural experiments" further weakens conclusions about their results.

In many complex experiments it is necessary to add controls for specific effects beyond observing the natural situation. In an experiment related to the simple removals described earlier, it was necessary to transfer specimens of *P. jordani* from one mountain range to another in the southern Appalachians. The purpose was to test for the effect of the introduced form on the local population of *P. glutinosus*, when it was substituted for the local *P. jordani*. An additional control was required, in order to confirm that the introduced *P. jordani* could survive and reproduce in the new area, in the absence of competition from either native form. Thus, more plots were established, from which both local species of *Plethodon* were removed, while introducing *P. jordani* from the distant mountain range (Hairston 1980b, 1983). The introduced salamanders survived on the control plots, thus validating the results of the experiment. In experiments using enclosures or exclosures, more elaborate controls may be necessary, in order to check for the effect of the manipulation on the outcome of the experiments.

Replication

Variability is all-pervasive in nature, and it is manifestly impossible to find identical locations for the different treatments to be employed in a field experiment. Therefore, in order to avoid possible unrecognized systematic differences among locations, it is necessary to assign locations to treatments randomly; that is, each time an assignment is made to a treatment, all locations should have an equal chance of being assigned. This procedure has the additional merit of avoiding possible bias by the experimenter. The only problem can occur in small experiments with few replicates, in which case chance may segregate one treatment to neighboring locations. Deliberate interspersion will avoid this problem, but reduces the purity of any statistical inference on subsequent analysis of the results. This subject is treated in detail by Hurlbert (1984).

The natural variability must be taken into account in interpreting the results, and the only means of assessing variability is to have two or more representatives of each treatment, including the controls. Several early experiments on root competition in forests suffered from failure to provide replicates; see, for example, Toumey and Kienholz (1931). Despite the apparently dramatic results of cutting roots around one plot, a comparison of the replicates in one such experiment in a 31-year-old loblolly pine stand (Korstian & Coile 1938) demonstrates the necessity of having them. At the start of the experiment in 1932, the two experimental plots to be trenched to minimize competition from tree roots had 16 and 6 species, and 119 and 80 individual plants, respectively. The control plot for the first had 21 species and 65 individuals, and the control plot for the second had 5 species and 48 individuals. During the next four years, the flora of the trenched plots increased in species and numbers: from 16 to 24 species in the first plot, and from 6 to 16 species in the second; from 119 to 741 individuals in the first plot, and from 80 to 1,213 individuals in the second. The two control plots decreased moderately in both number of species and number of individuals. The changes in species composition differed greatly on the experimental plots. On the first, the dominant species after four years, amounting to 26 percent of the total, was absent at the start; on the second, the dominant species at the start (90%) was also dominant at the end (82%). Thus, both the initial composition and the response to the same treatment varied greatly among replicates. It should be noted that the authors did provide sufficient details for this analysis to be made. The current dictates of space limitation frequently prevent the reader from obtaining such information.

If controls and experimentals were essentially alike at the start, a greater similarity among controls alone and among experimentals alone than exists between the groups at the end of an experiment is the first indication that the experimental manipulation has had an effect. The quantitative measure of those comparisons is the province of statistics. Although the subject is outside the scope of this book, it cannot be stressed too strongly that an understanding of the principles of statistics is absolutely essential before any kind of ecological experiment is undertaken. Throughout this book, statistical terms are used occasionally. A reader who is not familiar with statistics should nevertheless be able to understand the general meaning from the context. Knowledge of the exact technical meanings of the terms is not essential to understanding the point being made. Among the available array of texts, Sokal and Rohlf (1981) is authoritative, and Fisher (1960) and Siegel (1956) provide useful information in readily understandable form.

In planning an experiment, it is necessary to know how much replication to include. This depends on the amount of variability in the data, and correct assessment of the needed replication is a problem that can be solved only with the help of statistics. The estimate should be made during the period of establishing the initial conditions. It is quite possible that the amount of replication that is necessary is more than the time and other resources of the experimenter will allow. In that case, the planned experiment may have to be reduced in complexity, with reduced sophistication of the questions being asked. The trade-offs involved in such decisions are discussed in more detail in Chapter 3.

At this point, it is recognized that some large-scale ecological experiments are carried out under conditions in which replication cannot be achieved. A notable example is the experiment on whole lakes by Schindler (1974). His aerial photograph is thoroughly convincing that adding phosphate increases the phytoplankton biomass. Statistical "significance" was not determinable in that case, and was not attempted. There is nothing wrong with such experiments. What would be wrong would be a misleading attempt to use statistics to bolster the conclusion. The problem is discussed, with examples, by Stewart-Oaten, Murdoch, and Parker (1986).

Systematic variability: blocks

For some field experiments, it is known or strongly suspected that the locations of some parts of the experiment (plots) are different in an important way from others. Yet it may not be possible to locate sufficient replicates without encountering these differences. In such cases it is frequently possible to design the experiment so that all treatments, including controls, are represented in each kind of location. In my experiments on *Desmognathus* (Hairston 1986) it was necessary to place some plots along each of three streams. I worried that the streams might support different densities of the four species involved, and therefore I placed one plot of each of the three treatments on each stream, thereby establishing three blocks. The effect of any differences between streams could be removed from the analysis of results statistically, making for a more precise answer to the question of differences between treatments. Before starting the manipulations, there were five counts of the number of salamanders seen during night searches on each of the nine plots. For two of these sets of searches, the counts of *D. monticola* were as follows:

> Search 2: The plots on stream *A* had 1, 4, and 0; those on stream *B* had 7, 5, and 7; those on stream *C* had 3, 2, and 1.

> Search 4: The plots on stream *A* had 4, 3, and 2; those on stream *B* had 16, 4, and 5; those on stream *C* had 4, 6, and 8.

Data such as these permit an assessment of differences between blocks (streams, in this example), whether or not experimental manipulations have taken place. The actual assessment is a problem in statistics, but for the present it is sufficient to state that one of the two sets of searches showed that there was less than one chance in twenty that the differences were due to variation between plots on individual streams. Such a probability level usually is accepted as "significant" statistically. It was the data from search 2 that showed this difference – not at all obvious from a simple inspection of the numbers. There were, however, no statistically significant differences among the plots that were destined to be parts of the different treatments – a result that undoubtedly came from placing one plot for each treatment on each stream. The statistical tests would have been impossible without more than one plot per stream. When the experiments were concluded, it was found that the significant difference between blocks occurred no more frequently over all searches than would be expected from chance. Thus, the original worry need not have affected the design of the experiment, but that conclusion could be made only after the fact, and the block design was appreciated by a critical reader.

The use of blocks partially achieves the interspersion of treatments that was mentioned earlier, and randomization within blocks further ensures this.

Systematic variability: stratification of data

Different well-defined parts of a population may differ much less within the parts than a random sample of the whole population would reveal. An obvious example is provided by many attributes of the sexes. If an ecological experiment is designed to test a hypothesis about growth, the sizes of individuals are important. Among many species the sexes differ in size, and the data must be kept separate, because the combined data would incorporate an unnecessary amount of variation, and because changes in sex ratio at different times during the experiment could easily produce misleading results.

Keeping the data separate is called stratification, and there are many ways in which different subgroups can be recognized and the data stratified accordingly. An example is treated in some detail later, with children of different ages having different levels of parasitization – a common observation for many parasites. Obviously, the different age classes must be examined separately for the data to be meaningful. Although the overall proportion positive is less easily interpreted than the stratified data, it is needed in some compilations, and for it to be correct, the different age classes (strata) must be incorporated in proportion to their representation in the population.

Groups within a population may respond differently to an experimental manipulation. For example, in the experimental removal of *Plethodon glutinosus* described earlier, the mean densities of *P. jordani* on experimental and control plots did diverge in the last three years (Fig. 2.1), but the difference was not significant statistically because the differences between plots within treatments were great enough to obscure, in a statistical sense, the mean difference between treatments. However, the observed difference was entirely due to increases in the numbers of salamanders in the two youngest year classes, which created an interesting and statistically significant difference in the proportion of those young individuals. The obvious interpretation is that the removal of *P. glutinosus* permitted more reproductive output by the adult *P. jordani* than could be attained on the control plots. Stratifying the data by age classes revealed an important difference that was obscured in the gross population numbers. The implication of that result is that if the experiment had been continued for a sufficient number of years, the population means would also have been significantly different, as they were for the reciprocal experiment (see Chapter 4).

This raises the question of how long an experiment should be continued, or when one should be terminated. In the current example, a prior decision had been made that the experiment should last for the minimum duration of the life cycle of *P. glutinosus*, which has the longer generation of the two species involved. The duration of an experiment should be determined in advance, because of twin temptations: to stop when the results are pleasing, or to continue until they become so. Either procedure would violate proper scientific practice. The choice depends on the natural history of the organisms involved. Long-lived species should be given time to respond, as should those whose irregular pattern of reproductive success may dictate a long experiment so that bursts of successful reproduction will be included. For species in these two categories, brief experiments only rarely can give populational results; behavioral or physiological responses are the most one can expect. These were ignored by Bender, Case, and Gilpin (1984), who created an imaginary dichotomy between "pulse" and "press" experiments. In the real world, experiments can have any of an array of durations, with a variety of kinds of responses. Ecologists who are not thoroughly familiar with the organisms involved risk wasting a great deal of time.

Pitfalls in ecological experiments

Ecologists conducting experiments in the field, no matter how carefully the experiments have been planned, sometimes encounter unexpected difficulties either in the execution of the work or in the analysis of the results. These difficulties fall under several headings.

Pseudoreplication

Proper replication requires that replicates be independent of each other. That is, no measurement, count, or other observation on one replicate should have any influence on a similar observation on any other replicate. That is one of the most fundamental assumptions in the mathematics of statistical analysis, and yet there have been many studies in ecology in which that assumption has been violated (Hurlbert 1984). Hurlbert coined the term "pseudoreplication" to cover all of the various ways in which independence of replicates was not ensured in different studies.

One of the most obvious violations of the asumption of independence occurs when an experiment is continued over several sets of observations. Although the counts or measurements at any one time are truly independent of each other, the same counts or measurements on the same plots or other experimental units at successive times clearly are not independent, and must not be used as such in the statistical analysis of the experiment. The importance of the point lies in the fact that the statistical significance of an observed difference between the mean values of two treatments, say experimentals and controls, depends in part on the number of replicates involved. Thus, inflating that number with nonindependent observations constitutes pseudoreplication.

One form of pseudoreplication occurs when plots or other replicates of a given treatment are placed together, and apart from the replicates of another treatment (or control). This may happen deliberately, as for the sake of convenience, or accidentally, as when random assignment of locations results in replicates not being interspersed with those of other treatments. In either case, the replicates are less than truly independent, and the statistical probability calculated from the data therefore is suspect. These points were discussed earlier, and by Hurlbert (1984).

The commonest form of pseudoreplication is the use of several samples within a treatment unit to calculate the statistical probability of the effect of the treatment. Thus, counts of the individuals in different samples from a tank, or from a plot, are not completely independent of each other, because the measures reflect both the treatment to which the unit has been subjected and the local characteristics of the plot. In principle, it is not possible to separate the two influences. The same problem applies to measurement of the number of individuals within a plot. The solution is not as simple as Hurlbert suggested, and to understand the controversy it is necessary to have enough statistical background to include a knowledge of correlation and analysis of variance (ANOVA).

Ecological experiments often include several, or even many, observations on each experimental unit to which a treatment has been applied. For example, an experiment on density dependence might have two cages containing ten individuals and two cages containing twenty individuals. At the end of the experiment, each survivor is weighed. How many observations of the effect of density on growth have been made? In a strict sense, the answer is one per survivor, perhaps as many as sixty, but if the individuals are competing they are influencing one another's growth, and these observations are not independent. Within a unit, individuals may have a negative covariance. In the extreme case of only two individuals in a unit, if one grows large, the other must be small, if they are limited by resources. On the other hand, suppose one of the replicates of the low-density treatment is in a favorable habitat and the other replicate is in a less favorable habitat. In this case, individuals in a unit are expected to have a positive covariance. Only in the case of zero covariance among individuals in a unit can all measurements be taken as independent estimates of the effect of treatment. When intraunit correlations are positive, the use of all individuals in tests of significance runs the risk of a type I error, rejecting the null hypothesis when it is in fact true. Standard statistical practice would be to use the mean response of individuals within an experimental unit. In this case, one would have only four observations, two on the effect of each treatment on growth. When intraunit correlations are negative (as expected when responses reflect competition), use of only means may be too conservative, and there is a risk of a type II error, that is, accepting the null hypothesis when it is in fact false. In this case, the use of individual observations is in fact justified.

The F ratio of the mean square between replicates divided by the mean square among individuals within units is a measure of the sign of the correlation. If $F > 1$, then one should use population means; if $F \leq 1$ then the use of individual observations is justified (H. M. Wilbur pers. commun.)

Unwanted effects of experimentation and observation

The requirements of experimental design or of the question being asked have, in some instances, caused experimenters to use techniques that have affected the outcomes of the experiments. The commonest of these are "cage effects." These were first observed when attempts were made to include or exclude predators or grazers from experiments in the rocky intertidal habitat. For example, Connell (1961a) suggested that cages inhibited the grazing potential of caged limpets, and Dayton (1971) reported that algae growing on cages prevented desiccation under them and improved the survival of predatory nemerteans. An experiment on colonization by marine algae (Sousa 1979) yielded inconclusive results because cages designed to exclude herbivores became covered with algae and barnacles, preventing the establishment of algae within the cages. Shading and interference with the circulation of water or air have also been attributed to the presence of cages or even of roofless enclosures. Moreover, the use of fences to keep animals within experimental areas may well have the result of keeping their predators out or of selectively permitting flying predators access to the fenced area, while excluding earthbound predators. These effects are widely recognized at present as being undesirable properties of otherwise well-designed experiments.

It is commonly thought by ornithologists that mammal and snake predators follow the trails of investigators to nests that are visited regularly. The literature is less than unanimous. In two studies, one by Lenington (1979) on red-winged blackbirds (*Agelaius phoeniceus*) and one by Westmoreland and Best (1985) on mourning doves (*Zenaida macroura*), evidence was presented that survival was reduced by extra predation on frequently visited nests. Willis (1973) recorded a slight increase in predation early in the nesting cycle of bicolored antbirds (*Gymnopithys bicolor*) as an apparent result of his visits, but Gottfried and Thompson (1978) could not detect significant extra predation as a result of their visits to Japanese quail eggs placed in nests in a planned experiment. Proper precautions appear to negate this effect of the

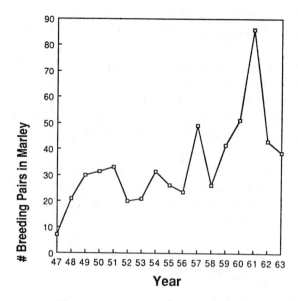

Figure 2.2. Fluctuations in the population of the great tit in Marley Wood, near Oxford, England. There was a surplus of nest boxes throughout the study. (From Perrins 1965.)

investigation itself (Nolan 1978). Another form of unintentional investigator effect on nesting success is documented in detail by Fetterolf (1983). He showed conclusively that routine study of the nests and chicks of ring-billed gulls (*Larus delawarensis*) caused significant decreases in number of eggs laid, hatching success, and fledging success. Those decreases were due to the effects of investigators' visits on the behavior of both adults and chicks.

Investigators working with hole-nesting birds sometimes place nest boxes in the habitat to facilitate the study. In the well-known long-term work on the great tit (*Parus major*) in Marley Wood, near Oxford, 200 nest boxes were put up in 1947 (Gibb 1950). The additional nest sites apparently shifted the limiting resource from nest holes to food and resulted in an increase in the population (see also Dhondt, Eyckerman, & Huble 1979). Although not mentioned by Perrins (1965) or Lack (1966), the change from a stable to an unstable limiting resource apparently resulted in an increase in the magnitude of fluctuations in the population (Fig. 2.2).

Trapping animals with bait can have several different unwanted effects on the outcome of the study. Some individuals become accustomed to the food provided in the trap, and thus become "trap-happy" – preventing the trap from taking an unbiased sample of the population. Others have the opposite reaction and become "trap-shy." The effect of such a behavioral reaction to the technique is rarely quantifiable, but it must be substantial, and it could lead to an erroneous interpretation of the results. Moreover, the time spent in a trap can well lead to reduced predation because of being protected by the trap, or to increased exposure to the elements, if provision is not made for nest material or for protective cover.

These examples of known or potential effects of the investigation itself, beyond any manipulations that are carried out, are not meant to be exhaustive, but to show the interested reader the kinds of problems that can arise and to stimulate careful thought prior to the start of a study.

Changes in controls

Natural areas have a tendency to vary in different directions, and such a divergence can cause problems in a long-term experiment. In the experiment involving transplanting salamanders (*Plethdon jordani*) described earlier, I predicted that one of the transferred populations would have a negative effect on the newly exposed population of *P. glutinosus* (Hairston 1973). The experiment was followed for eight years, with two plots being established where many individuals were introduced, and two plots remaining as unmanipulated controls. Unfortunately, the mean counts of *P. glutinosus* on the controls declined during most of the study (Hairston 1983), an observation that caused difficulty in interpreting the steeper decline in the mean counts of *P. glutinosus* on the experimental plots. In this case, there is a statistical test for comparing the rates of decline, but one can imagine situations in which the problem would be insoluble. This example is unlike the situation, already described, in which numbers on both control and experimental plots increased. In that case, there was not a significant difference in the rates of increase.

As a different kind of example, consider the results of an experiment in the control of a disease: schistosomiasis. One of the problems in controlling many tropical diseases is cost. These tropical countries are poor and lack the resources to do some of the obvious things. In this case, it was thought that because acquiring schistosomiasis requires active behavior on the part of people (getting into water with infective

Table 2.1. *Prevalence of schistosomiasis in four age classes in two villages*

Age (yr)	Control village			Experimental village		
	No. examined	No. positive	Prevalence (%)	No. examined	No. positive	Prevalence (%)
<3	56	1	1.9	46	0	0
3–6	115	13	11.3	92	7	7.6
7–10	109	43	39.5	90	35	38.9
11–14	79	47	59.5	74	35	46.7

Note: See text for full explanation.

snails; infecting snails by promiscuous disposal of feces), an aggressive campaign of health education might reduce the incidence of the disease.

In order to find out if such a program would have an effect, an experiment was set up in two villages with approximately equal proportions of children infected: 77 of 303 children (25.4%) in the village that was to be the focus of an educational campaign, and 104 of 359 (29.0%) in the village destined to be a control. The small difference is not significant statistically. For the purpose of this discussion, the absence of replication is ignored. The test consisted of examinations of children under 15 years of age, that group being accessible, as well as being the part of the population most receptive to health education. After 2.5 years of effort, the children were reexamined, with the following results: In the experimental village, 43 of 333 (12.9%) were found to be infected; in the control village, 75 of 322 (23.3%). The probability that the difference was due to chance is less than 1 in 1,000, a satisfying result, especially because the control village had not changed by a significant amount.

This crude analysis ignores the importance of age structure among the children, as well as the fact that the prevalence of schistosomiasis (percentage positive) increases with age. Broken down by age classes, the initial conditions are as shown in Table 2.1. The data show the sensitivities of these age classes to any measure reducing the rate of transmission. Thus, in the experiment, most of the members of each of the three youngest age classes would have moved into the next older class, and if transmission had been reduced, they would have diluted the older group with negatives. The data also show the importance of

Table 2.2. *Prevalence of schistosomiasis in each age class in the two villages after 2.5 years of health education in the experimental village*

Age (yr)	Control village				Experimental village			
	No. examined	No. positive	Prevalence (%)	Change (%)	No. examined	No. positive	Prevalence (%)	Change (%)
<3	47	0	0	−1.9	62	0	0	0
3–6	84	5	5.9	−5.3	106	1	0.9	−6.7
7– 10	112	29	25.9	−13.6	94	15	16.0	−22.9
11– 14	79	41	51.9	−7.6	71	27	38.0	−7.9

age structure in determining the crude prevalence rates reported earlier. A change in the representations of the different age classes in the population examined would alter the crude prevalence rate. An increased representation of the older children would increase the calculated prevalence of schistosomiasis, and vice versa. That is what happened, as the breakdown of the final data shows (Table 2.2). There was little difference between the two villages in the decrease in percentage positive at any age. The difference in overall percentages infected came almost entirely from a change in the relative representations of the age classes. In the experimental village, the two younger age classes increased from 45.6 percent of the total to 50.4 percent; in the control village, the representation of the same two age classes decreased from 47.6 to 40.7 percent. The result was that in the experimental village the overall parasite rate was diluted with the normal number of negatives among the younger children, whereas in the control village the parasite rate was inflated by the larger number of positives among the older children.

The change in age structure among the children examined could have brought about a statistically significant difference without any change in parasite rate in any age class. That can be confirmed by calculating the expected number infected at each age at the end of the experiment, assuming no change during the experiment. For the experimental village, the expected number is 77.67, or 23.3 percent of the 333 examined; for the control village, it is 101.62, or 31.6 percent of the 322 examined. That difference would have been "significant" statistically. Any claim of success in reducing the transmission of schistosomiasis would therefore have been spurious.

Examples of good design

The work of D. C. Smith (1983) is the first example discussed here of a field experiment designed and conducted in an excellent manner. Most experiments in fresh water have involved the use of enclosed spaces, with the ever-present risk that the enclosures themselves have influenced the outcomes of the experiments. This study, in contrast, was performed in naturally isolated bodies of water. They were rock pools near the shore of Lake Superior on two small islands associated with Isle Royale. The species of interest was the chorus frog, *Pseudacris triseriata*, which breeds in these pools.

Two factors endangered the tadpoles from the physical standpoint: desiccation in the smaller pools, and being swept out by wave action during storms for those pools low on the shore. Smith observed that there was virtually no survival of the tadpoles in either event.

No such accidental loss occurred in the larger pools far away from the shore, where tadpoles were rare or absent, and Smith considered two possible sources of tadpole mortality: predation and intraspecific competition. He identified three species of potentially important predators: larvae of the salamander *Ambystoma laterale*, nymphs of the dragonfly *Anax junius* (he has informed me that it was misidentified and is actually *Aeshna juncea*), and the dytiscid beetle *Rhanthus binotatus*. His study of the initial conditions showed that *Ambystoma* and *Anax* were confined to the largest pools high above the water's edge and that *Pseudacris* tadpoles were found in unexpectedly few of these pools, and in low densities where they occurred. No such negative relationship was observed between *Pseudacris* and *Rhanthus*, and although the beetles readily ate all sizes of tadpoles in the laboratory, only the smallest ones were affected in the field. Replicated laboratory experiments, in which two tadpoles of equal size were confined with one predator, established that *Ambystoma* could not eat large tadpoles (Fig. 2.3). The timing of breeding meant that there were few salamander larvae large enough to consume tadpoles, less than 5 percent of which were of a vulnerable size. The dragonfly nymphs were able to eat a larger array of sizes of tadpoles (Fig. 2.3), none of which were too large for the large nymphs.

In the field, *Anax* appeared to be abundant enough to have a strong impact on the tadpole populations, and Smith conducted two reciprocal experiments to test that hypothesis. He selected two large pools high up on the shore that contained dragonfly nymphs but no tadpoles, and two large pools lower down that contained tadpoles but no drag-

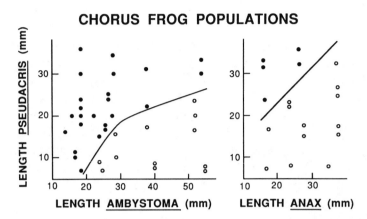

Figure 2.3. Relationships among total length of *P. triseriata* tadpoles, total length of predators, and vulnerability of tadpoles to predation in 200-ml laboratory containers. Tadpoles above the lines escape predation. Lines drawn by eye. Open circles indicate tadpoles eaten; solid circles indicate tadpoles surviving. (From D. C. Smith 1983.)

onflies. After measuring the volumes of all four pools, he removed the tadpoles from the lower pools and then reintroduced them at the same density for both pools. *Anax* nymphs were introduced into one of the two at a density comparable to the natural density. Nearly all *Anax* (at least 92.5%) were removed from one of the upper pools, and tadpoles were introduced into both at the same density as in the reciprocal experiment. The results were clear (Table 2.3). *Pseudacris* was eliminated by natural densities of *Anax*, but survived well where the predatory nymphs were absent or nearly so. The experiment revealed the reason for the virtual absence of tadpoles from seemingly acceptable pools that were large enough to nullify desiccation and far enough from shore not to be washed out by waves.

The next question concerned the factors controlling the populations of tadpoles in the remaining pools, which were transient enough to prevent successful colonization by the predators, but of sufficient duration to allow metamorphosis of the tadpoles to be completed. As part of determining the initial conditions, Smith sampled natural pools repeatedly. He found that growth was negatively correlated with density and that the length of the larval period was positively correlated with density. He carried out an experiment testing for the effects of density and food supply. Among the pools that qualified as acceptable, he established five blocks of four pools each. The pools within each

Table 2.3. *Dragonfly predation experiments*

			Natural numbers		Experimental numbers				
			Anax	*Pseudacris*	*Anax*	*Pseudacris*			
Pool	Treatment	Pool volume (liters)	19 June	18 June	19 June	19 June	25 June	2 July	10 July
Experiment A: dragonfly addition									
P1	No *Anax*	746	0	229	0	297	203	190	166
P2	*Anax*	330	0	102	33	132	17	1	0
			2 July	2 July	3 July	3 July	8 July	14 July	24 July
Experiment B: dragonfly removal									
P3	No *Anax*	283	92	0	7	112	58	58	57
P4	*Anax*	583	50	0	95	234	0	0	0

Note: Experiment A tests for the effect of *A. junius* on numbers of *P. triseriata* in pools initially occupied by *P. triseriata*. Experiment B tests for the effect of *A. junius* on *P. triseriata* in pools initially with *A. junius*. *A. junius* eliminated *P. triseriata* in both experiments.
From Smith (1983).

Table 2.4. *Data table for food and density experiment*

Treatment		Survivorship (%)	Larval period (d)	Growth coefficient First order	Growth coefficient Second order	Body length (mm)
Density	Food					
L	H	90.0	46	0.321	−0.017	12.74
L	L	42.9	63	0.119	−0.001	11.22
H	H	71.2	52	0.239	−0.026	11.52
H	L	24.6	70	0.101	0.176	10.74

Note: H indicates high; L indicates low. Body lengths are of stage 42 tadpoles, defined here to be at metamorphosis.
From Smith (1983).

block were carefully matched according to size, exposure, relative depth, height on shore, and location. Each block contained four treatments of the two factors: high and low levels of both density and food. Assignment of treatments within each block was random. The densities were set within the natural range, with the high densities being 2–6/l and the low densities 0.3–0.8/l. Within each block, the ratio of high to low density was the same for both food levels, which consisted of the regular addition of a small amount of rabbit chow for the high food level and the naturally existing supply for the low food level.

The effects of the treatments were assessed as survivorship, duration of larval period, body length at metamorphosis, and growth (from a second-order polynomial growth curve, the first-order coefficient being determined by the rate of growth, and the second-order coefficient being the departure from constant, arithmetic growth). Density had a statistically significant effect on all of the variables; food affected survivorship, the first-order growth coefficient, and body length at metamorphosis. The actual mean values under the different treatments are in Table 2.4. There was no significant effect of an interaction between density and food. Larval period and growth rate were affected by block differences, a result showing the wisdom of using a block design, as the statistical manipulation removed the variance due to block effects before the remaining treatments were analyzed.

In this study, the author met the requirements of experimental design in providing initial conditions, adequate controls, and sufficient replication. The use of a block design spread the treatments over the available array of conditions in an admirable way. He avoided the pit-falls described earlier, in not using pens, and in not using multiple measurements for each pool. It is noteworthy that the predation results were not analyzed statistically. It is not necessary to prove the obvious.

The second example of good experimentation was carried out in the laboratory (F. E. Smith 1963b). It is chosen as much for Smith's avoidance of circularity as for the experimentation per se. Smith pointed out that the principal difficulty in reconciling experimental data with the logistic model of population growth involved the universal occurrence of time lags in real population growth. Although they occur at all times, the lags are most obvious in the phenomenon of "overshooting" the carrying capacity of the experimental system. The reproductive process becomes irreversible, and having been initiated at a time when the population was well below the carrying capacity, the newly born young represent an excess. Their consumption of the limiting resource causes the carrying capacity itself to be lowered temporarily, and an oscillation is set up. The result is strong deviations from the logistic, especially in populations with an age structure.

He noted that many attributes of population growth had been studied by putting microorganisms into chemostats – continuous culture systems in which growth rates are determined by the rate of flow of nutrient resource into the system, compensated volumetrically by an equal outflow. Such a system is time-free. He devised an analogous system for animals with an age structure. His purpose was to test the hypothesis that without time lags the population could be described by the logistic equation. Smith's method was to grow *Daphnia* in such a way that continuous population growth was achieved at different rates of supply of algal suspension. The use of parthenogenetic animals allowed him to avoid dealing mathematically with males. He started with populations in 100 ml or less of culture fluid, which was changed daily and increased by a constant percentage. At the end of a week, each population was sorted to size, and each size class was reduced in numbers so as to return the system to its original volume and dilution. He kept this up until the size structure was "reasonably constant" – that is, until the stable age distribution could be assumed. Specimens not used to restart the cultures were preserved for future use.

For each population, he then had the imposed population growth rate per individual, $dN/N\,dt$, and the density of animals per 100 ml. These data could be used to test his original hypothesis. Because, from the logistic model, $dN/dt = rN(K - N)/K$, we know that as N, the

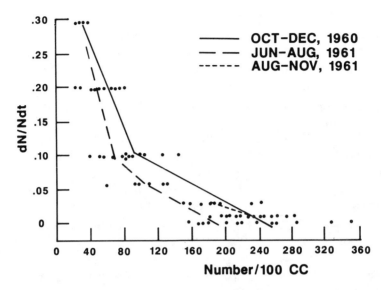

Figure 2.4. Observed densities of *Daphnia* at various specific rates of growth, using number of individuals as the measure of density. Data are combined from three sets of experiments, as shown. (From F. E. Smith 1963.)

number of individuals, increases, $dN/N\, dt$ decreases because $(K - N)/K$ becomes smaller and reaches zero when $N = K$, the carrying capacity of the system. The population growth rate per individual approaches r, the intrinsic rate of population growth, as N becomes very small. The relationship is linear. Therefore, if Smith's *Daphnia* populations had been following the logistic equation, his data points should have scattered around the straight line connecting r and K on a plot of $dN/N\, dt$ against N. They plainly did not do so (Fig. 2.4). Converting the numbers to dry weight (obtained from the animals preserved from the experiments) did not improve the fit, thus eliminating the possibility that the size structure gave inappropriate data.

He pointed out that in food-limited systems, the rate of supply of food and the rate of its utilization are items of more importance than are the carrying capacity and the unused part of the carrying capacity $(K - N)/K$. This being the case, the rate of utilization of food per unit biomass is not equivalent to the biomass as a proportion of the carrying capacity, because animals in a growing population use up more food per unit biomass than those at the carrying capacity, which would have just enough food to maintain themselves and replace deaths with

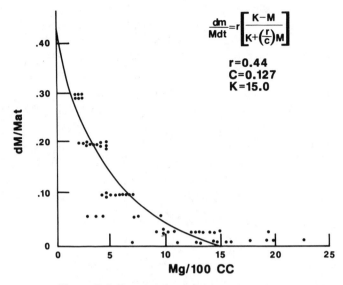

Figure 2.5. Dry-weight densities of *Daphnia* at various growth rates, compared with the proposed model. The data and curve were independently determined. (From F. E. Smith 1963.)

births. The necessary conversion of biomass into rate of food consumption requires the following modification of the logistic equation:

$$dM/dt = rM(K - M)/[K + (r/c)M] \qquad (2.1)$$

where M is biomass, K is M at saturation, and c is rate of replacement of mass in the population at saturation. Smith gives the full derivation of all terms, for which his paper should be consulted.

Equation (2.1) has three constants: r, c, and K. In order to test the validity of his equation, Smith took the excellent step of measuring them independent of his expanding populations and thus was able to use the populations for the test. To obtain an estimate of r, forty-eight individuals were raised separately from birth in an excess of food, giving forty-eight independent rates of increase, the mean of which was 0.44/day, with a standard error of 0.005. A mean value of K was obtained from two populations maintained at zero growth rate for more than two months. The two values were 15.1 mg/100 ml and 14.6 mg/100 ml, with a mean of 14.85 mg. The constant c was obtained from death rates and the loss of dry weight by starved individuals. The estimate was 0.127/day. Using these independently obtained constants, the model was compared to the observations on the expanding cultures (Fig. 2.5). The fit was quite good, and most ecologists would have been satisfied that the model had been validated, but in subsequent experiments using different algal densities, the model was found to be inadequate and Smith resorted to a different model (F. E. Smith, pers. commun.). This final twist to the account reveals the self-correcting nature of science in a way that dramatizes the experimental approach.

It is perhaps not fair to compare these experiments with field experiments, but it should be noted that the requirements of experimental design were met in all particulars, and the unusual rigor in the complete independence of the various measurements makes the work especially worthy of emulation.

An experiment that lacked important elements of design

The work of Morris and Grant (1972) is an example of work in which several of the requirements of experimental design were not met. I would have hesitated to cite it as an experiment were it not for Schoener's acceptance of the paper as an experiment in which interspecific competition was demonstrated (Schoener 1983). The purpose of the work was to look for competition between two species of microtine rodents, the meadow vole, *Microtus pennsylvanicus*, and the redback vole, *Clethrionomys gapperi*, with *Clethrionomys* excluding *Microtus* from some habitats. Certain aspects of the ecological distribution of these voles suggested the initial hypothesis of exclusion of *Microtus* by *Clethrionomys*. *Microtus* is a grassland species, whereas *Clethrionomys* is typically a woodland species. On islands where no *Clethrionomys* are present, *Microtus* is less selective of its habitat than on the mainland, where *Clethrionomys* is present. The plan was to give *Microtus* the opportunity to occupy habitats from which *Clethrionomys* had been excluded experimentally.

The experiment was conducted as follows: A two-acre plot containing both grassland and woodland was surrounded by galvanized metal 3 ft (0.91 m) high, 1 ft being sunk in the ground. Within this plot, all small mammals were removed by trapping in May 1968. Those captured were *Microtus*, ground squirrels (*Spermophilus tridecemlineatus*), jumping mice (*Zapus hudsonius*), and shrews (*Sorex cinereus*) (Morris 1972). From the standpoint of establishing the initial conditions of the experiment, it thus consisted of unoccupied, enclosed habitat. As far as the experimental enclosure was concerned, the initial trapping data could have answered their question, because no *Cleth-*

rionomys were present, and the distribution of *Microtus* in May must have shown where they were in the two habitats. The information is not given in this paper, nor in others on the same study (Grant 1972; Morris 1972). The absence of *Clethrionomys* from the enclosure raises the question of the suitability of the location for the experiment. The point may be relevant to the difficulty in establishing that species in a later phase of the study.

One of the flaws in the design of this experiment was the use of the same enclosure as the control for another experiment, testing the effect of the insecticide endrin on the population of another small rodent, *Peromyscus maniculatus*. Thus, when twelve *Microtus* were introduced after the general removals, twenty-two *Peromyscus* were also introduced. This was described by Morris and Grant (1972, p. 277): "Initially a few *Peromyscus maniculatus* were also introduced to the enclosure, in connection with another experiment (Morris 1972), but since most escaped immediately after introduction their generally brief presence is not considered a complicating factor." The paper referred to, however, shows that ten more were introduced (along with ten more *Microtus*) within the next month and that at least some of them remained throughout the first season of work, including some recruitment. *Peromyscus* varies geographically in its habitat, and the geographic race used was not specified. The possibility exists that even though less abundant than *Microtus*, it may have influenced the distribution of the latter. The number known to have been present at each trapping period has been added above the histogram (Fig. 2.6). *Microtus* increased in abundance to a total of sixty-three in the last trapping period. At no time were more captured in the woodland part of the enclosure than expected from the number of traps there, and in one period (of six), significantly fewer captures were made there than expected (Fig. 2.6).

No control enclosure was established, nor were there any replicates of the experimental enclosure. These were two serious omissions. We do not know what happened in the absence of the experimental manipulation, and we do not have any means of estimating the variation that may have occurred between enclosures treated alike.

At the beginning of the second season (June 1969), both *Clethrionomys* and *Microtus* were introduced into their appropriate habitats in the enclosure at densities typical of unrestrained populations. The actual numbers are not given, but the *Microtus* data for the four trapping periods are shown in Figure 2.7, and presumably *Clethrionomys*

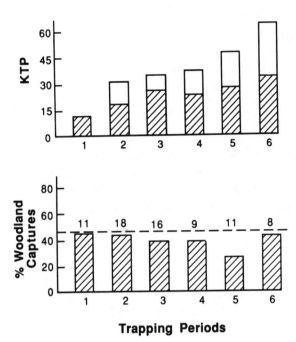

Trapping Periods

Figure 2.6. Known trappable population (KTP) of *Microtus* and percentage captures in the woodland in the first experiment. Unshaded portions of histograms indicate the number of animals trapped for the first time in each trapping period. The broken line indicates the percentage of traps in the woodland. Figures above the lower histogram show the number of *Peromyscus* known to be present. (From Morris & Grant 1972 and Morris 1972.)

had increased to thirty-seven in late July between the second and third trapping periods, as that number was reintroduced in August between the third and fourth periods. The reintroduction was followed by a "catastrophic decline," only seven being caught in the subsequent trapping period. The authors attribute the failure of *Microtus* to move out of the woodland (Fig. 2.7) to this reduction in numbers of *Clethrionomys*. The inconclusive nature of the results of that year's experiment was recognized, and the work was continued for a third season.

In 1970, there were twenty-two *Microtus* left from the experiment of 1969. These increased in abundance in the absence of *Clethrionomys* through August (Fig. 2.8). At that time, twelve *Clethrionomys* were introduced, and introductions were continued in an attempt to keep the number at that level. In 1968 and 1969, the experiments were ended in early to mid September, but in 1970, the observations were

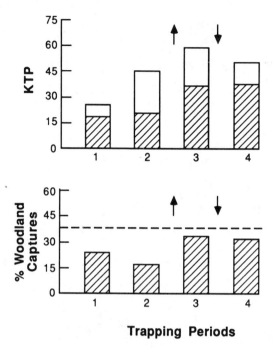

Trapping Periods

Figure 2.7. Known trappable population (KTP) of *Microtus* and percentage captures in the woodland in the second experiment. Upward arrows indicate the time of complete removal of *Clethrionomys,* and downward arrows indicate the time of reintroduction of *Clethrionomys.* Other information as in Figure 2.6. (From Morris & Grant 1972.)

continued until 3 December. As that was the only year with autumn data, comparisons are impossible.

The authors conclude that the results of the three experiments support the hypothesis of exclusion of *Microtus* by *Clethrionomys.* The data can equally well be interpreted as the result of intraspecific crowding by *Microtus,* if indeed any conclusion can legitimately be made.

To recapitulate, the flaws in this study were as follows:

1. The initial conditions were not given, though known from the initial trapping.
2. The presence of *Peromyscus* throughout the first season was not fully described.
3. There was no control. There were no *Clethrionomys* in the enclosure to begin with, yet their presence was in some sense considered to be a "control."

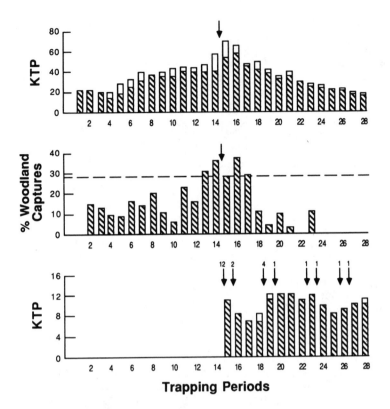

Trapping Periods

Figure 2.8. Known trappable populations (KTP) of *Microtus* (top histogram) and *Clethrionomys* (bottom histogram) during the third experiment. The middle histogram shows the percentage of captures of *Microtus* in the woodland. Arrows show times of introduction of *Clethrionomys*, and for the bottom figure, the number introduced. Other information as in Figure 2.6. (From Morris & Grant 1972.)

4. There was no replication.
5. There was an obvious alternative explanation in the high numbers of *Microtus* that were present when the confirmatory results were obtained in each year.

Synthesis

The requirements of experimental design do not need to be modified for ecological experiments, but certain of them do need to be emphasized. The requirement of clearly stating the initial conditions must be met, or there will be no possibility of using the conclusions from the experiment in making true predictions, because a prediction can be expected to be true only if the initial conditions are known.

"No control, no conclusion" is axiomatic in all experimentation, but it may not be easy to have and maintain satisfactory controls. This is especially true in field situations, where natural variation over time may cause the controls to become different from other treatments spontaneously. Complex experiments, of course, may require ingenious controls to take care of the various contingencies.

The great headache in ecological experimentation is natural variability of conditions, and the principal defense is sufficient replication. There has been a tendency to begin an experiment before enough time has been spent in measuring the variability and thus determining the necessary amount of replication. Some of the problems can be avoided by the use of a block design, or by stratifying the data so that significantly different parts of a population are analyzed independently.

Despite care in planning, there are still unexpected pitfalls in ecological experiments. The first of these concerns the problem of pseudoreplication. Baldly stated, this is the inflation of degrees of freedom beyond what is warranted by the design of the experiment. It happens when counts or other measures are made repeatedly in time, thus invalidating the assumption of independence. It also occurs where treatment and place are confounded, as when several samples are taken within treatment plots, and the variation among those samples is used in the statistical analysis. According to the strictest application of rules, we would be required to discard valuable information.

A second pitfall concerns the unwanted side effects of the experimentation itself. This may take the form of "cage effects." The dynamics of the population being followed may be altered through the experimenter's presence influencing the behavior of individuals of either the subject species or its predators or competitors.

Changes in controls during the course of an experiment may make them no longer valid. Natural areas have a tendency to vary in different directions, and such an event in a long-term experiment can cause problems. A second kind of problem in controls can be caused by inattention to such matters as changes in representation in stratified data, which can make important differences in the interpretation of results.

This chapter has presented descriptions of two studies that illustrate proper attention to experimental and other scientific requirements, as well as a description of one study in which so many rules were broken that the conclusions cannot be accepted.

3

Trade-offs in ecological experimentation

Introduction

Ecological experimentation has some characteristics in common with mathematical modeling in ecology, which has been stated by Levins (1968) to face the impossibility of simultaneously maximizing precision, realism, and generality [see a discussion of this problem by Hunt & Doyle (1984)]. Ecologists conducting experiments face analogous choices, in that providing confidence in a relevant ecological process may preclude its general application, or the requirements of a sophisticated experimental design may severely decrease realism, or the use of an elaborate design in the field may put the necessary amount of replication beyond the resources of the investigator. In each case, the ecologist faces a difficult choice. All of the choices should be made deliberately, because to let them be made by default can lead to a misinterpretation or to such an unfortunate effect as replication insufficient to yield a convincing (that is, statistically significant) result.

Generality versus confidence

Conclusions reached from ecological studies increase in value as they can be extended to more and more situations. Therefore, any factors reducing this generality should also incorporate sufficient benefits to offset the loss. Experience over a wide range of habitats might be offset by a thorough knowledge of the ecological processes taking place in one or a few. Anyone undertaking ecological experiments is faced with this dilemma. The experiments are needed to test hypotheses about the processes, but they necessarily limit the results of the tests to one or a few localities. One of the first field experiments, that of Connell (1961a,b), provides an example. The vertical zonation of marine organisms on rocky coasts is a common observation, and Connell's experiments on an island in the estuary of the River Clyde in Scotland showed that the lower limit of distribution of the barnacle

52

Chthamalus stellatus was determined by competition with another barnacle, *Balanus balanoides*. The upper limit of *B. balanoides* was set by physical factors, especially desiccation, to which *C. stellatus* was less susceptible. Predation by the snail *Thais lapillus* was not important at levels where ecologically significant competition between the barnacle species took place. Lower down on the shore, it consumed an appreciable proportion of the barnacles. The clear and convincing picture of the causes of zonation that came from Connell's work did not apply to other areas, even to such a place as Puget Sound in the state of Washington, where the same genera of barnacles and predatory snails were present. In that locality, *Balanus glandula* occupied the uppermost zone, whereas *B. cariosus* was found lower down (Connell 1970, 1971). *Chthamalus dalli* was found scattered throughout the intertidal zone. *Balanus glandula* was excluded from all but the uppermost zone by predation from *Thais emarginata*, which ranged higher on the shore than did *T. lapillus* in Scotland. *Balanus glandula* settled regularly over a wide range of the intertidal zone in large numbers each year and was shown to be competitively superior to *C. dalli* in caging experiments. The young *B. glandula* that had settled below the highest level were as regularly consumed. Presented with a dependable food supply, *T. emarginata* had become adapted to feeding higher in the intertidal than other species in the genus. Connell's explanation of the difference in ecological interactions was that in Scotland, where settling was less regular, such an adaptation would have led to starvation in some years. Apparently, in Puget Sound, *Chthamalus dalli* escapes predation because *B. glandula* is the favored prey, and *B. cariosus* becomes too large for snail predation after two years of growth. That did not happen often enough for interspecific competition among the barnacles to be a factor in determining their distribution.

The experiments in these two areas have revealed in each area the ecological interactions determining zonation. The interactions were so different that generalizing from either would be impossible, and generalizing from observation of the zonation alone would almost certainly be erroneous. Slobodkin (1986) has implied that we should not attempt to find solutions to large questions in ecology because of the complexity of the organisms and the world in which they live. Although the solutions of two decades ago were obviously too simplistic, I am not ready to abandon the hope of syntheses, at least for some environments. The field might yet produce another Darwin.

A second example will serve to illustrate the trade-off between generalization and local experimentation in a different way. The organ-isms are two species of terrestrial salamanders, *Plethodon jordani* and *P. glutinosus*, and an explanation of their altitudinal distributions in the southern Appalachians has been the object of research over a period of sixty years. *Plethodon glutinosus* is widely distributed over the eastern United States, and consists of a number of geographic forms that are distinguishable by color pattern, or enzymatically, or both (Highton 1983). In the southern Appalachians, it occupies lower elevations than does the endemic *P. jordani*, which is partially or com-pletely isolated at higher altitudes on a number of local mountain ranges. Early reports (Pope 1928; Bailey 1937) concentrated on geo-graphic data, but Pope (pers. commun.) believed that altitudinal dis-tributions would not be easy to interpret because the recorded loca-tions of both species included a wide range of altitudes.

My study in the Black Mountains of North Carolina showed *P. glu-tinosus* to be present at altitudes from 915 to 1,433 m, while *P. jordani* was found from 915 to 2,013 m (Hairston 1949). The overlap was thus 518 m, entirely consistent with literature records. However, my data had been taken in the form of detailed transects on different slopes of the mountains and those records showed that the altitudinal overlap was no more than 70 m on any single transect. The total reflected the variety of directions in which the slopes faced, with overlap at lower elevations on north-facing slopes and at higher elevations on south-facing ones. My interpretation was that the two species were kept apart by competition. Similar transects on other mountains in the southern Appalachians subsequently revealed that the altitudinal distributions of the two species differed among mountains. The situation in the Great Smoky Mountains of North Carolina and Tennessee was like that in the Black Mountains; in the Balsam Mountains of North Caro-lina, which are between the Blacks and the Smokies, the species over-lapped by at least 1,200 m (Hairston 1951). That observation required a different interpretation for the salamanders in the Balsams, and I concluded that competition was much less intense there than in the Blacks or Smokies. Extensive field work had led to two hypotheses about the interactions between the two species.

Experimental tests were proposed (Hairston 1973), and the experi-ments confirmed the hypotheses in that competition was shown to be more intense in the Great Smoky Mountains than in the Balsam Mountains (Hairston 1980a). The confirmation was satisfying, but still it is not known with certainty if the conclusions derived from the experiments can be extended to the remaining mountain ranges jointly occupied by the two species. The altitudinal distribution in the Black Mountains leads to the expectation that there is intense competition between *Plethodon jordani* and *P. glutinosus*, but the situation is complicated by the presence of a third species of large plethodon, *P. yonahlossee*, which presumably has requirements similar to those of the other two. It is not found in either the Balsam Mountains or the Great Smoky Mountains. Similarly, *P. jordani* and *P. glutinosus* coexist throughout the South Mountains, a small range isolated to the east of the rest of the southern Appalachians. The broad overlap in the South Mountains suggests that competition is less intense there than in the Smokies, as it is in the Balsams. It should be noted that *P. jordani* attains a considerably larger size there than it does elsewhere (R. Highton pers. commun.), and that could alter its relationship with *P. glutinosus*, which is larger than *P. jordani* in all other localities. These differences among localities, which are typical of many such situations, should cause us to be cautious about generalizing from even well-studied situations. We do not know how many detailed experiments must be carried out before the generality can be accepted. Perhaps some clear-sighted ecologist of the future will be able to use the accumulation of experimental evidence in at least one kind of habitat and produce the hoped-for synthesis.

Realism versus sophistication of experimental design

Ecological relationships are so complicated that in attempting to deal with them, we must, like Hercules fighting Hydra, put some of the heads under rocks while we contest with the others.

Dealing with more than one or two ecological questions at once requires a complex experimental design. The demands of statistical analysis are such that in complex experiments, variability within treatments should be kept nearly constant from treatment to treatment. Such an experiment permits a number of questions to be answered at once and also allows for the assessment of interactions between factors. The price to be paid is having a large number of experimental units in which the experimenter has a measure of control over the sources of environmental variability. The requirements are most frequently met in the laboratory, but there have been some examples of elaborate experiments that were carried out under seminatural conditions in the field.

Laboratory experiments

Laboratory experiments involve at least two conditions that raise questions about their ecological meaning. The first is the widely recognized simplified environments that must be used. This is an advantage, in that the conditions permit the experimenter to confirm or eliminate the importance of some factors that have been advocated as important from the theoretical standpoint. A good example is the large set of experiments on competition among an array of species of *Drosophila* conducted by Gilpin, Carpenter, and Pomerantz (1986). They concluded that competition was most likely exploitative, with some evidence for generalized interference, and none for specific interference. As might be expected from those results, nearly all combinations revealed transitivity of competitive success. That is, if species *A* wins over species *B*, and *B* wins over *C*, then *A* practically always wins over *C*. For *C* to win over *A* would require some form of highly specific competitive ability against *A*, an ability not involved in exploitative ability or generalized interference, such as secretion of a metabolite generally toxic to other species of *Drosophila*.

It is also noteworthy that Gilpin and associates found almost no evidence of niche partitioning in their simple laboratory systems. Coexistence among ten species competing at once never involved more than three species at the arbitrary end of an experiment; in the whole set of experiments, only five of the species were ever present at the end, and the authors argued that two of those would have gone extinct had the experiments continued longer. It is true, of course, that not many niche axes were available for the flies to partition, which is a partial explanation of the finding of the importance of exploitative competition. That was the nearly inevitable consequence of the simple laboratory environment.

The second condition that raises questions regarding the ecological meaning of laboratory experiments is the restricted array of species that can be used, especially the restricted array of *kinds* of species available for such work. Experiments on these species were of interest in the early days of ecological experiments, such as those by Gause (1934) or Crombie (1945, 1946) when the applicability of simple mathematical models was being tested. Practical considerations require that the species used in laboratory populations be both small and easily cultured. Thus, most ecological experiments in the laboratory have used such organisms as phage, bacteria, protozoans, algae, rotifers, cladocerans, and a restricted array of terrestrial arthropods: grain pests, fruit flies, a few mosquitos, and a few mites. These species, which seem to be preadapted to laboratory conditions, tend to be the adaptable "weeds." They lack the highly specific requirements that imply coevolution in organized communities. Few of them have been studied in the field to an extent that would allow us to suspect the factors determining their distribution and abundance. That is especially true of interspecific interactions, either competition or predation, that may have an influence on the sizes of their populations. The example of competition among the twenty-eight species of *Drosophila* from around the world demonstrates only that many of them compete in laboratory cream bottles, where they have little choice. The experiments tested no hypotheses derived from the ecology of the species, and no such hypothesis could have been tested, as that ecology is virtually unknown. It was not to be expected that they would reveal much of interest that could be applied to field systems where the species have evolved in the presence of competitors or predators.

In fact, it is difficult to find any population experiments conducted in the laboratory that were designed to test hypotheses generated from the ecology of the organisms as understood from field studies. The explanation advanced here is that field studies suggesting the importance of competition or predation have involved species that do not lend themselves to laboratory experimentation. Laboratory experiments testing field-generated hypotheses have involved not populations but individuals whose physiology or behavior was being investigated. Examples of that kind of work are the studies by Muller, Muller, and Haines (1964) on the effect of allelochemicals and Landa and Rabinowitz (1983) on differential susceptibility of plant species to herbivore feeding. The species involved could be kept alive during the experiments, but no attempt was made to culture them, and populational phenomena were not involved. There is no intent to denigrate such experiments. Many of them are revealing, but they are not relevant to the present subject.

Field experiments

Work conducted under field conditions almost automatically involves much greater realism than that conducted in the laboratory. The experiments are carried out where the natural situation contains the basis for proposing the hypothesis to be tested. Unless the postulated ecological phenomena are irregular in occurrence (Wiens 1977; Dunham 1980), any failure to demonstrate them means rejection of the hypothesis of their existence, or else means that the experiment was not adequate in design or execution. The requirements for any experiment depend on the question or set of questions to be answered. They are described in Chapter 2. For present purposes, it is sufficient to note that the number of experimental units depends both on the complexity of the design and on the variability of the data that are expected to be collected. Field experiments will automatically involve greater variability than laboratory experiments, and it can be assumed that the experimenter is limited in time and resources to the extent that the need for enough experimental units (plots, pools, or cages) to overcome the variability problem will limit the complexity of design and thus limit the sophistication of the kinds of questions that can be attacked simultaneously. Suppose, for example, that D. C. Smith (1983) whose experiment on tadpoles is described in Chapter 2, had needed to explore the effects of three levels of density or three levels of food. Neither would have been thought unusual as being of general interest. To have retained the same design would have required manipulating and monitoring half again as many pools, meaning perhaps more effort than was possible. To have explored three levels of both factors would have required 2.25 times as much effort. Keeping the effort approximately constant would have meant reducing the number of blocks, and hence the number of replicates, from five to either three or two. Anyone who has engaged in field experimentation will appreciate the danger of loss of statistical significance from the loss of replicates per treatment.

A second class of problems encountered in field experimentation can compound those already mentioned. These problems concern the necessary size of the experimental units. Except for trees, sessile or sedentary organisms pose few problems, the size of experimental units being determined by density and the number of individuals needed for adequate populations. It is the motile animals that cause difficulties. The necessity of knowing in advance the extent of movements is well illustrated by the experience of Schroder and Rosenzweig (1975). They investigated possible competition between the heteromyid rodents *Dipodomys merriami* and *D. ordii*. These granivorous species were similar in size and in terms of seeds eaten in central New Mexico, and although they showed differences in preferred vegetation, they were caught frequently at the same trap locations on grids where both kinds of vegetation were present.

The plan was to remove each species to two different levels on matched grids, retaining two grids as controls. A response of either species to the lowered population density of the other was to be interpreted as evidence of interspecific competition. Each grid covered 16.2 ha and consisted of 331 live traps set 25 m apart in a concentric hexagonal array. The diameter of the hexagon was 500 m, and none of the grids was fenced. The ten grids were placed at wide intervals over a total area of 3,108 ha. Captured rodents were marked with numbered ear tags, and those not to be removed experimentally were released at the trap sites. The most remarkable finding was the rapidity with which each species returned to its initial density on grids from which conspecific individuals had been removed. The opposite species responded to the removals to a negligible extent.

Intuitively, the sizes of the grids would appear to have been more than adequate for the experiment, as most small mammals are quite sedentary. That was not the case with these two species of *Dipodomys*, even though they reside in burrows. The new animals were adults that were distinguishable from the remaining residents only in the absence of ear tags, and hence the immigration could not be attributed to juvenile wandering in search of unoccupied habitat. Although recaptures between the widely spaced grids were rare, two instances show the remarkable vagility of *D. ordii*, at least. Between February and May, one individual had moved a distance of 9.5 km, and another had moved 5 km in one week. There was much more movement than had been anticipated, and despite the large size of the grids, they were inadequate to keep the populations reduced long enough to show an interspecific effect. Presumably, it would not have been feasible to enlarge the grids sufficiently without sacrificing important elements of experimental design, even had Schroder and Rosenzweig been aware of the extent of movements of individual animals.

Managed environments in the field

There are, of course, intermediate situations between the largely controlled conditions in laboratory experiments and the completely open conditions under which many field experiments are conducted. These may involve exclosures to keep out predators or competitors, with accompanying confinement of the experimental species and the general effect of such barriers on the physical environment, or they may involve outdoor containers in which there is control over all species introduced during the experiment, with accompanying loss of realism. The outstanding example of the use of outdoor containers to achieve definitive results is the work of H. M. Wilbur and his students (Morin 1983a; Morin et al. 1983; Wilbur et al. 1983). The use of numerous cattle tanks as surrogate pools permitted the establishment of carefully replicated but complex communities of amphibians and the accompanying array of plankton and macrophytes. Block designs controlled for potential effects of location within the hexagonal array of tanks. The elegance of experimental design was followed by sophisticated statistical analyses of the results, and the interaction of competition and predation in structuring the communities of tadpoles and plankters was revealed in impressive fashion. Pure competition among the tadpoles resulted in the group of metamorphosed frogs being dominated by *Scaphiopus holbrooki* and *Bufo terrestris*, with *Hyla crucifer* and *H. gratiosa* being nearly eliminated. With increasing numbers of the predator *Notophthalmus*, first *Bufo* and then *Scaphiopus* declined in representation, and *Hyla crucifer* assumed increasing prominence. Of equal interest was the relationship between competition and predation in their effects on the biomass of froglets produced. The presence of intermediate numbers of *Notophthalmus* reduced competition, and the tanks produced significantly greater masses of metamorphs than did those without predators or those with the maximum number.

There was some obvious loss of realism, in that natural pools do not remain the same size and depth. Wilbur (1987) added differential gradual draining as a manipulation in otherwise similar experiments, but the vertical sides of the cattle tanks remained an unrealistic element. Another unrealistic aspect of those experiments was the prevention of immigration and emigration, properties not shared with natural pools. Perhaps more important was the necessary limitation of the array of amphibian species used in the experiments. The most abundant four to six species of anuran tadpoles were chosen from a potentially interacting group of more than twenty species, and one or two species of predatory urodeles were chosen from an array of five or more. Thus, whereas we know a great deal about the ecological interactions in the tanks, the degree of correspondence between those events and competition and predation in the natural ponds is only partly known from an experiment undertaken by Morin (1983b) in the pond that inspired the work. Working with the two species of predators used in the tank experiments, he found that *Notophthalmus viridescens* preyed extensively on the eggs of *Ambystoma tigrinum*, reducing survival to hatching from 98.3 percent among eggs in the pond that were protected from

Notophthalmus to 3.5 percent among unprotected eggs. In the experimental tanks, *Ambystoma* larvae preyed on *Notophthalmus* larvae, and reduced their production to about 27 percent of the control numbers. Without the work in the natural pond, the mutual predation would have been unknown.

The natural predation by *Ambystoma* on anuran tadpoles is unknown, but it seems unlikely that it is as great as was observed in the experiments. A density of four *Ambystoma* larvae per tank (stated to be within the natural range of densities) eliminated all 1,200 tadpoles from each of three tanks and permitted only a total of 13 to reach metamorphosis from the remaining three tanks. Data were not provided on field survival rates, but 0.0018 seems intuitively to be low.

These experiments have resulted in a wealth of information about the effects of intraspecific and interspecific competition on growth, survival and duration of the larval period, as well as the potential of predation in ameliorating those effects. The difficulty is in translating what can be the interactions in nature into what they actually are. Seminatural experiments such as these provide one possible transition between variable and otherwise difficult natural situations and the unrealistically simple environments of the laboratory.

Sophistication of experimental design versus adequate replication in the field

A recurring theme in previous sections of this book has been that natural situations are variable and that the variability imposes a necessity to have sufficient replication to distinguish statistically between average differences among units that have been treated differently. In combination with the requirement that the units be large enough to accommodate the natural movements of a sufficient number of the animals being investigated, the need for multiple units imposes a strain on the resources of any investigator. The experiment of Menge et al. (1986a,b) involved monitoring thirty-two plots, each 0.25 m² in area, for three years. Their conservative estimate was that about 11,410 person-hours had been devoted to establishing and maintaining the study, and they acknowledged that they were unable to avoid pseudoreplication because of constraints on time and budget. For most of the experimental conditions, they maintained only two replicate plots. Fortunately, the effects of the manipulations were large, and two replicates were sufficient to show a number of interesting ecological interactions. With a greater, and not unusual, amount of variation between replicates, many of these effects could easily have been undetected, as in the equally sophisticated experiments of Hall et al. (1970) described in Chapter 7.

It is thus essential to establish the basic variability during the planning of an experiment, so that the choice of design can be made between an elaborate experiment that will test for several effects and their interactions and a simpler experiment that will give fewer answers but will have sufficient replication to ensure statistically satisfactory results. As an example of the difficulty in making the decisions, I have chosen the well-designed experiments of Stiven and Kuenzler (1979). They addressed the question of what affected the populations of two species of mollusk in salt marshes in the vicinity of Morehead City, North Carolina. The mollusks were the snail *Littorina irrorata*, which feeds by scraping surfaces, and the mussel *Geukensia demissa*, which is a filter feeder. Their hypothesis was that the animals were competing intraspecifically and that the most important resources were the deposits of detritus from the only important plant on the marsh, *Spartina alterniflora*, the salt marsh grass, and the periphyton on stems and the marsh surface. In the years 1974 through 1976 they carried out an intensive sampling program in three salt marshes, one of which (Calico Marsh) was heavily influenced by sewage effluent. In all three marshes, both species were strongly clumped in distribution, with mean densities being small fractions of the variances (Table 3.1). The distributions precluded the use of normal statistics in comparing the marshes, but the differences were striking, especially for *Littorina*. That observation forced a difficult choice in adhering to their experimental design.

The plan was to use nine treatments, consisting of three densities of the mollusks (normal, half normal, and twice normal) and three amounts of *Spartina* litter for each density. For use as a block, nine enclosures 10 m by 0.75 m were established in each marsh, there being no replication of any treatment within blocks. All mollusks of both species were removed for measurement and reintroduction. Unfortunately, the mean numbers removed in the different marshes differed by a factor of seven for *Littorina* and more than six for *Geukensia*, making the establishment of a single normal control density for all three blocks (marshes) impossible. Use of the observed mean density within each block would mean giving up the replication between blocks, and to use the same density for all would mean that the base-

Table 3.1. *Sampling data on two salt marsh mollusks over a period of two years*

Marsh	Month	Littorina			Geukensia		
		N	Mean	Variance	N	Mean	Variance
Tar Landing	10/74	25	18.6	506.25	25	3.6	20.25
	6/75	30	14.5	346.8	30	2.8	36.3
	10/75	30	11.3	202.8	30	5.7	218.7
	6/76	30	13.2	388.87	30	0.1	0.3
	10/76	30	11.4	346.7	30	0.4	2.7
Causeway	11/74	20	0.8	7.2	20	4.3	80.0
	6/75	30	2.3	24.3	30	2.0	58.8
	10/75	30	0.5	2.7	30	7.5	346.8
	6/76	30	0.7	14.7	30	2.3	19.2
	10/76	30	0.4	1.2	30	1.6	19.2
Calico	10/74	25	42.2	2304	25	2.4	20.25
	6/75	30	30.9	1598.7	30	2.4	58.8
	10/75	30	28.4	1555.2	30	1.6	14.7
	6/76	24	19.8	952.56	24	4.4	15.36
	10/76	30	30.7	4465.2	30	0.5	4.8

Adapted from Stiven and Kuenzler (1979).

line density, whatever was chosen, would be unnatural for two of the blocks. They chose the second alternative. For one block, the high density returned to the enclosures was below the mean number removed, and for another the low density introduced was nearly double the mean number removed. These statements apply to *Littorina*, but matters were little better for *Geukensia* (Table 3.2).

The results of these experiments are difficult to interpret. As far as survival was concerned, both species survived significantly better in Calico Marsh than in the other two (Fig. 3.1). This result was independent of the experimental manipulations, because Calico Marsh was intermediate between the others in premanipulation density. The sewage effluent may have had an effect on survival, or the greater distance from open bay water may have reduced the number of predators. Survival was related to the experimental manipulations in a few cases. *Littorina* survived better at lower densities in Tar Landing Marsh – the area where all experimental densities were below the natural density, a result that appears to be fortuitous. Similarly, survival of *Geukensia* improved in the expected directions in Causeway Marsh for

Table 3.2. *Existing densities per enclosure, and experimental manipulations of two salt marsh mollusks*

	Littorina			Geukensia		
	Tar Landing	Causeway	Calico	Tar Landing	Causeway	Calico
Mean no. removed per enclosure	342.2	46.9	150.2	21.8	8.2	53.2
No. returned at:						
Half density	75	75	75	14	14	14
Full density	150	150	150	28	28	28
Double density	300	300	300	56	56	56

Note: Each enclosure was 10 m by 0.75 m.
Adapted from Stiven and Kuenzler (1979).

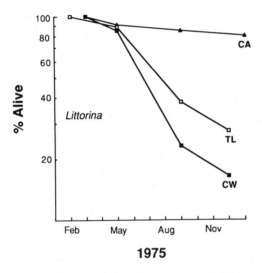

Figure 3.1. Survivorship trends for experimental populations of *Littorina* in Calico (CA), Tar Landing (TL), and Causeway (CW) marshes during the first experimental year, all treatments combined. (From Stiven & Kuenzler 1979.)

both density and added detritus, but note that all experimental densities there were three times that planned, relative to the local density.

It is easy to criticize this study with the help of hindsight, but the dilemma posed by the great variability in local densities of the mollusks would have required abandoning what was an excellent experimental design. In hindsight, it can be suggested that confining the experiment to one marsh would have answered the questions posed, but only for that marsh, and generality would have been lost. The actual densities were so different at the locations of the blocks that the use of more than one marsh would not have been feasible, even if the experiment had been redesigned so that fewer densities of mollusks or litter would be used, in the interest of increasing the number of replicates. The lesson to be learned is that it may be difficult or even impossible to devise experiments to answer every question we need answered.

Synthesis

Ecological experiments are nearly always conducted under conditions that force us to choose among alternative strategies for solving our problems. Some of the trade-offs come from the act of experimenting in the first place. Others come from limitations of time and other resources of the experimenter; still others come from the choice between levels of management of the environment in which the experiment is to be carried out.

Similar observations in different locations tempt us to provide a common explanation, but the hypothesis thus generated usually can be tested experimentally in only one place. A successful outcome gives confidence in the hypothesis, but the confidence may not be extendable to other areas. Two examples have been given in which it was known from separate experiments that generalizing from either would be incorrect or in which there was reason to question that further experiments in specific different locations would give the same results, even though the basic observations were similar to those in the locations of the experiments.

Experiments carried out in the field provide the assurance that results are applicable in the real world from which was derived the hypotheses that were tested. The price to be paid for the realism is that normally rather simple experimental designs must be followed, because the variability of most factors requires a number of replicates, and for motile animals the size of experimental units must be large enough to ensure a relatively small proportion of emigration and immigration. Experiments that are designed to detect several ecological phenomena and their interactions require low variances among replicates and control by the experimenter over the sources of such variance. That nearly always means that the experiments must be carried out in the laboratory. The disadvantages of laboratory experiments involve the simple environments that must be used and the limited kinds of species that can be carried through a sufficient number of generations for completion of the experiment. Both of these features greatly reduce the realism of the study. Seminatural experiments may offer a reasonable compromise between field experiments and those conducted in the laboratory. They allow both a larger degree of experimenter control than is true in the field and a greater degree of complexity and hence realism within the experimental units than can be achieved in the laboratory.

A third trade-off faced by ecologists is the choice between adequate replication to assure statistical significance of results and a sophisticated design that theoretically will answer a complex set of questions. Assuming that resources and effort are available to the usual extent, the variation ordinarily encountered in the field may require more replication than can be sustained in a complex experiment. Nature has no stake in our understanding its interactions, and it may not be possible to carry out all desirable experiments.

4

Experiments in forests

Introduction

Humans are terrestrial. Our experience is almost exclusively with that environment, and we should therefore have an intuitive understanding of terrestrial situations that is superior to our grasp of aquatic situations, whether freshwater or marine. For that reason, I have begun this description and criticism of ecological experiments with those performed on land. One of the themes of this book is that many generalizations in ecology are unlikely to hold across environments that differ in major ways. A consideration of the results of observations and experiments suggests that on land, interactions among the elements of the biota will be distinctive for at least the following categories: forest, prairie, desert, and tundra. Further subdivisions may be necessary.

A conventional and logical arrangement of the experiments to be described is to consider them in the context of the trophic level on which they were conducted, starting with the decomposers. It is recognized that it is not always possible to make the assignment cleanly. For example, in taking prey, most predators do not discriminate between herbivores and smaller predators, but for a considerable majority of the experiments, the assignments are reasonable. No attempt is made to describe all of the experiments on any trophic level. Those experiments selected either illustrate the interactions of greatest interest, or are examples of problems that face experimental ecologists, or represent good or bad experimental design.

Forests present practical difficulties for a number of kinds of experiments, and fewer have been conducted in forests than in more accessible habitats. In considering the results of experiments in old fields and other successional areas once forested, it is necessary to keep in mind the successional nature of the communities, because some of the processes hasten the end of the stage, and others tend to stabilize the situation. Descriptions of experiments in successional communities and in arid environments are deferred to later chapters.

Interactions among decomposers

In most terrestrial habitats, litter does not accumulate, despite the fact that more than 90 percent of the production falls to the ground uneaten. In tropical rain forests, the litter disappears very rapidly; in temperate forests, the decay requires two or more years. The eventual complete decomposition means that decomposers as a whole – the fungi and bacteria – are limited by the supply of litter and that competition must be taking place among them. It is not surprising that the literature on these organisms has emphasized competition, as seen in recent compendia (Wicklow & Carroll 1981; Frankland, Hedger, & Swift 1982).

An early experiment with five different fertilizers in pine plantations near Reading, England (Hora 1959), gave a result that strongly suggested competition between two species of basidiomycetes, though the detection of competition was secondary to the purpose of the experiment. Hora established five fertilized plots, each ten by twenty yards, in each of three forests. After the first season, he placed a control plot beside each experimental plot. The fertilizers were "hydrated lime," superphosphate, ammonium sulfate, potassium nitrate, and a "complete" commercial fertilizer. After the first year, the lime plot was retained, and all of the other experimental plots were treated with complete fertilizer, so as to obtain some replication, although statistical analysis was not reported. All plots were surveyed weekly, and each fruiting body was removed. Thus, after the initial removal, all data were for "toadstools" appearing during the week.

Interest here centers on two species, *Lactarius rufus* and *Paxillus involutus* (Fig. 4.1). Whether in control plots or in those receiving fertilizer, changes in abundance of the two species were in opposite directions in nine-tenths of the periods over which they were measured. In the control plots, *Lactarius* production declined in the second year, whereas *Paxillus* production increased in all but one plot between the first and second years. Lime obviously affected both species adversely, but the remaining treatments increased the performance of *Paxillus*. If the other fertilizers were favorable to *Lactarius*, it was only in the first year, and even that is doubtful. The obvious explanation of these results is that the two species compete and that different conditions favor their respective competitive abilities. It is possible to explain the data as reflecting opposite adaptations by the two species, but it should be noted that opposite responses to two different environmental fac-

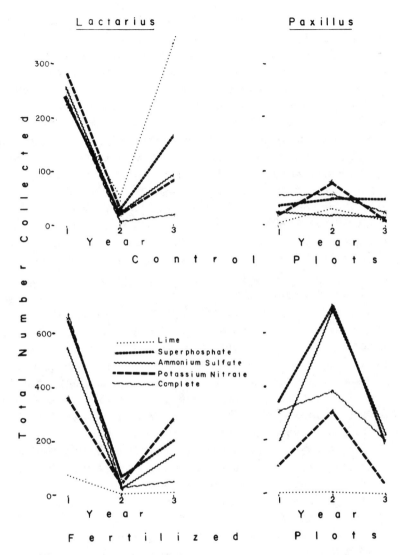

Figure 4.1. Changes in the abundance of two species of mushrooms, *Lactarius rufus* and *Paxillus involutus,* under several different fertilizer regimes and the controls for each regime. Each point is the total for all weekly collections for the year. The different regimes, except for lime, which was kept separate, were all treated with the "complete" fertilizer after the first year. (Adapted from Hora 1959.)

tors (years and most fertilizers) and the same response to another (lime) would be required to sustain that explanation.

Fungi are prominent in bringing about the decay of wood. Intraspecific competition in the basidiomycete *Fomes cajanderi* was investigated by Adams and Roth (1969). They found that ice-damaged Douglas fir (*Pseudotsuga menziesii*) supported multiple infections by genetically incompatible strains twenty-two years after the damage. The strains were distinguishable by the pigmented lines demarking the zones of contact as they grew together, whereas compatible strains grew together without such lines. The observation on sections of naturally infected heartwood was confirmed by culturing the distinguishable strains on agar and finding the same pigmented lines. All incompatible strains from three different trees were then paired on agar. One tree harbored three strains, one harbored four, and the third harbored eight strains. Adams and Roth pointed out that poorly located strains could not penetrate farther into the decaying heartwood that had already been occupied and were the losers in competition. They found that secondary infection was extremely rare, and they concluded that practically all of the competition was intraspecific.

Competition is not the only interaction taking place in the decay of wood. Blanchette and Shaw (1978) conducted an experiment on the effects of a combination of nitrogen-fixing bacteria and yeast along with different fungi as compared with the effects of the fungi alone and the combination of bacteria and yeast alone. They used chips from a mixture of conifers, some less than 1 year old, some 1–2 years old, and some 25 years old. Four weighed replicates of each age group for each combination of decomposers, plus uninoculated controls, were placed in quart jars and autoclaved. All except the controls were then inoculated with certain basidiomycetes alone (the brown-rot fungus *Poria placenta* and the white-rot fungi *Coriolus versicolor* and *Hirschioporus abietinus*), a mixture of cultures of *Enterobacter* spp., *Saccharomyces bailii*, and *Pichia pinus* alone, or combinations of each fungus with the bacteria–yeast mixture. The jars were sealed in polyethylene bags and incubated for five months. Two replicates of each treatment were kept for scanning electron microscopy; two were dried, and the weight loss during incubation was determined. The amounts of fungal chitin were determined by measuring the amount of glucosamine chemically.

Weight loss from decay caused by the fungi alone averaged up to 40.12 percent – from 11.43 times to 41.54 times the loss from the bacteria–yeast mixture for the first two age classes of chips, and from 1.40

times to 28.15 times for the old chips. In all cases, the mixture that included a fungus caused a greater weight loss than did the fungus alone, the difference amounting to 3–9 percent for most comparisons, but rising to 27 percent for one comparison in the second age class and to 370 percent for one comparison in the old age class. Glucosamine measurements followed the same pattern. The brown-rot fungus was about twice as effective in the decay process as were the white-rot fungi. All comparisons between means were statistically significant. Scanning electron microscopy showed the bacteria and yeasts to be closely associated with the fungal hyphae where lysis of the wood cell walls was taking place.

These experiments revealed the primary role of fungi in wood decay, but also showed the synergistic effect of fungi and the other microorganisms. No test was made for competition among the fungi.

In some locations, dung is a significant component of the ecosystem. It is likely to be more so in grasslands or savannas than in forests, but caterpillar frass can be more than negligible. Harper and Webster (1964) investigated the competitive basis of fungal succession on rabbit pellets – a conveniently packaged example of herbivore dung from a species inhabiting woodlands as well as open areas. They placed ten individual freshly deposited pellets on sterilized, moist filter paper in petri dishes and readily confirmed the sequence of appearance of fruiting bodies, with the phycomycetes appearing after two or three days, the ascomycetes after five or six days or longer, and the basidiomycetes and some pyrenomycetes after nine days. Imperfect fungi appeared simultaneously with the other groups. In general, the early ones disappeared over a period of three or four weeks. That the differences in time of appearance were not related to the latent period of germination was shown experimentally by breaking the spore dormancy of several species in each group and observing the time required to germinate. There also was no correlation between the time of appearance and the growth rate of hyphae.

The effects of the ascomycete *Ascobolus viridulus* and the basidiomycete *Coprinus heptemerus* on the phycomycete *Pilaria anomala* were investigated in the following experiment: A single spore of each was placed on replicate sterile pellets in the combinations *Pilaria* only, *Pilaria* plus *Ascobolus*, *Pilaria* plus *Coprinus*, and all three species. Thirty pellets were used for each combination. *Pilaria* fruited successfully on all thirty pellets in the first two combinations for all days 2–14. Thus, *Ascobolus* could not be shown to have an effect on the fruiting of *Pilaria*. With *Coprinus*, the result was quite different. By day 6, the number of pellets with *Pilaria* fruiting declined to twenty-eight, and that continued through day 10, when only two pellets had fruiting *Pilaria*. With all three species in combination, the decline in fruiting began on day 7 and dropped to three pellets on day 11.

In a similar experiment involving the inoculation of ten pellets by each species separately and all pairs of the three, fruiting of *Ascobolus* was strongly inhibited by the presence of *Coprinus*, fruiting on only two of the ten pellets inoculated with both species. The remaining combinations gave results similar to those from the first experiment. A third experiment, using a different phycomycete, *Pilobius crystallinus*, involved recording the numbers of sporangia produced by the three species alone and in all combinations; it showed *Pilobius* reproduction to be reduced in the presence of both *Ascobolus* and *Coprinus*, and *Ascobolus* reproduction was reduced in the presence of *Coprinus*. Again, *Coprinus* reproduced equally well alone and in the presence of the other two species.

The mechanism by which *Coprinus* suppressed the other two fungi was investigated by Ikediugwu and Webster (1970). A sterilized cellophane disk was placed on dung agar in a petri dish and inoculated with either a germinated spore of each of two species or a small agar block of mycelia from cultures of each of two species. There were at least five replicates of each combination (*Coprinus heptemerus* and *Pilobius crystallinus* or *C. heptemerus* and *Ascobolus crenulatus*). With *P. crystallinus*, the inocula were placed "5 cm apart"; with *A. crenulatus*, they were 1 cm apart. One day after inoculation, observations of the individual hyphae were made with a microscope. Wherever the hyphae of the two species came into contact, the cells of *Pilobius* or *Ascobolus* were killed in a specific way. The hyphae lost opacity, and also lost turgor pressure. The necessity for direct contact with *C. heptemerus* was tested by placing a disk of sterilized cellophane on top of a growing colony of that species and inoculating the disk with *A. crenulatus*. There were three replicates; controls used the cellophane on top of a colony of *A. crenulatus*. In a reverse experiment, a colony of *C. heptemerus* growing on cellophane was placed on top of a colony of *A. crenulatus*. Hyphae of *A. crenulatus* were affected in both experiments, the effect being more severe when the colony of *C. heptemerus* was placed on top of the other species. The experiment left no doubt that a damaging substance had diffused through the cellophane. Attempts to characterize it failed.

Harper and Webster (1964) conducted one experiment on the effect of dung bacteria on the reproduction of *Pilobius*. In contrast to the results obtained by Blanchette and Shaw (1978) on the decay of wood chips, they found that when ungerminated fungus spores were placed on sterilized pellets in the presence of a suspension of the bacteria, production of sporangia was delayed by one day, and the total production of sporangia over eighteen days of incubation was much reduced. When pregerminated spores were used, the delay was observed, but not the reduction in total sporangia.

Herbivorous and litter-feeding invertebrates are the major contributors of feces in forests, and it is of interest that a succession parallel to that observed by Harper and Webster (1964) was observed by Nicholson, Bocock, and Heal (1966) on the fecal pellets of the millipede *Glomeris marginata* from a mixed deciduous woodland in Lancashire. Similar observations have been made regarding the decay of deciduous litter itself (Hering 1965, 1967), as well as the litter of the major herbaceous contributor of litter, bracken (*Pteridium aquilinum*) (Frankland 1966, 1969). None of those studies included experiments on competition, but Frankland suggested that competition was responsible for absence of the fungus *Polyscytalum fecundissimum* from natural litter, although it readily decomposed bracken litter that had been sterilized.

The other group of decomposers comprises the bacteria. Competition within the group was investigated by Lowe and Gray (1972, 1973). They isolated 209 strains of coccoids from two soil horizons (A_1 and C) in a pine forest in Lancashire and conducted 179 tests on them, in order to classify them by the methods of numerical taxonomy. Five of the strains, each selected to be typical of a taxonomic cluster, were selected for the competition experiments. Suspensions of pairs of strains were introduced into sterile screw-cap bottles, each containing 10 g of sterile soil from one of the horizons (unsterilized soil inhibits germination and growth of most soil microflora – see Chapter 5). The suspensions gave a total of 10^6 bacteria per gram. Each experiment was run in triplicate, controls consisting of each strain introduced alone. The bottles were incubated for seven days at 25 °C, and the contents were assessed by the dilution plate count technique. Lowe and Gray gave complete data for the combination of one strain and each of the other four, and expressed the yield in competition as a percentage of the yield alone (Table 4.1). Growth on soil from the two horizons gave similar, but not identical, results, and the different combinations of strains gave yields ranging from 8 to 95 percent of the controls, show-

Table 4.1. *Effects of competition between isolates of soil bacteria having different degrees of taxonomic similarity*

| | | Relative density of soil bacteria | | | |
| | | A_1 horizon soil | | C horizon soil | |
A49 vs.:	Similarity %	A49	Opponent	A49	Opponent
A21	75.2	45	87	58	78
A81	54.6	48	8	32	13
A34	58.9	90	95	75	83
C39	84.3	17	38	26	33

Note: For each pair of isolates, the density after one week of growth in competition is given, as a percentage of the density after one week of growth alone. One strain (A49) was grown in competition with four others. Percentages estimated from the original graphs in Lowe and Gray (1973).

ing that competition was severe between some strains and negligible between others. It is noteworthy that taxonomic similarity gave no clue to the intensity of competition. The pair most alike and the pair least alike gave the two strongest effects.

Competition among decomposers has thus been found frequently, and it has been argued (Brian 1957) that the production of antibiotics is related in the evolutionary sense to the competitive advantage of the organisms producing them. Because most of the experiments on antibiotics and other inhibiting factors in soil have been carried out on soils other than those from forests, description of those experiments is deferred to Chapter 5.

Plant competition

A debate over the relative importance of competition among tree crowns for light and among tree roots for water and nutrients led to a number of experiments. The first of these involved trenching around plots in forests to cut the roots of surrounding trees and to release any plants on the plots from their competition, as discussed briefly in Chapter 2. Most of these experiments involved single plots and their control plots. One such plot was followed for eight years in a stand of white pine (*Pinus strobus* L.) in New Hampshire (Toumey & Kienholz 1931). The plot, which was 2.74 m by 2.74 m, was first trenched to a depth of 0.92 m in 1922, and then retrenched in 1924,

Table 4.2. *Effects of trenching a square plot 2.74 by 2.74 m to a depth of 0.92 m*

Parameter	Trenched plot			Untrenched plot
	1922	1925	1930	1930
No. individuals	388	640	1882	267
No. species	12	27	31	25
Height (cm); average maximum for each 0.093 m²			21.3	6.35
Density of ground cover (%)			48.4	2.9
Density of total vegetation (%)			80.0	8.1
Average height of white pines (cm)			36.07	6.6
Average height of hemlocks *(Tsuga canadensis)* (cm)			95.76	6.6

Note: The trenching was repeated at two-year intervals. The location was a mature stand of white pine *(Pinus strobus)* in New Hampshire.
From Toumey and Kienholz (1931).

1926, and 1928. In the initial trenching, 825 roots were cut, and the necessity of retrenching was shown by the 126 roots cut in 1924, and the 136 cut in 1926. The control plot was split, its two halves being on opposite sides of the trenched plot. The trenched plot was mapped initially, most plants being located exactly, but some clumps of grass and of moss were recorded by area. The mapping was repeated in 1925 and 1930. For all observations, the total ground cover of small herbaceous plants, the projected crowns of taller plants, and the heights of all plants were recorded. Unfortunately, no such data were recorded for the control plot at either of the first two mappings. The vegetation was assumed to be similar to that on the trenched plot at the start of the experiment. Photographs taken of the trenched plot and surrounding ground confirm in a qualitative way the initial similarity and the subsequent divergence of the trenched plot from the two halves of the control plot. The results of the experiment are summarized in Table 4.2. Were it not for the lack of replicates and the failure to obtain quantitative data for the control plot before 1930, the effect of trenching would be much more impressive.

The most impressive of the early experiments were those of Fabricius (1929). His experiments were conducted in two areas: a mature spruce forest and a mature forest of Scotch pine. In each area, he used rows of small (0.5 m²) circular plots in three locations: inside a mature forest (full shade), near the edge of the forest (half shade), and nearby but not influenced by the trees. In the first two rows, one-third of the plots were trenched to a depth of 25 cm to cut roots. The trenches were refilled. Each plot had seeds of a tree species sown on it, each species being replicated eight times. Comparison of the results on trenched and untrenched plots showed the effect of root competition for water; comparison of the results under different amounts of shade showed the effect of crown competition for light. Both factors proved to be important, the responses to each differing among tree species. All were affected favorably by trenching, but spruce and fir were less affected by shade than were larch, pine, and beech. The effect of each factor depended on the availability of the other. This experiment was excellent in design and execution. There were adequate replicates of each treatment, and the design made it possible to test both hypotheses in an objective manner.

Those experiments and the experiments reported by Korstian and Coile (1938) established the effect of competition among forest trees. It is noteworthy that the positive results of trenching were obtained in conifer forests, whether in Europe or in central North Carolina. The same experiment in two different oak forests (*Quercus stellata–Q. marilandica*, and *Q. alba–Q. vetulina–Q. rubra*) and in a forest of red gum (*Liquidambar styraciflua*) and yellow poplar (*Liriodendron tulipifera*) gave essentially negative results. Although dependent on negative results from unreplicated plots, the tentative conclusion is that in deciduous forests other factors are more important than root competition. Among these are shading and the well-documented effect of phytotoxins from living or dead foliage, as described later.

An interesting and ingenious experiment on intraspecific competition in the crowns of young forest trees has recently been reported by Jones and Harper (1987). In a grassland site in northern Wales, they planted 4-year-old birch (*Betula pendula*) trees in three triangular patterns, so that each member of a trio was 20 cm away from the other two. When planted, they were 61–106 cm high, and members of a trio were chosen to be matched in height. There were thus three replicates of the basic design. The branches facing the other members of the trio were in close contact over an arc taking up 60 degrees of a circle. This was the high-interference zone. The arcs covering 60 degrees on either side of the first zone were designated the medium-interference zone, and the remaining half-circle facing away from competitors was the low-interference zone. New primary branches were produced on the main axis each growing season. The youngest set was at the top of the crown, and progressively older sets were located down the main axis. Data were taken with respect to the age of the primary branch and the interference zone in which it was located. At the start of the experiment in the spring of 1980, and at the end of the growing seasons of 1980, 1981, and 1982, censuses were taken of all buds, their locations, their status (alive or dead), and the locations of all lateral branches. The status of each shoot (whether short or long) was also recorded. In the analysis of the data, trees were considered as blocks; the comparisons were between the numbers of buds (total and living) per branch, the percentage of buds starting the growing season as long shoots, and the percentage of long-shoot buds surviving to the end of the growing season. For the first three censuses, the total numbers of buds per branch were significantly different between trees and between the ages of branches. Only at the last census, at the end of year three, did the interference zone make a significant difference. The number of living buds responded to interference at the end of years two and three, with significantly fewer in the high-interference zone. There was also an age–zone interaction, with the number of living buds declining more after earlier branch ages in the high-interference zone than in the low. This was brought about by greater bud mortality on older branches and in the high-interference zone. Because new buds can appear only on long shoots, it is through these that growth can occur. Production of long shoots was greatest in branches 2 years old and away from competing trees. Older branches were more shaded, and the ones in the high-interference zone were especially so; the interpretation was that shading brought about the observed results.

The experiment showed in detail how differences in shape between trees in forests and in the open come about through differential growth of parts, brought on by competition for light. The statistical analysis gives some cause for concern, as the assumption of independence among buds and branches may be difficult to sustain, and the tables make it clear that the assumption was made. Up to 582 independent observations are implied for one year's census.

Some of the experiments on competition among forest trees were flawed by lack of replication, but the overall results leave little doubt that competition is important and ubiquitous.

The experiments on herbaceous forest plants have elucidated relationships other than competition, although interspecific competition has been implied in some of the discussions. These studies have involved the effects of elements of the physicochemical environment on the distribution, growth, and seedling establishment of common species, as well as the direct effects of chemicals produced by the trees.

Pigott and Taylor (1964) explored the effects of nutrients on the nettle *Urtica dioica* in Derbyshire and Cambridgeshire. Previous work had shown that the species contains a high concentration of nitrogen in its above-ground tissues, a characteristic that had led to the conclusion that the distribution of *Urtica* was primarily controlled by nitrogen. Pigott and Taylor recorded the ecological distribution of *U. dioica*, *Mercurialis perennis* (a second perennial), and the perennial grass *Descampsia caespitosa* in a wooded area in Derbyshire. *Mercurialis* formed dense beds on limestone scree slopes, *Urtica* occurred in narrow bands on deep mull at the foot of the slopes, and *Descampsia* occupied colluvial loam on the flat bottom below the slope. Analysis of the aerial shoots of the three species confirmed that *Urtica* contained much higher levels of nitrogen than the other two species; it also contained higher levels of phosphorus. The top 10 cm of soil under each of the three species contained nearly the same concentrations of inorganic nitrogen, although the limestone fragments under *Mercurialis* reduced the amount per unit area. Thus, the availability of nitrogen did not appear to account for the observed distribution of *Urtica dioica*, and Pigott and Taylor decided to compare its performance on the addition of nitrogen with that on the addition of phosphorus. They sowed fruits of *Urtica* in pots containing soil from areas dominated by each of the three species. Using nine replicates for each treatment, they added nitrogen to one set, phosphorus to another, both to a third, and all nutrients except phosphorus to a fourth. Controls had no addition of nutrients. The necessity of phosphorus for growth on all soils except that on which *U. dioica* regenerated naturally was abundantly confirmed (Table 4.3). A second similar experiment confirmed the results and also showed that *Mercurialis perennis* grew nearly as well without the addition of phosphorus as with it, and the growth of *Descampsia caespitosa* was unaffected by any fertilizer treatment.

These well-designed experiments gave convincing results, but the authors noted that greenhouse experiments frequently are misleading as a guide to the natural situation, and they conducted the following field experiment: Three pairs of matched plots, each 1 m square, were placed in areas dominated by *Mercurialis* and were seeded with *Urtica dioica*. One member of each pair was fertilized with $Ca(H_2PO_4)_2$ to a concentration slightly below that in soils where *U. dioica* grew luxuri-

Table 4.3. *Dry weight (mg) of* Urtica dioica *plants grown from seed on woodland soils*

		Addition				
Natural dominant	Soil type	None	$Ca(H_2PO_4)_2$ (10–20 mg P)	NH_4NO_3 (10–20 mg N)	$Ca(H_2PO_4)_2$ + NH_4NO_3	All except P
M. perennis	Mull	6±2	92±11.5	5±1	125±21	5±1
M. perennis	Protorendzina	1	248±26	1	282±31	1
D. caespitosa	Gleyed mull	4±1	214±16	6±2	235±25	—
U. dioica, no regen.	Mull	44±32	—	—	—	—
U. dioica, no regen.	Mull	67±5	251±55	—	—	—
U. dioica, abundant regen.	Mull	41±5	30±9	—	—	—

Note: Glasshouse experiments with soil in plastic pots. The other "natural dominants" were *Mercurialis perennis* and *Descampsia caespitosa*. Nine replicates in each treatment.
From Pigott and Taylor (1964).

antly. Two of the areas were in adjacent parts of the same wood in Cambridgeshire, one in an area of low light intensity, and the other in an area that received more light. The third area was dense shade in the wood in Derbyshire where the original field observations had been made. The results revealed a strong positive interaction between the fertilizing and light intensity. At high light intensity, the plants reached an average dry mass of 15.2 g without phosphorus, and 177.7 g with it; in low light, the averages were 2.0 and 10.5 g, respectively. In dense shade, *Urtica* plants could be found only on the fertilized plots, but they were few even there.

This study is notable for permitting the rejection of a widely accepted explanation of the distribution of a common plant, and it strikingly demonstrates the necessity for both greenhouse and field experiments.

A second example of an experiment requiring the rejection of an obvious explanation for the ecological distribution of a woodland herb was provided by Martin (1968). *Mercurialis perennis* is characteristic of well-drained woodland soils in England and on the Continent, as has been mentioned in the experiments of Pigott and Taylor (1964). Martin, noting its absence from poorly drained soil, tested its ability to occupy such areas in the absence of *Primula eliator*, the species of herb typical of areas subject to waterlogging in the spring. In May 1963, he removed blocks of soil 50 by 50 cm and 12 cm deep to make a trench from 0.5 m inside a *Mercurialis* colony down a bank to 2 m within a *Primula* area. Blocks of *Mercurialis* "turf" were then placed in the trench, and the vigor and density of shoots were recorded over the next year. Little change was observed throughout 1963 in the plants that had been moved to the base of the bank, except that they were slightly smaller than those placed within the natural distribution of *M. perennis*. It was in the spring of 1964 that the new shoots in the *Primula* area were found to be stunted and yellowish in color and to have reduced leaf area. The root systems of these plants were found to be impaired, in some cases to the point of their having no roots, although there was evidence that the roots had been extensive. Although unreplicated, the experiment gave strong evidence that *Mercurialis perennis* was physiologically incapable of existing in the area of spring waterlogging.

Martin also reported the result of an experiment begun by A. S. Watt in 1946. Watt established three quadrats in a *Mercurialis* area, and three in a *Primula eliator* area. One quadrat in each area had the soil level raised 15 cm, one had the soil level lowered 15 cm, and one was a control. In each quadrat, he planted three *M. perennis* plants, three *P. eliator* plants, and three *Primula vulgaris* plants. In 1947 there was a marked difference between the species on the quadrats in the *Primula* area. *Mercurialis* grew well in the raised plot, barely survived in the control, and did not survive in the lowered plot. Martin repeated the observations in 1964 and found that the raised plot was dominated by *M. perennis*, with some *Primula* present; the control was dominated by *Primula*, with one plant of *Mercurialis* present; no plants were present on the plot where the soil level had been lowered. In the *Mercurialis* area, *M. perennis* was dominant on all plots, but less abundant on the lowered plot. The results were thus similar to those of Martin's own experiment, but again there was no replication.

In a search for the physiological basis for the ecological response of *M. perennis*, Martin conducted experiments on its response to manipulated amounts of deionized water, oxygen, CO_2, manganous ions, and ferrous ions, all of these being different in well-drained and waterlogged soils. Because the other experiments gave negative results, only the one involving water and ferrous ions is described here. Eight seedlings were grown in acid-washed sand under each of these conditions: waterlogged with deionized water, and waterlogged with 5, 10, and 15 ppm ferrous sulfate. After three weeks, the only plants remaining alive were those in sand waterlogged with deionized water. The others had died at rates relatable to the concentrations of ferrous sulfate. Martin was able to show that water-soluble iron was present in significantly greater amounts in the *Primula* area than in the *Mercurialis* area. This was a thorough investigation in which competition was shown not to be important in the restriction of *Mercurialis* and in which the physiological tolerance of the species was shown to be ample for all conditions except for the concentration of soluble iron.

It has been demonstrated repeatedly that foliage, both living and fallen, contains substances that inhibit germination and growth of many herbaceous species. Observing that a number of species of herbs grew sparsely or not at all under a canopy of sycamores (*Platanus occidentalis*), Al-Naib and Rice (1971) conducted a thorough study of the phenomenon. They first obtained quantitative data showing that the densities of seven species under the edge of sycamore canopy and at increasing distances away were significantly less than directly under the canopy. They then established six shaded areas 2.5 by 1.5 m and showed that many of the species grew as well under artificial shade equal to the density under sycamores as they did in open sunlight. Moreover, samples of soil from beneath the trees were at least equal to those obtained from away from the canopy in soil moisture, total nitrogen, total phosphorus, iron, copper, and zinc. Thus, it was not possible to attribute the observed distribution of the herbs to competition for those substances.

Al-Naib and Rice conducted two sets of experiments testing for the effects of sycamore leaves on the germination and growth of eight species of herbs, as well as one experiment testing for the effect of soil from beneath the trees. For each species in each of the first two sets, ten experimental and ten control pots were provided with a mixture of soil and sand as a base. For the first pair of experiments, ground decaying leaves were added to the experimental pots in an amount about one-sixth that at leaf fall; an equivalent amount of ground peat moss was added to each of the controls. For the second pair, a leachate was prepared by spraying a fine mist over sycamore branches and catching the drip on plastic sheets. This leachate was used to water the experimental pots as indicated by the soil condition in the pots. Control plots received the same amount of water from the supply for the mist. In the final experiment, litter was removed, and the bare soil was taken with little disturbance for use in pots. The experimental soil was collected under the sycamores; the control came from elsewhere. For all experiments, fifty seeds were planted in each pot, except for *Ambrosia psilotstachya*, for which naturally growing seedlings were transplanted because of the difficulty of obtaining artificial germination. After germination was complete, each pot was thinned to the five largest plants, which were allowed to grow for three weeks, after which they were oven-dried and weighed.

All experiments resulted in significant depression of both germination and growth. Only with the leachate did any species fail to be affected (Table 4.4). In that treatment, *Elymus virginicus* and *Panicum virgatum* were unaffected. Al-Naib and Rice then went on to identify the chemicals causing the effect, and they tested the purified phytotoxins on the germination of *Amaranthus retroflexus*. This amounted to 15–51 percent of the germination on controls among seven different chemicals. The most effective was scopoletin, and the least effective was isochlorogenic acid.

The results from this excellent study are clear. The interpretation of this and similar studies is still controversial. Some botanists see an adaptive role and call the chemicals allelopathic, the implication being

Table 4.4. *Effects of leaf leachate of sycamore on germination and seedling growth*

Species	Exp. no.	Mean oven-dry weight of seedlings (mg)			Germination (% of control)
		Control	Test	F_s	
Ambrosia psilotstachya	1	937.0	358.5	133.3[a]	—
	2	823.0	321.5	127.5[a]	—
Andropogon glomeratus	1	181.8	178.2	2.2	70
	2	157.7	92.0	8.7[a]	63
Andropogon virginicus	1	283.4	201.8	4.8[a]	77
	2	313.3	215.9	6.2[a]	71
Cynodon dactylon	1	189.8	18.6	92.7[a]	61
	2	165.9	15.0	86.9[a]	53
Elymus virginicus	1	102.5	100.5	1.4	97
	2	87.4	84.3	3.2	91
Panicum virgatum	1	155.3	150.3	2.2	95
	2	124.2	121.2	1.8	98
Setaria viridis	1	296.7	187.5	21.8[a]	64
	2	329.9	232.5	33.4[a]	52
Tridens flavus	1	944.6	371.0	48.5[a]	67
	2	861.1	298.0	18.0[a]	74

[a]Weight significantly different from control at .05 level or better.
From Al-Naib and Rice (1971).

that they evolved as mechanisms for competitive interference. Others prefer the term "phytotoxin," and call attention to the possibility that they are metabolic by-products or defenses against herbivory.

Herbivory and secondary interactions between herbivores and forest plants

Damage by herbivores

It is widely recognized that terrestrial herbivores rarely consume more than 5–10 percent of the primary production (Strong et al. 1984b), and this is especially true for the dominant forest trees. The exceptions nearly always involve introduced species of herbivores that have thereby escaped from their natural complement of predators and parasites. Kulman (1971) reviewed the extensive literature on damage done to forest trees by insect defoliators and included a plea for proper experimentation before conclusions are attempted. His list includes many more examples for conifer forests than for hardwoods, reflecting the increased frequency of herbivore outbreaks in northern forests, but unfortunately he does not distinguish between introduced pests and native pests. Crawley (1983) gave a thorough, balanced account of herbivory and the related interactions between plants and animals.

The common and currently popular alternative explanation for the small fraction of production consumed by herbivores is that the plants contain chemicals that either repel them or result in depressed growth, thus providing mechanisms capable of controlling the level of herbivory. This section considers experiments involving the interactions.

The *Eucalyptus* forests of Australia provide the best-documented example of major, sustained herbivory (Fox & Macauley 1977). In contrast to the small proportion of foliage eaten in forests in the North Temperate Zone, at least 20–60 percent defoliation in both eastern and western Australia has commonly been reported. It has been suggested that the much smaller insectivorous bird fauna is responsible for these observations (Strong et al. 1984b, quoting P. A. Morrow), but other explanations are available. Loyn et al. (1981) conducted an experiment in a 3-ha area where defoliation by psyllid Homoptera had been endemic. They suspected that interspecifically territorial birds (bell miners, *Manorina melanophrys*) were defending an area containing more psyllids than they could consume. The birds were trapped with mist nets and removed to a distant area. Apparently as a result, eleven other species of insectivorous birds entered the area and consumed a much larger fraction of the insects than the bell miners had. The damage to the foliage stopped, and even though this was an unreplicated experiment with inadequately described controls, it does provide an alternative hypothesis to the lack of an avian insectivore fauna. The general applicability of either hypothesis remains unknown.

An experimental test of the hypothesis that insect herbivory was suppressing productivity of *Eucalyptus* was provided by Morrow and LaMarche (1978). The growth of eleven control trees of each of two species (*E. pauciflora* and *E. stellulata*) in the Snowy Mountains of southeastern Australia was determined by tree-ring analysis over a twenty-five-year period: 1952–76. In 1972, an additional three trees of each were selected. One branch of each of these six trees was sprayed weekly between December 1972 and March 1973 with a broad-spectrum, nonpersistent, nonsystematic, contact insecticide, the remaining part of each tree being protected by temporary shields. No further spraying was carried out, and after three years the sprayed branches and matching unsprayed branches were cut, and their growth was determined from tree rings. The sprayed branches of both species showed highly significant increases in growth in the three years after treatment, in contrast to the five preceding years. The average increase was twofold for *E. pauciflora* and more than threefold for *E. stellulata*. The unsprayed branches of the experimental trees had experienced a lesser but statistically significant improvement in growth as a result of the treatment. Branches from the eleven control trees revealed that they had not grown better during the experimental period than they had during the previous twenty years. It is clear from this experiment that growth suppression by insect herbivores was important, and had been continuous for at least twenty-five years. The use of tree rings gave important information about the initial conditions, and the experiment was adequately replicated and well controlled.

The situation in Australia is anomalous from the standpoint of the effect of protective chemicals. *Eucalyptus* is well known to contain high concentrations of such chemicals, and the fact that the trees are much more extensively defoliated than those elsewhere is evidence that insects are able to evolve mechanisms to circumvent the effect (Crawley 1983).

One of the most widely quoted studies of herbivory and the response of trees is that of Feeny (1970). Although the extent of damage to the trees was reported anecdotally, there can be little doubt that the winter moth (*Operophtera brumata*) causes extensive defoliation of oaks (*Quercus rober*) in England during early spring in some years; see the photograph by Feeny (1970). There is one brood per year, after which the fifth-instar larvae pupate below the surface of the soil. Even when there is extensive defoliation, the trees respond by producing further shoots, and the photosynthetic area is restored by late June. Although timber production is reduced in such years, the effect on the forest is not disastrous. This system has been the subject of much correlative research, especially of a quantitative and mathematical nature (Varley, Gradwell, & Hassell 1974; Hassell 1980; Anderson & May 1981), but experiments have been few. Feeny's work involved the suitability of the oak leaves as food for the winter moth at different times during the season. His first experiment was to expose twenty-five fourth-instar larvae to leaves collected on 16 May and twenty-five to leaves collected on 28 May. In order to make the test, he delayed hatching by keeping the eggs at 4 °C, and he froze both sets of leaves at -20 °C. The leaves were of necessity kept frozen for different periods to synchronize with the growth stage of the caterpillars. The larvae were fed on thawed leaves and weighed at short intervals until pupation. Freshly thawed leaves were provided at each weighing. The results of this experiment were dramatic. Larvae fed on early leaves grew normally, and the mean weight of the twenty-one pupae was highly significantly greater than the mean weight of the ten individuals surviving to pupate after feeding on the mature leaves. Ten of the former produced normal adults, whereas none of the latter did. A second experiment, in which early leaves and mature leaves were dried, ground to powder, and used to prepare an agar-based food, showed nonsignificant differences in growth of larvae fed the two kinds of food. Feeny concluded that the increased toughness of the mature leaves (which he measured with a "penetrometer") was the reason for the outcome of the first experiment.

Feeny went on to measure changes in concentrations of sugars, water, protein, and tannin in the leaves over the course of a season. The glucose concentration did not change appreciably. Water content decreased markedly, and protein concentration decreased to about 60 percent of the initial. Tannin increased greatly, and in another experiment he showed that it was not assimilated by the larvae. His conclusion was that tannins provide protection from herbivores, and although he did not make the statement that the winter moth population is controlled by the changes in oak leaves, he did state that the apparent excess of food for herbivores is not necessarily available as suitable food for phytophagous insects or other herbivores. However, his data show that at least thirty-eight species of Lepidoptera complete their growth on mature oak leaves (July or later). Thus, the potential for defoliation is present throughout the season.

Although no experiments have been conducted to test the hypothesis, there is evidence that the population of the winter moth is controlled by density-dependent predation during the pupal stage (Varley et al. 1974). A spectacular if crude experiment showed that regulation of a population of the winter moth that had been introduced into Nova Scotia was achieved by the introduction of two of its parasitoids from England (Embree 1971). The principal agent was *Cyzenis albicans*, which apparently was prevented from regulating the winter moth population in England because it was subject to the same predation as the parasitized pupae of the moth (Hassell 1980).

In a thorough study of herbivory on perennial forest herbs, Rausher and Feeny (1980) and Rausher (1981) conducted experiments on the plants *Aristolochia reticulata* and *A. serpentaria* and on herbivory by the larvae of the pipevine swallowtail butterfly, *Battus philenor*. The location was a longleaf pine (*Pinus palustris*) forest in Texas. Two factors were used: density of *A. reticulata* and exposure to the larvae. Four plots were established, but because two densities of the plants were to be used, and the same number of plants in all treatments were desired, the plots could not be the same size. All *A. reticulata* growing on the plots were dug up, and the planned densities (101 per plot) were established anew. The densities were within the natural range for the habitat. The experimental plants were dug up in December, after the above-ground parts had died back. The soil was washed from the roots, which were then blotted dry, weighed, and transplanted. The position of each plant was marked. Two of the plots (one of high density, one low) were surrounded by aluminum barriers to prevent larvae from crawling in. All plants were censused weekly March September of the first year and March–June of the second year. Each leaf that had been eaten was recorded (to the nearest quarter) on each occasion. Butterfly eggs that had been deposited on the protected plants were removed. All surviving plants were dug up in early July of the second year, and the soil was washed from their roots, which were freeze-dried. The effects of the treatments were assessed as leaves present or eaten, mortality of the plants, growth of the roots, and (for the second year, because flowering and seed production are underground) seeds produced. There was only one weak effect of density on any of the measures, either directly or as part of an interaction. Plants exposed to butterfly larvae had many fewer leaves than did the protected plants in both summers. Mortality was low for both treatments: 9 percent for exposed plants, and 3 percent or less for protected plants. The difference was significant. Growth, measured as final dry mass of roots compared with initial dry mass (calculated from the initial damp weight), was significantly greater among protected plants than among plants exposed to herbivory. Despite great variation among plants within treatments, seed production was also increased significantly by protection from the larvae.

This experiment suffered from the obvious confounding of the effects of place and treatment, because there was no replication. The probabilities were calculated from individual plants, which were not independent because of the confounding. Nevertheless, the differences were large enough to look convincing; the authors calculated that about 45 percent of the annual leaf crop was consumed by the larvae.

Herbivory was not the only interaction investigated. Rausher (1981) observed that in late spring, *Battus* larvae disappeared from *A. reticulata* plants much more rapidly than from *A. serpentaria*, and adult butterflies preferentially laid eggs on *A. serpentaria* at that season. Larvae were observed leaving the *reticulata* plants, and death could account for only part of the difference. He conducted experiments to test the acceptability of *reticulata* leaves of different ages, and the larval growth rates when fed on the same leaves. In mid-April and again in late May, he clipped forty plants at ground level, placed them in a special container of water immediately, and brought them to a laboratory, where he placed three second-instar larvae on each plant. By tracing the outlines of all leaves at the start and again when all three larvae had left the plant, he was able to calculate the leaf area that had been eaten. April larvae consumed a much greater leaf area during the thirty-minute trial than did May larvae, and the difference was statistically significant. This was related to the time they remained on the plants: virtually all in April, but less than 25 percent remaining on the late May plants. Because the leaves become tougher with age, and the fraction of young leaves declines rapidly in late April, Rausher concluded that the toughness of the leaves (due to reduced water content), combined with a drop in nitrogen content, discouraged the larvae from feeding and showed that no other factor, such as digestibility-reducing compounds, was involved. In contrast to the observations and experiments on *Aristolochia reticulata*, there were no seasonal differences in consumption of the leaves of *A. serpentaria*. Rausher found that *serpentaria* leaves did not increase in toughness as the season progressed.

By feeding larvae from a culture on either young leaves of *A. reticulata* (mean dry matter = 17.13%) or old leaves (mean dry matter = 28.81%), Rausher was able to compare the resulting growth with the amount of leaf tissue actually consumed. The approximate digestibility was estimated as the difference between weight ingested and weight of feces, divided by the weight ingested. By appropriate calibration, he eliminated consumption rate and compared the growth rates on equivalent amounts of leaf tissue. Growth was significantly faster on young leaves; 28.1 percent of the biomass of young leaves was converted into larval tissue, compared with 13.1 percent of old leaves.

In these experiments, the individuals, whether of plants or of larvae, were chosen at random and were therefore independent of each other, thus making the statistical analyses valid. Only in the first set of experiments was the effect of density tested. Because no effect was found, it is not possible to assign a causative relationship between any of the interesting factors and the regulation of the population of insects or that of the food plants.

Response by forest trees to herbivory

The chemicals incorporated in the leaves of oaks and in a great many other plants have been shown to have deleterious effects on at least some of their herbivores. The nature of these chemicals and their physiological effects are the subjects of a large literature (Rosenthal & Janzen 1979; Crawley 1983; Denno & McClure 1983). Of even more ecological interest is the set of interactions in which the plants are stimulated by herbivory to produce higher levels of defensive chemicals. Some of these interactions are described in Chapter 5. As far as the interactions between trees and their herbivores are concerned, the following examples have been selected to illustrate both the interactions and the kinds of experiments conducted.

Bryant (1981) observed that snowshoe hares (*Lepus americanus*) at the peak of their population cycles in Alaska browsed a number of deciduous trees (*Betula papyrifera, Populus tremuloides, P. balsamifera,* and *Alnus crispa*) so completely that they produced adventitious shoots in subsequent years; de Vos (1964) had made similar observations on Manitoulin Island in Lake Huron. Bryant further observed that the hares seemed to avoid feeding on the adventitious shoots (Bryant & Kuropat 1980), and he devised an experiment to discover the basis. He measured the nitrogen, phosphorus, and resin contents of adventitious shoots and of mature-form twigs of all four species. These species grow in clones, and he was thus able to avoid genetic heterogeneity within the treatments for the twenty-five clones of each species tested. The adventitious shoots contained significantly greater amounts of all three test chemicals than did the mature-form twigs. His next step was to test the hypothesis that it is the extra resins that make the shoots unpalatable. The resins were extracted from dormant adventitious shoots of all four species, and dilutions of the extracts were painted onto mature-form stems of *Salix alaxensis*, which does not naturally contain resin and is a palatable food of the hares. The dilutions ranged from zero resin to 160 mg g^{-1} dry weight, which is less than the normal amount in the adventitious shoots. Bundles of these treated stems, along with natural controls and controls exposed only to the diluent, were placed in the field in locations that had been baited with mature-form twigs of each of the four test species. The results were expressed as the percentages of the available dry matter that had been eaten after twenty-four hours. Nearly 100 percent of both kinds of control stems were consumed, whereas the resin-treated stems were eaten in inverse relationship to the concentration, with virtually complete rejection of stems having more than 8 percent resin. The experiment leaves no doubt that the browsing-stimulated growth contained enough extra resin to make normally palatable species unacceptable to the hares. Bryant also found that *Alnus crispa* and *Populus balsamifera* produced significantly more repellent resins than did *P. tremuloides* and *Betula papyrifera*. An incidental finding was that the extra nitrogen and phosphorus were not involved in the repellant property.

In at least two experiments it has been demonstrated that the physical damage by herbivore defoliation stimulates the trees to produce chemicals that have adverse effects on the herbivores. Haukioja and Niemela (1979) simulated herbivory by tearing some of the leaves of four mountain birch (*Betula pubescens*) trees two or three times per week. Intact leaves were collected from the same stems, and control leaves were collected from neighboring trees. Larvae of seven species of insects were reared on the leaves, each larva being kept in a separate plastic tube (except for the gregarious *Eriogaster*) and fed daily. At least fifty larvae were used for each species. The species were chosen to represent the full season when the birch trees have leaves. They were, in order of date of pupation, *Oporinia autumnata, Brephos parthenias* (both geometrid Lepidoptera), *Pristiphora* sp., *Pteronidea* sp., *Trichiosoma lucorum,* and *Dineura virididorsata* (all Hymenoptera), and *Eriogaster lanestris* (a lasiocampid lepidopteran). The response was assessed as the date on which each larva pupated, the weight of the pupa, and the mortality of each species under experimental and control treatments. Pupation was significantly delayed for both sexes of *Oporinia* and *Brephos* which had been fed intact leaves from the experimental trees. The Hymenoptera were all males, because the eggs from which they were reared were from unfertilized females. Pupation was significantly delayed in *Pristiphora* and *Pteronidea*. Thus, all four species in which pupation normally began in July or early August were adversely affected by the "induced" leaves. The weight of pupae of *Oporinia* grown on induced leaves was significantly less than that of those grown on control leaves. The weight of the remaining species was not affected by the treatment. The survival of *Pteronidea* was significantly worse on induced leaves than on controls. No other species could be shown to be affected. The late summer species were unaffected by the treatment, and the authors were of the opinion that only during the period when the leaves were growing was there an induction from damaged leaves to intact leaves on the same tree. These experiments were amply replicated and carefully controlled.

Not all tests of the induction hypothesis have been made in the subarctic, although it is clear that more stimulus comes from that area because of the higher frequency of outbreaks of herbivores there. In temperate forests, outbreaks are infrequent and, as mentioned earlier, are nearly always caused by introduced species. An example of simulation of the effect of the gypsy moth (*Lymantria dispar*) was provided by Wallner and Walton (1979). They artificially damaged the leaves of black oak (*Quercus velutina*), cutting off one-third of the surface on each of three dates. Gray birch (*Betula populifolia*) was treated similarly, except that whole leaves were removed on three dates. The dates of removal corresponded to the majority of larvae reaching the third, fourth, and fifth instars. Eighteen trees of each species were chosen, and half of them were defoliated in the first year. These nine trees, plus six of the remaining trees, were defoliated in the second year. Gypsy moth eggs were collected in three widely separated areas. After hatching, five first instar larvae were placed into plastic petri dishes, three of which were mounted onto every tree so that a twig was enclosed in each dish. As each source of larvae was represented, there were nine experimental containers on each tree. The petri dishes were examined every other day; dead larvae were removed, and the cause of death was determined. Pupae were removed, taken to the laboratory, weighed, and sexed. The responses, measured separately for the two sexes, were weight at pupation, developmental time, and mortality (third instar to pupation) under defoliation versus controls (first year), and controls versus one and two annual defoliations (second year).

Leaves on defoliated trees affected the larvae adversely. The mean weight of pupae on experimental trees was lower by a highly significant amount than was the mean on control trees. The result was confirmed in the second year, although there was no apparent further reduction from the second defoliation of oak trees. Developmental time was not affected by the treatment, except through an interaction with tree species, with larvae raised on oak showing a small effect, and those raised on birch showing a slight inverse effect. Mortality was significantly higher among larvae raised on defoliated trees, although the pooling of data from larvae of different geographic origins, which were significantly different in other responses, would be frowned on by statistical purists.

There was adequate replication, and controls were properly planned, but the unbalanced design in the second year, with the reduction in the number of control trees, apparently produced some anomalous results, such as larger pupae among those raised on twice-defoliated oaks than among those raised on once-defoliated oaks. There was, however, a convincing demonstration of the effect of experimental defoliation during the year in which it was taking place.

It is easy to conclude from these experiments that the increased production of "defensive" chemicals by defoliated plants is an adaptation to the presence of the herbivores. There is, however, an alternative explanation for the phenomenon. Tuomi et al. (1984) called attention to the normal balance between nutrients and carbon fixation by trees in nutrient-poor soils and to the physiological stress caused by defoliation. The effect of defoliation is that there is an excess of carbon and a deficiency of nutrients, and this situation can last for several years (Bryant, Chapin, & Kline 1983). The excess of carbon cannot be diverted to growth under conditions of nutrient stress, and the carbon is then used in the production of phenolic secondary metabolites. The hypothesis of Tuomi and associates was that although these secondary metabolites did have adverse effects on defoliating herbivores, that effect was incidental to the physiological state of the trees. They tested the hypothesis by examining available data obtained from fertilizing mountain birch (*Betula pubescens*) to different amounts as a means of decreasing nutrient stress, and cutting one-third to one-half of the roots to increase it. They found a significant difference in the percentages of phenolics in the leaves under the different treatments, and they pointed out that the relation to the percentge of nitrogen was an inverse relation. They also found that the levels of phenolics remained significantly above control levels for three years after defoliation, although nitrogen levels were not statistically distinguishable from controls after the second year. The negative effect on a forest lepidopteran (*Epirrita autumnata*) continued for four years. It is noteworthy that the authors proposed two means whereby the hypothesis could be falsified. First, fertilization in connection with defoliation should shorten the relaxation time of carbon-based resistance, and carbon-based allelochemicals should not decrease to the original level until nutrient stress is relaxed. Second, the long-lasting responses to defoliation should not occur in nutrient-rich soils. It will be of much interest to monitor the outcomes of these predictions, which appear to be properly a priori.

Herbivore adaptation to defensive chemicals

As already noted, it would be most surprising if herbivores, particularly forest insects, were unable to adapt to the presence of defensive chemicals at least as rapidly as the plants adapt to the effects of herbivory. The physiological mechanisms by which the various chemicals are detoxified or sequestered provide the basis for a large literature, much of it irrelevant ecologically. There are numerous papers concerning the ability of laboratory rats to detoxify chemicals, and there is a further large literature on the mechanisms whereby insects become resistant to insecticides. For example, Krieger, Feeny, and Wilkinson (1971) tested the larvae of thirty-five species of Lepidoptera for the presence of gut epoxidase, an enzyme involved in detoxifying aldrin. It was present in amounts that varied directly with the variety of their food plants, the maximum levels being found in those species feeding normally on eleven or more families of plants. They hypothesized that the natural function of such enzymes was to detoxify defensive chemicals that were present in the tissues of their food plants.

The experiments to be described in this section were selected for their ecological relevance as well as for other interesting features. They constitute only a small sample from the great variety of mechanisms that have been evolved by herbivores to neutralize the effects of defensive chemicals. At least two broad classes of mechanisms are involved: detoxification and avoidance of uptake into the sensitive relevant cells. Insects with the latter ability frequently store the chemical in their tissues or in specific organs, extruding the chemical when attacked by predators.

The plant kingdom has many species that contain chemicals known as phytoecdysones because they are chemically similar to the moulting hormones of insects (ecdysone). Phytoecdysones interfere physiologically with the normal metabolism of insects and upset the regular sequence of increases and decreases in the secretion of ecdysone occurring during the life history. Hikino, Ohizumi, and Takemoto (1975) investigated the ability of the silkworm (*Bombyx mori*) to avoid this effect. The normal food plant of these larvae is mulberry (*Morus* sp.),

Table 4.5. *Distribution of radioactivity in 3-day-old fifth-instar larvae of silkworm after injection or oral administration of ^{3}H-ecdysterone (0.5 µg/3 µl per gram)*

Organ	Distribution (%)[a] at time after administration				
	15 min	1 h	4 h	8 h	24 h
Injection					
Body tissues	30.3	31.4	13.9	9.5	6.5
Hemolymph	48.3	28.2	16.5	11.0	2.9
Gut	21.4	37.4	38.6	19.3	9.4
Oral administration					
Body tissues	17.1	12.5	11.9	5.9	4.2
Hemolymph	25.4	20.1	13.4	9.5	2.2
Gut	57.5	66.8	36.0	18.8	2.0

[a]Percentage of incorporation against total recovered radioactivity.
Reprinted with permission from *Journal of Insect Physiology* 21, Hikino et al., Detoxication mechanism of *Bombyx mori* against exogenous phytoecdysone ecdysterone. Copyright © 1975, Pergamon Journals Ltd.

which contains ecdysterone, a common phytoecdysone. Their technique was to synthesize ecdysterone, incorporating ^{3}H, and to administer the compound to living larvae, either through a feeding tube or by injection into the hemolymph. To test for the ability of a specific tissue to catabolize ecdysterone, they removed the fat bodies from fifty larvae, homogenized them, and incubated the homogenate with the synthesized compound for two hours.

At 15 min, 1 h, 4 h, 8 h, and 24 h after administration of the radioactive compound to living larvae, samples (three to five individuals) were killed, and the amount of radioactivity was measured by scintillation counting for each of three portions: body tissues, hemolymph, and gut. The results (Table 4.5) show marked decreases after 1 h. The compound was taken up rapidly from the hemolymph, appearing in appreciable amounts in both body tissues and gut after 15 min. The amount in the gut continued to increase for 4 h. Following oral administration, the gut continued to contain more than half of the radioactivity for 1 h. In the body tissues and hemolymph, radioactivity declined after 15 min. The decreases in amount of radioactivity were attributed to excretion into the feces. From the standpoint of protection of the insect, there was an equally important effect in the catabolism of the compound in the tissues. Ecdysterone is broken down into two major catabolites, which the authors designated as "Compound A" and "Compound B." On chromatographic examination of the tissues, hemolymph, and gut of animals that had been injected with ecdysterone and also those that had had it administered orally, Hikino and associates showed that most of the radioactivity that they had detected in the earlier experiment was in fact due to one of the two catabolites. They further conducted a bioassay of the possible effects of these compounds over a period of 24 h. The test was conducted by exposing isolated abdomens of the fly *Sarcophaga peregrina* to extracts from silkworm larvae at 0, 1, 4, and 24 h after injection with ecdysterone. Relative to the activity at the start, the activity of the extracts declined to 40 percent after 1 h and less than 13 percent after 4 h. Thus, it was concluded that the catabolites were ineffective and that the silkworm rapidly inactivates the phytoecdysone in its diet, in addition to excreting it directly.

The ability of some species to avoid the effects of poisonous substances is remarkable, in that it involves the absence of measurable amounts of the enzyme Na^+-K^+-ATPase in most tissues. Vaughan and Jungreis (1977) conducted experiments on three species of Lepidoptera (*Hyalophora cecropia*, *Danaus plexippus*, and *Manduca sexta*), all of which feed on plants containing glycosides – chemicals that are normally highly toxic, through inactivation of the relevant enzymes. Injection of the cardiac glycoside ouabain into the haemolymph of *D. plexippus* produced no observable effect in living specimens. The chemical was not inactivated, as could be demonstrated by chromatographic analysis of the hemolymph 48 h after injection. The enzyme does function in the neuronal tissues of all three species, as could be shown by homogenizing the heads and measuring the lowered (by 62–68%) ATPase activity in the presence of ouabain. Thus, it was the failure of the tissues to take up the glycoside that caused its lack of effect in vivo. These insects have the interesting property that their epithelia lack the enzyme Na^+-K^+-ATPase, and their hemolymph contains very low concentrations of Na^+ and high levels of K^+. Vaughan and Jungreis experimented with neuronal tissues exposed to ouabain and increasing concentrations of K^+. The concentration of K^+ necessary to protect the activity of the enzyme was within the normal range for hemolymph. These interesting experiments provide a convincing explanation for the ability of the insects to feed on plants that are poisonous to most animals, and they further lead to an understanding of how *D. plexippus*, for example, can sequester the chemical in its own tissues and thus be protected from its predators.

A second and more direct example of how herbivores use chemicals produced by plants for their own protection is the storage of such compounds in special organs, from which they can excrete the material to repel predators when attacked. Morrow, Bellas, and Eisner (1976) investigated this characteristic of a number of species of sawflies (Hymenoptera, Pergidae) that feed on *Eucalyptus* in Australia. The larvae of these insects have diverticular pouches of the foregut in which an oily substance is stored. They regurgitate this liquid when attacked, and most species exhibit group behavior in which they may array themselves in a circular clump with the heads facing out, or form a cluster and smear the oily fluid on their backs. Morrow and associates extracted essential oils from the leaves of *Eucalyptus pauciflora, E. stellulata,* and *E. viminalis,* subjected them to gas-liquid chromatography and compared the recorded traces with those obtained by chromatography of extracts of the oily liquid obtained by pinching larvae that were feeding on the same trees. In all cases the traces were essentially identical, even when two trees of the same species had slightly different essential oils. The oils in the food leaves were obviously the source of the stored fluids in the diverticular pouches.

The effects of the fluids on potential predators were tested both on Australian forms and on insect predators in the United States. The Australian meat ant, *Iridomyrmex purpureus,* readily attacked individual larvae of two species of pergids, *Perga affinis* and *Pseudoperga guerini.* The larvae regurgitated fluid, arched back, and applied the fluid directly onto the the ants or onto the locations of ant bites. Ants receiving the fluid, or approaching larvae with it on their bodies, walked away and performed cleaning behavior. If the ants received enough of the fluid, they were essentially immobilized and probably fatally affected. As might have been anticipated, the larvae were not completely immune to all predators. The ant *Myrmica pilosula* was able to attack small individuals and even small groups of such individuals by coming from the rear, but other prey were always preferred if they were available. The reduviid heteropteran *Leana australis* was able to attack groups of *Pseudoperga guerini* successfully by landing in the center of a group, thus avoiding alarming the whole colony.

Two American predatory vertebrates, Swainson's thrush (*Catharus ustulatus*) and the grasshopper mouse (*Onychomys* sp.), were presented mealworms that had been dabbed with a streak of discharge from sawfly larvae. Caged birds were fed treated mealworms in random sequence, one among three or four untreated mealworms. All 159 untreated mealworms were eaten, but only 13 of 55 treated worms. The rejection rate increased during the trials, only 2 of 12 being touched in the last part of the tests. The grasshopper mouse was less discriminating. It ate all 68 untreated mealworms offered, and 16 of 34 treated individuals. "Field mice" ate only 2 of 31 treated mealworms, while consuming all 73 that had not been treated.

These observations and experiments demonstrate convincingly that the sawfly larvae have made an evolutionary response to the noxious essential oils in the leaves of their food trees. They not only are unaffected by the oils but also have co-opted the oils for their own defense.

The final example of herbivore adaptation to defensive chemicals is that of the black pineleaf scale, *Nuculaspis californica*, on ponderosa pine, *Pinus ponderosa* (Edmunds & Alstad 1978). This insect infests the trees in outbreak numbers when dust or inadvertent spraying with insecticides kills its normal control agent, the hymenopteran parasitoid *Prospatella* sp. Under outbreak conditions, there is an extraordinary variability in the density of scales on different individual trees. Spraying insecticides on plots of trees results in a quick return to the situations on individual trees that prevailed originally: Previously heavily infested trees become heavily infested within a few years, those lightly infested become lightly infested, and uninfested trees remain so. Reciprocal grafts between infested and uninfested trees retain their original characteristics. An important characteristic of the outbreaks is that there is a strong correlation between the population density of scales and the age of the tree: In one study of 667 pines, 10 percent of those under 3 m high, 19 percent of those between 3 and 7.5 m high, and 67 percent of those over 7.5 m high were heavily infested. These observations led Edmunds and Alstad to hypothesize that

(i) individual trees vary in the defensive phenotypes which they present to scale insects;

(ii) selection over many generations produces scale insect populations which are increasingly adapted to the defensive character of their host tree (that is, the insects track individual hosts); and

(iii) selection of scale insects for maximum fitness on one tree is maladaptive with respect to the prospect of establishing colonies on trees of different defensive phenotype. The result should be a series of semi-isolated subpopulations, or demes, on individual pine trees. (p. 942)

They tested the hypothesis by transferring infested branches from individual trees in one area to uninfested trees in another area just before scale reproduction. The donor trees were in a dust-induced outbreak in Spokane County, Washington, and the receptors were located in a "clean" area 25 km distant. The branches came from ten donor trees, and three were attached to each of ten receptor trees in such a way that first-instar larvae could easily move onto the new leaves of the receptor. An index of survival on the receptors was devised, relating the abundance after one week to that after nine months (overwinter). The survival indexes were compared statistically for between donors, between receptors, and for the interaction. All were significant, a result that was consistent with the original hypothesis. In order to test the alternative hypothesis that differences among trees reflected a decline in resistance to scale attack with age, a second experiment was conducted. Again, ten donors and ten receptors were used, and the receptors were selected to represent a range of ages from 13 to 78 years. Two branches were transferred from donor to each receptor. After nine months, the means of the survival indexes from each receptor were compared with tree age. The alternative hypothesis required a positive correlation, but none was found. A third experiment involved comparing within-tree transfers onto treated branches to between-tree transfers. Within-tree indexes, as well as absolute numerical counts, gave much higher values and much lower variability than between-tree values, again confirming the hypothesis of demes differing in adaptation to the defenses of individual trees. Edmunds and Alstad pointed out that the evidence for genetically different populations was based on inference only, but because all of the experiments involved two generations of scales, any other interpretation is unlikely.

The experiments were well planned and executed, and the results were definitive. The phenomenon uncovered could occur only when the host plant had a vastly longer life than the herbivore.

The experiments that have been described demonstrate the complexity of the direct effects of herbivores, and especially the coevolutionary reactions by both plants and the animals that feed on them. Damage due to outbreaks of native herbivores in boreal forests is more prevalent than in temperate forests, where most of the damage is done by introduced species. The exception is in the *Eucalyptus* forests of Australia, a finding that would not have been expected, considering the plentiful protective chemicals in those trees. The well-documented ability of folivores to adapt to chemical defenses causes the critical reader to question the widespread belief that plant defenses prevent herbivore damage.

Competition among folivores and among sap feeders in forests

Intraspecific competition in a lepidopteran leaf miner species was investigated by Bultman and Faeth (1986). The location was an open oak woodland in central Arizona. Emory oak (*Quercus emoryi*) was fed on by a species of *Cameraria* that was found by sampling to be highly variable in distribution. Some branches supported significantly more leaf miners than would have been expected by chance, although the larvae were distributed among individual leaves in a manner not distinguishable from random. It should be realized that only about 2 percent of the leaves were mined by this species, and the effect on the trees must have been negligible; in fact, nearly half of the branches sampled supported no mines. In the experiment, twenty-four individual terminal branches (about 400 leaves per branch) were caged with fine-meshed screening before bud break. After the leaves flushed, twelve cages received relatively high numbers of adults (9 females and 3 males), and twelve received low numbers (2 of each sex). Counts of miners in the experimental cages revealed that the low-density treatment produced an average of 5.18 per 100 leaves, and the high-density treatment produced an average of 18.97 per 100 leaves. These were 2.51 and 9.19 times the natural density. Survival was significantly better at low density (16.6%) than at high (9.7%), and it was also significantly better on singly mined leaves (14.0%) than on those with more than one mine (5.6%). There was, however, no interaction between these effects. The differences between the two treatments were entirely due to differences among singly mined leaves – an anomalous result. This experiment shows that density effects can be obtained with crowding sufficiently greater than is observed in nature, especially when the herbivores are protected from predators and parasites.

In his review of experiments on interspecific competition through 1982, Schoener (1983) listed only four examples for forest herbivores, aside from granivores and nectar feeders. Two of these (Grant 1969; Morris & Grant 1972) were only partly in woodland. The Morris and Grant experiment is criticized in Chapter 1.

An additional example, which appears among Schoener's references, but not in his table, is an excellent study by McClure (1980) on two species of scale insects, *Fiorinia externa* and *Tsugaspidiotus tsugae*, feeding on hemlock, *Tsuga canadensis*, in Connecticut. McClure expected to find competition because of the distribution of the two species in Fairfield County. Both species had been introduced, probably at New York, and the prevailing winds blew from that direction (southwest). *F. externa* was absent from the six northeastern townships, but was present on all trees sampled in the five southwestern townships, and at intermediate frequencies in the intervening twelve townships. *T. tsugae* was present in all townships, but was less frequently encountered than *F. externa* in the nine southwestern townships. At twenty localities studied for three years, both species were present originally at all twenty sites. The total initial density was high: an average of 53.39 scales per 100 youngest needles, with a range at different sites from 4.5 to 127.8. After one year, *T. tsugae* had declined in relative abundance at eighteen sites and had disappeared from one. After another year, it was present at only six of the sites and had declined in relative abundance at all of them.

In three successive seasons, McClure exposed young hemlocks in a greenhouse by placing infested branches on them at the dates (7–8 June for *F. externa*, 21–22 June for *T. tsugae*) when colonization was maximal. Replicated sets (five or six replicates) were exposed to each species alone and to both species. The densities achieved experimentally were somewhat higher than the natural densities, but not excessively so. The range was 74.5 to 288.0 (both species), 10.0 to 138.0 (*T. tsugae* alone), and 37.5 to 170.5 (*F. externa* alone), all per 100 young needles. McClure used the ranges of densities to calculate correlations of survival, fecundity, and parasitism against density for each species alone and in the presence of the other for two successive years. For *F. externa*, survival and fecundity were negatively correlated in both years with its own density, both alone and with *T. tsugae*. There was no significant correlation of either trait with the density of *T. tsugae*. Parasitism was significantly correlated with the density of *F. externa* alone. In combination with *T. tsugae*, parasitism on *F. externa* was correlated with the total density of both scales, but not with its own density, nor with that of its competitor. For *T. tsugae*, neither survival nor fecundity was negatively correlated with its own density, but in both years they were negatively correlated with the density of *F. externa* when in the presence of that species. Parasitism was positively correlated with the density of *T. tsugae* alone and with the combined densities of both species when they were together. Thus, *F. externa* had a strong negative effect on *T. tsugae* by all three measures; the reverse effect was found only for parasitism.

The experimental results, which were obtained from a good design and adequate replication, confirm the expectation of competitive superiority of *F. externa* that was based on field observations. This example is especially noteworthy because McClure (1986) followed this work with studies in Japan, the location from which the two species of scale had been introduced. He found that in natural forests there, the level of infestation by the two species was innocuous – never as high as it was in Connecticut. His data showed that the scales had the potential to reach injurious densities, but did not do so because two hymenopterous parasites, *Aspidiotiphagus citrinus* and *Arrhenophagus albitibae*, regularly killed 90.2 to 94.2 percent of both scale species. This is a classic example of species that become forest pests when introduced into a distant area, from which critical native enemies are excluded.

There have been two other examples of experiments for which demonstrations of competition among forest herbivores were claimed: the case of leafhoppers (*Erythroneura* spp.) on American sycamore (*Platanus occidentalis* L.) (McClure & Price 1975), and the case of moose and hare on the vegetation of Isle Royale, Michigan (Belovsky 1984). McClure and Price made detailed counts of seven species of leafhoppers on sycamore leaves in two riparian forests in Illinois. In one of the forests, samples of 100 leaves for each sample at the time of maximum density revealed that the average was less than 2 females per leaf among half of the samples, 2–6 per leaf among one-quarter of the samples, and more than 6 females per leaf among the remaining samples. The overall average was 72 adults per ten leaves. The samples were taken up to a height of 4 m from five well-separated trees. Other data showed that the density was much less above that height and was negligible above 12 m, although the trees were 20–30 m high. Densities were much lower at the second site, where the overall average was three adults per ten leaves. The authors attributed the difference to heavy rains at the site of low density. Their experiment consisted of placing cages over single leaves, and introducing specimens according to the following numbers of males and females per cage: 1, 2, 6, 10, and 14 for single-species experiments, and 2, 6, 10, and 14 each of males and females for mixed-species experiments. The densities were realistic for the season of maximum abundance in the high-density location. Each experimental density was replicated five times. The response was measured as the number of male progeny produced per female, as only males could be identified to species in the mixtures.

Significant differences were observed between the responses of the seven species when caged alone at the two lowest densities, but each species performed almost equally well at those two densities. The differences between species disappeared when six or more adults of each sex were together, and no young were produced at the highest density. Eight different combinations of species were used. In all cases, each species performed better when equally crowded with another species than in single-species experiments, although not all of the differences were significant. McClure and Price interpreted these results to show interspecific competition and claimed that competition was an important regulating mechanism for *Erythroneura*. The experiments were properly replicated, and the controls were adequate for the interspecific effects, but not for any cage effects, such as the exclusion of predators and parasitoids. They provided observations on parasitization, showing that the natural parasite rate was low for most of the species, and they argued that the failure of the rate to change with host density was evidence against a density-dependent effect. There can be little doubt that their experiment confirmed the existence of competition at densities reached on one quarter of the leaves of the lowest 20 percent of the branches in the month of maximum density in one of the two study areas. Their hypothesis that the remainder of the tree was unsuitable habitat was not tested, and their finding that the inner leaves supported fewer leafhoppers than the outer canopy is evidence to the contrary. We are left with meager evidence on the mechanisms determining the density of these insects in the forests.

Belovsky's study (1984) of consumption of forage by moose (*Alces alces*) and snowshoe hare (*Lepus americanus*) on Isle Royale in Lake Superior made ingenious use of the difference in the appearance of the twigs after each species had fed. Most of the work was not experimental, and the primary purpose was to apply the Schoener (1974, 1976, 1978) competition equations to data from the moose–hare system. The actual evidence that the two species compete depended on a negative correlation between the number of twigs removed per plant by each species in a series of plots, two of which had been fenced to exclude moose. The remaining thirteen plots were open, and some of them were in locations where hares were absent or nearly so. The graph presented by Belovsky reveals that although there is a statistically significant negative relationship over the fifteen plots, the statistical effect is produced by the four extreme points. The remaining eleven points cannot be construed as contributing to the correlation. In view of the complexity of both moose and hare populations with respect to their predators (Mech 1966, 1974; Jordan, Botkin, & Wolfe 1971; Brand, Keith, & Fischer 1976), the claim of competition between them without a better experiment than the one described is difficult to sustain.

A revealing experiment on forest herbivores was conducted by Strong (1982, 1984), who worked with tropical leaf beetles (hispine Chrysomelidae) living on the abundant understory plant *Heliconia*. This is a perennial monocot, a close relative of the banana, and it grows in clumps. Leaves appear singly, and at first they are tightly furled. As they open, the beetles enter at the tip and begin to feed on the tender, still rolled-up parts. Fully opened leaves are unsuitable locations for the beetles, and they leave before unfurling is complete.

Strong collected fifty-three samples, each consisting of a number of leaves from a nearly pure clump of one species of *Heliconia*. He identified and counted the beetles in each sample and analyzed the data for associations between species among the individual leaves. The analysis consisted of calculating the signed square root of chi-square for the forty-six samples having two or more species present. The values ranged from -2.5 to $+2.2$, with a distribution not distinguishable from normal. There was no indication of a tendency for the species to segregate among the leaves in a sample.

To test the implied assumption that the species did not distinguish among leaves, Strong conducted the following experiment: He created a fairly dense stand of pure *H. imbricata* and put plastic bags over the tips of developing leaves as soon as they appeared and before they started to unfurl. When they opened to 2 cm, he removed the bags and introduced predetermined numbers of one species into half of the leaves and the same numbers of a second species into the other half. Colonization by the free community then took place until the leaves began to open enough to stimulate departure of the beetles. This took place after either twenty-four or forty-eight hours, giving him four different experimental "samples." The signed square root of chi-square for these four ranged between -0.5 and $+1.0$ and fell symmetrically near the center of distribution for the natural samples. Inasmuch as he chose the leaves to be as much alike as possible and assigned treatments at random, he believed that he had eliminated any between-leaf heterogeneity. A second method of analyzing the data was to calculate partial correlation coefficients between densities of the species, taken two at a time. This gave him a large number of coefficients, of which only four were significantly negative, whereas twenty-two were significantly positive (most were nonsignificant). The experimental communities were typical of the group as a whole. Again, there was no evidence of segregation between the species, as would have been expected had they been competing.

A laboratory experiment in which protected beetles were offered either pieces of newly opened leaves or undamaged parts of leaves from which the beetles had emigrated revealed no preference, demonstrating that the leftover parts were still acceptable as food. Strong concluded that there was no competition among the species and, furthermore, that the populations were most likely kept below carrying capacity by predation, probably by parasitoids. Although much of this study was observational, rather than experimental, properly controlled and replicated experiments were used to test hypotheses derived from the observations.

The experiments on competition among forest herbivores leave serious doubt about its importance in the community. Only the experiment of McClure gave unequivocal evidence for interspecific competition severe enough to support resource depletion as a mechanism limiting the populations of the herbivores, and his work was on introduced species, which could be expected to be exceptional.

Effects of enemies on forest herbivores

Competition among bird species has played such an important part in the development of ecological theory that it is surprising that their impact on presumed resources has been largely neglected. An exception is the experiment of Holmes, Schultz, and Nothnagle (1979). They constructed ten large netting cages (6 × 6 × 2 m) in Hubbard Brook Forest in New Hampshire. The cages were placed over the understory shrubs (*Acer pennsylvanicum*), and ten matching areas were selected as controls. The mesh was fine enough to exclude birds, but not insects. The arthropod populations were followed by counting the numbers on 400 leaves in each cage and on each control plot. Caterpillar numbers were greater inside the cages than on the control plots throughout June, July, and August, and on two occasions the difference was statistically significant, as was the overall mean. Despite the temporal pseudoreplication involved in the overall mean, the effect of excluding birds was convincing. Moreover, the seasonal variation in generations among insects would have greatly reduced any autocorrelation between successive samples from the same cages and plots and

Table 4.6. *Fate of leaf miners examined on trees from which invertebrate predators were excluded, compared with two sets of control trees*

Condition	Total mines examined	% preyed on	% vacated	% dead (unknown causes)
Predators excluded	141	4.3	72.3	23.4
Control 1	39	25.6**	48.7*	25.6 (NS)
Control 2	197	42.6**	42.1**	15.2 (NS)

Note: Significances of differences between treatment and controls [comparison of percentages, Sokal & Rohlf (1981, p. 607)] are as follows: NS = not significantly different ($p > .05$); *$p < .01$; **$p < .001$.
From Faeth (1980).

thus brought about greater independence. Other arthropods (Coleoptera, Homoptera, Hemiptera, and Arachnida) were not significantly different in abundance inside and outside the cages.

Strong effects of invertebrate predators on herbivorous insects have been demonstrated in two experiments. In the first, Faeth (1980) excluded the ants *Crematogaster ashmeadi* and *Pseudomyrmex brunnea* from oaks (*Quercus nigra*) in a pine–oak stand in northern Florida. He applied a sticky insect barrier to the trunks of ten trees and followed the fate of the lepidopteran leaf miner *Eriocraniella* sp. on those trees, on ten control trees in the same stand, and on ten more controls 1.7 km distant. He was able to identify mines from which the insects had emerged successfully, those that obviously had been preyed on, and those whose inhabitants were dead from unknown causes. His results (Table 4.6) leave no doubt that ground-dwelling predators constituted an important source of mortality. Deaths from unknown causes did not differ significantly among the three groups of trees. Perhaps the most interesting aspect of this study is the low natural density of the leaf miner (less than two mines per 100 leaves). The ants must be unusually efficient at locating them. Faeth cites an estimate that at least 10 percent of leaves must be mined for bird predation to be energetically profitable.

A similar experiment was carried out on forest trees by Skinner and Whittaker (1981), who examined the effects of ants on caterpillars and aphids on oaks and maples. After observing that some areas in Cringlebarrow Wood in northwest England contained populations of ants, whereas others did not, and that the areas where ants (*Formica rufa*)

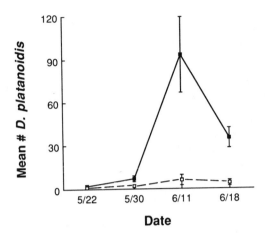

Figure 4.2. Seasonal variation in mean number of *D. platanoidis* per shoot on six banded and six unbanded shoots at Thrang Wood. Vertical bars represent 1 s.e. (From Skinner & Whittaker 1981.)

were active had significantly fewer caterpillars per 100 shoots than did those where ants were absent, they excluded ants from a series of shoots of sycamore trees (*Acer pseudoplatanus*) at nearby Thrang Wood by banding the bases of the shoots with a material that prevented the ants from reaching the buds. Numbers of herbivorous insects per shoot were followed from mid-May to mid-June on experimental and control shoots (Fig. 4.2). By early June, there was a significant increase in the abundance of the aphid *Drepanosiphum platanoidis* where ants had been excluded.

As part of the study of the butterfly *Battus philenor* and its food plants described earlier, Rausher (1981) assessed the effect of predators on the survival of *B. philenor* larvae. He selected 120 *A. reticulata* plants and assigned them randomly to one of four treatments: early season plants protected by screening, early season controls, late season protected plants, and late season controls. In addition to screening, the protected plants were surrounded by sheets of plastic onto which a sticky substance was applied in three strips to prevent ground-dwelling predators from reaching the plants. A significantly greater proportion of larvae remained on the protected plants until the third instar (early season = 0.778, late season = 0.482) than on the controls (early season = 0.366, late season = 0.103). The difference between seasons was also significant, but the interaction between treatment and season was not.

Experiments excluding flying predators from forest trees are impractical in many cases, but one such experiment, never before reported, was conducted at the University of Michigan by Professor D. G. Shappirio. Professor Shappirio was engaged in neurohormonal research on the large cecropia moths (*Hyalophora cecropia*), and raised them on native cherry trees. He had found that in order to recover any cocoons, he had to cover the trees with insect netting before he placed eggs on the trees, thus protecting the growing caterpillars from predatory and parasitoid insects, as well as from birds. He demonstrated the effectiveness of the netting by setting out eggs in his routine fashion on covered trees and on additional cherry trees with no netting. It was the original intention to count the ratio between cocoons recovered and eggs set out under both conditions. Counts were unnecessary, as not a single caterpillar survived to pupate where they were unprotected by the netting. Because several trees were chosen at random for each condition, it was a valid experiment, and a convincing one. Professor Shappirio concluded that in nature, the species must survive in situations where the caterpillars are less exposed, as in dense thickets.

All of the experiments showed that predators and/or parasitoids had highly significant effects on the populations of forest herbivores, in some cases even though the latter were present in remarkably small numbers.

Competition among forest granivores

The reasons for distinguishing between herbivores that feed on foliage or sap and those that feed on seeds have been explained elsewhere (Hairston 1964). Many of the former are specialists on single species or small groups of related species of plants, and rarely do they enlarge their diets to include animal food. The latter, in contrast, normally feed on a variety of seeds, and in a number of cases, they become predators, especially in seasons when young are being reared. Failure to recognize the importance of this distinction has led several authors to consider the hypothesis of lack of competition among "herbivores" false, most recently Sih et al. (1985).

Three studies, one on birds and two on rodents, concluded that competition was involved. Williams and Batzli (1979a) worked with bark-foraging birds in a forest in Illinois. Three species of woodpeckers, red-headed (*Melanerpes erythrocephalus*), red-bellied (*M. carolinus*), and downy (*Picoides pubescens*), plus the white-breasted nuthatch (*Sitta carolinensis*), were observed in two upland forests and the intervening and adjacent lowland forest. The four species depend on mast, corn, and other seeds to different degrees in the winter. The red-headed woodpecker stores this food in cracks in bark and defends an interspecific territory aggressively; the red-bellied woodpecker uses much the same food, but neither stores food nor defends a winter territory; the downy woodpecker is much more insectivorous than the other two, but feeds on seeds occasionally; the nuthatch feeds on seeds and stores them in cracks in bark. The experiment was conducted to test the hypothesis that red-headed woodpeckers, which are primarily birds of upland forests, exclude red-bellied woodpeckers and nuthatches from that habitat and prevent downy woodpeckers from foraging in the upper branches of trees. Preliminary observations showed that both upland forests were occupied by red-headed woodpeckers and that one pair of red-bellied woodpeckers foraged in the adjacent lowland forest, along with white-breasted nuthatches. Downy woodpeckers were present in the upland forest, but most of their activity was below the height at which the red-headed woodpeckers normally foraged. The experiment consisted of removing the red-headed woodpeckers from one of the two upland forests and monitoring both forests for two years. The pair of red-bellied woodpeckers occupied the upland forest from which the red-headed woodpeckers had been removed and foraged at the heights favored by the absent species. The same was true of the nuthatches. Downy woodpeckers foraged higher in the trees in the experimental forest, but remained at lower levels in the control. In the second year of the experiment, the acorn crop "failed," and the red-headed woodpeckers emigrated. The authors did not report any change in the distributions of the remaining species during that unmanipulated absence, but the same thing had happened in the year before the experiment began, and they had observed appropriate shifts then (Williams & Batzli 1979b). The absence of replication in this study and the use of data on individual birds to calculate probabilities are causes for concern, despite the apparent confirmation of expectations.

Chipmunks are typical granivores, eating seeds mostly, but taking animal food when it is available. Chappell (1978) conducted a removal experiment in an area in the Sierra Nevada of California, where two species, *Eutamias amoenus* and *E. minimus*, have a parapatric distribution along the boundary between a pine–mountain mahogany forest, inhabited by *E. amoenus*, and a sagebrush community, inhabited by *E. minimus*. A continuous grid of live traps, set 40 m apart in a rectangular array of fifteen traps by eleven traps and covering both habitats, was used to establish preliminary data for a full active season. In the second year, one-third of the grid was used to remove all *amoenus*, the middle third was used as an unmanipulated control, and the remaining one-third was used to remove *minimus*. Because each third covered both habitats, the response was measured as the invasion of the habitat that was not typical of the species at the location. Probably because of a wet summer in the first year and a mild intervening winter, both species were at least twice as abundant at the start of the experiment as they previously had been. The effect of removing *amoenus* was a significant increase in the percentage of captures of *minimus* in the forest over the preliminary data and over the controls during the experiment. For *amoenus*, removing *minimus* gave a significant increase in captures in sagebrush over those in the experimental part of the grid the year before. During the experiment there was no significant difference between the experimental and control parts of the grid. In addition to that difference between the species, *minimus* established territories in the forest during the experiment, whereas *amoenus* made only temporary excursions into the sagebrush. Observation positions were used to obtain information on the behavior of the chipmunks, and it was clear that in interspecific encounters, *amoenus* was nearly always the winner, although intraspecifically *minimus* was as aggressive. Chappell concluded that the asymmetrical result of the experiment was due to the inability of the behavioral dominant to tolerate the dry sagebrush habitat physiologically, whereas there was no such barrier preventing *minimus* from occupying the forest in the absence of *amoenus*.

The result of the experiment seems clear enough, despite the absence of replication. The shifts within the experimental grids were more convincing than differences between them.

The final experiment in this group is that of Montgomery (1981), involving two species of wood mice, *Apodemus sylvaticus* and *A. flavicollis*, in a mixed deciduous woodland in Gloucestershire, England. Three trap grids were set up in woodland known to have populations of both species. The grids had two live traps set at each point in a seven-by-seven-point square, the points being 10 m apart. Trapping was carried out for twelve months before any manipulation, thus establishing good baseline data. From January through July, *A. sylvaticus* was removed continually from one grid, and *A. flavicollis* from another, with the third retained as a control. The period was chosen to coincide with the most critical time during the annual cycle of both species and thus was most likely to give a positive result. A statistically significant effect of removing *A. sylvaticus* on the abundance of *A. flavicollis* was claimed, but the graph of results does not show an impressive effect, as Montgomery acknowledged. The lack of replication and the statistical analysis involving repeated samples from the same grid (thus lacking independence) make the result less than convincing.

Although all three experiments with forest granivores claimed to have found interspecific competition, all were flawed in their lack of replication. Experiments with better design are needed, as are experiments dealing with granivorous invertebrates, such as weevils feeding on acorns.

Interactions among forest predators

Birds

Because competition between species of birds has figured so largely in community and biogeographic theory, it is important to present a critique of the experiments bearing on the subject. Such experiments are difficult, because flight makes enclosures impractical and increases the complication of immigration and emigration, and because manipulating bird populations is either forbidden legally or frowned on socially. About half of such experiments have involved great tits and blue tits in England, Belgium, or Holland. It is characteristic of work on these species that an excessive number of nest boxes has always been provided, and the possibility exists that the normally limiting resource of nest holes has been replaced by food or some other factor.

The first experiment looking for an effect of any kind of manipulation was that of Krebs (1971). In one of two areas within Wytham Wood, near Oxford, he added sunflower seeds in large amounts during one winter, after following the populations of great tits and blue tits for eight years. Krebs claimed an effect on the breeding density of blue tits (Fig. 4.3). It is important to note the absence of replication and the fact that the populations of the two species had been diverging in density for five years. Were it not for other experiments on these species, the conclusion that they compete would be unjustified.

In their study in Belgium, Dhondt and Eyckerman (1980) took advantage of the difference in size between the two species, the great tit being appreciably the larger. After a number of years during which

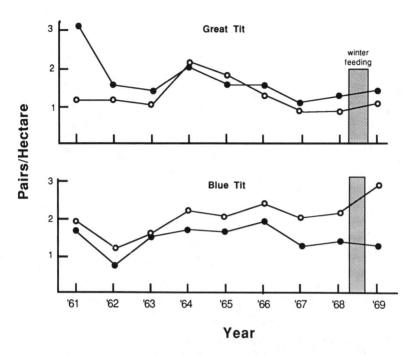

Figure 4.3. Effect of winter feeding on breeding density. Breeding density was measured by counting the number of birds breeding in boxes, except in the case of the Bean Wood great tits, where, because the population was disturbed by shooting some birds before the breeding season, the breeding population was taken as the number of territorial pairs before shooting. Open circles: Bean Wood, where excess food was provided during the shaded period. Solid circles: Marley Wood, which received no excess food. (From Krebs 1971.)

the nest boxes could accommodate either species, they chose one of two areas as experimental and reduced the diameters of the entrance holes to a size too small for great tits. In one of the rare examples of repetition of a field experiment, during the next year they chose a second pair of areas and did the same thing (Fig. 4.4). The density of blue tit pairs showed a dramatic increase above preexperimental years in both experiments. The calculation of statistical significance involves temporal pseudoreplication in both experiments, but the repetition of the experiment, with the same result, increases one's confidence in the result. Great tits had evidently been excluding blue tits from nest boxes that they would have occupied in the absence of the former. Dhondt and Eyckerman (1980) described a similar experiment by Löhrl (1977) that gave a similar result.

Minot (1981) carried out an experiment testing for an effect of blue

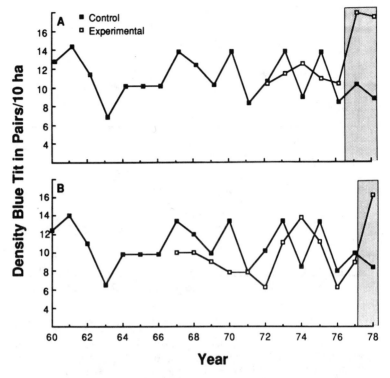

Figure 4.4. Breeding densities of the blue tit (pairs/10 ha) in experimental and control areas. Note that in both experimental areas (A, Gontrode; B, Soenen) the blue tit density increased after the experimental manipulation (shaded) of the nest boxes. (From Dhondt & Eyckerman 1980.)

tits on great tits. He removed blue tit nestlings from Bean Wood and introduced them into nests in Marley Wood, keeping Broad Oak Wood as a control (Table 4.7). There were no replicates of any treatment. The response of great tits was measured as the mean fledging weight, and the results of the experiment are shown in Table 4.8. Removing blue tit nestlings was claimed to have a statistically significant effect on the fledging weight of great tits, compared with those on either the control area or the area where the nestlings were added. The problem with this analysis is the confounding of the experimental treatment with the individual area, negating the independence of observations within areas and giving reason to question the validity of the statements of probability.

The next experiment was not strictly in a forest, being in disturbed habitat with grass and trees. It is included here because of the excellent

Table 4.7. *Summary of removal experiment in 1979*

Section	Great tits	Blue tits
Removal area: Bean Wood	1.06 pairs ha^{-1} 18 nests 15 successful broods	2.18 pairs ha^{-1} 37 nests 33 broods 346 young removed
Supplemented area: Marley Wood	0.66 pair ha^{-1} 30 nests 27 successful broods	1.56 pairs ha^{-1} 68 nests 60 broods Young increased by 45%
Control area: Broad Oak Wood	0.73 pair ha^{-1} 26 nests 22 successful broods	1.26 pairs ha^{-1} 45 nests 37 broods

From Minot (1981).

Table 4.8. *Results from removal experiment, great tit fledging weights*

Section	Mean fledging weight (g)	Standard error	Sample size
Removal area: Bean Wood	19.94	0.27	14
Supplemented area: Marley Wood	18.75	0.18	25
Control area: Broad Oak Wood	19.03	0.14	21
Control vs. removal	$t = 3.25,$	$p < 0.01$	
Control vs. supplemented	$t = 1.17,$	NS	
Removal vs. supplemented	$t = 3.72,$	$p < 0.001$	

From Minot (1981).

design. Högstedt (1980) was able to add potential competitors to test for competitive effects between magpies, which build their nests, and jackdaws, which nest in cavities. He placed three nest boxes in the territory of each of a number of magpies, and followed an equal number of control territories. The nest boxes were occupied promptly by jackdaws. Högstedt recorded the effects of the presence of jackdaws on clutch size, number of fledged young, number of broods with at least one fledged young, and mean nestling weight of magpies (Table 4.9). The significant effects were all manifest after hatching and involved survival and growth of the nestlings. Because nest sites were not involved, and no mention was made of interspecific aggression, it is

Table 4.9. *Breeding results for experimental and control pairs of magpies*

Parameter	Experimental group	Control group	p (two-tailed)
Start of laying (median date; day 1 = 1 April)	20	21	NS
Clutch size	6.50±0.30	6.48±0.18	NS
Mean weight of clutch	64.7±4.0	67.1±2.3	NS
Mean of mean nestling weight within brood, age 21–25 d	182±7	208±4	<0.02[a]
No. of started breedings (N)	18	38	
No. of hatched clutches (% of N)	10 (56%)	23 (61%)	NS
No. of broods with ≥ 1 fledged young (% of N)	3 (17%)	16 (42%)	<0.04[b]
No. of fledged young per successful brood	2.0±0.58	4.0±0.26	<0.05[a]
No. of fledged young per breeding attempt	0.33±0.20	1.68±0.34	<0.001

Note: Figures are given ±s.e.; NS, not significant.
[a] Mann–Whitney U test.
[b] Fisher exact probability test.
From Högstedt (1980). Reprinted by permission from *Nature* 283:64–6. Copyright © 1980 Macmillan Journals Limited.

Table 4.10. *Breeding results for individual females in experimental and control conditions in the same territory*

Female	Start of laying (day 1 = 1 April) E	C	Clutch size E	C	Clutch weight E	C	No. of fledged young E	C
1	17	8	6	7	45.0	50.4	0	3
2	20	23	6	6	60.0	61.2	2	3
3	25	29	5	6	52.5	63.0	0	3
4	26	28	7	7	68.6	70.0	1	1
5	13	11	7	7	77.0	79.1	0	0
6	21	16	6	6	64.2	62.4	0	0
7	20	28	8	7	—	—	0	4
8	—	—	—	—	—	—	0	0
9	—	—	5	6	—	—	0	4
p	NS		NS		NS		$t_8 = 2.78$	
							$p < 0.05$	

Note: E, experimental; C, control; —, data missing; NS, not significant.
From Högstedt (1980). Reprinted by permission from *Nature* 283:64–6. Copyright © 1980 Macmillan Journals Limited.

most likely that the effect of jackdaws was through competition for food.

This experiment was repeated in the second year, with experimental and control territories reversed. The procedure not only provided the important element of repetition but also permitted a comparison of a number of the same females under experimental and control conditions (Table 4.10). This was an ingenious, well-designed experiment, and the results are conclusive.

Altogether, it appears that interspecific competition is common among related species of forest birds, even though some of the experiments were flawed in one way or another, largely through lack of replication.

Lizards

Other forest predators that have been the subjects of experiments testing for interspecific competition are the lizards of the genus *Anolis* in the West Indies. Many extensive studies on geographic distributions, size relationships, and habitat assortment have led to the conclusion that past competition is responsible for much of the pattern and that, at present, food limitation is common. The situation is summarized by Ehrlich and Roughgarden (1987).

Because of the local distribution and the unusually similar sizes of *A. gingivinus* and *A. wattsi pogus* on St. Maarten, and the quite different situation for *A. bimaculatus* and *A. wattsi schwartzi* on St. Eustatius, Pacala and Roughgarden (1982, 1985) conducted experiments testing for competition between both pairs of species. The design was such that only the effects of the two smaller subspecies (*pogus* and *wattsi*) on their respective coexisting congeners could have been detected. I have criticized these experiments elsewhere (Hairston 1987), but the nature of this book requires that I repeat the criticisms. On each island, four square plots (12 × 12 m), were surrounded by fences 1.15 m high, topped by an overhang of plastic to prevent exit or entrance. The plots were further protected from movement by strips 2 m wide on both sides of the fences, where all vegetation was cut to a maximum height of 0.25 m. All anoles were removed from the plots, the average numbers being, for St. Maarten, 70.5 *gingivinus* and 41.25 *pogus*, and for St. Eustatius, 31.5 *bimaculatus* and 73.25 *schwartzi*. The experiments were started with the introduction onto all plots on St. Maarten of 60 *gingivinus*, and, in addition, 100 *pogus* on two of them. On St. Eustatius, 60 *bimaculatus* were placed on all four plots, with 100 *schwartzi* on two of them. The experiments permitted measurement of the performance of *gingivinus* with and without *pogus* (expected to show a large difference) and the performance of *bimaculatus* with and without *schwartzi* (expected to show little difference, if any). The experiments continued for about 3.5 months, the responses measured being growth rate, egg volume per female, prey volume per lizard, mean prey size, increased perch height, and survival. For all responses except survival, statistically significant differences were claimed between the performances of *gingivinus* on plots with and without *pogus*, whereas *bimaculatus* showed no such differences. For all of these, the individual lizards were used in the statistical calculations, instead of the plot means. As has been noted, that practice confounds place with treatment and constitutes pseudoreplication. For growth rates, the difference for *gingivinus* is still statistically significant if the plot means are used, but that is not true for the difference for egg volume per female. For prey volume and mean prey size, the differences shown by *gingivinus* look convincing, despite the pseudoreplication, but the great differences between replicate plots in the case of *bimaculatus* are causes for worry.

Nevertheless, the case looks reasonably convincing until we examine the numerical relationship between the mean numbers removed and the numbers placed on the plots at the start of the experiments. For *gingivinus* on St. Maarten and *schwartzi* on St. Eustatius, the discrepancy is not great (70.5 : 60 and 73.25 : 100, respectively). For *pogus* on St. Maarten, the ratio was 41.25 : 100, thus more than doubling any natural competitive effect, and biasing the experiment in the direction consistent with the initial hypothesis. Exactly the reverse bias was introduced on St. Eustatius. For *bimaculatus*, 60 individuals were introduced to replace an average of 31.5, thus bringing about marked intraspecific crowding. This was exacerbated by the cleared lanes inside the fences, as they reduced the area acceptable to that large species to less than half of the total plot, further crowding the already doubled natural density. It is small wonder that *bimaculatus* declined rapidly in numbers and had to be restocked twice. The failure to obtain evidence for interspecific competition on this species can easily be interpreted as any such effect being overwhelmed by excessive intraspecific crowding. The lanes did not affect *schwartzi*, which normally perches at an average height of 0.03 m – one-eighth that available in the cleared lanes (Roughgarden et al. 1981). The results of this pair of experiments were much less convincing than was claimed. The experiments represent the sacrifice of realism to rigid adherence to a preconceived design.

A more realistic experiment that showed the competitive effect of *gingivinus* on *pogus* was carried out on a small islet near St. Maarten (Roughgarden, Heckel, & Fuentes 1983). *Anolis wattsi pogus* was naturally absent from coastal parts of St. Maarten, and from the islet. It was introduced into each of two plots, and the resident *gingivinus* were removed from one of them. The survival of *pogus* was twice as high on the *gingivinus*-removal plots as on the control. The general suitability of the habitat on the islet for *pogus* was shown by the observation of hatchlings there, and its natural absence from there and from the lowland was most likely due to competition from *gingivinus*. One could wish for replication, and two reports of the experiment disagree on whether or not there was any. The original paper is as reported, but Ehrlich and Roughgarden (1987, p. 344) state that "at some sites, the resident *A. gingivinus* were removed; at other sites, the residents were left undisturbed."

Despite flawed experiments and unclear reporting, the evidence supports the existence of interspecific competition among these tropical forest lizards.

Salamanders

Among predators of the forest floor, the purely terrestrial salamanders of the genus *Plethodon* have been the subjects of the most experimentation. Jaeger (1971a) was impressed by the nearly mutually exclusive distributions of *P. cinereus* in the forest and *P. shenandoah* in the adjacent talus slopes in the Blue Ridge Mountains of Virginia. His hypothesis to explain the situation was that *P. cinereus* was the superior competitor and that *P. shenandoah* was superior physiologically in the dry talus location. He set up three 1-mm screen enclosures in forest soil and each of three types of talus: type I with no soil, type II with shallow soil, and type III with deeper soil. Two cages were 1 m by 0.5m by 0.5 m deep, and each was provided with ten specimens of one of the two species. The third cage was twice as wide, and had ten specimens of both species, an arrangement that preserved the same density in all cages. No salamanders survived one week in type I talus. Where each species was alone, *P. shenandoah* survived better than *P. cinereus* in type II talus and survived as well in type III talus and forest soil. In cages where both species were present, *P. cinereus* had significantly better survival in soil, better survival in type III talus, and worse survival in type II talus. The two last differences were not statistically significant. Although lacking replication, the experiment appeared to establish the competitive superiority of *P. cinereus* in soil. Jaeger (1971b) in testing the hypothesis that *P. shenandoah* was better able to retain water, suspended ten individual specimens of each species in 1-mm mesh containers in a refrigerator at 17 °C and 20 percent relative humidity. Controls consisted in suspending identical containers so that the bottoms were barely submerged in water. All individuals were weighed hourly after the start of the experiment. The controls showed no change in weight; in dry air, *P. cinereus* had lost a significantly greater proportion of its initial body weight after most time intervals, thus confirming the physiological superiority of *P. shenandoah* under dry conditions.

One of my sets of experiments on two other species of *Plethodon* in North Carolina is described briefly in another context in Chapter 3. The purpose of these experiments was twofold: to test the hypothesis that competition was stronger on mountain ranges where the altitudinal overlap between *Plethodon jordani* and *P. glutinosus* was narrow than where the overlap was wide and to permit a choice between two theories regarding the course of evolution for competing species (Hairston 1973). Although logically the evolutionary question would have been answered after the test of the competition hypothesis, for practical reasons the experiments were conducted simultaneously.

Plethodon jordani is endemic to the southern Appalachians, occupies the higher elevations, and is divided into a number of isolated or partly isolated populations, some of which are distinguishable by several characters: color pattern, size, tooth counts, and degree of sexual dimorphism (Hairston & Pope 1948). The populations intergrade freely wherever their distributions come into contact. *Plethodon glutinosus* is widely distributed over the eastern United States, and consists of a number of distinguishable populations (Highton 1972, 1983). There appear to be no differences among the parts of the population concerned in this study. Highton (1983) has applied the name *teyahallee* to this population, but has not shown that it is specifically distinct from most adjacent populations. Therefore, I continue to use the original name. In the southern Appalachians, the species occurs throughout the lower elevations and reaches 1,500 m or more in some locations, especially on south-facing slopes. In the Great Smoky

Mountains of North Carolina and Tennessee, and in the Black Mountains of North Carolina, *P. jordani* and *P. glutinosus* occupy parapatric distributions, occurring together only in a narrow altitudinal band 70–168 m wide. In the Balsam Mountains of North Carolina, the two species occur together over an altitudinal range of at least 1,365 m. In all locations, *P. jordani* is much more abundant than *P. glutinosus*, six to eight times as abundant in my experimental areas.

To test the hypothesis that competition was responsible for the narrow overlap, and therefore must have been stronger there than in the area of wide overlap, octagonal experimental plots 24.384 m in diameter were established at the same elevations in the overlap zones of the Great Smoky Mountains and the Balsam Mountains. At each location, *P. jordani* was removed repeatedly from two plots, and *P. glutinosus* from two. Three plots were followed as controls. Removals and counts were performed six times during each active season (mid-May to late September or early October) for five years (Hairston 1980a). In the Great Smoky Mountains, the removal of the more abundant *jordani* resulted in a significant increase over controls in the average number of *glutinosus* throughout the third, fourth, and fifth years. In the Balsam Mountains, where competition was expected to be weaker, there was a significant effect on the number of *glutinosus*, but only at the end of the fourth year and during the fifth year. Removal of *glutinosus* from plots in the Smokies resulted in an increase in the number of *jordani*, but it was not significantly above the control density. In the Balsams, *jordani* did not increase above the control density. Removing *glutinosus* caused a significant increase in the proportion of the two youngest year classes of *jordani*, an increase that was much greater in the Smokies than in the Balsams. The experiments confirmed the original hypothesis of stronger competition in the zone of narrow altitudinal overlap. Temporal and sacrificial pseudoreplication (Hurlbert 1984) were avoided by the use of a statistical model using multivariate analysis of variance (Hairston 1980a,b).

The evolutionary question was a choice between the competing theories of selection for reduction of competition through niche partitioning and selection for increased competitive ability. I took advantage of the color difference between the red-cheeked *jordani* in the Smokies and the gray-cheeked form in the Balsams (Hairston 1973, 1980b, 1983). Transplanting the two forms reciprocally would be expected to show the effect of each on the population of *glutinosus* with which it had not coevolved. After removing the local *jordani* from two plots in each experimental area, collections from the distant location were introduced. *Plethodon jordani* from the area of strong competition in the Smokies would be expected to have little effect on Balsam Mountains *glutinosus* if the latter had evolved through niche partitioning to have requirements different from those of *jordani*. On the other hand, if Smokies *jordani* had evolved specific interference mechanisms against *glutinosus*, the latter form in the Balsams would be expected to be adversely affected by the introduction. *Plethodon jordani* from the area of weak competition in the Balsams would have little effect on *glutinosus* in the Smokies under either hypothesis. If Balsams *jordani* had undergone niche partitioning, it would have requirements different from those of the Smokies *glutinosus*, and if the latter had evolved interference mechanisms against its local *jordani*, it would benefit from the substitution of a form that had not evolved such mechanisms. The results of the experiments support the hypothesis of the evolution of interference mechanisms in the Smokies. In the Balsams, after a period when it was difficult to get the introduced *jordani* established, the population of *glutinosus* declined significantly, relative to control populations (Fig. 4.5) (Hairston 1983). In the Smokies, the population of *glutinosus* increased to a level significantly above control populations, much as it did on plots where the only manipulation was removal of the local *jordani* (Fig. 4.6) (Hairston 1980b).

A noteworthy feature of these studies was the publication of the complete design of the experiments, along with the interpretations of all possible outcomes, before the work was begun, thus assuring the a priori nature of the hypotheses being tested (Hairston 1973).

Competition among some species of woodland salamanders has been well demonstrated experimentally, but not all combinations can be shown to compete. The remaining four or five species in the forest in my experiments showed no effect of the removal of either *P. jordani* or *P. glutinosus* (Hairston 1981).

Invertebrates

There is a deficiency of good experimental evidence on the interactions among predaceous or parasitoid insects in forests, especially the latter, and the deficiency represents a serious gap in our understanding of that ecosystem. Nevertheless, there have been several studies of competition among predaceous forest invertebrates. Spiders have been attractive subjects of experimentation because of

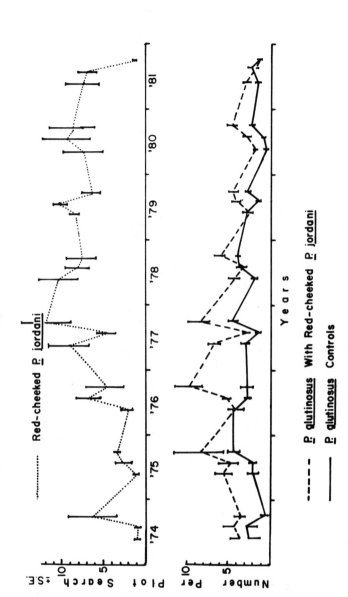

Figure 4.5. Effect of the highly competitive red-cheeked *P. jordani* on *P. glutinosus* in the Balsam Mountains, where competition between *P. glutinosus* and the local gray-cheeked *P. jordani* is not intense. [From Hairston (1983), in *The American Naturalist.* Copyright © 1983 The University of Chicago Press.]

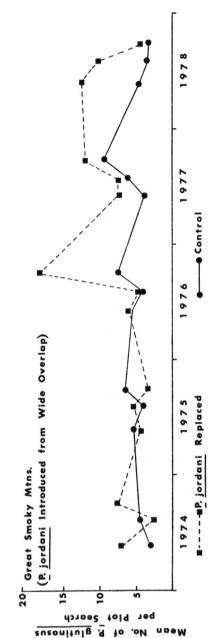

Figure 4.6. Average number of *P. glutinosus* per plot search where *P. jordani* from an area of wide altitudinal overlap were being substituted for *jordani* in an area of narrow overlap. For the experimental data (broken line), each point represents the mean of four searches; for the controls (solid line), each point represents the mean of six searches. (From Hairston 1980b.)

their conspicuous webs, which make them relatively easy to observe. They are among the few forest invertebrate predators to have been subjects of experiments testing for competition. There is good evidence of food limitation, but competition, either intraspecific or interspecific, has been detected only minimally (Wise 1975, 1979, 1981). Wise's experimental design was to construct open frames of wood, 4 by 1.6 by 1 m, which he placed at least 10 m apart in a mixed deciduous–pine woodland in Maryland. Within the frames, he attached dead branches of the kind normally used by the two species (*Mecynogea lemniscata* and *Metepeira labyrinthea*) for constructing their webs. He introduced different numbers of spiders into the frames, which were open to movement in and out. Thus, excessive crowding was avoided. Although slightly smaller nearest-neighbor distances were maintained in some of the frames than were observed in nearby forest, Wise observed that most of the densities were within the natural range. The range of densities in different frames were 1–13 for *Mecynogea* alone, 1–7 for *Metepeira* alone, and 2–19 for the two species together. Responses to differences in density were measured as survival and as the number of eggs per egg sac. There were weak but statistically significant intraspecific effects. Density explained 2 percent of the variance in survival of *Metepeira* and 1 percent of the variance in number of eggs per sac for *Mecynogea*. There were no detectable effects of interspecific density levels. The experiment was well designed and carefully conducted, and the conclusions appear justified. In a previous experiment, Wise showed that supplementing food by placing fruit flies in webs increased fecundity by a significant amount, thus confirming food limitation for both species. Apparently the natural density of flying insects is kept at low levels by other factors, such as bird predation, and the effect of spiders on the supply is not detectable.

There is good experimental evidence that spider populations in spruce forests suffer substantial amounts of bird predation themselves. Two experiments in that habitat in southwestern Sweden gave essentially the same results. In the first, Askenmo et al. (1977) placed net bags of two different meshes (1 mm and 10 mm) over randomly chosen branches of spruce trees (*Picea abies*) in October and collected the branches the following March. Both mesh sizes excluded birds, but the larger mesh allowed emigration and immigration of spiders of all sizes. Randomly chosen branches that were not protected were collected from the same trees at the start of the experiment, and another set of unprotected branches was collected at the end of the experiment. The branches came from two randomly chosen heights on each tree. Eighteen branches were chosen for each of the four sets, for a total of seventy-two. Care was taken to avoid loss of specimens in the process of collection. Spiders were counted and measured as to the length of abdomen and cephalothorax. The mean density of spiders at the start of the experiment was 26.5 per branch; at the end of the experiment, the mean density on unprotected branches was 11.4, whereas in coarse mesh bags the mean was 34.3, and in fine mesh, 17.5. The coarse mesh contained significantly greater numbers than either the controls or the fine mesh, between which the differences were not significant. When the spiders were classified by size, both coarse and fine mesh contained significantly more large specimens than did the controls, whereas there was no significant difference between treatments for small spiders (< 2.5 mm long). The authors attributed the difference to differential predation on large spiders by birds.

Gunnarsson (1983) conducted a similar experiment, but restricted the height of the experimental and control branches to 1.5 to 2.5 m above the ground. He also added bags (1-mm mesh) into which he added spiders to test for density dependence. As far as the predation part of the experiment was concerned, his results were much like those of Askenmo and associates, the overwinter mortality being 88 percent on unprotected branches and 68 percent in bags with normal density. He also reported significantly greater mortality (93%) in bags with initially raised density. The total numbers in these bags at the start of the experiment were raised to levels 5.2–20.3 times those on control branches from the same tree, and the results of the density test are best attributed to these unnatural levels, as the range of densities among control branches was from 6.2 to 29.9 per kilogram of branch – a maximum factor of 4.8.

Among other groups, carabid beetles are prominent invertebrate predators of the forest floor. An experimental analysis of intraspecific and interspecific competition among them was conducted by Lenski (1982, 1984) in the southern Appalachian Mountains. Lenski conducted two experiments. In the first, he constructed eighteen small square enclosures with aluminum edging, each 1.5 m on a side; six of them in an area recently clear-cut for timber, six placed 30–50 m inside an adjacent hardwood forest, and six placed 100 m inside the forest. Plastic cups placed inside the enclosures were used as pitfall traps. These were left open for seven consecutive days, trapping out all or nearly all resident specimens of *Carabus limbatus*. The traps were then closed, and two, four, or eight *C. limbatus* were added to the enclosures in a balanced design. The beetles had been marked individually by clipping tarsal claws. After seven days, the traps were reopened, and the remaining beetles were removed and weighed on an analytical balance. Body mass had been shown to be a sensitive indicator of foraging success. Although the finding was not pertinent to the density experiment, beetles from the enclosures in the forest were significantly heavier than were those from the enclosures in the clear-cut area. There was a significant effect of density on body mass in the forest, as well as a significant interaction between location and density, the latter having no effect on body mass in the clear-cut area. There also was a significant effect of density on the proportion recaptured, which declined with increasing density. Having established density dependence with realistic densities of *C. limbatus* under natural conditions, Lenski (1984) conducted another experiment in a nearby forest. He constructed ten larger square enclosures, 6 m on a side, surrounded with aluminum edging. He used the natural density of *Carabus limbatus*, but added four individuals of *C. sylvosus* to each enclosure, because that species, while present at the original location, was absent, although the forest was quite similar. Half of the enclosures were designated randomly as "food-supplement," the remaining ones being controls. Pitfall traps were used to collect the beetles from the enclosures during four periods ranging from eleven to twenty-eight days over the season when *C. limbatus* were active before estivation (mid-April to late July). The captured beetles were brought to the laboratory in separate vials, given individual marks, and weighed on an analytical balance. Those *C. limbatus* from food-supplement enclosures were given two mealworms (*Tenebrio* sp. larvae) and allowed to feed for two hours, after which all specimens were returned to their original enclosures. No feeding was done in the enclosures, and the *C. sylvosus* were not fed. Responses to the treatment by *C. limbatus* were measured as average mass of recaptures, activity (captures/day at risk), survival, reproduction by females (larval captures/female, date of larval capture, tenerals per female, and date of teneral capture), and mass, activity, and survival of teneral individuals. The effects on *C. sylvosus* were measured as average mass of recaptures, activity, and survival.

The results of this experiment were dramatic, as illustrated by the mass of nonteneral *C. limbatus* (Fig. 4.7), a result that was duplicated by tenerals (individuals whose exoskeletons had not hardened and darkened before capture). The activities of both nonteneral and teneral

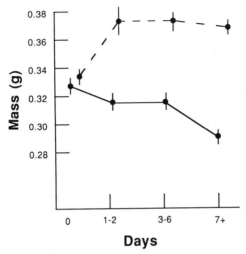

Figure 4.7. Mean ($\pm$ 1 s.e.) body mass of all nonteneral *Carabus limbatus* captures as a function of days since first capture. Solid line indicates control; dashed line indicates food supplementation. (From Lenski 1984.)

individuals of this species were significantly less on food supplement enclosures, indicating that much of the activity was associated with foraging. All of the measures of reproduction were significantly favored on food supplement plots, except for the date of capture of tenerals. *Carabus sylvosus*, despite not receiving food directly, was significantly heavier on food supplement plots than on controls. It thus benefited from the feeding of *limbatus*, presumably because of the lowered foraging activity of that species. Taken together, Lenski's two experiments established food limitation of *Carabus* and interspecific competition for that food. The density effect was important, because species can respond to food additions without any density-dependent response, because the ease of obtaining the food may be what is involved. The analysis of the experiments was noteworthy for its deliberate avoidance of pseudoreplication.

The experiments on forest predators varied in quality, but most groups showed interspecific competition to be present, although not for all combinations of species within the group. Spiders were alone in not showing competition, and there was good experimental evidence that at least some of them were strongly affected by secondary predation from birds.

Summary

There has been a remarkable consistency in the results from nearly all experiments in each trophic level in the forest ecosystem. Decomposing fungi and bacteria compete with each other, the competition most frequently involving interference. Forest trees compete, both through their roots and their crowns, but plants of the herbaceous layer appear to be limited more by specific conditions, such as the distribution of waterlogging or particular nutrients, than by interspecific competition. The experiments have revealed a complex set of relationships between forest herbivores and plants, with the latter producing (apparently) adaptive defensive chemicals, and the former evolving mechanisms to evade the chemicals by one means or another. Native folivores or sapsuckers have not been shown to compete, and the negative effect of predators on them has been demonstrated repeatedly by experiments. Most experiments have shown competition among the forest predators, spiders being the exception, probably because they themselves are the prey of birds. Thus, experiments in forests have shown relationships to be tight and consistent, and it should be possible to build a precise theory on the general principles already expressed.

5

Experiments in terrestrial successional communities

Introduction

Much of the area that was once forested, especially in the North Temperate Zone, is now either under cultivation or undergoing some stage of secondary succession. Such areas are more convenient for experimentation than forests themselves, because the vegetation is low enough to be accessible. A perusal of the table of information amassed by Schoener (1983) on field experiments reveals the large number of experiments that have been conducted in fields, meadows, or pastures – sixty-six species or groups of plants involved, compared with thirty-eight in forests – and it should be recognized that the experiments in pine forests reported by Korstian and Coile (1938) (Chapter 4) were in a late stage of succession.

The distinction between mature and successional stages is not trivial, as a comparison of the results reported by Schoener (1983) reveals: Of the 38 species in forests, 33 showed competition "always," 2 "sometimes," and only 3 "never." In contrast, of the 66 species in fields, meadows, or pastures, less than half (29) showed competition "always," 25 "sometimes," and 12 "never." The difference is highly significant statistically ($p < .001$). Despite the lower frequency of interspecific competition among plants in successional locations, the descriptions of experiments follow the same order as in Chapter 4, because that procedure will permit comparisons of the interactions causing the differences between forest communities and successional communities. Excellent experiments have been conducted in deserts and other arid areas; they are deferred to Chapter 6, because many of the interspecific relationships are unique to such habitats.

Nearly all of the communities considered in this chapter were in locations that had been subject to intense human disturbance. They ranged from garden or farm soil through old fields, pastures, and meadows. Simple timbering, though drastic at the time, results in a quick return to forest in most areas, unless followed by clearing for agricul-

128

ture. All experiments in forests, including some in late successional stages, have been included in Chapter 4.

Interactions among decomposers

The fact that dead organic matter does not accumulate in most terrestrial situations, despite large annual increments, has been cited as evidence that competition must exist among decomposers (Chapter 4). Evidence from more nearly direct sources was provided by Clark and Paul (1970). They pointed out that one-fifth of the substrate available in grassland soils would be consumed in producing one generation of new cells of the decomposers present, and hence there could be only five generations per year among organisms with the potential to reproduce within hours. They also measured CO_2 production from field soils and found it to be only $\frac{1}{35}$ to $\frac{1}{10}$ of that produced by an equivalent biomass of decomposers in laboratory populations at equilibrium densities. It should not be surprising, therefore, that so many appropriate experiments have revealed strong negative effects among decomposer species.

Tribe (1966) obtained some interesting results from his laboratory experiments on competition among six species of fungi from soil at the Cambridge University Farm. Soil fungi are divisible physiologically into "sugar fungi," which lack cellulase, and cellulolytic fungi, which are capable of decomposing that common plant structural component. The ability of the six species to grow on cellulose as an energy source permitted Tribe to conduct easily observable experiments, using cellulose film (cellophane) as a substrate. Small pieces 1.0 by 0.5 cm were boiled to remove plasticizers, autoclaved, and placed on sterilized clean sand in petri dishes, six pieces per dish. The sand was saturated with a solution of nutrient salts, and the ends of the cellophane strips were inoculated with the competing species in all pairs. The species were *Rhizoctonia solani, Botryotrichum piluliferum, Stachybotris atra, Trichoderma viride, Fusarium oxysporum,* and *F. culmorum.* After five weeks, the pieces of film were examined microscopically to determine the competitive dominant. Single-species controls were used to assess the relative cellulolytic activity of the competitors. The results (Table 5.1) show that competitive ability and cellulolytic activity were unrelated. *Stachybotris atra,* which dominated all of the other species in competition, was intermediate in its ability to break down cellulose, and *R. solani,* the most rapid consumer of cellulose, dominated only

Table 5.1. *Fungi dominant after five weeks' competition in paired cultures on cellulose film*

	R. s.	B. p.	S. a.	T. v.	F. o.	F. c.
R. solani	(1)					
B. piluliferum	R. s.	(2)				
S. atra	S. a.	S. a.	(3)			
T. viride	T. v.	T. v.	S. a.	(4)		
F. oxysporum	F. o.[a]	B. p.	S. a.	—[b]	(4)	
F. culmorum	F. c.[a]	B. p.	S. a.	T. v.	—	(5)

[a]*R. solani* and the fusaria coexisted equally, but most of the *R. solani* mycelium was dead by five weeks and overgrown by the fusaria.
[b]Mutual coexistence.
Note: See text for full scientific names. The numbers in parentheses show relative cellulolytic activity. From Tribe (1966).

one other species. The table further shows that the relationships did not exhibit transitivity. *Botryotrichum piluliferum* dominated both of the *Fusarium* species, and both of them dominated *R. solani*. Had the relationships been transitive, *B. piluliferum* should have dominated *R. solani*; instead, the reverse was found.

Tribe did not specify how many replicates of each combination he used. The fact that six cellophane strips were placed in each petri dish suggests that replication was ample. The laboratory environment required no controls, except that each species be demonstrated to grow alone.

Experimental outcomes such as those can best be explained as the result of interspecific interference. Two forms have been demonstrated among decomposers: antibiotics and a more general nonspecific effect called fungistasis. The discovery that many soil actinomycetes and fungi produce antibiotics provided a stimulus to experiments on interspecific interactions, only slightly delayed by the claim that antibiotics were irrelevant to soil ecology because thay had not been demonstrated to be produced or active under field conditions. That argument was shown to be incorrect, first by the experiment of Wright (1956). She introduced pieces of wheat straw 1 in. (2.54 cm) long into an acid podsol from Hertfordshire that had been inoculated with a spore suspension of *Trichoderma viride*, a fungus known to produce the antibiotic gliotoxin in the laboratory. After seven days, the straws and the soil immediately surrounding each were recovered and extracted with ether. The extracts were identified as gliotoxin by paper chromatography and tested for antibiotic activity by exposing agar seeded with *Bacillus subtilis* to them. The width of the zone of bacterial inhibition gave an estimate of the amount of gliotoxin present. Individual straws were found to contain thirteen times as much antibiotic (by weight) as the surrounding soil. A similar experiment with soil only slightly acid (*p*H 6.3) gave negative results.

The phenomenon of fungistasis was demonstrated by Dobbs and Hinson (1953). It had been observed earlier that cellophane buried in soil was not satisfactory as a method for observing growth of fungi, but when it was placed between glass slides that were separated at one end with a glass fiber and held together with rubber bands, fungal hyphae appeared on the cellophane. The following experiment tested the hypothesis that the soil itself inhibited growth of fungi. Boiled and autoclaved pieces of cellophane were dusted or sprayed with spores of known soil fungi and folded over the spores. A lump of soil was then pressed around the folded cellophane so that part of the latter extended beyond the soil. No spores germinated on that part of the cellophane in contact with the soil, but those on the part extending away from the soil did so. The method was applied to fifteen soils, representing forest soils, grassland soils, waterlogged soils, and subsoils, and complete inhibition was obtained in every case. The same result was obtained on a total of fifteen species of soil-inhabiting fungi. Substitutes for soil, namely, kaolin, alumina, and slate dust, reduced germination, but did not extinguish it. Wet filter paper, sand, and silica had no effect. Heating moist soil in a water bath at 60 °C for one hour removed the inhibitory effect, as does autoclaving the soil. That result suggests that inhibition comes from organisms in the soil, but it is possible that at least part of the release from inhibition comes from nutrients released from the bodies of the organisms killed in the process. Support for that view comes from the observation that the addition of glucose, even in traces (0.1%), allowed some germination to take place, an effect that disappeared after three days. However, the inhibition is restored to sterilized soils by inoculation with nonspecific soil microorganisms, and even by some that do not produce known antibiotics (Lockwood 1977). Griffin (1962), for example, inoculated autoclaved grassland soil with fifteen different fungi and bacteria, and then exposed water agar for nine days through a cellophane sheet placed between the agar and the soil. The cellophane and the soil were then removed, and the agar was inoculated with the test fungus *Gliocladium fimbriatum* and incubated at 0.45 °C (33 °F) for one month. Three replicates of each test were used. Whereas controls of autoclaved soil and water agar had little or no inhibitory effect on germination and mycelial growth of *G. fimbriatum*, all of the experimental soil organisms inhibited that species to varying degrees. All fifteen species had been grown previously in direct contact with *G. fimbriatum*, and only three could be shown to have an antagonistic effect by causing a zone of inhibition around its colony. Those three were known to produce antifungal antibiotics. Thus, the fungistatic effect observed was produced by at least nine species of nonantagonistic fungi and three nonantagonistic bacteria. These laboratory experiments were well planned and controlled and adequately replicated. Transfer through cellulose film indicates that small molecules are involved, and many antibiotics seem to be ruled out by the observation that their production is stimulated by the addition of glucose.

There can be no doubt that interference among decomposing organisms is widespread, and that phenomenon, in combination with the observed shortage of substrate relative to the number of organisms involved, is most obviously explained as an evolutionary response to the competition for resources.

Interactions among successional plants

For most of the history of ecology as a self-conscious field, the process of succession has been regarded as a key to the dynamics of natural communities, and it should not be surprising that the interpretations of succession by ecologists have differed strongly. Connell and Slatyer (1977) have classified these interpretations into models: the facilitation model, in which early-arriving species alter conditions in such a way that the establishment of later-arriving species is favored; the tolerance model, in which later-arriving species are able to exploit decreased levels of resources; the inhibition model, in which all species resist invasion by competitors, the latter being able to become established only when the earlier arrivals die or are damaged. Some experiments have explicitly tested these models.

Experiments on successional communities can be classified as work in communities that were being allowed to continue in succession and work in communities being held in some intermediate stage, either by repeated mowing or by grazing. The literature in both areas is quite large, and only a small sample can be described here. In both, the experiments have involved the use of fertilizers, removal of selected species, and transplanted individuals of a selected group of species. Although the results of some of them are interesting, almost no greenhouse experiments have been described, and the same applies to those involving the use of pots. I have not found descriptions of experiments in areas undergoing primary succession.

Unmanipulated secondary succession

An experimental test of the three models of succession was conducted by Hils and Vankat (1982) in a first-year old field in southwestern Ohio. They noted that in many descriptions of old fields, the pioneer species are annuals, which are then followed by perennials. The design of their experiment was to remove annuals and biennials from one set of plots, perennials from another set, and separately to remove certain species dominating each class: *Erigeron annuus* and *E. canadensis* (annuals, both separately and together) and the perennials *Aster pilosus* and *Solidago canadensis* (removed together). Under the facilitation model, removal of annuals and biennials was expected to cause a decline in the biomass of perennials. Under the inhibition model, the opposite was expected: an increase in the biomass of perennials. The tolerance model predicted no significant change in perennials on the removal of annuals and biennials. Removal of perennials was expected to be followed by an increase in the biomass of annuals under the facilitation model, but no change under the other two.

In the experiment, four replicate plots, 5 by 10 m, were assigned randomly to each treatment. Removals were by hand, either by pulling the plants up or by cutting them at ground level when gentle pulling was unsuccessful. At least three removals were performed on each plot, starting in late May. After the first frost, results were assessed by clipping all plants on five 0.25-m² quadrats in each experimental plot, randomly located. Materials from the quadrats in a plot were combined, sorted to species, air-dried at 80 °C for 24 h, and weighed.

The results showed no statistically significant differences between any treatment plants and the controls (Table 5.2). The high heterogeneity in the field obviously contributed to the failure to demonstrate any effect of the treatments, but the magnitude of the differences among means suggests that even with sufficient replication to obtain statistically significant results, the importance of such effects would be

Table 5.2. *Above-ground biomass values (mean ± s.d.) by growth form for each treatment and control*

	Above-ground biomass (g/m^2)						
		−Erigeron canadensis		−E. canadensis and E. annuus	−Aster pilosus and Solidago canadensis	−Annuals and biennials	−Perennials
	Control	−E. canadensis	−E. annuus				
Annuals	103 ± 37	80 ± 26	87 ± 35	95 ± 26	91 ± 26	—	70 ± 14
Biennials	29 ± 45	33 ± 24	52 ± 43	20 ± 27	62 ± 41	—	100 ± 99
Perennials	205 ± 11	200 ± 66	235 ± 53	200 ± 29	135 ± 62	232 ± 59	—
Unidentified material	27 ± 27	32 ± 22	30 ± 24	25 ± 29	33 ± 26	25 ± 28	23 ± 22
Total	363 ± 37	344 ± 87	403 ± 58	340 ± 41	321 ± 135	257 ± 87	193 ± 96

Note: Treatments are listed by the species removed.
From Hils and Vankat (1982).

unimpressive. Thus, the danger of claiming a null result when an effect was present ("type II error") was diminished, as far as ecological interpretation was concerned. Hils and Vankat stated that their results supported the tolerance model of competition in this early successional stage. The experiment was thoughtfully planned, with appropriate controls and adequate replication.

The reasons for the heterogeneity of vegetation on old fields was explored by Tilman (1984) in some elaborate experiments with a number of nutrients. Tilman made the assumption that competition was universal in the community in which he worked, a sandy area north of Minneapolis, Minnesota. He cited the work of Hils and Vankat as supporting that assumption, despite the negative results of their removal experiments. He was interested in testing his "resource ratio hypothesis," which predicted that "plants will be separated along a gradient of two limiting resources if plants are competing for the resources and if there are 'tradeoffs' in the competitive abilities of the plant species for the resources" (Tilman 1984, p. 1445).

In his first experiment, Tilman applied pure nutrients to 0.25-m^2 plots on a field eight years after cessation of cultivation. The plots were widely separated by unfertilized strips 2 m wide, and treatments were assigned randomly. The nutrients were NH_3NO_3, H_3PO_4, K_2O, $MgSO_4$, and $CaCO_3$. In June, each was supplied to some plots separately (nitrogen 26 g/m^2, phosphorus 4.8 g/m^2, potassium 32 g/m^2, magnesium 8.7 g/m^2, and calcium 5.7 g/m^2), and in combinations described later. There were fourteen control plots, and three supplied with each kind of nutrient. On 25 September, the vegetation was cut at ground level and dried to constant mass. Only the plots supplied with nitrogen yielded significantly more than did the controls, thus establishing that element as limiting. The same nutrients were supplied in combination to more plots, in order to test for the effect of multiple additions. The kinds of additions were made in paired sets of plots, one set of the pair receiving all nutrients, and the other set having one nutrient omitted. The plots receiving no nitrogen yielded no more than the controls. For the other pairs, the statistical tests were between the members of each pair. The plots receiving all nutrients yielded significantly more than did those receiving all except magnesium. The other pairs showed no significant differences in yield. Replication was ample, being from seven to sixteen plots per treatment. Tilman argued that the increased availability of nitrogen allowed the plants to use more of the other nutrients and that under those conditions magnesium became limiting.

His second experiment set up gradients of nitrogen and magnesium as two nutrients for which the plants appeared to compete, thus qualifying them as tests for his hypothesis. The field was converted to a first-year field by thorough disking (light plowing with a disk harrow), and the experiment continued for two years. Thirty-six plots, each 3 by 3 m, separated by 2-m walkways, were assigned to six treatments in a latin-square design. This assures random assignment of treatments in both rows and columns across the field, permitting the statistical removal of any effect of systematic heterogeneity in case part of the field is more fertile than the rest. The treatments were as follows: (*A*) nitrogen 13.6 g/m², magnesium 0; (*B*) nitrogen 10.2 g/m², magnesium 0.9 g/m²; (*C*) nitrogen 6.8 g/m², magnesium 1.9 g/m²; (*D*) nitrogen 3.4 g/m², magnesium 2.9 g/m²; (*E*) nitrogen 0, magnesium 3.8 g/m²; (F) control, no addition. The results were assessed by clipping the vegetation on predetermined quadrats, sorting to species, and drying to constant mass. Soil samples were collected in both years and analyzed for total N and extractable Ca, Mg, and K. In July of the second year, twenty pairs of measures in each plot were made of the light intensity at the soil surface and above the vegetation.

The results of this experiment were complex, and they cannot be given here in their entirety. Soil analyses made in April, just before the treatment, showed negligible differences in levels of nitrogen and magnesium among the plots. At the end of the growing season, the expected gradient of magnesium was found, but the gradient in nitrogen, although detectable, was less impressive. The treatments were repeated in the second year, and in July the magnesium gradient was essentially repeated. The nitrogen gradient was even less conspicuous than it had been at the end of the first year.

In both years, there was a highly significant treatment effect on total above-ground biomass. There were differences in which treatments gave the most yield: *A*, *B*, and *C* in the first year, and *B*, *C*, and *D* in the second. As could be expected, light penetration to the soil surface was inversely related to total biomass in the second year, with treatments *E* and *F* having the greatest penetration, and *B*, *C*, and *D* the least. The difference between productions in the two years would be readily explainable had the level of magnesium been depressed in treatment *A* in the second year, but that was not the case, and the explanation must rest with the different species compositions in the two years. Those species with an appreciable fraction of their total production in treatment *A* in the first year were virtually absent in the second. They were *Chenopodium album, Setaria glauca, Ambrosia artemisiifolia,* and *Mollugo verticillata.* The dominant *Agrostis scabra* in treatment *A* in the second year was insufficient to make up the difference. Only one species, *Aristida basiramea,* was among the six most productive in both years, and it reached its peak production in the control plots in both years. Events in the control plots show that succession was more important than the treatments. Excluding *Aristida,* all of the other five species dominant in the first year showed a decline in the control plots in the second year; all of those dominant in the second year showed an increase in the controls from the first year. One species yielded its maximum production at the high-nitrogen end of the gradient. This was *Agrostis scabra* in the second year, and statistical analysis showed a significant downward trend to the other end of the gradient. The reverse was true of *Aristida basiramea,* which had its maximum yield in the high-magnesium end of the gradient, also in the second year. The remaining dominant species having statistically significant trends all reached maximum production in the plots receiving intermediate amounts of both nitrogen and magnesium. Presumably, a consistent increase and decrease in effect along the gradient resulted in statistical significance for the trend.

The prediction of the "resource ratio hypothesis" was clearly met in the second year, as the species did array themselves differentially along the established gradient, and there were few cases of haphazard response to the nutrients. Whether or not this effect was related to the marked change in species composition is unknown. Tilman concluded that some of the heterogeneity in distribution of old-field plants was explained by his results. The experiments were sophisticated in design and execution. Had they not been, it seems likely that many fewer effects would have been detected.

Pairwise competition among old-field species was the subject of an experiment by Miller and Werner (1987). In their field in southwestern Michigan, five species made up more than 90 percent of the biomass: *Ambrosia artemisiifolia* and *Chenopodium album* are upright annuals; *Plantago lanceolata* is a rosette-forming perennial; *Trifolium repens* is a creeping perennial; and *Agropyron repens* is a perennial grass. The field was plowed in the autumn; before emergence in the following spring, 202 quadrats, 1.3 by 1.3 m, were marked out in a randomized block design. After emergence, all but two species were removed from each quadrat, and the members of the pair were regulated by selective removal or seeding to give all combinations of none, half-natural, nat-

Table 5.3. *Responses of focal species to the presence of associated species*

Focal species	Associate species					Mean response
	Ambr.	*Agro.*	*Plan.*	*Lepid.*	*Chen.*	
Year 2, midsummer						
Ambrosia	1.00b	0.91b	0.86b	0.75b	0.88b	0.85
Agropyron	—	—	—	—	—	—
Plantago	0.22b	0.21b	1.00c	0.68c	0.66c	0.44
Trifolium	0.17b	0.20b	0.34bc	1.00c	0.94c	0.41
Chenopodium	0.27b	0.28b	0.41b	0.49b	1.00b	0.36
Mean effect	0.22	0.40	0.54	0.64	0.82	
Year 2, autumn						
Ambrosia	1.00b	0.94b	1.03b	1.02b	1.04b	1.01
Agropyron	0.37b	1.00c	0.86c	0.95c	1.16c	0.84
Plantago	0.23b	0.36b	1.00c	1.08c	0.73c	0.60
Trifolium	0.22b	0.27b	0.67c	1.00c	0.90c	0.51
Chenopodium	0.08b	0.16bc	0.43cd	1.15d	1.00d	0.46
Mean effect	0.22	0.43	0.75	1.05	0.96	

Note: Values are expressed as a proportion of growth in monoculture (the principal diagonal). Values in the same row followed by different letters are significantly different at the $p < .05$ level.
From Miller and Werner (1987).

ural, and twice-natural densities. There were at least five replicate quadrats for each combination. The response of each species was measured in midsummer by nondestructive morphological measures of ten individuals in the center 1 m^2 of each quadrat. This was converted to biomass by correlating the same measures with dry weights of thirty individuals from outside the experiment after they had been measured in the same way. The method was not satisfactory for *Agropyron*. The final response was obtained in October by harvesting all individuals in the center (0.6 × 0.6 m) of each plot and obtaining the dry weight. When the biomass of each species growing in the presence of another was represented as a proportion of its growth in monoculture, the results (Table 5.3) showed that the resistance to competition was positively related to the competitive impact on the other species, giving a hierarchy of competitive ability. This hierarchy was not disturbed by the refinement of varying the densities of competing pairs of species. In monoculture, all five species showed a reduced mean biomass with increasing densities. In combination, there were four significant negative relationships between the mean biomass of one species and the yield of the associate species: increased density of *Agropyron* significantly affected *Plantago*, *Trifolium*, and *Chenopodium*, and increased yield of *Plantago* had a negative effect on *Chenopodium*. Despite its competitive position, increasing the yield of *Ambrosia* did not add to the simple effect of its presence, probably because its yield was high even at low densities, and further increases could not increase the already strong effect.

These experiments were well designed, with adequate replication. The relationships within this first-year old field were clearly demonstrated, and the completely transitive arrangement probably is characteristic of early succession.

Taking all of these studies together, competition among plants in early secondary successional habitats has been shown to exist, but the interactions may be weak, and in at least one experiment, they could not be shown to exist. In this, the situation is markedly different from that in forests.

Arrested secondary succession

In Britain and northern Europe, some areas have been kept as grasslands by grazing for a very long time, perhaps since the Neolithic (Tansley 1953). When protected, such areas quickly become converted to woodland through the normal processes of succession, but as long as the grazing continues, the composition of the vegetation remains virtually constant over wide areas (Mitchley & Grubb 1986). In eastern North America, agricultural practices have not remained so constant, but much the same effect is achieved by regular mowing. The dominant grasses are mixed with both annual and perennial herbaceous species, and the means whereby these mixtures remain stable has attracted the attention of many plant ecologists.

Berendse (1983), noting that fertilization results in a decrease in species richness, conducted a series of experiments in a hayfield to test for the effects of intraspecific competition, interspecific competition, and niche differentiation in the normal maintenance of the species composition. The location was on the slope of a dike along the IJsselmeer in the Netherlands. The field had been mowed (harvested) in June and September for ten years, with no fertilizer being applied. The experiments involved two of the dominant species: the grass *Anthoxanthum odoratum*, and the perennial forb *Plantago lanceolata*. Three separate experiments were carried out, two of them on plots 30 by 30 cm, located so as to ensure adequate densities of the two species, but with actual treatments assigned at random. In the first experiment, a replacement series was established by selective removal of all plants except (a) twenty rosettes of *Plantago*, (b) ten rosettes of *Plantago* and eight tussocks of *Anthoxanthum*, and (c) sixteen tussocks of *Anthoxanthum*. These were replicated five times in each of two series, one with a nutrient solution added and one with only tap water added. The design permitted analysis by the classical de Wit diagrams, in which the yield of each species in the different combinations gives the importance of interference or niche differentiation. If the yield per plant in combination is less than that with an equal density of conspecifics, there was interference; if the yield per plant in combination is greater than when alone, there was differential use of resources by the two species. The results for two harvests in each of two successive years (Fig. 5.1) show that *Plantago* throughout the experiment had the same weight per plant in the mixture as it did alone. During the course of the experiment, *Anthoxanthum* increased its yield per plant in the mixture, relative to that in monoculture. For both species, fertilization greatly increased the yield.

In the second experiment, Berendse established a range of densities of both species in monoculture. There were three replicates at each density. In combination with the monoculture parts of the first experiment, there were three densities of *Anthoxanthum* (4, 8, and 16 tussocks per plot) and four of *Plantago* (5, 10, 20, and 40 rosettes per plot). Strong intraspecific density dependence was shown in the yields, which averaged virtually the same amount per plot over all densities, although there was a weakness in the large amount of variation within densities. This intraspecific competition, combined with the effect of fertilizer, demonstrated that nutrients were limiting populations in this field and that the plants competed for them.

A most interesting result was obtained by the third experiment, in which ten plots, 50 by 50 cm, were located in undisturbed parts of the hayfield. Five of these were fertilized like the replacement series, the other five receiving tap water. Fertilization increased the yield by 70–80 percent, but more interesting were the effects on *Plantago* and *Anthoxanthum*. On the unfertilized plots, *Plantago* constituted about 30 percent of the above-ground biomass. On the fertilized plots, the absolute yield declined to less than one-fourth of that, and its representation declined to less than 5 percent. *Anthoxanthum* also declined, but to a lesser degree: 30 percent to 16 percent. Thus, competition with

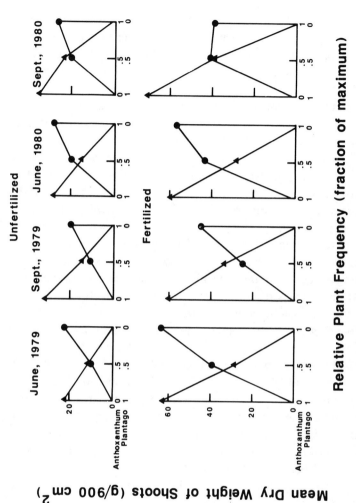

Relative Plant Frequency (fraction of maximum)

Figure 5.1. Mean dry weight (g) of shoots per plot (900 cm²) related to relative plant frequency for monocultures and mixed cultures of *Anthoxanthum* (filled circles) and *Plantago* (triangles) that had been fertilized with a nutrient solution or left unfertilized. On the first three harvests, the plants were clipped 2.5 cm above the soil surface; on the last harvest (September 1980), the plants were cut at the soil surface. (From Berendse 1983.)

Anthoxanthum could not be the cause of the decrease in prominence of *Plantago*. The balance between these two species under unfertilized conditions, apparently possible because of differential use of resources, were upset by the species that were better able to use the increased supply of nutrients.

This series of experiments is praiseworthy because of the overall plan, as well as the good experimental design. Removal experiments in natural vegetation are subject to criticism because the effect of the bare area itself frequently is ignored. Berendse's use of monoculture density series, plus fertilized and unfertilized plots in undisturbed areas, constituted an excellent control on that unwanted feature of the basic experiment. The importance of continuing the experiment for two years is shown in the increase in the performance of *Anthoxanthum* in mixtures, relative to its per-plant performance alone.

Grubb (1982) showed that a period of two years was inadequate for determining the course of interspecific interactions in regularly mowed grasslands. In a survey of nine roadsides in Cambridgeshire, he found a remarkably consistent pattern of relative abundances, with seven species (five grasses and two dicotyledons) being ubiquitous or nearly so, and constituting more than 88 percent of the total mowed biomass. Grubb established a garden experiment in which seedlings of four species were planted in plots 1.5 by 1.5 m. The species were the grass *Arrhenatherum elatius*, the overwhelming dominant in the community, two other grasses (*Dactylis glomerata* and *Festuca rubra*), and the dicot *Plantago lanceolata*. The last three species apparently were chosen for growth forms, rather than for prominence in the community, as *Plantago* had been found in only three of the surveyed roadsides. There were two replicates for each of the following treatments: single species, *Dactylis* planted with each of the others, and all four planted together. The plots were in blocks of four, and each block was surrounded by a "guard row" of *Dactylis* – an arrangement that was not explained. The plots were harvested annually, and detailed data were obtained on the dry weight of each species in each plot after one, two, six, and eight years.

The results for the first two years were much alike. By comparing performances in the presence of other species with performances in monoculture, Grubb found that the yield of *Dactylis* was greater than expected, and that of *Arrhenatherum* was also greater, but less so than *Dactylis*. *Plantago* in the mixtures yielded less than expected, and the yield of *Festuca* was greatly reduced in the presence of other species.

The yields of all species except *Arrhenatherum* were lower after the second year, but the pattern was still much the same as far as interspecific effects were concerned. Great variation between replicate plots, apparently related to previous use of the area, precluded any more definitive statement of results.

The community changed markedly between the second and sixth years. Early in the experiment, *Dactylis* was a dominant, but in the interim, *Arrhenatherum* spread into all plots and after six years made up 77.86–96.87 percent of the biomass in all treatments, including those where it had not been planted initially. It had also displaced *Dactylis* from much of the guard-row part of the design. The eighth year saw some recovery of *Festuca* and a further decrease in the relative abundance of *Dactylis*. As in the early stage of the experiment, differences between replicates were prominent features of the data.

Although revealing the value of long-continued experiments, this study lacked adequate replicates, and the reader is left uninformed of the reasons for some choices, such as the failure to use all of the most ubiquitous and abundant species, and the choice of *Dactylis* as the one species to pair with the others. It was impossible to obtain data for the third and fourth years because the investigator was out of the country, but they were nevertheless the crucially important years for observing the shift to *Arrhenatherum*, which brought the experimental system into line with the naturally occurring system.

In a widely cited experiment, Putwain and Harper (1970) used selective herbicides to remove different potential competitors of the sorrels *Rumex acetosa* and *R. acetosella* in two grasslands in Wales. In one location, in which the species of interest was *R. acetosella*, sheep continued to graze throughout the experiment; the other, in which *R. acetosa* was prominent, had been surrounded with a sheep-proof fence for two years. At each location, five replicate blocks were established, and within each block there were five plots 90 by 90 cm. Four different chemical treatments were used for the selective removals. One killed all grasses, one killed all nongrass species except *Rumex*, one killed all plants except *Rumex*, and one killed only the adult sorrel plants. The fifth plot was a control. In addition to the herbicide treatments, each plot was divided into four subplots, three of which were seeded at progressive densities of the appropriate species of *Rumex*. The treatments were applied in June 1965, and the seeds were sown in August (ungrazed plots) and September (grazed plots). Counts were made on the numbers of mature plants and the numbers of seedlings over the periods July–March (ungrazed) and June–June (grazed). The plots were harvested in July, 1966, and dry weights were obtained for the two *Rumex* species.

Removal of all other plants resulted in significant increases in the numbers of mature *Rumex* individuals in both locations, and the differences between the experimental plots and the controls were maintained throughout the experiment. The same treatment also resulted in significant increases in the numbers of seedlings, but most of the increase in *R. acetosella* occurred in the spring following the start of the experiment, in contrast to *R. acetosa*, which sprouted in the fall. There was a major difference in the responses of the two species to elimination of the grasses. In the case of *R. acetosa*, there was an increase significantly greater than those on the plots from which all other plants were eliminated, but *R. acetosella* showed no such response. Seedling densities of both species increased in response to the elimination of grasses. Yields of dried biomass gave results much like those for the total numbers of mature plants of both species. Putwain and Harper offered no explanation for the different responses of the two species to the elimination of grasses and did not mention any possible effect of the confounding of the treatments with grazing. From the standpoint of design, the study is best considered as two separate experiments, each with a good design, but the confounding of species differences with the effect of grazing precludes interpretation beyond the obvious one of release of *Rumex* from competition.

An unusually complete experiment was conducted by Fowler (1981) in a grassy field in North Carolina. The field had been maintained for about thirty years by mowing to a height of 5 cm once a month from April to October. The vegetation was a mixture of species, some introduced from Europe, some from South America, and some native. Thus, some combinations had been in association for many years, whereas others were new. Ten blocks were established, each containing twelve plots 90 by 100 cm, among which treatments were assigned at random. Within blocks, each of the seven most abundant species was removed from one plot by hand, one plot was treated with herbicide to remove all grasses, one was treated to remove all dicots, and the soil in one was steam-sterilized to kill all plants. Treatments were continued for two years. As the species made up two seasonally distinct groups, records were made in April and September of the final year. Two plots in each block were retained as unmanipulated controls, one for each season. Data consisted of measures of percentage cover of each species over a rectangle 34 by 12 cm in the center of each plot.

The results were not exciting, and perhaps that in itself is their greatest interest. Fourteen of the seventy-two pairwise effects were statistically significant, but the magnitudes of the effects were low and much alike, whether statistically significant or not. There was no evidence that the community could be separated into groups of competing species, and the competition that was detected was diffuse. There was no obvious relationship of competition to species of common geographic origin. No mention was made of the potential effect of mowing on the suppression of competitive winners. The experiment was carefully designed and more comprehensive in the removal of different single species than is most such work. As Fowler pointed out, detection of spatially distinct competitive groups [not found in a direct analysis of the vegetation (Fowler & Antonovics 1981)] would have required replication within blocks.

Experiments bearing on biogeography

The distributions of many species have been correlated with various climatic features (Pigott 1975), and it is tempting to attribute the cause to the physiology of the organisms. Superficially, the distributions of *Sedum telephium* and *S. rosea* in Great Britain appear to be determined by climate. *Sedum rosea* is a northern and alpine species found at elevations down to 450 m above sea level in the Pennines and the Lake District of England. The distribution overlaps slightly with the lowland *S. telephium*, which is found as high as 460 m. Woodward (1975) and Woodward and Pigott (1975) conducted a series of experiments testing the hypothesis that the distributions were determined by the effect of climate on growth. Only two of these experiments can be described here. They chose a series of altitudinal sites from 25 m to 625 m above sea level, and a plot was set out at each elevation. The plots were arranged so that the two species were planted in pairs 5 cm apart, with rows of such pairs separated by rows of plants of a common grass, *Sesleria albicans*. The heights of both species, and their plant cover, were recorded after four months of growth. *Sedum telephium* responded to the altitudinal gradient in the expected way. Plant cover declined linearly from 0.24 dm² at 25 m to about-one tenth of that at 625 m, and plant height declined similarly from 65 mm to 25 mm. *Sedum rosea* was virtually unaffected by differences in altitude. Plant cover was close to 0.035 dm² at all altitudes, and plant height declined only from 27 mm to 15 mm as altitude was increased. A second series of experiments was conducted in growth chambers, where environmental conditions could be controlled. Seedlings were planted individually in pots, fourteen replicate pots for each condition. Temperature was regulated so that in one condition the day temperature was 15 °C and the mean was 11.7 °C. *Sedum telephium* had a larger leaf area (15 cm²) than *S. rosea* (7 cm²), and the total dry weight of its plants (95 mg) was almost twice as great (50 mg for *rosea*). At slightly lower temperatures (day, 12.5 °C, mean 10 °C), the growth of *S. rosea* was not significantly different, but that of *S. telephium* was reduced to a leaf area of slightly less than 5 cm², and the dry weight to less than 30 mg. Thus, a small difference in mean temperature reversed the relative growth abilities of the two species. These experiments demonstrate that the two distributions cannot be explained by the physiology of the two species alone. *Sedum telephium* did appear to respond physiologically in the expected way, but *S. rosea* was virtually unaffected by differences in altitude or realistic differences in temperature, and its absence from lower altitudes must have been due to competition.

A different kind of biogeographical concern has to do with the way in which the number of species changes with the size of the area considered, as well as the ecological implications of the relationship. For the most part, this question has been attacked from a purely descriptive standpoint, with the complications of confounding factors, such as those accompanying island size or habitat differences in contiguous areas. Such studies have not standardized the total area covered by islands of different sizes and thus have not been able to address such questions as the relative desirability of different sizes of refuges in conservation.

Quinn and Robinson (1987) conducted an experiment in which many of the complications were eliminated. They chose a field in the Central Valley of California and set up square plots of three different sizes: 2 m², 8 m², and 32 m². Two-thirds of the plots were fenced, and the remainder were exposed to grazing by sheep. The numbers of plots were arranged so that the total area was the same for each size: thirty-two plots of 2 m², eight plots of 8 m², and two plots of 32 m² for the fenced plots, and half of those numbers for the grazed plots. The vegetation consisted of introduced annual grasses, which appeared to be a stable community, not a successional stage. Observations were of three types and continued over two years. The first was biweekly vegetation surveys, consisting of 2-m² quadrats in the two larger plots and whole plots of the small ones. These were used to estimate plant cover, but all species were recorded, whether they were within the quadrats or not. Only reproducing plants were counted. The second observation was of the seed rain, with seed traps set in the plots for one month on each of three occasions. Seeds were identified to species and counted. The third observation was of the seed bank, made from soil samples once during the first year. Seeds are important, of course, in a community of annuals.

The vegetation surveys confirmed the usual species–area relationship. The mean number of species per plot increased with plot size. In the second year, the means for fenced plots were 8.3 for small plots, 11.9 for medium plots, and 14.5 for large plots; for grazed plots, they were 9.5 for small plots, 10.0 for medium plots, and 14 for the single large plot. However, the total number of species involved showed the reverse pattern. Among fenced plots, the small ones held a total of 29 species, the medium ones 26 species, and the large ones 20. In the grazed area, the small plots had a total of 26 species, the medium ones 16 species, and the large plot 15 species (the discrepancy from the "mean" of 14 was not explained). The relative abundance of the species within sampling plots of the same size was used to calculate a diversity index, which estimates how nearly the abundances conform to a perfectly uniform abundance among the species. In aggregate, the small plots showed a greater diversity, whether grazed or not. The seed data did not reveal surprises. There was a significant correlation between the seed species richness and that of the standing vegetation for all three sizes of plots.

This was a most interesting approach to experimental biogeography. By eliminating some of the complexities of natural situations, and still finding the classical species–area relationship, Quinn and Robinson revealed important relationships. Although, as they stated, their results are not relevant to the preservation of particular species such as large vertebrates, there is a clear indication that many small reserves may harbor a greater diversity of genetic material than will a few large ones.

Herbivore–plant interactions

Experiments on the various kinds of interactions between plants and their herbivores are described in Chapter 4. Here, the emphasis is on experiments revealing differences between the interactions in successional communities and those in forests.

The effect of grazing in the maintenance of an intermediate stage in succession has been mentioned. Domestic animals are outside the province of this book, but the rabbit is considered, even though it was introduced into England some centuries after the Norman Conquest. One of the early ecological experiments consisted of erecting rabbit-proof enclosures on the South Downs near the border of Sussex and Hampshire (Tansley 1922; Tansley & Adamson 1925). In the winter of 1908–9, two enclosures, 820 m² and 390 m², were constructed 600 m apart. Each one was placed with one edge just within the wood, the rest of the enclosure extending 25–30 m into the grassland. Rabbits had grazed the turf down to a height of 1–2.5 cm, but by the summer of 1909, the height inside the fences was 12.5 cm in one enclosure and 14 cm in the other. Detailed surveys of the vegetation were made in 1909, 1914, and 1920. Shortly after the start of the experiment, a deliberate reduction of the rabbit population was undertaken, with the result that by 1914 the turf outside the enclosures had increased to 2.5–5 cm high near one enclosure and to 4–8 cm near the other. Inside, there had been a further increase in height to 10–15 cm and 15–22.5 cm, respectively. Grazing by domestic animals (first sheep and then cattle) kept the turf outside the enclosures to a height of 4–9 cm in 1920, whereas inside the turf was 15–30 cm high in the first enclosure and 20–25 cm high in the second. The species composition of the herbaceous vegetation changed relatively little during the eleven years, but the relative abundance of grasses increased inside the second enclosure. In 1920, they composed 41.6 percent of the wet weight outside and 67.2 percent of the wet weight inside. Changes in the representation of woody plants were more dramatic than those in the herbaceous plants. In 1909, the larger plot had no woody plants within the grassy part; in 1914, there were 11, representing five species; in 1920, there were 125 plants of eleven species, and it was clear that the grassland would be replaced first by *Crategus* scrub and then by ash woodland. Events in the second enclosure were similar, but even more rapid. Including the edge of the wood, there were 19 woody plants of four species in 1909, and 225 plants of fifteen species in 1914. By 1920, *Rubus leucostachys* had spread and smothered some other woody plants at the edge of the wood, but there were many more woody plants in the grassy area, and the edge of the wood had encroached by 14 m on the grassy part of the enclosure. The eventual fate of the area in becoming woodland was clear. The replicated results were thoroughly convincing and should have called attention to the fact that interactions among the plants were not the sole ecological consideration in

these grasslands. Herbivory generally, and selective herbivory especially are important in this partly artificial community. It remains for
speculation whether rabbits would have as great an effect in the
absence of human interference in the form of the initial clearing for
domestic animals, and in partial protection from their natural
enemies.

The importance of differential herbivory by the same species of
chrysomelid beetle on two species of *Rumex* was tested experimentally
by Whittaker (1982). *Rumex crispus* was observed to be rare on a
gravel bank beside a stream in Lancashire, but *R. obtusifolius* was present in a density of seventy plants per 100 m², in company with seven
other species of vascular plants. The beetle, *Gastrophysa viridula*, was
capable of three generations in a season, but some of these failed in
floods. It fed on both species of *Rumex*, but its effect was more severe
on *R. crispus*, and Whittaker tested the hypothesis that this herbivory
kept *crispus* from being present on the gravel bank. He grew seventy
R. crispus from seeds in gravel-filled pots for ten weeks in a greenhouse
and acclimated them for two weeks out of doors. He then drew ten
plants at random for harvesting to determine the dry weights of above-
ground and below-ground parts, and he planted the remaining sixty in
a rectangular grid on the gravel bank. Alternate rows of ten plants each
were designated experimental, which *G. viridula* were allowed to colonize from the naturally occurring *R. obtusifolius*, and control, from
which all beetles and their eggs were removed by hand at intervals of
no more than three days. After each generation of beetles, ten experimental and ten control plants were chosen at random and harvested
to measure the dry weights of above- and below-ground parts. The
experiment was conducted in 1978, when the second generation was
eliminated by flooding. Harvests were accordingly made on 30 June
and 21 September. On both occasions, the control plants had significantly greater dry weights of both above-ground and below-ground
parts, despite the fact that the third generation of beetles was present
in low numbers after postflood colonization of the gravel bank.
Because one generation of beetles had been missed, there remained ten
R. crispus plants of each group. These were marked and left in place
over winter, when further flooding occurred. After the floods, two of
the grazed plants and five of the controls remained. The experiment
was repeated in 1980, when the first two generations of beetles were
completed successfully on the gravel bank. The second generation was
present in small numbers, and the third generation was lost by flood-

ing. The plants were harvested on 19 June and 24 July. The 19 June harvest gave the same result as the two in 1978: Control plants weighed significantly more than grazed ones. There was a nonsignificant difference in the same direction for the 24 July harvest. In this experiment, there remained nine grazed plants and thirteen controls, and again these were followed through the next winter and spring, when five of the grazed plants and twelve of the controls had survived the winter floods. Overall survival was better than in the first experiment, but the difference was in the same direction. Whittaker claimed a statistically significant difference in survival, but his test involved sacrificial pseudoreplication (the difference between years was sacrificed for the test). Whittaker's interpretation was that the herbivory alone could not account for the absence of *Rumex crispus* from the bank, because no plants were killed directly. The loss through root-weakened plants being washed away meant that a combination of herbivory and flooding accounted for the original observation.

Although any differences between gravel banks were not considered, the experiment was thoughtfully planned and executed. In most other experiments, the herbivores were removed by insecticides, as described later. This was done only once in these experiments, when visits to the site could not be made at a time when the beetles were especially active.

The use of insecticides to eliminate herbivorous insects in experiments on succesional communities is naturally time-saving, compared with hand removal. An early experiment by Shure (1971) revealed some of the complications that can arise from the use of insecticides. Shure created four new fields in central New Jersey by disking in April. An organophosphate was applied to two of the fields in early May, after which all of the fields were disked again to create a soil residue in the treated fields. The experiment was repeated in the next year. An area 10 by 20 m was marked in the center of each field, and within each area five quadrats 50 by 50 cm were harvested at two-week intervals. On three occasions during the summer, a sweep-net method was used to assess the insect population. From the standpoint of its purpose, the experiment was a failure. Insect populations were no lower on the treated fields than on the controls, and the diversity was slightly higher on the treated fields. Nevertheless, in the first year the biomass of plants was greater on treated fields, although within-treatment differences were so great that the difference was significant only early in the season. The density of plants and the vegetation diversity were significantly higher on treated areas in the first year. Neither density nor biomass showed any consistent differences in the second year, which Shure attributed to the higher rainfall leaching the insecticide out of the soil more rapidly. The increase in plant density on treated areas in the first year apparently was a secondary effect of toxicity of the insecticide on an early-growing dominant, *Convolvulus sepium*, which was significantly reduced on the treated areas.

The elimination of insect herbivores by insecticides does permit elaborate experimental designs, such as that used by Brown et al. (1987a) on three communities of different ages at Silwood Park, Berkshire. The communities were one, two, and seven years old, and the legumes *Vicia sativa* and *V. hirsuta* were prominent in all three. Extensive suction sampling of insects on both species obtained nine species that fed on leaves and stems, nine that fed on flowers, and five that fed on fruits. *Vicia hirsuta* supported many more sucking individuals than did *V. sativa*, and the reverse was true of leaf-eating insects. Twenty plots 3 by 3 m were located in each community. The plots were separated by 2 m in the first-year site, and 3 m in the other two. Ten plots were systematically allocated to Malathion treatment (sprayed at ten-day intervals from April to October). The remaining plots in each site were sprayed with water. Rabbits were fenced out of the sites, and slugs were poisoned with bait pellets placed around the bases of the experimental plants, of which up to five of each species were marked in each plot.

These plants were examined at two-week intervals throughout the growing season, and records were made of plant height, number of leaves, number of leaves damaged by insects, and number of reproductive structures. The youngest leaf was marked, and the turnover of leaves was assessed by calculation of life expectancy. Insect damage was recorded according to a scale related to percentage of leaf area removed. At intervals, 100 leaves were removed at random from each species in each treatment. Damage was recorded on the same scale as for the marked plants; the number of leaflets was recorded; and the leaves were oven-dried. Seed pod size, the number of seeds per pod, and total seed weight were recorded. By all measures, plants that had been treated with insecticide performed significantly better than did the controls. It is perhaps a quibble to complain that plots were assigned to treatments systematically, rather than randomly, as the data make statistics superfluous in most cases. Brown, Leijn, and Stinson (1987b), noting Shure's results (1971), tested the effect of the insecticide on an array of successional plant species and could detect no significant effect. The plants tested did not include the two species of *Vicia*, however.

There appears to be an arithmetic discrepancy between the text and the data as given for *V. sativa*. This is fully detectable only for the plants in the first-year site. The maximum numbers of leaves per plant are shown to be 83 percent greater on the control plots than on the insecticide-treated plots. Elsewhere, the mean numbers of leaflets per leaf were shown to be 21 percent greater on insecticide-treated plants. The control plants suffered insect damage that could be roughly estimated to be an average of 24–25 percent of the leaf area, from the relationship between damage rating and leaf life expectancy. Combining these figures, it is estimated that the leaf area on the control plants should have been 14 percent greater than that on the insecticide-treated plants. Yet the latter were stated to have had highly significantly greater biomass. One can visualize possible explanations, but the discrepancy was not discussed.

Not all studies work as planned. Natural events may overtake plans, but the latter are sometimes carried out regardless. An example is the study by McBrien, Harmson, and Crowder (1983) of an outbreak of three species of chrysomelid beetles (*Trirhabda*) on goldenrod, *Solidago canadensis*, the usual dominant in successional communities of intermediate age in northcentral North America. The outbreak was observed in an abandoned hayfield in southern Ontario, where six plots 15 by 6.7 m were staked out. The plant and insect populations were followed for five years. Plant populations were sampled twice each summer by the nondestructive method of estimating the percentage ground cover on each of five quadrats 50 by 50 cm, randomly placed within each plot. Insect populations were sampled with fifty sweeps with a 30-cm net every two weeks during the summer. *Trirhabda* larvae were the principal insects of interest, and the population was reported as the largest collection in any year. In June and July of the fourth year, and May of the fifth year, three of the plots were treated with Carbaryl, a cholinesterase inhibitor. In June of the fifth year the plots were again treated with the insecticide Malathion to control an outbreak of aphids. The remaining three plots were retained as controls. The data were reported for one control plot and one experimental plot, and hence there was no replication of treatments, as far as the reader was concerned. In the summer of the third year, the maximum number of larvae collected reached more than 5,000 in the control plot and about 3,000 in the experimental plot. In the fourth year, when insecticide treatment began, the larval populations had fallen to around 200 on the control plot and around 400 on the experimental plot, most likely because *Solidago* had fallen from 50–65 percent cover early in the study to less than 10 percent. A beneficial effect on *Solidago* was claimed, but the cover had already begun to increase by the time of application of the insecticide, and the larval population on the control was so low that it is difficult to attribute the failure of *Solidago* to recover there to *Trirhabda*. Evidence was presented that grasses had already begun to increase before treatment on the insecticide plot, and that kind of event on the control plot could easily account for the failure of *Solidago* to recover there. Some conclusions might be possible with data from all six plots, but it is reasonable to suppose that such data would not have supported the interpretation.

Despite problems with the design and execution of experiments on the effects of herbivory on the growth and composition of successional plants, there is good evidence that the effect is greater than the effect of herbivores on forest trees (Chapter 4).

Plant defenses against herbivory have been the subject of a voluminous literature during the last two decades (Wallace & Mansell 1976; Rosenthal & Janzen 1979; Crawley 1983; Denno & McClure 1983). A distinction has been found between the nature of these allelochemicals in herbs, on one hand, and their nature in shrubs and trees, on the other. Futuyma (1976) surveyed the literature and found that families of plants that were primarily herbaceous contained a much greater array of secondary compounds than did families of primarily woody plants. Nearly all of the latter (eleven of thirteen) contained phenolics, but other compounds were scattered widely: Representatives of five families contained quinones, three contained cyanogenic glycosides, three contained coumarin glycosides, three contained alkaloids, one contained saponins, and none contained acetylenes or sulfur compounds. Among thirteen herbaceous families, representatives of ten contained alkaloids, nine contained quinones, six contained saponins, five contained phenolics, five contained cyanogenic glycosides, five contained coumarin glycosides, three contained acetylenes, and three contained sulfur compounds. In general, woody species contain such substances as tannins and phenolics, which are energetically costly to produce, but have effects on the physiology of a wide range of organisms, including, of course, herbivores, but also presenting problems to their producers. Such defenses would not be lethal, but would slow the growth and development of the herbivores, which would not be expected to specialize because of the chemicals. The compounds found in herbs characteristic of early succession have smaller molecules, are less costly to produce and store, and have specifically poisonous effects at low doses. They are lethal, and to consume the plant, a herbivore would have to have a specific mechanism for detoxifying, rapidly excreting, or sequestering the compound. Such herbivores should specialize on particular plant families, and Futuyma found that 88 percent of the 110 species of butterflies of the eastern United States that fed on herbaceous vegetation were restricted to single families of plants, whereas 68 percent of the 53 species feeding on woody plants were thus restricted. Among the hawkmoths (Sphingidae) of the United States and Canada 13 of 14 species (93%) feeding on herbs are confined to one family, whereas 26 of 42 species (62%) feeding on woody plants are restricted to one family.

Several experiments have tested the implications of these observations. Cates and Orians (1975) and Otte (1975) independently tested the palatability of arrays of plant species to generalist herbivores. Two species of slugs, *Ariolimax columbianus*, native to western Washington state, and *Arion ater*, introduced from Europe, were the herbivores used by Cates and Orians. The slugs were starved for the night prior to testing and were presented individually with six leaf disks of 3.8 cm^2 (not the 38 cm^2 stated). The disks were alternated, three from the test species and three from a highly palatable control. After overnight exposure, the logarithm of the amount eaten from the test species was rated as a proportion of the logarithm of the amount eaten from the control. The average score of 12 to 36 tests per species was the palatability index. Cates and Orians tested 18 species of early successional annuals, 45 species of early successional perennials, and 17 species of late successional and climax plants for palatability. The average indexes for the two slug species were not significantly different for any category of plants. The average palatabilities of the different categories were strikingly different. For early successional annuals, the palatability averaged 0.96 ± 0.09 for *Ariolimax* and 0.99 ± 0.14 for *Arion*; for the early successional perennials, the average indexes were 0.77 ± 0.30 for *Ariolimax* and 0.69 ± 0.36 for *Arion*; and for late successional and climax plants, the figures were 0.46 ± 0.45 for *Ariolimax* and 0.40 ± 0.39 for *Arion*. There was a marked decrease in palability with the progress of succession, and the differences were statistically significant, despite the large variation within categories.

Otte (1975) tested the palatability of 125 native species of plants and 24 introduced species for three native species of grasshoppers, *Schistocerca emarginata, S. obscura,* and *S. americana.* He placed 100 nymphs of one species in a gauze cage and allowed them to feed for at least two days on 2–5 species of plants cut in local habitats near Austin, Texas. He took care than one species was edible, so as to serve as a standard. Palatability was recorded on a scale from 0 (no feeding) to 5 (complete defoliation). All three species were generalist feeders, and they fed at least minimally on 36–89 species, in proportion to the number to which they were exposed. Otte's results were the reverse of those of Cates and Orians. He pooled palatability categories 0–2.5 as low and categories 2.5–5 as high. Native early successional plants rated low for 52 of 64 species (81%); native midsuccessional plants rated low for 37 of 49 species (76%); native late successional or climax species rated low for 4 of 11 species (36%). The last were significantly different from plants of the two earlier stages. He also presented the data according to life history. Among native annuals, 44 of 49 species were rated low, and 5 high; among 45 native perennials, 29 were rated low, and 16 high; among 31 native trees, shrubs, and vines, 21 were rated low, and 10 high. The annuals were significantly different from the plants having the other life histories. For neither classification were the three species of grasshoppers significantly different from each other. Otte conducted experiments testing the association between edibility of eight plants and the ability of *S. americana* to survive, grow, and mature when fed those plants exclusively for ninety days. Survival was 54–73 percent on five species of plants whose palatability had rated 3 or higher, and it was nil for those rated 2 or below. Similarly, most of the grasshoppers that were fed on the relatively palatable species reached maturity, whereas none of the others did. The mean weight of surviving individuals followed the other trends.

Otte was puzzled by the contrast between his results and those of Cates and Orians. He suggested that the much greater mobility of *Schistocerca* allowed the grasshoppers to be selective feeders and still be generalists. Both sets of experiments were well planned, and the quality of the experimentation cannot be the reason for the difference. It is true that even within categories, palatability varied between species over the full range of possible values, except for the early successional species tested by Cates and Orians, where the range was 0.83 to 1.08 for *Ariolimax.* Discounting such remote possibilities as an important difference in the way succession works in Washington and Texas, one can only suppose that some factor or factors were overlooked. Otte did not starve his specimens before exposing them to the plants, and that might account for the generally lower palatability that he found, but the discrepancy would not account for the very different pattern. Further experimentation will be required to resolve the questions raised.

Both of the preceding experiments were performed on generalist feeders. Scriber and Feeny (1979) selected the butterfly family Papilionidae as representing an array of species, some feeding on forbs (dicotyledonous herbs), and others feeding on woody plants. Moreover, some are specialists, confined to single families, and others feed on plants belonging to a number of families. They wanted to test two hypotheses: (a) Larvae grow better and mature faster when feeding on the leaves of herbaceous plants than on the leaves of woody plants, because the latter are more fibrous and contain tannins. (b) Larvae of species that are specialists grow better and mature faster than larvae of generalists. They grew larvae of nine species of Papilionidae on forty-five species of plants. Three species were specialists on one plant species each; another was known to feed on twenty-two confamilial plants. One species of butterfly fed on thirteen species of plants representing nine families; other species were intermediate in degree of specialization. In a few experiments, abnormal food species were used. Varying numbers of replicate experiments were conducted for the different combinations, but in only 5 of 127 was there no replication. Growth, consumption rate, efficiency of conversion of ingested food, efficiency of nitrogen utilization, and duration of instars were recorded for each experiment.

Superficially, both hypotheses were confirmed. Larvae that fed on forbs grew faster and had shorter instars than did those feeding on woody vegetation, and specialists performed better by at least one of the two criteria than did intermediate species or generalist feeders. There was a difficulty, however, in that the classes were confounded, with forb feeders being specialists, and generalists feeding primarily on woody plants. Scriber and Feeny attempted two further experiments to separate the hypotheses. The southern army worm, *Spodoptera eridania*, a noctuid lepidopteran, was used as a forb-feeding generalist, and members of another group of Lepidoptera, the bombycoid moths, were used because their feeding habits included specialists, intermediate forms, and generalists on a number of species of trees and shrubs. The data for *S. eridania* generally supported the hypothesis that feed-

ing on early succesional forbs led to more growth and faster development than feeding on the leaves of shrubs and trees. Specialization
appeared to be a secondary phenomenon, but the extra taxonomic distance weakens the conclusion. The bombycoid moths gave results that
supported neither hypothesis, because variation within conditions was
great, and growth differences were small. The fastest-growing larvae
included species in all three categories.

When these studies are considered together, general conclusions are
difficult to draw. There is no doubt that many species of herbaceous
plants contain chemicals that are highly toxic to herbivores, but the
effects of these chemicals on herbivore growth are not always as great
as their existence would lead one to expect. The obvious reason for the
discrepancy is in the adaptation of the herbivores to their food plants.

Competition among successional herbivores

Several reviewers have commented on the paucity of examples of
competition among terrestrial folivores (Lawton & Strong 1981;
Schoener 1983; Strong et al. 1984a). I have chosen the following examples from among those claiming to have detected competition. In successional or grassland habitats, both mammals and insects have been
objects of experimentation.

Joule and Jameson (1972), working in a herb-dominated habitat in
southern Texas, removed the herbivorous cotton rat (*Sigmodon hispidus*) from one 3.6-ha plot and removed the granivore *Reithrodontomys fulvescens* plus the mixed herbivore *Oryzomys palustris* from
another plot; they left two plots as controls, where all small mammals
were live-trapped and released. All plots were separated by paved
roads. One of the control plots was immediately between the two
experimental plots; the other was slightly more distant across a wider
paved road. At biweekly intervals from 30 January to 22 May, traps
were set; all individuals captured were weighed and marked, and those
not from removal plots were released. The numbers of captures were
pooled for three periods, and the data tested for differences in two
ways: first, among all four plots and among the three periods; second,
for the three plots from which the species concerned was not removed.
Inasmuch as the removals were moderately successful in reducing the
respective populations, both *Sigmodon* and *Reithrodontomys* showed
significantly different populations among the four plots. When tested
for the effect of removing the other species, neither showed an effect –

not surprising, in view of the lack of replication. Changes in mean weight were not easily interpretable. Significant increases were observed for female *Sigmodon* on the plots from which the other two species were removed, and both males and females of that species had significant weight gains on the control plot that was situated between the two experimental plots. For the remaining individuals on the plot from which *Sigmodon* had been removed, there was no observable change – an anomalous result, because intraspecific effects should have been greater than interspecific effects, especially as *Sigmodon* is the largest of the three species and was originally the most abundant. The other two species did not change significantly in weight. The results of this experiment provide no convincing evidence of interspecific competition.

A second experiment in the same habitat was better designed (Cameron 1977; Cameron & Kincaid 1982; Kincaid & Cameron 1982). There were two replicate plots for each treatment: *Sigmodon* removal, *Reithrodontomys* removal, and controls. *Oryzomys*, the least abundant of the three species, was not involved in this experiment, despite the fact that its food is intermediate between the foods of the other two. The experiment was continued for three years, with density, demographic responses, movement, differential habitat use, and food being monitored. Density and survival showed the reverse of what was expected; both were lower on the experimental plots. Movement was greater on experimental plots, apparently in response to the artificially created density gradient. There was no evidence of a niche shift in response to the manipulation, but *Reithrodontomys* did make greater use of the vertical component of the habitat in the presence of *Sigmodon* than in its absence. After a great amount of effort, the evidence for interspecific competition was weak at best.

Competition among herbivorous insects has been claimed in a few cases, of which two examples are described here. Gibson and Visser (1982) conducted an experiment on two species of mirid Heteroptera in a grassy common in Wytham Woods, near Oxford. *Notostira elongata* and *Megalocerea recticornis* both fed on a number of species of grasses, but only *M. recticornis* could feed on *Arrhenatherum elatius*, which was rare in the location of the four experimental plots. The octagonal plots had a diameter of 5 m, giving each an area of 17.7 m^2. Three of the plots were fenced with plastic fences, which were found to be effective barriers to the nymphs, which cannot fly. The fourth plot was an unfenced control. Based on previous research in the same area, more than 1,000 *M. recticornis* nymphs were expected to hatch in each area, but *N. elongata* had experienced a decline of six years' duration, and only four or five were expected to hatch in each plot. The density of *N. elongata* was increased on two of the fenced plots by the addition of 1,700 nymphs collected from another field, giving a density of 96 m^{-2}, similar to the density from which they came, but 340–425 times the density in the experimental field, and 6.4 times the density six years earlier. Because of the scarcity of *A. elatius*, sixteen blocks of turf of this species, 25 by 25 cm, were substituted for the natural turf in one of the two plots to which *N. elongata* was added. Similar areas of turf were dug up and put back in the two remaining fenced plots. The insect populations were sampled by a suction method. Ten samples covering 0.093 m^2 each were taken at random on alternate days in each plot. The mirids were identified, counted, and returned. The method did not appear to harm them.

Despite an attempt to choose plots that were alike, the unfenced control had a density of grasses that was only 75 percent of the average for the other three plots. The number of first-instar *M. recticornis* caught on that plot was only about one-sixth of the number caught on the other three plots, and the calculated survivorship was appreciably higher there (40.0% vs. 25.2%). On the two experimental plots, the calculated survival of *M. recticornis* was 25.5 percent where its exclusive food plant was substituted for 1/17.7 of the natural turf, and 12.0 percent where the same amount of natural turf was dug up and replaced. Taken together, these figures suggest that the substitution of its exclusive food over 5.6 percent of the area was sufficient to counteract the effect of 1,700 individuals of the putative competitor and was also sufficient to more than double the survivorship of *M. recticornis*. The loss of the small area to a food plant that it could not use did not have a demonstrably deleterious effect on *N. elongata*. Its survival was about one-third better there than on the plot where the natural turf was dug up and put back. The effect of the excessive density of *N. elongata* was apparently to reduce survival to less than one-fifth of the survival of *M. recticornis*, although its survival on the control plots was not reported, and the survival at natural density remains unknown.

Gibson and Visser (1982) interpreted their results to mean that *M. recticornis* was adversely affected by competition from *N. elongata*. If the interpretation was correct, the effect was most likely attributable to the excessive introduction of the latter. The lack of replication, especially combined with the natural differences among plots, is reason to question any interpretation.

The second claim of interspecific competition among folivores is that of Stiling (1980). He worked with leafhoppers of the genus *Eupteryx* in South Wales. The two species, *E. cyclops* and *E. urticae*, are confined to stinging nettles, and the vegetation consisted of nettles, grasses, and thistles. The conditions of the experiment were artificial in that the insects were caged with potted nettles. A range of densities of both species, alone and in combination, was used in the experiments. The numbers released into the cages represented realistic field densities, and the experiments were continued for eight days. The leafhoppers left characteristic spots where they had eaten the leaves. The area eaten was recorded for each species alone, and *E. urticae* showed a significant decrease in amount of leaf eaten per insect with increasing density. For *E. cyclops*, the relationship was negative, but nonsignificant. Of more interest were the observations on the relationship between the number of eggs laid per female and density. The eggs were dissected out of the plants and hatched, and the nymphs were identified to species. There were significant negative relationships between the number of eggs laid per female and the density of each species, and the negative slope became significantly steeper in cages where the other species had been added. In both cases, however, the reduction in fecundity per female was greater for intraspecific increases in density than for an equal increase of the other species.

For the experimental conditions, the evidence for competition was convincing, but there were no controls for cage effects, and the possibility of predation and parasitism was eliminated by the cages. In observational studies, Stiling found egg parasitism by the hymenopteran *Anagrus*, as well as the nymphal parasites *Aphelopus*, a dryinid hymenopteran, and *Chalarus*, a pipunculid dipteran. The egg parasite showed a strong density-dependent effect, but the nymphal parasites did not. Nevertheless, the egg parasite could have prevented competition from being effective, and that is as valid a mechanism for the determination of the abundance of the leafhoppers as is interspecific or intraspecific competition.

Predation in successional communities

Several experiments have tested the effects of predators on herbivore populations in successional communities. All have involved insects. Eickwort (1977) investigated the reasons for the scarcity of the milkweed leaf beetle, *Labidomera clivicollis*, in view of the fact that its close chrysomelid relative *Leptinotarsa decemlineata*, the Colorado potato beetle, is an abundant pest. *Labidomera* feeds exclusively on

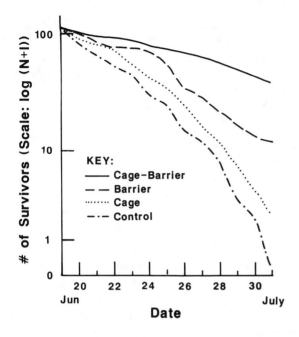

Figure 5.2. Log survivorship curves of larvae in the first field experiment. (From Eickwort 1977.)

milkweeds, *Asclepias* spp., and Eickwort tested the suitability of three species for growth of the larvae. The larvae grew equally well on two of them, and she chose *A. incarnata* for field experiments because the adults oviposited preferentially on that species and were more abundant on it than on *A. syriaca*. The habitat chosen was a roadside clearing in upstate New York. The vegetation, in addition to a dense stand of *A. incarnata*, was a mixture of herbaceous species. Sixteen plants were selected to have the same numbers of leaf nodes and to be separated from each other. They were assigned at random to four treatments: unprotected controls, those protected from ground-dispersed predators by an aluminum barrier surrounded by a ground sheet and covered with a sticky substance, those protected from flying predators by a nylon cage suspended 20 cm above the ground, and those protected from both creeping and flying predators. The only predators not successfully excluded were spiders, but they affected all treatments equally. Newly hatched larvae of *Labidomera* were placed on each plant, and their survival was followed for twelve days, at which time all 112 larvae on the control plants were dead. The results (Fig. 5.2) showed that ground-dispersed predators were more effective than fly-ing predators and that larvae protected from both survived best. There were statistically significant differences between survival on plants with each kind of protection and survival on those without that pro-tection. Daily mortality from ground-dispersed predators was 0.1875, and that from air-dispersed predators was 0.0305. Eickwort recognized that absolute mortality was not necessarily the factor regulating the population, but argued persuasively that other potential sources of reg-ulation were unlikely to be effective. The experiment was well de-signed, with adequate replication and proper controls.

Aphids are abundant herbivores, sometimes reaching outbreak numbers. Edson (1985) carried out a complex experiment on two spe-cies of *Uroleucon* in an old field in Piedmont North Carolina. Both *U. nigrotuberculatus* and *U. tissoti* feed primarily on one species of gold-enrod, *Solidago altissima*, and during the study they were the only abundant herbivores feeding on that species. The two aphid species are easily distinguished by color, and they normally use different means of dispersal. The dark red *U. nigrotuberculatus* disperses by alates, which congregate on the new plant in large colonies. The pale green *U. tissoti* occurs in numerous small colonies, which result from the deposition of a few young on each of several plants; it also tends to walk from plant to plant more than does *U. nigrotuberculatus*. Edson trans-planted goldenrod plants into 3.8-liter plastic containers, and after the field was mowed she replanted the containers either singly or in sepa-rate patches of ten. Single plants and the centers of patches were spaced in a grid about 11 m apart. Plants in the patches were 30 cm apart. The pattern was established to reveal ecological differences that could be brought about through the different dispersal methods normally used by the two species. Edson used a two-factor (planting pattern and pred-ator removal) randomized block design for her experiment. After removing all aphids, she placed a single adult of each species on each plant, and then replaced all dead adults for the next three days. There-after, she removed daily, by hand, all aphid predators from half of the plants, a practice that she showed was 68 percent effective for cocci-nellids, 59 percent effective for dipteran eggs and larvae, and 34 per-cent effective for neuropterans. All plants were censused for aphids every four days early in the experiment and every six days later.

In analyzing results, Edson divided the period of observation into three parts: the early period (first four censuses), when the aphid popu-lations were increasing exponentially, regardless of treatment; a middle period (next four censuses), when they had stopped growing and had begun to decline; a late period (last five censuses), when many of the plants with reduced predation were obviously in poor condition (Fig. 5.3). Predator removal had a significant positive effect on both species during the second period, demonstrating that natural predation was controlling the populations. During this period, there was also a significant effect of the dispersion pattern of the plants, with aphid abundance being greater on plants in dense patches than on those planted separately. The condition of the plants during the third period was analyzed in two different ways. The heights of plants under the two treatments were compared, and a highly significant effect of predator removal was found, with the increased densities of aphids having retarded growth, specifically in the dense patches. There was no effect of plant dispersion on plant height, however, showing the absence of a crowding effect. The second analysis consisted of a visual record of the appearance of the leaves, whether normal and green, malformed and yellow, or intermediate in appearance. There was a significant relationship with the density of aphids per plant, the normal plants having the fewest. Thus, the natural predation had protected the plants from the deleterious effects of aphid damage.

This was another example of a well-designed and well-executed experiment with clear results. Not all experiments on predation in successional habitats have given such definitive answers. In this, and in Eickwort's experiment (1977), the aim was to protect one or two species of herbivores from all of their predators. In the experiments described next, single species of predators were manipulated, and all species of herbivores were followed.

Hurd and Eisenberg (1984a,b) added different numbers of mantids (*Tenodera sinensis*) to plots on a field in Delaware. The field previously had contained no mantids because of annual mowing. Twelve plots 20 by 20 m were established and randomly assigned to one of four treatments: high density (oothecae added to give an average of 12,595 hatchlings), medium density (average of 4,189 hatchlings), low density (average of 1,303), and control (none added). Plots were separated by mowed strips 10 m wide, and each plot was surrounded by a strip of plastic mulch 1 m wide, made further effective by a band of sticky material. The distribution of the plots on the field was planned to keep the vegetational assemblage constant (Fig. 5.4). The effect of chance on small numbers is clearly seen in the clustering of control and high-density plots at the center of the area and the wide dispersal of

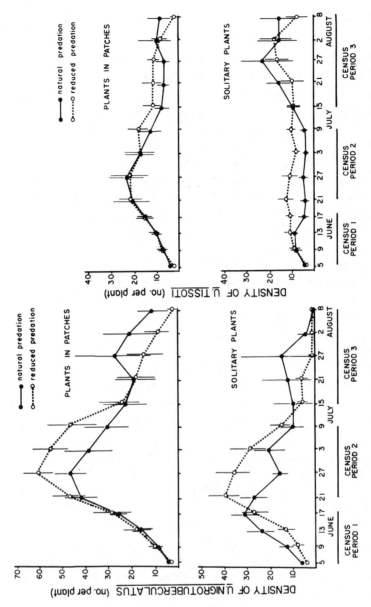

Figure 5.3. Effects of predator reduction on the density of *Uroleucon nigrotuberculatus* (left) and *U. tissoti* (right) at both plant spacings. Data are means ± 1 s.e. (From Edson 1985.)

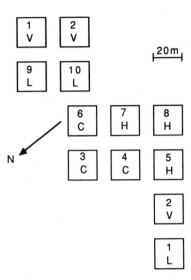

Figure 5.4. Plot design for field density manipulation. C = control (no mantids), L = low density (*x*), V = medium density (3*x*), and H = high density (9*x*). (From Hurd & Eisenberg 1984a.)

the low- and medium-density plots. Data on mantid abundance and dispersal show no significant effect of this distribution of plots, but it is an example of the problem discussed by Hurlbert (1984), who advocates deliberate interspersion of treatments in preference to random assignment when the number of plots is small. The responses of the herbivores and the other predators were not reported in a way that permitted testing for the possible effect of plot distribution, but only high-density plots showed any effect, and it was not stated whether the failure of the low- and medium-density plots to show an effect was due to higher variances there or to a lesser response. The arthropod populations were sampled on five dates, using a suction sampler along randomly chosen vertical transects in each plot.

There was a huge increase in the total biomass as a result of the introduction. On the high-density plots seven weeks later, the ratio of carnivore biomass to herbivore biomass was between 1.2 and 1.3, whereas on the control plots the ratio was about 0.2. The ratio remained higher throughout the eighty-three days of the experiment, significantly so for all samplings except one. The mean herbivore biomass was greater on control plots than on high-density mantid plots for four of the five samplings, significantly so for the first and last samplings. The mean number of herbivores was higher on the controls only for the last two samplings (significantly so for only one). The non-mantid carnivores followed fairly similar patterns, the biomass and the mean abundance each being significantly higher on control plots on one of the last two samplings. That suggested that the mantids, which were much the largest carnivores by that time, were preying on at least some of the naturally occurring carnivores and thereby potentially blurring the outcome of the main experiment.

Aside from the plot placement already discussed, the principal criticisms of the experiment concern the use of an exotic predator, which although present in the eastern United States was not present on the field, and the high densities actually used. Notice that the low and medium densities had no effect, even though they raised the level of carnivore biomass to at least 1.3 and 4 times that on the controls. Therefore, the unimpressive effect of predation was achieved by the use of an unrealistic density.

A similarly weak effect of predators was found by Heads and Lawton (1984), who protected the extrafloral nectaries of bracken, *Pteridium aquilinum*, by ringing the stems with tape, which was then smeared with tree-banding grease. Fronds were chosen in pairs, one ringed and the other kept as a control. Fifty-six pairs were selected in one area near York, and the insect populations were censused on seven occasions over the three months June–August. The manipulations were successful in reducing ant activity, but only one species of herbivore increased significantly on the fronds that had been protected from ants. Heads and Lawton concluded that ant predation was feeble relative to other factors, even for that species.

Competition among predators in successional habitats

There appear to have been few experiments testing for competition among these predators. Pontin (1961) discovered that the production of alate queens of the ant *Lasius flavus* was proportional to the distance between colonies in a calcareous grassland in Berkshire. Further analysis showed that where the colonies overlapped with underground galleries of *L. niger*, the relationship still held, but that for an equivalent production of alate queens a significantly greater distance between *L. flavus* colonies was required. He tested the hypothesis of interspecific competition by poisoning one colony of *L. niger* and then following alate queen production by the colonies of *L. flavus* that overlapped its distribution. All showed an increase, which was significantly

Table 5.4. *Calculated biomasses of the alate queens produced by* Lasius *in the three years 1966–8*

	Biomass (g)		
	1966	1967	1968
Transplanted *L. flavus* (F.)	47	25.4	d21.5
L. flavus with neighboring *L. flavus* removed	19	u21	42.7
L. flavus with added *L. flavus* neighbors	56	d14.8	u37
L. niger with *L. flavus* removed	8.4	6	u24.4
L. niger with added *L. flavus*	7.7	d0.7	u17.6
L. flavus controls	140.4	d64.6	u167
L. niger controls	37.8	37.3	47.4

Note: Letters preceding values indicate the direction of those changes (u, up; d, down) that have $p = .05$ of occurring by chance. The experimental transplants were performed between the 1966 and 1967 collections. From Pontin (1969).

different from changes shown by colonies not in the immediate vicinity of the poisoned *L. niger* colony. The manipulation was, of course, unreplicated. Eight years later, Pontin (1969) reported a second experiment on the same two species, but on a different kind of soil – an acid sandy soil overlying clay. The situation was complicated by the presence of a third species, *Myrmica scabrinodis*, a predator on *L. flavus*, which occupied part of some of the mounds of that species. The major experiment involved only the two *Lasius* species. Pontin was able to transplant whole colonies of *L. flavus* with minimal disturbance. After obtaining data on alate queen production for one year, he transplanted a number of colonies so as to remove them from the vicinity of some *L. niger* colonies and place them close to others. The move also changed the relationships of the surrounding colonies of *L. flavus*. Pontin presented data for the year before the manipulation, the year of the manipulation, which took place in March, and the year after that. It was an unfortuante circumstance that the great majority of all colonies of *L. flavus* had reduced production of alate queens in the year of the manipulation, including twenty-six of forty controls, two of five with neighbors removed, all seven with neighbors added, and five of the six transplanted colonies. Similar declines applied to *L. niger*, with two of five controls, both with *flavus* neighbors removed, and all three with *flavus* neighbors added. The overall pattern is clearest in Table 5.4, which presents the data in terms of the calculated biomass of the queens produced. All of the interspecific effects changed in concert with the controls, and in the second year of the experiment, all treatments increased alate queen production, except for the colonies that had been moved. Without a clearer difference from the controls, it is difficult to accept the claim that interspecific competition was demonstrated.

Spiders are prominent predators in old fields, and differences between the species had been proposed as evidence that competition had been responsible for selection favoring the differences. Horton and Wise (1983) conducted carefully designed experiments in two successive years, testing for interspecific competition between the orb-weaving species *Argiope aurantia* and *A. trifasciata* in an old field in Maryland. They used a randomized block design. Twelve unfenced plots, 12 by 12 m were laid out in two blocks, each with unreplicated treatments. The plots were surrounded by mowed strips 1.5 m wide. Treatments were increased density (two to three times the mean density in the field), natural density, and density reduced to about one-half natural. High-density interspecific effects were obtained by adding specimens removed from plots designated as intraspecific and adding them to high-density plots, additional specimens being obtained in nearby fields as required. Because the removals had to be repeated at each census (repeated at intervals of 1.5–2 weeks), these plots were treated as low-density plots of the species removed. In the second year, the experiment was repeated, but the plots were reassigned to treatments. The manipulations were begun in June, using immature spiders. In the second year, all spiders were removed from all plots initially, and the planned densities were established on the denuded plots. Observations made at each census were number and locations of the webs of each species, height above ground of the center of the orb, the family and size of all prey found in each web, and the length of the spider. The repeated censuses showed that the manipulations were successful during the first part of each summer; high-density plots had significantly more spiders than natural-density plots, and except for *A. aurantia* in the first year, the latter had significantly more than the low-density plots.

Argiope trifasciata placed its webs higher in the vegetation than did *A. aurantia*, regardless of the treatment, and early in the first year of the experiment, both species responded to increased density by placing their webs higher. This was an intraspecific effect, as there was no effect of species composition on web height, and no interaction between density and species composition. The density effect was not observed in the second year. Probably as a result of web placement, the two species captured significantly different proportions of the major orders of prey, *A. trifasciata* capturing more Homoptera (85% Cicadellidae), and the larger *A. aurantia* capturing more Orthoptera (91% Acrididae) and Hymenoptera (63% Apidae). There were no treatment effects on the proportion of webs with prey (17% for *A. trifasciata*, 22% for *A. aurantia*) or on the major taxa of insects captured. The second year was one of drought, and although both species grew during both seasons, both were smaller in the second year, with *A. aurantia* being affected significantly more than *A. trifasciata*. There were no treatment effects on growth. Survival of *trifasciata* was significantly depressed by high density in the first year, but there were no other treatment effects on survival.

Horton and Wise thus found no evidence for interspecific competition, and they argued that the experiment provided much better evidence than the observational data used by previous investigators to sustain the interpretation that the observed differences in habitat and prey utilization were results of natural selection to reduce competition. It should be noted that their experimental design carried the implied assumption that interspecific effects would be unimportant, and after the fact, that turned out to be the case, but it does appear to have been a design that could have backfired.

Summary

Unlike the experiments in forests, those in successional habitats have not been consistent within trophic levels. The picture is of a weak imitation of the relationships in forest ecosystems. Although the decomposing fungi and bacteria compete as strongly as they do in forests, the remaining trophic levels have provided exceptions, mostly in negative results. Competition does not appear to be universal among successional plants, and when found has sometimes been weak. Herbivores have more impact on plants than they do in forests, and they also sometimes compete with each other, rather than being held in check by predators, as Edson's aphids were (Edson 1985). Competition among predators does occur, but not universally. Considering the overall results in successional communities, it is clear that the authors of HSS were wise to state that "As in the original paper, we except '. . . successional stages, in which the failure of decomposition hastens the termination of the state'" (Slobodkin et al. 1967).

6

Experiments in arid environments

Introduction

Deserts and semideserts are characterized by a striking difference from nearly all other terrestrial environments. Except for brief periods following rare rains, most of the ground is bare, shrubs and some perennial grasses being the only obvious vegetation. This has important implications not only within the producer trophic level but also for the interactions between the producers and primary consumers. Annual plants, which form a nearly negligible fraction of the vegetation in undisturbed parts of better-watered regions, assume a major importance in those deserts that have been investigated ecologically. The reason for the prominence of annuals lies in the resistance of their seeds to the harsh conditions that prevail in deserts most of the time. Thus, the reservoir of seeds left from past brief periods of favorable weather is vital to the maintenance of that ecosystem, and the magnitude of the reservior determines the abundance of the seed-eating animals that are so characteristic of many deserts.

The shrubs and perennials in such areas have deep roots, which spread far beyond the spans of their canopies, and frequently the roots of neighboring shrubs actually touch, even though there is much bare ground between the branches. The distribution usually is attributed to the potential for obtaining as much water as is possible, and competition for water is commonly claimed for arid-land plants as reviewed by Fowler (1986). Thus, at shallow depths of soil, there is space available for occupancy by the shallow-rooted annuals at any time when conditions permit the germination of their seeds.

Experiments on competition among shrubs and other perennials

As was the case with many ecological experiments in the field, the early work was carried out in the interest of potential application.

170

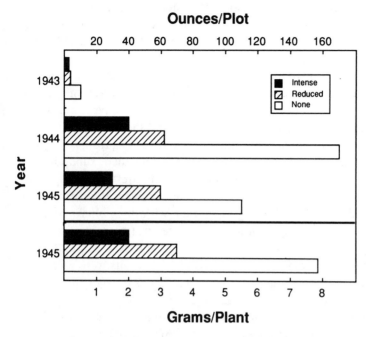

Figure 6.1. Effects of competition from sagebrush *(Artemisia tridentata)* on annual production of herbage by twenty species of perennial arid-land plants. (From Robertson 1947.)

A good example is provided by the experiments of Robertson (1947), who was interested in improving grazing range in northern Nevada by replacing sagebrush *(Artemisia tridentata)* with grasses or legumes. The competitive effect of sagebrush was tested against twelve native species of perennials, and eight Eurasian species. For "intense competition," natural sagebrush was cleared from two strips 2.74 by 64.04 m (3 × 70 yd). In each strip, one plot 3.05 m long was allotted at random to each species to be tested. Carefully selected seeds were sown in four uniform rows. For "reduced competition," the treatment was identical except that trenches 25.4 cm deep were dug between the plots and the surrounding sagebrush, thus reducing the effect of the roots of that species. For "no competition," a square covering 4,051 m² (one acre) was completely cleared, and two sets of plots of the same size as those for the other treatments were established within the central fifth of the clearing. All plots were harvested at the 5.08-cm (2-in.) level annually for three years. The overall results were impressive (Fig. 6.1), and all individual species gave similar results, although the rates at which they responded to the treatments differed. The negative effect of sagebrush was clearly established, and the experimental design was adequate for the purpose. No pseudoreplication can be detected in the reported statistical analyses.

Also with the apparent aim of improving grazing, this time in Arizona, Cable (1969) investigated the competitive interactions among perennial grasses (largely *Trichachne californica*), the perennial semi-shrub *Aplopappus tenuisectus* (burroweed), and the annual grass *Bouteloua aristidoides*, after killing the dominant shrub *Prosopis juliflora* (velvet mesquite). Thus, the experiment concerned subdominant plants. The paper refers to the spread of mesquite; although not explicit, the implication is that overgrazing brought about the situation. A randomized block design was used, with three blocks of plots, each plot being 0.915 by 4.88 m. Seven different treatments involved removing plants so as to leave each type alone and in all combinations. The plots were maintained for four years, and results were measured as annual herbage production (for grasses), crown area (for burroweed), basal area of perennial grasses, and stem growth for all groups. The three groups responded in markedly different ways (Fig. 6.2). Some of the annual differences reflected rainfall, which was 377.7 mm in 1961, 287.5 mm in 1962, 334.5 mm in 1963, and 389.1 mm in 1964. Burroweed increased every year under all treatments, suggesting strongly that release from competition by mesquite was most important, although there were no controls for that treatment. It also fared better in combination with annual grasses than by itself – a result not easily explained. Perennial grasses responded slowly, and only in the last year did one species reach a significantly greater production alone than in any combination. The immediate response of annual grasses was dramatic, but thereafter their performance was slow, and the different treatments had little effect. Overall, the results revealed less competition than might have been expected. It is possible that the less-than-dominant status of the species involved was responsible. The experiment was well designed and apparently carefully carried out. It is not possible to determine whether or not the statistical analyses were appropriate, although the reference to "significant at $p = .10$" (p. 32) is not reassuring.

The effects of adult desert shrubs on seedlings of a second species were investigated by Friedman (1971) in the Negev desert of Israel. Nine seedlings of *Artemisia herba-alba* were planted at each of three distances (50 cm, 100 cm, and 200 cm) from the stems of five individ-

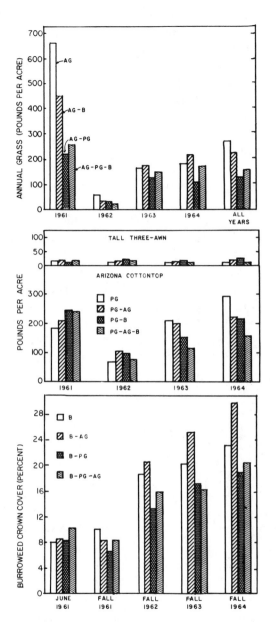

Figure 6.2. Effects of competition among annual grass, perennial grasses, and burroweed when all had been protected from competition from the dominant shrub *Prosopis juliflora* (velvet mesquite): top, annual grass; middle, perennial grasses; bottom, burroweed. (From Cable 1969.)

uals of *Zygophyllum dumosum*, which were selected to have a diameter of 100 cm. Control seedlings were planted at least 10 m from any living perennial. The seedlings received 500 ml of water at three and six days. Those not becoming established were replaced for a period of a month. In addition, twenty-nine naturally established seedlings were followed. They were located at distances of 40–176 cm from adult *Zygophyllum*. Growth of the seedlings was followed for fourteen months, and survival for nineteen months.

The results were clear. *Zygophyllum* inhibited the growth of all seedlings out to a distance of at least 200 cm, whether transplanted or growing naturally. Even at that distance, the growth rate of the experimentally planted seedlings was never more than 40 percent of that for the control seedlings, and for most of the duration of the experiment the growth rate was less than 10 percent of that for the controls. Seedlings at distances of 100 cm or less were much alike in performance, whether planted or growing naturally, growth being very slow. Mortality was related to proximity to *Zygophyllum* for transplanted seedlings, 47.6 percent at 50 cm and 33.0 percent at 200 cm for the first year. No mortality was observed among the naturally established seedlings. The experiment was well designed. Both naturally growing and experimental controls were used, and there were enough replicates, although no statistical analyses were reported, and variance among replicates cannot be discovered by the reader.

Friedman attributed the effect of the larger shrub to its exploitation of water reserves, but no measurements of soil moisture were taken, the conclusion being based on the density of roots at different distances from the stem.

Not all experiments in arid areas have been conducted with the attention to the requirements of experimental design that was given by Robertson (1947), Cable (1969), or Friedman (1971), as previously described. Whitford et al. (1978) sprayed a herbicide over a 9-ha area of Chihuahuan desert in New Mexico. Pretreatment measurements of vegetation were made in July 1971. After applications of herbicide in September 1971 and 1972, they followed the decrease in shrub cover and the increase in grass cover in 1973 and 1975. All measurements were made on nine belts 5 by 100 m, one in each hectare of the treated area. In 1975, belt transects on a control area were surveyed. The control area was 1 km distant from the sprayed area, and more belts were established at the borders of the sprayed area. Statistical analysis was performed, comparing percentage plant cover pretreatment, in the treated area (1975), in the border belts (1975), and in the control area (1975). For the most prominent shrub, creosote bush (*Larrea tridentata*), pretreatment and treatment borders were found to be alike statistically and with significantly greater cover than the treated and control areas, which were also different from each other. For a second shrub, *Flourensia cernua*, the pretreatment survey showed significantly greater cover than the treated area, and both had significantly less cover than the border and control areas, which were alike. For the most abundant grass species, *Muhlenbergia porteri*, the border and control areas were alike in having less cover than the treated area and more than the pretreatment survey. The second most abundant grass, *Sporobolus flexuosus*, had significantly less cover in the pretreatment survey than after treatment, on the border areas, or on the control area, all of which were alike.

Most of the mistakes in design are obvious. The failure to establish a control area at the time of the pretreatment survey meant that spontaneous changes could not be monitored. The control area was not like the treated area was during the pretreatment period, or else it diverged as much as the treated area did after spraying. Choosing plots within the treatment and control areas constituted pseudoreplication, because differences in place and treatment were confounded. This casts doubt on the validity of the statistical analysis. All of these problems appear to be reflected in the variety of statistically significant differences, and they lead one to question the conclusions.

Gurevitch (1986) was interested in the local distribution of the perennial C_3 grass *Stipa neomexicana* in a semiarid area in Arizona. She observed that it occurred only on dry ridge crests, where grass cover was low, and was not found lower down the slopes in moister areas, where the total grass cover was considerably greater. She hypothesized that it was excluded from the apparently more favorable area by competition from *Aristida glauca* and, perhaps, other perennial C_4 grasses. Her experiments were conducted at the top of the ridge, midway down, and in the wash (dry stream channel) at the bottom of the slope. At each location, an area was "chosen at random and divided into 10 blocks, each of which was subdivided into 16 approximately equal subunits. Treatments were randomly assigned to subunits" (pp. 47–8). A treatment consisted of selecting either a *Stipa* or an *Aristida* plant and removing all grass within 0.5 m. There were

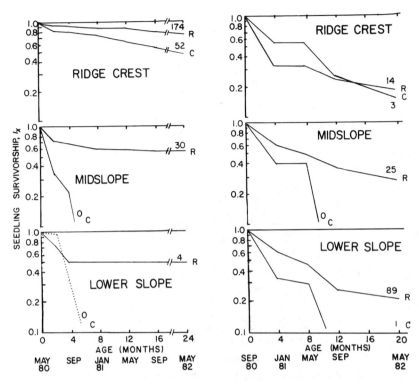

Figure 6.3. Survival of *Stipa* (left) and C$_4$ seedlings (right) in presence and absence of competing grasses, except for a single specimen. Three locations of differing exposures to drought were the sites of the experiments. Dotted line: results based on <4 seedlings. (From Gurevitch 1986.)

twenty replicates, either treated or control, for each species within the ten blocks at each location. Control plants, also selected at random, had no surrounding grasses removed.

Gurevitch followed responses to the treatment in several ways: establishment, growth, and survival of seedlings within the 0.5-m radius of each mature plant, and the growth and reproduction of the mature plants. *Stipa* seedlings could be identified, but all C$_4$ seedlings had to be considered as a group. Both showed significant increases in all three measures as the result of the treatment, and it should be noted that she did not treat the individual seedlings as replicates, thus avoiding pseudoreplication. The effect on survival is shown in Figure 6.3. Neighboring grasses clearly had a powerful effect, so much so that only

Table 6.1. *Estimated numbers of flowers per plant in control and removal treatments at the three topographic positions for* Stipa *and* Aristida (*n* = 20)

A. Number of flowers per plant

Position	Treatment	Stipa		Aristida	
		Mean	95% CI[a]	Mean	95% CI[a]
Ridge crest	Control	1.45	2.02	65.15	49.29
	Removal	13.30	4.44	72.90	98.35
Midslope	Control	4.05	2.63	263.15	156.76
	Removal	28.65	13.99	343.00	162.53
Lower slope	Control	35.45	13.96	149.85	85.94
	Removal	58.85	22.06	419.95	175.45

B. Univariate analyses

Factor	Stipa		Aristida	
	F	p	F	p
Treatment	19.611	<.005	5.506	<.05
Position × treatment	0.630	NS	3.266	NS
Position × treatment				
Linear effect	0.847	NS	6.120	.05
Quadratic effect	0.412	NS	0.412	NS

[a]95% confidence interval.
From Gurevitch (1986); includes correction of second number in last column.

on the dry ridge crest was there any appreciable survival among the control seedlings. At all locations, *Stipa* survived better than did the C_4 plants, but there were very few present initially on the lower slope. Mature plants of both species grew significantly more at all three locations when not surrounded by other grasses, and there was also a strong effect of the removal of competitors on reproduction, expressed as the number of flowers per plant (Table 6.1).

A revealing observation concerned the soil water potential on the ridge and in the wash over a wetting–drying–wetting cycle. During the dry period, the measurements showed that the soil in the wash had significantly less water potential than that on the ridge, despite receiving more during the wet period. Gurevitch attributed this to the water demands of the larger number of plants on the lower slope and argued that it was competition for the water that tended to confine *Stipa* to

Table 6.2. *Estimated finite rates of increase (λ) for populations of*
Stipa neomexicana, *and some components of* λ.

	Ridge crest		Midslope		Lower slope	
	Control	Removal	Control	Removal	Control	Removal
λ	0.928	1.035	0.827	0.923	0.591	0.875
χ_{max}	40	50	30	50	20	50
α (yr)	16	8	9	6	6	2
l_α	0.35	0.50	0.10	0.40	0.05	0.30
ΣB_x	0.031	0.102	0.017	0.018	0.001	0.005

Note: χ_{max} = maximum age; α = age at first reproduction; l_α = survivorship to reproductive age; ΣB_x = annual number of seedlings surviving to 1 yr per mature plant. From Gurevitch (1986).

the ridge crests. She backed up the assertion by calculating the finite rate of increase for *Stipa* at all three locations for both control and experimental conditions (Table 6.2). On the ridge crest, the value was close to the expected 1.0 for control plants as well as for plants protected from competition. Proceeding down slope, the experimental plants continued to come close to a theoretical population balance, whereas the control plants showed an important decrease, indicating that the population could not maintain itself there. The design, execution, and analysis of this experiment were very good, and the final means of confirming the original hypothesis through estimates of the population dynamics was ingenious.

A physiological approach to competition in desert shrubs was taken by Fonteyn and Mahall (1981). To test the prevalent hypothesis that desert plants compete for water, they conducted removal experiments on the two dominant shrubs in the Mojave desert of California: *Larrea tridentata* and *Ambrosia dumosa*. A 2.5-ha site was chosen, and within it, forty nonoverlapping 100-m² circular plots were located, so that each contained at least three *Larrea* and eleven *Ambrosia* plants. In addition to control plots with no plants removed, they established plots containing a single individual of the test species, plots with all naturally occurring individuals of the test species, and plots containing a single individual of the test species surrounded by all naturally occurring individuals of the other species. Thus, there were four treatments of each species, making five replicates of each. The design allowed Fonteyn and Mahall to separate the effects of interspecific competition from the effects of intraspecific competition. The responses of the plants to the treatments were assessed by making predawn measurements of plant xylem pressure potentials of the monitored plants, which were those on which the plots were centered. The xylem pressure potential just before dawn is thought to reflect soil moisture availability and thus to reflect the competitive effect of neighboring plants. Thus, if competing plants are making water less available, the pressure, measured in bars, will be lower (more negative) than if the monitored plant is alone. The results during a drying period after a rain show that for both species the control plants had significantly lower xylem pressure potentials than did the experimental plants in any treatment, and those with no competing plants nearby had the highest potentials (Fig. 6.4). Fonteyn and Mahall pointed out that for most of their measurements, the effect of interspecific competition for water was greater than the effect of intraspecific competition. Because the experiment was well designed to test that specific point, it is necessary to consider the implications, especially because the effect was in both directions. Fonteyn and Mahall mentioned the possibility that there were allelopathic root interactions. Direct evidence for the existence of allelopathic chemicals in *Larrea* is equivocal (Knipe & Herbel 1966), but the alternative is for each of the two species to be more efficient in taking up water than the other – an obvious impossibility. The question of allelopathy has been difficult to settle directly and has been controversial; see discussions by Harper (1977), Heisey and Delwiche (1985), and Fowler (1986). From the standpoint of this book, the experimenters, although ingenious, have sometimes failed to consider a sufficient array of alternative hypotheses.

The studies described in this section leave no doubt that desert perennial species compete with each other and that water is the most important resource for which they compete.

Experiments on annuals

Some interactions between desert perennials and annuals are apparently beneficial to the latter, but there does not appear to have been an experimental test; see the review by Fowler (1986). A negative effect of a perennial shrub, *Artemisia herba-alba*, on associated species of annuals was demonstrated experimentally by Friedman, Orshan, and Ziger-Cfir (1977) in the Negev desert of Israel. Twenty-five plots, each 2.5 by 2.5 m, were chosen at random on a north-facing slope where *Artemisia* was dominant. Five plots were allocated to each of five treatments. As shown in Table 6.3, three treatments involved

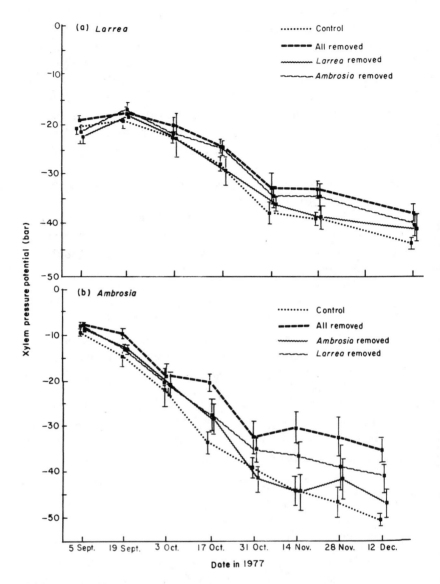

Figure 6.4. Differential effects of removal treatments on stem xylem pressure potentials of (a) *Larrea tridentata* and (b) *Ambrosia dumosa* during autumn 1977. Bars are ±s.e.; *n* = 15. (From Fonteyn & Mahall 1981.)

Table 6.3. *Numbers and dry-matter yields of annual plants per 0.25 m²*
in variously treated plots, March 1975[a]

	Treatment	North-facing slope		South-facing slope	
		No. of annual plants	Total dry matter (g)	No. of annual plants	Total dry matter (g)
(i)	All perennials removed	7.5 ± 3.0**	6.5 ± 2.2**	19.1 ± 5.6*	12.2 ± 2.4
(ii)	All perennials pruned	3.2 ± 1.0*	1.1 ± 3.2	17.7 ± 6.0*	9.3 ± 2.4
(iii)	Soil between perennials hoed	2.7 ± 0.8	1.8 ± 0.5*	11.0 ± 3.6	5.9 ± 2.6
(iv)	All perennials removed, and soil between them hoed	8.7 ± 3.2**	5.9 ± 2.8**	12.5 ± 5.8	8.3 ± 2.6
(v)	Control	1.2 ± 0.4	0.6 ± 0.2	11.9 ± 2.6	10.8 ± 4.4

[a]Mean of five plots ± standard error. Significance level of difference from control: *$p <$ .05; **$p < .01$.
From Friedman et al. (1977).

removing or pruning the perennials; in a fourth, the soil between the shrubs was hoed; the fifth treatment was an undisturbed control. Measurements were made in an area 0.25 m² in the center of each plot. All experimental manipulations caused a statistically significant increase in the number of annual plants or in the total dry matter of annuals, or both. A matching experiment on a south-facing slope, where *Zygophyllum dumosum* was the shrub involved, produced a very slight effect, as the table shows. The experiment was properly designed, with adequate preliminary data, good controls, and care taken to avoid edge effects.

The difference between the results suggested that simple competition for water or some other resource was an insufficient explanation. Friedman and associates then conducted experiments testing the hypothesis of allelopathy. Seeds of four common annuals were allowed to germinate in moist chambers, where they were behind filter paper that touched water in which there were shoots of *Artemisia* or *Zygophyllum*, or under conditions where they were exposed to the same air as the shoots. Ten seeds were placed in each chamber, but replicate chambers were not mentioned. The data show no effect of *Zygophyllum*, but a reduction of 94–95 percent in the germination of *Stipa capensis* and a reduction of 96–98 percent in the germination of *Helianthemum ledifolium* when *Artemisia* was present, either by immersion or as a volatile. There was a 50 percent effect of *Artemisia* on *Zygophyllum* germination, but there was none on the germination of either of two varieties of *Medicago lacinata*. The artificiality of the conditions leaves uncertain whether or not there is a significant allelopathic effect in nature.

Competition among desert annuals was found by Inouye (1980). His experiment in the Sonoran desert of Arizona consisted of establishing five quadrats 1.0 by 0.5 m, and removing all seedling annuals from half of each plot weekly for six weeks during a period when 6.1 cm of rain fell and germination was maximal. The plots were placed to avoid the influence of perennials, which covered only 30 percent of the area. Censuses of seedlings were made on the undisturbed half of each plot when removals were being made on the experimental half. In every case, the cumulative number of germinating seedlings was greater where removals were being carried out. The absolute differences ranged from 67 to 505, and the ratio "Thinned/Control" ranged from 1.85 to 9.15. Despite the variation, the difference was significant. The experimental design was adequate to establish the conclusion that existing seedlings inhibit further germination. The mechanism is unknown.

In the Chihuahuan desert, the commonest annual, *Eriogonum abertianum*, has the unusual phenology of germinating during the winter rains, but maturing and setting seeds during the summer rains. Its effect on the normal summer annuals was tested by Davidson, Samson, and Inouye (1985). Four plots 10 by 10 m in size were established before the summer rains, and all annual plants were censused. Two of the plots were selected as experimental, and all *E. abertianum* were removed. Two months later, the plots were censused. There were dramatic and highly significant increases in the numbers of all of the five most abundant summer annuals, again demonstrating strong competition among desert annuals.

Experiments on the effects of primary consumers on plants of arid areas

Folivores

The effects of the grasshopper *Hesperotettix viridis* on two species of Compositae were investigated by Parker (1985) and Parker and

Table 6.4. *Vulnerability to herbivory in* G. microcephala
*plants of different sizes: data on mortality and flowering
during the summer of 1980 for yearling and mature* G.
microcephala *plants protected or unprotected from
grasshopper feeding damage*

	Protected plants		Unprotected plants	
Plants dying by September 1980[a]				
	(%)	(No./group)	(%)	(No./group)
Mature plants	0	20	4.9	81
Yearlings	6.9	29	33.3	210
Flower heads in September 1980[b]				
		(No./plant)		(No./plant)
Mature plants				
Mean ± 1 s.e.		1,310 ± 159		3 ± 1
Range		352–2,713		0–80

[a]The mortality among unprotected yearlings was significantly higher than that for all other groups (log likelihood ratio test, $p < .005$).
[b]No yearlings flowered in 1980.
From Parker (1985).

Root (1981). The location was a long-undisturbed grassland in New Mexico. *Gutierrezia microcephala* is a successional shrub that is able to resist replacement by perennial grasses for long periods. Parker (1985) protected twenty-nine yearling plants and twenty mature plants under cages of window screening. Five plants were covered with screening above and on the south side to control for shading and other cage effects, and large numbers of plants served as untreated controls. The cages were placed in mid-June, earlier in the summer than grasshopper damage occurred. By early September, virtually every unprotected plant had suffered severe defoliation, including the five with dummy cages. Survival among yearlings was significantly better among protected plants than among controls, as was flowering among the mature plants (Table 6.4). A smaller companion experiment on the locally uncommon biennial *Machaeranthera canescens* showed that all twelve plants provided with dummy cages died of defoliation by the grasshoppers, whereas only three of thirteen caged plants failed to survive the summer, and the survivors all produced flowers (Parker & Root 1981). Parker (1985) suggested that attack by *Hesperotettix viri-*

dis and a root-boring beetle, *Crossidus pulchellus*, hastened the replacement of *Gutierrezia* by perennial grasses. The experiments were well designed and controlled, but the long-term effect remains unknown, because of highly variable populations of the herbivore.

Seed eaters

Two floristically different deserts in Arizona have been the sites of experiments on the effects of granivores on the densities of annual plants. The first experiment was conducted in the Sonoran desert and was incidental to a test of the hypothesis of competition between granivorous rodents and ants, to be described later (Brown, Davidson, & Reichman 1979a; Brown, Reichman, & Davidson 1979b). The four treatments, each replicated twice on circular arenas 36 m in diameter, were as follows: without rodents, without ants, without either, and control. The manipulations themselves were successful. Three years after the start of the experiment, three replicate 1-m² quadrats for each of four subtreatments were established within each arena (Inouye et al. 1980). The subtreatments were as follows: addition of 29 mm of water over two weeks, thinning to reduce plant density to one-third, watering and thinning, and control. In locating the quadrats, perennial shrubs were avoided. No effect of the rodent and ant exclusions were apparent one year after the start of the basic experiments. Two years later, with subtreatments incorporated in the analysis, there were statistically significant differences between the effects of rodents and ants (Table 6.5). In all cases except one, the removal of either granivorous rodents or ants, or both, resulted in increases in the abundance of the different annual species. The example of *Euphorbia polycarpa*, which was reduced in abundance by the removal of rodents, was explained as being due to competition from large-seeded species on which the rodents feed by preference. A detailed follow-up of this experiment (Davidson, Inouye, & Brown 1984) is presented in Table 6.6. Where present, rodents reduced the populations of annuals with large seeds (1.1 mg or more), whether ants were present or not. Where rodents were excluded, ants significantly reduced the populations of annuals with small seeds (0.7 mg or less).

These are most interesting results, though marred by the obvious pseudoreplication of having three quadrats of each kind within each main arena, and by the absence of data on initial densities. The probability levels should therefore be treated skeptically.

Table 6.5. *Effects of removal of ants or rodents or both on densities of certain annual plant species, all plants, plant biomass, and two measures of species diversity*

	+Rodents + ants	+Rodents − ants	−Rodents + ants	−Rodents − ants	Effect of removal of: Rodents	Ants
Initial census (29 Jan. 1977)						
1. Large plants	1.00 (35.8)	0.98	2.08	2.35	Increase ($p < .01$)	NS
2. Small plants	1.00 (292.5)	3.30	3.32	3.17	NS	Increase ($p < .01$)
Final census (2 Apr. 1977)						
3. *Erodium cicutarium* (seed mass = 1.6 mg)	1.00 (1.8)	1.83	7.03	16.11	Increase ($p < .01$)	NS
4. *E. texanum* (seed mass = 1.6 mg)	1.00 (0.6)	0.88	2.07	0.78	Increase ($p < .05$)	NS
5. *Euphorbia polycarpa* (seed mass = 0.2 mg)	1.00 (0.6)	2.00	0.14	0.29	Decrease ($p < .02$)	NS
6. *Filago californica* (seed mass = 0.04 mg)	1.00 (142.1)	1.90	1.43	2.59	NS	Increase ($p < .05$)
7. *Lotus humistratus* (seed mass = 1.5 mg)	1.00 (11.4)	1.14	2.43	5.22	Increase ($p < .01$)	NS
8. All plants	1.00 (209.6)	1.35	1.34	1.94	Increase ($p < .05$)	Increase ($p < .01$)
9. Dry mass *(all species)*	1.00 (5.8)	1.07	2.09	2.17	Increase ($p < .01$)	NS
10. Species diversity (*H*)	1.00 (2.78)	0.73	0.99	0.89	NS	Decrease ($p < .05$)
11. Species (*E*) evenness	1.00 (0.53)	0.77	1.99	1.04	NS	Decrease ($p < .05$)

Note: Values given are ratios of treatment to control (+Rodents + Ants) means. Numbers in parentheses are mean values for unthinned plots, except for plant biomass and the two measures of diversity, which are for control plots. Statistical analysis was by ANOVA; NS = not significant.
From Inouye et al. (1980).

Table 6.6. *Mean population densities of large-seeded and small-seeded plants under different regimes of seed predation by ants and rodents*

Rodents	Seed size[a]	Plant density (No./400 cm²)[b]		Effect of ant removal (p)[c]
		Ants present	Ants absent	
Present	L	94.4	72.5	<.414
		38.5	39.8	
	S	148.6	173.3	<.089
		347.6	90.0	
Absent	L	176.5	178.0	<.352
		97.4	157.0	
	S	32.6	114.6	<.002
		22.1	233.8	
Effect of rodent removal (p)	L	<.001	<.000	
	S	<.001	<.454	

[a]L, large-seeded annuals; S, small-seeded annuals.
[b]Two replicates for each experimental treatment.
[c]ANOVA, with replicate plots treated as separate grouping variables.
From Davidson et al. (1984).

The second experiment was conducted in the Chihuahuan desert (Davidson et al. 1985). Again, the primary design concerned competition among the granivores, two replicate plots 50 by 50 m being established for each treatment, which were the same as in the previous experiment, except that all plots were fenced, and those not intended to exclude rodents were provided with sixteen holes each. Pseudoreplication was again involved in the design, there being eight permanent census quadrats in each plot. These quadrats were originally 0.5 m² in area, but the area was halved for the last two years of the five-year experiment. In order to make the data comparable, counts from these two years were doubled, although that increased the variance. A more acceptable practice would have been to divide the counts from the first three years by two, and randomly assign zeros to half of the fractional counts. A third problem was the failure to establish initial conditions. The graphs showing the abundances of different annuals or groups of them over time do not show indications of variance, and the first data points are different enough in some graphs to cause concern. These problems are sufficiently troublesome to cause us to accept only the most conservative of the conclusions based on the elaborate statistical analysis. Removal of both ants and rodents clearly brought about increases in some of the annual plants. The ratio of the number of large-seeded plants on rodent-removal plots to the initial density was at least as great as 1,000-fold in these experiments, and up to 157-fold in similar experiments (Brown et al. 1986). These are results that are of great interest in understanding the desert ecosystem, as discussed in Chapter 9.

Experiments on competition among desert granivores

Rodents

In what is one of the most interestingly titled papers on eco-logical experiments, Munger and Brown (1981) described the exclu-sion of kangaroo rats (*Dipodomys* species) from plots by means of "semipermeable fences": those provided with holes of a size large enough to admit small rodents (1.9 × 1.9 cm), but too small to admit any species of *Dipodomys*. In the Chihuahuan desert, four such plots were established, 50 by 50 m, as were four control plots with holes large enough to admit all granivorous rodents (6.5 × 6.5 cm). The experiment was preceded by a three-month period of trapping with all holes large enough to admit all species, thus establishing the proper baseline data. Then, repeated trapping eliminated all three species of *Dipodomys*: the largest, *D. spectabilis* (125 g), plus *D. ordii* (47 g) and *D. merriami* (40 g). The results were significant, though fluctuating, increases in the abundances of the small granivores above control den-sities, in contrast to unchanged numbers of *Onychomys*, an insectivo-rous genus (Brown & Munger 1985). This is impressive evidence of a competitive effect, and the statistical analysis avoided temporal pseu-doreplication. A further experiment excluding only *D. spectabilis* has yielded promising but statistically nonsignificant increases in the abundances of the other species of *Dipodomys* after two years.

The importance of the food resource was investigated by the addi-tion of 96 kg of seeds per year to each of eight of the quarter-hectare plots in a complex design involving two sizes of seeds, 6 mg and about 1 mg, and two schedules of addition of the mixture. There were two replicate plots of each treatment. For all treatments the results were the same: a significant increase in the abundance of *D. spectabilis*, and significant decreases in the abundances of *D. ordii* and *D. merriami*. The remaining granivorous rodents decreased in abundance by non-

Table 6.7. *Energetic compensation by desert rodents to supplemental seeds and to removal of selected rodent species*

		Experimental treatment	
	Seed addition	Removal of *D. spectabilis*	Removal of all 3 *Dipodomys* species
Energy made available (kJ/d)[a]	3,060	201.4	439.7
Energetic response (kJ/d)[b]	91	49.4	33.2
% compensation[c]	2.9 (by all 8 sp. of granivorous rodents)	33.8 (by 7 sp. of smaller granivorous rodents)	9.5 (by 5 sp. of small granivorous rodents)

[a]For seed-addition treatments, calculated as the metabolizable energy in the added millet. For other treatments, determined by calculating how much the removed individuals would have consumed, based on their total biomass.
[b]Determined by calculating the consumption of the indicated groups, based on their measured increase in total biomass.
[c]For the rodent-removal experiments, percentage compensation was calculated as follows: [(1977–8 energy consumption minus 1978–82 energy consumption for the average of the removal plots) minus (1977–8 energy consumption minus 1978–82 energy consumption for the average of the control plots)] divided by (metabolizable energy of added seeds or energy consumption of the rodents removed).
Note: Rodent compensation for the additional food energy made available never exceeded 34%.
From Brown and Munger (1985).

significant amounts. As Brown and Munger pointed out, the result strongly suggests some form of behavioral interference by *D. spectabilis*. For whatever reason, the species favored by the removal of competitors or the addition of food did not increase their consumption of the presumed limiting resource in proportion to the calculated benefit (Table 6.7).

Rodents and ants

Logically, if any granivorous species compete, all of them should, provided that exploitation is the basis of the competition. Thus, it was anticipated that some of the combinations of rodents and ants would be found to compete, as both are conspicuous granivores

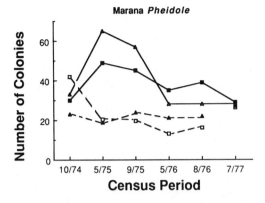

Figure 6.5. Changes in density of *Pheidole* spp. (including *P. xero-phila tucsonica, P. sitarches,* and *P. gilvescens*) on two rodent-removal plots (solid lines) and two control plots (dashed lines) at Marana, Arizona, over a 2.75-year period. (From Davidson et al. 1984.)

in the desert. Two experiments have been reported. The first, in the Sonoran desert, has been described in the section on the effects of granivores on annual plants. The results showed 70.8 percent more ant colonies on rodent exclosures than on controls, a statistically significant result (Brown et al. 1979a). The authors claimed 19.8 percent more rodents on the ant-removal plots than on the controls, but the significance of that result has been challenged on methodological grounds by Galindo (1986), and the correction has been accepted by Brown and Davidson (1986). The problem was an inappropriate statistical test, as well as large variations among replicate plots.

The effects of granivorous rodents on ant populations were eventually found to be much more complex than was originally thought (Davidson et al. 1984). After the removal of rodents had caused an initial increase in the density of ants, the effect of competition by large-seeded annuals on the small-seeded ones began to reduce the number of the small seeds favored by ants. As a consequence, ants of the genus *Pheidole* eventually declined in abundance to control levels after three years (Fig. 6.5).

In the Chihuahuan desert, a similar experiment yielded inconclusive results. One species of ant, *Pheidole xerophila*, increased significantly in the absence of rodents, but other species of ants decreased, and the removal of ants had no effect on rodent populations (Davidson et al. 1985).

Experiments on desert insectivores

Spiders

In a study significant for both ecology and the theory of territoriality, Riechert (1981) used the spider *Agelenopsis apertia*, a sheet-web builder of western North America. Each web has an attached funnel, which runs into a protected feature of the immediate environment. The funnel is used to escape from unfavorable thermal conditions. She worked in two areas, a desert grassland in New Mexico, and a riparian habitat in Arizona. She measured the availability and consumption of prey, and the time available for foraging. In the desert grassland, an average of 27.2 mg of prey were available per day to these annual spiders during maturation and egg production. Densities averaged 42 adults per 1,000 m². A number of species of insects were captured, mostly folivores (Locustidae, Noctuidae, and Chrysomelidae) and sapsuckers (Cicadellidae). The other major component was the Sarcophagidae (Riechert & Tracy 1975). In the riparian habitat, food was more abundant, an average of 79.6 mg being available per day, with spider densities being about 110 adults per 1,000 m².

Riechert had observed that these spiders were intolerant of near neighbors and that they maintained territories with a median size of 3.8 m² in the desert grassland and 0.6 m² in the more favorable riparian habitat. She was interested in three questions about the territories: Is territory size fixed? Are there "floaters" in the population and where? Is reproduction confined to the holders of territories? The first question involves the compressibility of territories – a characteristic that has been observed in a variety of other kinds of animals (Wilson 1975) in response to resource availability. In one set of experiments, Riechert captured thirty-two adult female specimens in the desert grassland for each experiment and divided them into two groups, each with sixteen isolated individuals. One group ("satiated") was fed 250 mg per day for each spider; the other ("deprived") was fed 20 mg per day each. In different experiments, this schedule was maintained for one, two, or four weeks. For each experiment, three square enclosures 2 by 2 m were set up. The third enclosure was used for freshly caught adult females, which presumably had received the current natural food of 40 mg each per day. Each enclosure had sixteen equally spaced screen cones sunk flush with the ground, and one previously marked spider was confined to each until construction of webs had started, after which they were no longer confined to the cones. The whole enclosure

Table 6.8. *Trial-end spider density and spacing in field versus experimental contexts for two populations of* Agelenopsis aperta

	No. of web owners		Mean distance between webs (cm)	
	Grassland	Riparian	Grassland	Riparian
Field estimates	2	8	109 ± 11	42 ± 3[a]
Experimental results				
1. Control	2	7	112	55
2. Food deprivation				
1 wk	2, 1		100, —	
2 wk	3, 2		141, 104	
4 wk	2	8, 8, 8	162	54, 52, 57
3. Satiation				
1 wk	1			
2 wk	2, 1		120, —	
4 wk	2	9, 8, 8	162	51, 52, 57
Lifetime	2, 1			

Note: Desert grassland in south central New Mexico, and desert riparian in southeastern Arizona. Feeding-level durations represent pretrial feeding period. Similar feeding levels were maintained during trials completed within the experimental enclosures. Spider density at the start of a trial equaled 16 individuals per enclosure, and each trial lasted 2 wk. Replicate runs separated by commas.
[a] Means and standard errors for field populations.
From Riechert (1981), in *The American Naturalist.* Copyright © 1981 The University of Chicago Press.

was covered with a cheesecloth canopy to restrict immigration and emigration and to provide a suitable thermal environment. During the whole experiment, the spiders were provided with the three different amounts of food daily. The enclosures were opened daily, the location of each spider was checked, and any resting on the canopy were removed. Some twenty-six agonistic interactions between individuals were observed during the daily observations. Spiders collected in the riparian habitat were treated in the same way, except that only the four-week preexperimental feeding was used. The results (Table 6.8) are clear. The number of web owners and the distances between webs after two weeks are completely consistent with territories of sizes that are fixed and unresponsive to the different rates of supply of food. The only differences were in the sizes of webs, with satiated individuals constructing significantly smaller webs than deprived individuals.

To answer her second question, Riechert conducted a removal of all residents that she could capture (36 of 44) on a grid of 900 m² in the desert grassland. The territory holders in the surrounding area had been marked, so that newcomers could be identified as unmarked floaters or moving residents. Within fourteen days, nineteen newcomers were located, of which only one had been marked. Floaters were shown in another test to be largely located within existing territories, remaining in cracks or other refuges.

The final question, of the relative reproductive success of territory holders and floaters, was answered by marking the former in an area and constructing drift fences with can traps to catch floaters. Each spider was marked and weighed, and placed on the other side of the fence. Recaptures allowed Riechert to calculate weight gain or loss per day for both territory holders and wanderers. All of the territory holders gained weight during the test, but a minority of the floaters did so, the median change in weight being negative for them. Riechert concluded that few floaters would survive long in that state and that only the territory holders contributed to the future population.

Lizards

In contrast to a considerable literature suggesting, on the basis of indirect evidence such as niche partitioning, that interspecific competition has structured communities of desert lizards (Pianka 1967, 1975; Pianka, Huey, & Lawlor 1978), three experiments testing that hypothesis have given less than convincing results in confirmation (Dunham 1980; Smith 1981; Tinkle 1982). Dunham's experiment in the Chihuahuan desert of the Big Bend National Park in Texas involved mutual removals of *Sceloporus merriami* and *Urosaurus ornatus*. They were selected for experimentation because they were abundant and were the only species of the twelve present in the area that were small, saxicolous, diurnal insectivores, and therefore were potential competitors. Dunham chose six rocky habitats that were isolated by unsuitable terrain and randomly assigned two of them to each of three treatments: control, *Sceloporus* removal, and *Urosaurus* removal. The smallest habitat covered 0.53 hectare; the largest covered 1.02 ha. Starting in May 1974, the plots were censused at least monthly during the summer months through 1977. All lizards captured were weighed, toe-clipped, and sexed. Except for those to be removed, they were released near the point of capture. Response to the experimental manipulation was assessed through population density, survival, individual growth, foraging success, and prehibernation lipid storage.

The four years of the study differed greatly in rainfall, 1974 and 1976 being above the long-term average, 1975 and 1977 being below. This observation is most important in Dunham's interpretation of his results.

Dunham reported that the density of *U. ornatus* did not differ significantly on control and experimental plots at the beginning of the experiment in 1974 and that there were significantly larger populations on the *S. merriami*-removal plots in 1975 and 1976, but not in 1977. Removing *U. ornatus* had no effect on the density of *S. merriami*. He was cautious in claiming an effect of competition, because of the method of estimating density (capture–recapture), as well as the high variance between replicates and the lack of statistical tests for analyzing all of the data.

The data on survival are difficult to interpret, and that may well be because the individual lizards were treated statistically as the experimental units, rather than the plots. Thus, both simple and sacrificial pseudoreplications were involved. For *U. ornatus*, significantly better survival through the first year of life was reported on the experimental plots from 1974 to 1975, but on the control plots from 1976 to 1977. For first-year *S. merriami*, survival was significantly better on the experimental plots from 1975 to 1976, but the treatments were not different in the other two periods. Adult *U. ornatus* survived significantly better on the control plots from 1974 to 1975 and from 1976 to 1977, whereas the reciprocal result was found for *S. merriami:* survival was significantly better on the experimental plots from 1975 to 1976. If the two species really responded to the treatments, they clearly responded differently both to treatment and to years.

Growth was assessed by using repeated snout–vent length measurements on individuals and assuming that growth followed the logistic equation. The calculated asymptotic sizes did not differ between treatments or between wet and dry years for either species. For *U. ornatus*, a significantly higher mean specific growth rate on experimental plots was claimed for the two dry years pooled, but not for the wet years. The experiment had no effect on the specific growth rate of *S. merriami*. In this analysis, individuals were again assumed to be the experimental units, instead of the plots, and the analysis was further complicated by pooling data from alternate years, thus ignoring both differences between replicate plots and differences between years. Inas-

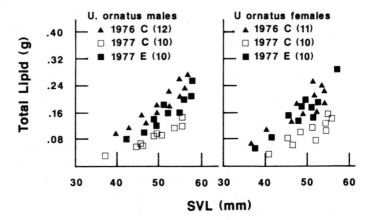

Figure 6.6. Data showing a significant (ANCOVA) treatment effect on total prehibernation body lipid in male and female *U. ornatus* in 1977. (From Dunham 1980.)

much as the claimed effect on *U. ornatus* was essential to Dunham's interpretation of his study, these criticisms are serious.

Direct observations of feeding strikes were used to assess foraging success. The relevant test showed that in 1976, *U. ornatus* foraged at a significantly higher rate on the plots from which *S. merriami* had been removed than on the control plots. This was true in June, when insects were scarce, but not in August, when they were five times as abundant. There was no treatment effect on the success of *S. merriami*. As with survival and growth, the analysis was flawed because individual lizards were used in establishing degrees of freedom.

To obtain data on food consumption and fat storage, Dunham collected specimens in similar habitat no more than 2 km from the experimental plots. These were assumed to be comparable to animals on the controls. At the end of the experiment in October 1977, some specimens were collected on the experimental plots for comparison with those collected elsewhere. Stomach contents were weighed, and stored fat was measured.

Stomach contents correlated significantly with the number of arthropod prey determined by an objective sampling method. Because the sampling was performed only on control plots, the result is not directly applicable to the experiment.

Dunham regarded his results on prehibernation fat storage by *U. ornatus* as his most convincing evidence for an effect of removing *S. merriami*. Analyses of covariance were performed on both sexes of

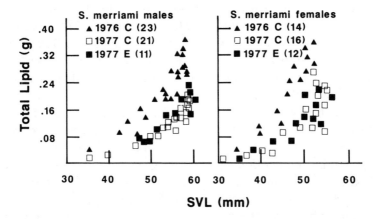

Figure 6.7. Data showing the absence of a significant (ANCOVA) treatment effect on total prehibernation body lipid in male and female *S. merriami* in 1977. (From Dunham 1980.)

both species relating lipid content and body mass as a function of snout–vent length and the following conditions: controls in a wet year (1976), controls in a dry year (1977), and experimentals in the dry year. The results are shown graphically in Figures 6.6 and 6.7. Statistical analysis confirmed the visual impression. For both sexes of *U. ornatus*, the group of points that is distinctly below the others are the controls for the dry year. The experimentals for the dry year were not significantly different from the controls in the wet year. In contrast, the set of points that is distinct in the case of *S. merriami* is the controls in the wet year. They are distinctly above both controls and experimentals for the dry year, and the latter are not significantly different. Both treatment and years were important for *U. ornatus*, but only years for *S. merriami*. Dunham concluded that he had demonstrated exploitative competition for resources and that this was likely to be important only in dry years. If correct, the conclusion supports the contention of Wiens (1977) that competition is irregular in occurrence, especially in highly variable environments.

The basic design of this experiment was very good. The first census seems to have been adequate for baseline data; controls were provided, and there were replicates of each experimental treatment. The handling of the data was flawed throughout, specifically in treating individuals as the units of experimentation, thereby confounding treatment with location. The differences between replicates were important in the only data provided: those on estimates of population density, a most important measure of suitability of the local environment. This aspect of the study should have alerted the experimenter to the necessity to use the plots as the units of experimentation. Because of this error, it is uncertain whether or not there was an experimental effect, an uncertainty that is emphasized by the failure to obtain a significant result on *S. merriami*.

Smith (1981) investigated competition between two lizard species in an Arizona woodland. Although not in a desert location, one of the species was *Urosaurus ornatus*, the one found by Dunham to be affected by competition. The second species was *Sceloporus virgatus*. Like Dunham, Smith had six plots, two for each of three treatments: controls, *Urosaurus* removals, and *Sceloporus* removals. They were separated by fences 38 cm high, across which movement was minimal.

The responses to the manipulations were assessed by population size, survivorship, and growth. No significant changes in numbers were found on plots from which the other species had been removed, in comparison with the numbers on control plots. Survivorship was compared for two age classes of both sexes of both species over three years. There were thus twenty-four statistical tests. In two cases, survival was found to be significantly higher at the .05 level on experimental plots – a proportion suspiciously close to the single one expected by random chance. Moreover, in eleven cases, survival was higher on controls, and there was one tie. The most convincing feature was that both of the tests were for the young females of both species in the same year. However, inasmuch as the tests were by chi-square, rather than by a parametric test on the proportions, individuals, rather than plots, were used as the units of experimentation – a mistake not made in analyzing growth.

Urosaurus ornatus showed no significant differences in growth, either between treatments or between years. Young *Sceloporus virgatus* (both sexes) grew significantly more in the two wet years than in the dry year, and young females grew more rapidly during the dry year on experimental plots than on controls. There was a significant treatment–years interaction. Although pseudoreplication was avoided, there were at least twenty-two statistical tests of growth, raising the suspicion of nonvalidity of the positive results.

A third experiment on competition among lizards of the American Southwest was conducted by Tinkle (1982) in a riparian habitat near the Sonoran desert in Arizona. He observed that *Sceloporus undulatus* was decidedly less arboreal there, in the presence of the highly arboreal

S. clarki and *Urosaurus ornatus*, than it was on another study area in Utah, where those two species were absent. After four summers of study, he divided the Arizona habitat into a control area and an experimental area and removed *S. clarki* and *U. ornatus* from the experimental area for three years. Briefly, there was no effect of the removals on the ecological distribution, abundance, survival, or size of *S. undulatus*, and neither the absence of replicates nor the confounding of treatment with place need obstruct the interpretation.

All three authors expected to find interspecific competition when they began their experiments, but the expectation was met only marginally in two of the three studies, and a case can be made that competition was not convincingly demonstrated, even to the limited extent claimed. There are numerous lizard predators in the areas, some highly specific, as was recognized, and the existence of this well-defined group of secondary predators is a factor that must be taken into account in understanding the ecosystem of the arid environments of the American Southwest.

Scorpions

A comparison of the population estimates and individual sizes of animals reported by Dunham (1980), Tinkle (1982), and Polis and McCormick (1987) reveals the interesting information that the biomasses of lizards and of scorpions in desert environments are comparable – around 1 kg or more per hectare each. The interactions involving scorpions are thus significant, and the experiments of Polis and McCormick to uncover interspecific interactions gave surprising results. The experiments were performed in the Mojave desert of California.

Paruroctonus mesaensis, by far the most abundant species, was tested for food limitation. Twenty-one field-caught gravid females were isolated in large plastic containers with enough sand for them to construct burrows, and the containers were placed in the field. They were fed crickets ad libitum. Three months later, they were compared with eighteen gravid females that had been living under field conditions. They were 28 percent heavier than the field individuals, and their embryos, though no more numerous, were 83 percent larger. Both differences were highly significant.

They removed *P. mesaensis* from 300 quadrats 10 by 10 m over a period of twenty-nine months and followed sixty randomly chosen quadrats of the same size as unmanipulated controls. The effort was successful. The mean density on the removal plots at the end of the experiment was 0.21 per plot; on the controls, it was 3.95 per plot. There were three other species of scorpions on the plots, one of which (*Hadrurus arizonensis*) was not abundant enough for the effect to be tested statistically. Both of the other two species increased dramatically: *Paruroctonus luteolus* to six times the density on control plots, and *Vaejovis confusus* to a 30 percent greater mean density. Both differences were significant statistically. Polis and McCormick presented good evidence that the response was due to release from predation, rather than from competition. On five dates over the duration of the experiment, they placed pitfall traps in experimental and control plots. Inasmuch as scorpions detect prey by the vibrations of their movements, this was a better technique than the use of sticky traps, which would have caught flying prey as well as terrestrial ones. On no occasion were the mean catches significantly different in the two areas. Moreover, observations of foraging success detected no differences among any of the species on control versus experimental plots. This, and ample other evidence, means that scorpions are food-limited, but not in a density-dependent manner. This group of predators is limited in abundance by intragroup predation, including cannibalism by the most abundant species. There is no evidence of an important impact on the rest of the ecosystem. It is possible to criticize the unbalanced designs of these experiments (21 fed females compared with 18 wild controls; 300 experimental removal plots versus 60 controls). Had the statistical analysis been of a highly sophisticated kind, the design might have caused problems. However, there appears to have been no such problem. The replication was ample, and adequate controls were provided. The amount of effort required to carry out the experiments must have been great.

Summary

In deserts, there appear to be three sets of species that are almost completely independent of each other from the standpoint of ecological interactions: first, the perennial plants, the herbivores that depend on them, and their predators; second, the annual plants and the granivores that depend on their seeds; third, the insectivores and their prey and predators. Further experimentation may continue to support the hypothesis of the independence of the three groups, but the hypothesis should certainly be tested. Within each group, the ecological relationships are well documented. The perennials compete with each other; the only folivore demonstrated to reduce the population of a perennial feeds on a successional species; and experiments are needed testing for the effect of predation on the folivores of the dominant perennials. The annuals are adversely affected by each other and by the perennials, but there are also effects of the granivores on the annuals and competitive effects of the granivores on each other. Possible effects of predators on the granivores have not been explored experimentally. The last is true of the effect of predation on lizards, which might explain the general absence of competition among these ecologically similar animals.

7

Experiments in fresh water

Introduction

It is conventional to classify freshwater habitats as lakes, ponds, and streams. That will serve well here, because many of the specific problems being attacked are quite different, and many of the techniques used in conducting experiments in these three kinds of habitats are different. The separate conditions have resulted in experimental designs specific to the habitat, even when the problems have been much the same in principle.

In the case of bodies of water large enough to be considered lakes, most ecological thinking has concentrated on the plankton. This is the general term designating drifting algae and small animals whose vertical movements may be important, but whose horizontal movements are insignificant from the standpoint of their ecology. Although fish predation on zooplankton is important in many lakes, the ecology of the plankton frequently has been studied independent of the fish and other large animals in the lake, and a number of experiments were carried out on the assumption that the important external influence was the supply of nutrients to the system. The edges and bottoms of lakes have entered limnological thought largely through the bacterial mineralization of nutrients that arrive at the bottom in the form of dead organisms. These nutrients are recycled when the lake becomes isothermal and the water can be mixed by the wind. Mixing is largely prevented in summer because the upper level of water becomes warmer and lighter than the deeper water and tends to be circulated by the wind as the mostly independent epilimnion. The transition between the warm upper layer and the cool lower depths is quite abrupt and is known as the thermocline. In the upper layer, the epilimnion, light is ample for photosynthesis, but the nutrients tend to become depleted relative to the deeper hypolimnion. This vertical stratification makes an important distinction between deep lakes, on one hand, and shallow lakes and ponds, on the other.

200

In ponds, the ecological impacts of bottom organisms and those on the pond margins are relatively much greater than is true of lakes, and the importance of the plankton is thus diminished, relatively at least. From the standpoint of experimental design, ponds are more easily replicated than lakes, and some of the most sophisticated and interesting experiments have been conducted using replicated ponds. The emphasis of experiments in ponds has also been more on macroorganisms, such as fish and amphibia, than has been the case in lakes.

Streams provide very different conditions and more severe challenges to experimenters than do lakes and ponds. Replicates and controls are difficult to arrange, and meteorological events, especially rain, can have far more serious consequences than is true for quiet waters. Many an experiment has been destroyed by heavy spates.

The ecology of ponds and streams is directly influenced by species that spend only part of their lives there. Many insects are aquatic only in their immature stages, and their dispersal depends on the winged adults. Amphibians normally spend most of their adult lives on land, where they are not always regarded as important ecological elements, but their larvae have been shown to have strong effects on the ponds where the eggs are deposited.

There have been experiments on the ecology of each of these habitats. Such experiments are the subjects of this chapter.

Experiments in lakes

Nutrients and algae

The importance of nutrients to the ecology of lakes is attested by the common classification into oligotrophic (nutrient-poor) and eutrophic (nutrient-rich) types. The nutrients concerned are almost universally considered to be nitrogen and phosphorus, and a large amount of limnological work has concerned the importance, both absolute and relative, of these two elements and the means by which they are recycled through the ecosystem. Schindler's experiment (1974) in fertilizing two nearly independent lake basins with nitrate and sugar, and adding phosphate to one of them, is mentioned in Chapter 2. The dramatic difference between the two was illustrated by a photograph taken from an airplane. The absence of replicates does not appear to have detracted from an acceptable conclusion, although the result immediately raises the question of why the herbivorous

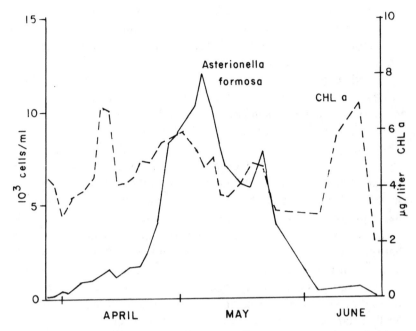

Figure 7.1. Cell counts of *Asterionella* and concentrations of chlorophyll *a* in Egg Lake during spring 1976. Plotted are the averages of 0.5-m and 1.5-m depths. (From Lehman & Sandgren 1978.)

plankton did not keep up with the algae. Because the bloom was of a blue-green "alga," *Anabaena spiroides*, it may not have been acceptable as a food for the local herbivores. A second explanation could be the effect of predators, and a time lag in the population dynamics of the herbivores remains a possibility. Further experimentation will be necessary before a choice can be made.

A small lake on an island in Puget Sound was found by Lehman and Sandgren (1978) to show the interesting property that there was a change in the nutrient limiting algal growth during spring and early summer. From late April to late May, the dominant alga was the diatom *Asterionella formosa* (Fig. 7.1). It accounted for more than 70 percent of the number of cells and for nearly all of the two maxima of chlorophyll *a*. Other species of algae were responsible for the chlorophyll *a* in early to mid-April, and still others created the peak in June. The rise of *Asterionella* numbers was associated with seasonal low concentrations of NO_3-N, NH_3-N, and PO_4-P. Before the dominance of the diatom, NO_3-N had been present in concentrations between 200 and 250 micrograms per liter. By early May, it had declined to less than 50. In April, the concentration of PO_4-P began an increase from about 1 microgram per liter to between 6 and 8 by the end of May. Lehman and Sandgren conducted three experiments in 18-liter polyethylene bags, testing the effect of adding either phosphate or nitrate, or both in combination, on the density of *Asterionella*, the density of all other algae, and the concentrations of chlorophyll *a* and of diatom-silicon. Replicate bags were used for each condition and were suspended in the lake at a depth of 1.5 m, the depth from which the water had been taken. The experiments ran 19–23 April, 9–13 May, and 19–22 May. The first experiment resulted in increases above levels in the control bags for chlorophyll *a*, diatom-Si, and *Asterionella* cell counts in bags that had received additions of PO_4-P, with or without NH_3NO_3, but undetectable effects of the addition of NH_3NO_3. The density of algae other than *Asterionella* was unaffected by any treatment. The next two experiments showed no effect of adding PO_4-P, but strong effects of adding nitrogen, especially in combination with PO_4, all responses being positive. The experiments demonstrated that the correlation between the abundance of *Asterionella* and the changes in concentrations of the two nutrients was actually due to a change in limiting factors. Lehman and Sandgren presented evidence that the marked increase in PO_4-P came from leakage out of two species of macrophytes that were growing rapidly over an appreciable part of the lake bottom. The experiments were well timed and properly controlled and replicated. Although the replicates responded alike in nearly all cases, no statistical analysis was presented, and that is a flaw in what was otherwise good work.

Although the response of the plankton to nutrients is quite predictable in oligotrophic lakes, as shown later in the experiments of Neill (1981, 1984), Barica, Kling, and Gibson (1980) found the effect of adding nitrate and ammonia to a shallow hypereutrophic lake in Saskatchewan to be subtle and not fully in accord with the hypothesis being tested. The lake and a nearby pond had regularly experienced blooms of the blue-green alga *Aphanizomenon flos-aquae* every summer. The blooms were invariably followed by a crash of the algal population, resulting in a depletion of the oxygen and massive fish kills. Like other blue-greens, *A. flos-aquae* fixes nitrogen, and the hypothesis was that it could take advantage of the low N : P ratio (3–4 : 1) in these bodies of water and thus outcompete the chlorophyte species and produce a nonsustainable biomass. It was postulated that the addition of NH_4

and NO_3 would allow the chlorophytes to compete well with the blue-greens and avoid the population crash and the following oxygen depletion.

Three experiments were conducted in successive years in the lake. In 1976, three pairs of clear plastic tubes, 2 m in diameter and 3 m deep (the maximum depth of the lake), were installed, with floating collars and bottoms driven into the lake bottom. Before the appearance of *A. flos-aquae*, two of the tubes were treated with ammonium chloride, and two with sodium nitrate, in both cases sufficient to raise the N : P ratio to about 15 : 1. Two tubes were retained as controls. The additions were made weekly until the summerkill of mid-August, except that the ammonium chloride was added twice weekly at the end of July and early August, in an apparent attempt to arrest the bloom of *A. flos-aquae*.

The control tubes and the open lake experienced the typical bloom and summerkill, with blue-green algae composing virtually 100 percent of the phytoplankton after mid-July. The two pairs of experimental tubes eventually had a complete dominance of blue-greens, but at a somewhat slower rate, and the chlorophyll *a* concentrations were 144–151 g/liter, in contrast to the 555 in the controls and 470 in the open water of the lake. Eventually, the bloom collapsed in the experimental tubes as well as elsewhere, but there was a delay of about sixteen days. Oxygen concentrations were similar in all tubes in August.

A single large plastic tube 10 m in diameter ("limnocorral") was constructed in 1977, but the experiment was a failure because the unusually warm spring stimulated an early appearance of the bloom of *A. flos-aquae*, both in the lake and in the limnocorral, despite the application of ammonium nitrate in a concentration equal to the combined NH_4 and NO_3 additions of the previous summer. In 1978, a second limnocorral was constructed to act as a control. Ammonium nitrate was added as in 1977, starting well before the bloom of blue-greens was anticipated. Unfortunately, the lake developed the bloom six weeks later than usual, and summerkill conditions never appeared. Fertilization apparently changed the species composition of algae from *A. flos-aquae* to another blue-green, *Microcystis aeruginosa*, which appeared in abundance while the lake and the control corral were still dominated by chlorophytes. Despite the lack of replication, that effect was reasonably convincing, but its relevance to the original hypothesis is obscure.

At the same time as the second limnocorral experiment was conducted, a nearby pond with a history similar to that of the lake was treated with ammonium nitrate in a concentration ten times that in the experiment. No *A. flos-aquae* bloom developed, and the phytoplankton was dominated first by cryptomonads and then by chlorophytes. Fish survival was good. Because there was no control and no replication, the meaning of this result is unclear, as there was no summerkill in the lake (the nearest approach to a control). Barica and associates acknowledged that the treatment was not a satisfactory method of avoiding fish kills, although the results were interesting from the limnological standpoint. Nitrogen additions had some of the expected effect, but factors other than nutrient deficiency must have been involved in the collapse of the bloom.

Nutrient recycling

A highly sophisticated study of the immediate sources of nutrients during the summer in the epilimnion of Lake Washington was conducted by Lehman (1980). Some nutrients were brought in by streams, by runoff, and even by the air; others came from diffusion from the hypolimnion. Lehman addressed the question of how much immediate recycling through the zooplankton contributed to the maintenance of the algal–zooplankton system. Lake Washington had been studied intensively for nearly forty years by W. T. Edmondson and his students, and outstanding baseline data were available. Lehman was able to calculate the input of nutrients from allochthonous sources, and data on thermal and concentration gradients across the thermocline permitted him to calculate the rate of diffusion of nitrogen and phosphorus from the hypolimnion. His first experiment was designed to estimate the rate at which different densities of zooplankton caused the accumulation of nutrients, as well as the depletion of algae. The method was to enclose 20 liters of lake water in each of a number of polyethylene bags. In some, the abundance of zooplankton was artificially increased by amounts ranging from 15-fold to 55-fold. Other bags held the normal zooplankton abundance. The concentrations of nutrients and the abundance of phytoplankton were monitored in samples taken from the bags at intervals, the last sample being taken 30 h after the start of the experiment. The concentration of nutrients increased approximately linearly with time in each of the bags with elevated densities of zooplankton (Fig. 7.2). The algal abundance (expressed as the concentration of chlorophyll *a*) was higher initially than that in the control bags because of the retention of large colonies of *Botryococcus* along with the zooplankton, which was obtained by hauls with a coarse plankton net. Lehman argued that *Botryococcus* was too large to be used as food by the animals, but it may have absorbed some of the nutrients released by excretion or egestion. The slopes of the changes in nutrient concentrations were the observed rates of nutrient regeneration by the zooplankton. No replication was mentioned, but the clear relationship at 30 h between nutrient concentration and experimental density of zooplankton is reassuring.

Lehman pointed out that the calculated regeneration rates would have been influenced by the balance between remineralization by the zooplankton and the known rapid uptake by the phytoplankton, and before the rate of regeneration could be properly compared with inputs from outside the lake and from the hypolimnion, some estimate had to be made of the correction necessary for the uptake by the phytoplankton. To accomplish this, he made use of the knowledge that at high concentrations of nutrients, the rate of uptake by phytoplankton becomes saturated, so that by adding nutrients to the experimental polyethylene bags in quantities about fifteen times the ambient, the unknown uptake could be held relatively constant for short periods of time. Bags with and without added zooplankton could then be compared for the change in concentration of nutrients. In this second experiment, zooplankton concentrations were raised fivefold to ninefold (Fig. 7.3). The desired regeneration rate, independent of the uptake rate, could be calculated from the change in concentration, the density of zooplankton, and the mean concentration of phytoplankton. Lehman's paper should be consulted for the mathematical details. The results were close to those calculated from the simpler first experiment.

When calibrated against the mean concentration of zooplankton above the thermocline during the summer, the rates of regeneration were 4.0 mg PO_4–P m^{-2} day^{-1} and 20.5 mg NH_3–N m^{-2} day^{-1}. These values were compared with averages of observations made over seven or more summers of 0.344 mg PO_4–P m^{-2} day^{-1} and 7.34 mg NH_3–N m^{-2} day^{-1} from all other sources. The results of this study demonstrated the importance of regeneration of nutrients by the zooplankton to the productivity of the epilimnion during the summer months. Lehman pointed out that because the zooplankton graze different species of algae preferentially, they may be simultaneously suppressing some

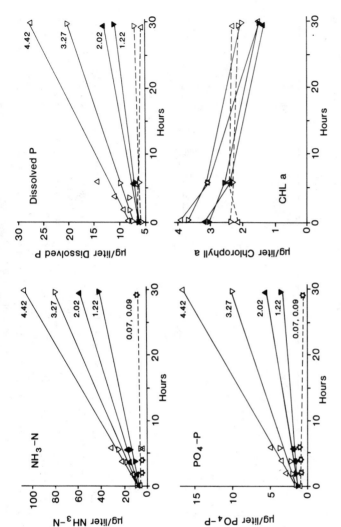

Figure 7.2. Concentrations of several substances inside plastic-bag enclosures incubated in Lake Washington, 15–16 September 1977. Zooplankton abundances given as milligrams dry weight per liter. [Reprinted from Lehman (1980), in *Evolution and Ecology of Zooplankton Communities*, edited by W. Charles Kerfoot, by permission of University Press of New England. © 1980 by Trustees of Dartmouth College.]

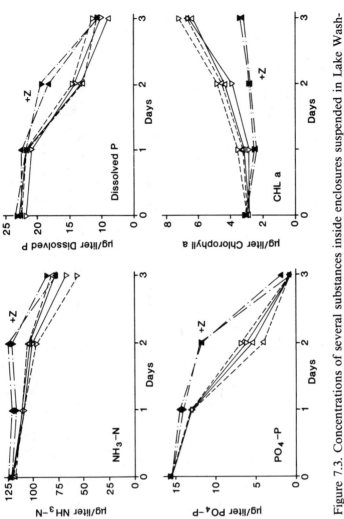

Figure 7.3. Concentrations of several substances inside enclosures suspended in Lake Washington, 29 September–2 October 1977. Concentrations of inorganic P and N were artificially elevated in all bags at start of experiment; +Z denotes bags that received added quantities of zooplankton (0.62 and 0.69 mg dry weight per liter). Abundances in other enclosures were 0.08 and 0.16 (solid line) and 0.10 and 0.04 (dashed line) milligrams dry weight per liter. Different symbols distinguish replicates. [Reprinted from Lehman (1980), in *Evolution and Ecology of Zooplankton Communities*, edited by W. Charles Kerfoot, by permission of University Press of New England. © 1980 by Trustees of Dartmouth College.]

species and fertilizing their competitors, thereby having a major impact on the species composition of the phytoplankton.

These experiments, though lacking replication, were based on a large amount of background information about the lake, and the ingenious use of knowledge of algal and zooplankton physiology make the study impressive.

Food-chain interactions within the plankton

The ecosystems of most lakes involve four well-defined trophic levels: phytoplanktonic producers, herbivorous zooplankton, planktivorous fishes, and piscivorous fishes. There are also predaceous zooplankters, which are preyed on by planktivorous fishes, thereby blurring a potential fifth trophic level, as the fishes do not discriminate between herbivorous and predaceous plankters. The dynamics of this system are simplified in those lakes from which fishes are absent. Such a situation was exploited by Neill (1981, 1984) and Neill and Peacock (1980) in oligotrophic Lake Gwendoline in British Columbia. The herbivorous plankton consisted of the rotifers *Chonochilus* sp., *Keratella* sp., *Kellicottia* sp., and *Polyarthra* sp., and a number of species of Crustacea, including the cladocerans *Daphnia rosea*, *Holopedium gibberum*, *Diaphanosoma brachyurum*, *Bosmina longirostris*, and *Chydorus* sp., and the copepods *Diaptomus kenai*, *D. leptotus*, and *Tropocyclops prasinus*. The predators were the midge larvae *Chaoborus trivittatus* and *C. americanus*, plus the rare copepod *Cyclops bicuspidatus*. Unlike their congeners elsewhere, the two species of *Chaoborus* did not migrate down into the bottom sediments during the day. That was a happy circumstance for the experiments, which were conducted in clear plastic tubes 1.55 m in diameter and 6, 10, or 14 m long for different experiments. They were suspended from the top with floating collars, and were securely closed at the bottom.

The tubes were pumped full of lake water that had been filtered to exclude zooplankton, but not phytoplankton. The composition of the plankton in the tubes was manipulated according to the design of the experiment concerned. There were two replicates for each treatment. The effects of nutrients on the crustacean community were tested with and without predatory midges (Neill & Peacock 1980). In these experiments, the crustaceans were added to the tubes in densities equal to the average for the lake. The low fertilizer level was also the level in the lake. Additional fertilizer (NaH_2PO_4, KNO_3) was added at 14 times the natural level and at 66–330 times the natural level.

At the highest level, and without *Chaoborus*, the abundance of crustaceans was 5.5 times the natural level after three months. The species composition and relative abundance had changed little from that in the controls. The populations of solitary rotifer species responded quickly to fertilization, increasing to ten times the initial level with the medium amount, and to more than 100 times the initial level with the high amount, whereas populations in the open lake and in the bags without fertilizer declined to less than one-tenth of the initial level.

With *Chaoborus* present, the abundance in the tubes with high levels of fertilizer was only twice that in the controls, and the species composition had changed radically to one of nearly pure *Chydorus*. This result may be related to the sessile habit of *Chydorus*, which commonly clings to surfaces (possibly the plastic walls of the tubes in this case), rendering it less accessible than other plankters to the open-water-feeding *Chaoborus*. At the medium level of fertilizer, the predator had almost no effect on the crustacean community, either on total abundance or on the relative abundances of the different species. The striking difference in the effect of *Chaoborus* at medium and high levels of fertilizer was explained by Neill and Peacock as being related to differences in survival with increasing fertilization (Fig. 7.4). Examination of the crops of the different instars showed that the first-instar larvae had fed exclusively on rotifers and the nauplii (early larval stages) of copepods. In the absence of fertilizer, both of these kinds of prey were rare, and their rarity caused a "bottleneck" in the survival of the early stages of *Chaoborus*. Regarding the addition of fertilizer, the rotifers increased appreciably with medium fertilization, and by two orders of magnitude at high levels of fertilization. Their interpretation of this information was that the fertilizer allowed the phytoplankton to increase, which temporarily released the rotifers from competition. Without this added food supply, most of the first-instar *Chaoborus* larvae starved. Their survival meant that the population could break through the "first-instar bottleneck," and the higher densities of later instars, which preyed on the herbivorous crustaceans, kept those populations well below the levels attained without *Chaoborus*.

In a second paper, Neill (1981) further explored the effects of *Chaoborus* predation on the different species of the crustacean community, although it is anomalous that there was no more discussion of *Chydorus*, which dominated the community in the presence of both fertilizer and the predator. The experiment, conducted in tubes 14 m long,

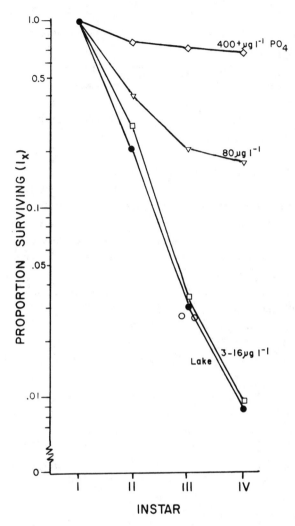

Figure 7.4. *Chaoborus trivittatus* survivorship by instar in experimental enclosures receiving different fertilization treatments. Points are conservative estimates based on peak instar I abundances because egg abundance was unreliably censused. [Reprinted from Neill & Peacock (1980), in *Evolution and Ecology of Zooplankton Communities*, edited by W. Charles Kerfoot, by permission of University Press of New England. © 1980 by Trustees of Dartmouth College.]

revealed the importance of temperature differences in two successive summers, as well as the effects of three levels of *Chaoborus* density: none, natural, and three times natural. The summer of 1976 was abnormally cool; the summer of 1977 was unusually warm. The manipulations were performed in May of each year, and through the summers the population densities of these six species of crustaceans were followed: *Daphnia rosea, Diaphanosoma brachyurum, Holopedium gibberum, Bosmina longirostris, Diaptomus kenai,* and *D. leptotus.* The *Chaoborus* densities remained at the experimentally set densities during both summers, except for a burst of first- and second-instar larvae in June, followed by a small increase in third and fourth instars at the end of July. The manipulation was much more effective in the cool summer than in the warm one. In July 1976, five of the six species showed statistically significant effects of predation. The only exception was *Holopedium*, which has a thick protective gelatinous coating on its carapace, although the peak July densities of *Daphnia* given in the appendix (56.3 for no *Chaoborus*, 46.9 for natural density, and 56.0 for triple density, all in thousands per square meter of surface) suggest some kind of artifact. In July 1977, only *Bosmina* and *Diaphanosoma* could be shown to be affected by the experimental densities of the predators. After July in both years, other factors became more important than predation, as crustacean reproduction more than compensated for those losses, and the early differences disappeared. The difference in responses in the two years was explained as being the result of lowered reproductive rates of the crustaceans early in the cool year, allowing the *Chaoborus* to keep their populations depressed, whereas in the warm year most of the crustaceans reproduced fast enough to overcome the predation. The rotifer populations responded inversely to the manipulation of *Chaoborus*, decreasing significantly in abundance in the predator-free tubes, and increasing 10-fold to 100-fold in the presence of enhanced *Chaoborus* densities. Thus, the known predation by *Chaoborus* on the rotifers was insufficient to hold their populations in check. It should be remembered that unlike the crustaceans and rotifers, *Chaoborus* could not respond numerically to the increase in its food supply within a single year.

These responses by the rotifers prompted experiments in 1978 and 1979 on the possible competitive effects of *Daphnia rosea* (the predominant cladoceran) and the possible predatory effects of the copepods *Diaptomus leptotus* and *D. kenai*. The experiment involved quadrupling the natural *Daphnia* density in two tubes, excluding *Daphnia* from two, excluding the copepods from two, and leaving two as controls. Small amounts of fertilizer (one-tenth that in the medium level of the earlier experiment) were added every two weeks to prevent the populations from going through the usual summer crash. The results of the experiment were clear (Fig. 7.5). The copepod-removal

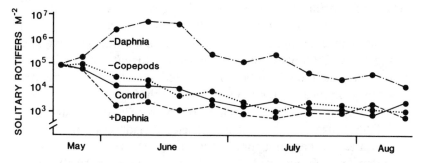

Figure 7.5. Mean densities of all solitary rotifers combined, excluding *Conochilus*, in four replicated experimental treatments in enclosures in 1978. (From Neill 1984.)

Table 7.1. *Analysis of variance of log-transformed densities of solitary rotifers (all species pooled) in mid-June 1978 after manipulation of crustacean densities one month previously*

Source of variation	d.f.	Mean square	$F_{3,4}$	p
Treatment	3	20.8207	99.849	<0.001
Error	4	0.2085		

Daphnia removed	Copepods removed	Control	*Daphnia* added
$6.3 \times 10^6 \text{ m}^{-2}$	$3.6 \times 10^4 \text{ m}^{-2}$	$3.2 \times 10^4 \text{ m}^{-2}$	3.1×10^5

Note: Boxes join mean rotifer densities in treatments for which there were no statistically significant differences by Student–Newman–Keuls test.
From Neill (1981).

tubes and the controls supported essentially the same densities of rotifers, but excluding *Daphnia* permitted rotifer populations to rise to 250 times that in the controls, and adding *Daphnia* caused the rotifer populations to fall below the controls by a significant amount (Table 7.1). The experiments left no doubt that competition from the cladocerans was the most important factor determining the abundance of solitary rotifers and that, except for brief periods and unusual densities of predatory midges, the community dynamics of this fish-free lake were determined by the scarcity of nutrients.

The experiments were thoughtful in plan, and the series followed a logical sequence, as results of the earlier ones were used as the basis for further elucidation in later years. The design was good, with adequate replicates and controls. A good point was the comparison of the controls with conditions in the open lake. Experiments using clear plastic tubes are not always so successful. In eutrophic lakes and ponds, the plastic tends to become covered with algae or sessile rotifers, thus complicating the interpretation of the results.

The competitive effect of a cladoceran on rotifers demonstrated by Neill (1984) suggested that different species of cladocerans might compete with each other. In laboratory environments, this is readily demonstrated (e.g., Frank 1952, 1957; Kerfoot & DeMott 1980). In the field, the possibility was investigated in small containers (3.5 liters) by Lynch (1978) in a natural pond in Minnesota. In an old, man-made lake in New Hampshire, DeMott and Kerfoot (1982) used large enclosures, 2 by 2 m, and 3 m deep. Most pond experiments are described in a later section, but these two studies complemented each other, and they are both considered here. Lynch had observed that there was a regular sequence of an increase in the abundance of *Daphnia pulex* in July, followed by a concomitant decline in its abundance and an increase in the abundance of *Ceriodaphnia reticulata*. He used clear plastic cylinders with two netting windows near the upper ends to allow some mixing with water in the pond. The cylinders were suspended at a depth of 0.5 m in an area free of rooted vegetation. Predetermined numbers of *Daphnia pulex* and *Ceriodaphnia reticulata* were introduced with filtered pond water. Single-species controls started with ten individuals; mixed species started with at least ten of each, some having each species at a numerical advantage of 20 : 10 or 30 : 10. All conditions were replicated. In the first experiment, conducted in late July and early August, *Daphnia* became extinct in all planned mixtures by the twenty-fifth day, although the control containers were supporting an average of ninety-five individuals each. In the second experiment, which was started immediately after the end of the first, Lynch added *Bosmina longirostris* to the system, providing replicated controls for all three species separately, and replicated experiments starting with ten individuals of each species in all combinations. The results of the two experiments are given in Table 7.2. None of the three species was lost from any combination, and at the end of the experiment, *Daphnia* was maintaining larger populations when with either *Ceriodaphnia* or *Bosmina* than when alone. The result was thus in strong contrast to that of the first experiment. The three-species combination produced fewer total cladocerans than did

Table 7.2. *Mean final densities (individuals/liter ± 0.95 confidence limits) of cladocerans in the two competition experiments*

Treatment	Daphnia	Ceriodaphnia	Bosmina	Daphnia + Ceriodaphnia	Daphnia + Bosmina	Ceriodaphnia + Bosmina	Daphnia + Ceriodaphnia + Bosmina
Experiment 1 (14 Aug.)							
N	3	3		9			
Daphnia	95.0 ± 19.0			0 (80)			
Ceriodaphnia		462.0 ± 53.4		265.0 ± 42.3 (193)			
Experiment 2 (10 Sept.)							
N	3	3	2	2	3	3	4
Daphnia	19.0 ± 10.8			48.0 ± 14	38.3 ± 15.4		17.5 ± 6.7
Ceriodaphnia		262.0 ± 40.2		61.5 ± 16		137.0 ± 29.1	2.8 ± 2.6
Bosmina			202.0 ± 127.6		6.3 ± 6.2	89.7 ± 23.5	12.2 ± 5.6

Note: Numbers in parentheses under *Daphnia + Ceriodaphnia* in Experiment 1 are the final densities in one chamber in which the two coexisted. Number of replicates denoted by *N*.
From Lynch (1978).

any other containers, except for the *Daphnia* controls. Low populations were associated with high death rates of immature specimens,
rather than with unfavorable conditions for adults. Lynch attributed
the difference between the two experiments partly to the sensitivity of
the feeding rate of *Daphnia* to high temperatures, which frequently
exceeded 25 °C during the first experiment, but dropped below that
level before the second experiment. He also made extensive analyses
of the algal populations in the experimental tubes and found that
Daphnia was favored by an increase in the abundance of flagellates
when in combination with either of the other two species. Despite his
efforts, however, many of the results remain unexplained and may be
related to interactions among the algae.

The effect of flagellates was the opposite of that found by DeMott
and Kerfoot (1982), who demonstrated a specialization by *Bosmina*
for feeding on these forms. Five years of observations on the plankton
of their mesotrophic (moderately nutrient-rich) lake had shown that
the species composition of the cladoceran community was virtually
unchanged, despite seasonal fluctuations. The lake was used as a pri-
vate fishing club and was stocked with trout (*Salmo gairdneri* and *Sal-
velinus fontinalis*). Two experiments in six large enclosures were carried out. In the first, four were used as exclosures, two being fertilized
regularly at five-day intervals for forty days, starting in late July, and
two being retained as controls. The purpose was to test for any effect
of fish predation on the populations and also for possible competition
between *Daphnia rosea* and *Bosmina longirostris* in the absence of
fish. The remaining enclosures had rainbow trout added (two in one
enclosure, eight in the other), to test directly the effect of fish predation
on the composition of the cladoceran community. The same control
enclosures served as for the fertilization experiment.

In the absence of fish, fertilization produced increases in the abundances of both *D. rosea* and *Bosmina*, but gave inconsistent results
between the two enclosures for *Diaphanosoma brachyurum* (Fig. 7.6).
For most of the year, the densities of *D. rosea* and *Bosmina* in the
control pens were much like those in the lake, but *D. brachyurum* was
significantly more abundant inside than out until mid-August, after
which the numbers in the enriched enclosures declined to undetectable
levels. None of these results can be interpreted to demonstrate interspecific competition among the Cladocera. The experimental introduction of trout gave inconclusive results (Fig. 7.7), at least in part
because there was no replication of either trout density. The three species had different population trajectories. Considering the differences

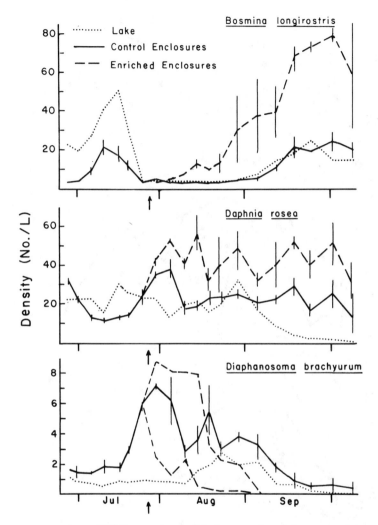

Figure 7.6. Comparison of cladoceran dynamics among lake, control, and enriched-enclosure populations. Bars show ±s.e. for replicate enclosures; arrows indicate the first nutrient additions to two enriched enclosures. *Diaphanosoma* population trajectories in the two enriched enclosures are plotted separately. (From DeMott & Kerfoot 1982.)

between the two controls, *Bosmina* populations were not convincingly different between the controls and either the two-trout or the eight-trout enclosure during the first month of the experiment. Thereafter, the populations in the control enclosures were lower than in the pres-

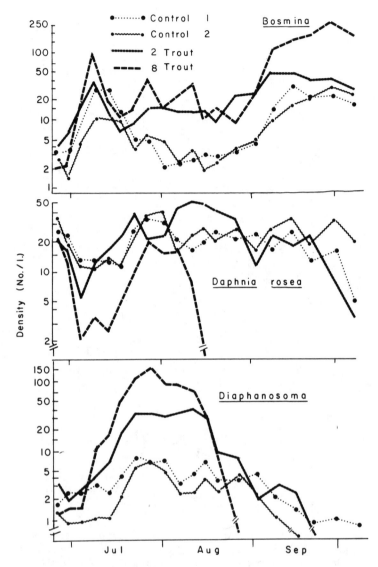

Figure 7.7. Comparison of cladoceran population dynamics among trout and control enclosures (note log scale). (From DeMott & Kerfoot 1982.)

ence of trout until mid-September, when the number of *Bosmina* in the two-trout enclosure converged on the controls. The reponse of *Daphnia* was less intepretable. In the two-trout enclosure, the population was never demonstrably different from the controls. With eight trout, the *Daphnia* population changed erratically, first declining, then increasing to control levels, then dropping to an undetectable level by late August. In the presence of trout, *Diaphanosoma* first increased and then disappeared from the samples at about the same time as *Daphnia*. DeMott and Kerfoot interpreted these graphs as indicating some competitive effect of *Daphnia* on *Bosmina*, with other factors having an impact, and as suggesting a "strong and direct conflict between *Daphnia* and *Diaphanosoma*." Caveat emptor! There is no means of detecting the variation within either trout treatment, and trout are not effective planktivores, as DeMott and Kerfoot acknowledged in their description of the site.

Their experiments on selective feeding by the different species of cladocerans provided an explanation for the weakness of the competitive interaction between *Bosmina* and *Daphnia*, in addition to at least partially reconciling the apparent contradiction with the outcome of the experiments conducted by Lynch (1978). DeMott and Kerfoot (1982) used different radioactive labels for bacteria and algae in natural lake water. Bacteria were labeled with ^{3}H-acetate by incubation in the dark for 24 h; algae were labeled with ^{14}C-bicarbonate by incubation in the light for 7–10 h in jars suspended in the lake at a depth of 1 m. Zooplankton freshly collected were combined with the labeled food items in 3.8-liter jars, which were sealed and suspended in the lake. This was done on 31 July 1979 and repeated on 22 August. By the second experiment, there had been a significant change in the algal community, from a July predominance (82%) of algae difficult for *Bosmina* to consume (*Sphaerocystis*, *Asterococcus*, and *Oocystis*) to a situation in August when flagellates were as abundant as the "resistant" forms. At the time of the August experiment, a second type was performed, substituting a monospecific culture of *Chlamydomonas* for the naturally occurring algae. The different labeling was used to determine the amounts of bacteria and algae that had been consumed. The ratio of algae to bacteria was used as a selectivity coefficient for each of four species of Cladocera: *Daphnia rosea*, *D. pulicharia*, *Diaphanosoma brachyurum*, and *Bosmina longirostris* (Table 7.3). The two species of *Daphnia* were similar in taking algae at about 2.5 times the rate at which they took bacteria, regardless of the composition of the algal part of the experiment. *Diaphanosoma* was less selective, but consistent among the experiments. The major contrast was for *Bosmina*, which shifted from preferring bacteria (when the algal community consisted largely of "resistant" species) to a strong selection of algae when

Table 7.3. *Feeding selectivity coefficients for in situ grazing experiments with radioactively labeled natural and introduced food particles*

| | Labeled particles | | | |
| | Algae/bacteria | | Chlamydomonas/bacteria | |
Cladoceran	(31 Jul. 1979, 3 h)	(22 Aug. 1979, 3 h)	(22 Aug. 1979, 3 h)	(22 Aug. 1979, 10 min)
Daphnia rosea				
Adults	2.37 ± 0.29 (5)	2.38 ± 0.13 (6)	2.66 ± 0.04 (3)	2.19 ± 0.08 (3)
Juveniles	1.91 ± 0.17 (6)	1.98 ± 0.12 (6)	2.33 ± 0.02 (6)	2.06 ± 0.09 (6)
Daphnia pulicaria				
Adults	2.38 ± 0.11 (6)	3.06 ± 0.12 (6)	2.30 ± 0.04 (3)	2.62 ± 0.28 (3)
Juveniles	3.66 ± 0.29 (6)	2.17 ± 0.10 (6)	2.40 ± 0.09 (7)	2.14 ± 0.07 (6)
Diaphanosoma brachyurum				
Adults	1.81 ± 0.08 (6)	2.00 ± 0.09 (4)	1.88 ± 0.03 (4)	1.47 ± 0.09 (6)
Juveniles	1.67 ± 0.04 (3)	1.45 ± 0.02 (3)	1.74 ± 0.03 (3)	1.42 ± 0.11 (4)
Bosmina longirostris				
Adults	0.74 ± 0.047 (4)	3.44 ± 0.12 (6)	11.6 ± 1.1 (6)	10.0 ± 0.97 (8)
Juveniles	0.41 ± 0.024 (3)	2.89 ± 0.22 (4)	6.48 ± 0.63 (5)	6.99 ± 1.1 (5)

Note: Mean selectivity ± standard error. A value of 1.0 indicates no selectivity, >1.0 "preference" for algae, and <1.0 "preference" for bacteria. Number of replicate scintillation vials is given in parentheses. From DeMott and Kerfoot (1982).

half of the community consisted of flagellates, and an overwhelming preference for *Chlamydomonas*. In the laboratory, DeMott and Kerfoot fed *Bosmina* and *Daphnia* on different concentrations of radioactively labeled *Chlamydomonas* and found that at densities of 15×10^3 cells per milliliter and below, *Bosmina* had a significantly higher ingestion rate than *Daphnia* after the sizes were adjusted to per-unit biomass. Thus, when flagellates are rare, *Bosmina* can obtain them more efficiently than *Daphnia*, but the latter is able to use other algae more efficiently. The special ability of *Bosmina* lies in the morphology of its feeding apparatus, which can be more selective than that of *Daphnia*.

Lynch (1978) had found that *Daphnia* was favored by flagellates, but he did not distinguish between sizes of flagellates, and DeMott and Kerfoot asserted that it was the small species that specially benefited *Bosmina*. There is thus some room for agreement.

Vertebrate predation

The kinds of competitors among herbivorous plankton species seem most frequently to be associated with either the absence or the deliberate exclusion of fishes. The impact of fish predation on the plankton community was investigated by Hrbáček (1962). He took advantage of some fish management efforts to observe their effects on many aspects of the limnology of the six water bodies involved. There were three eutrophic pools ("backwaters") on the floodplain of the Elbe in Czechoslovakia. Poltruba Pool, with a surface area of 1,800 m², was flooded to varying degrees in successive years: not at all in 1954; enough to cause a weekly turnover of water at times in 1955; enough to cause a daily turnover of water at times in 1956. Bezednice Pool, 4,800 m² in surface area, was not flooded during the study, nor was Velká Azimova, 380 m² in surface area. Poltruba was poisoned to eliminate unwanted species of fish in 1955, and again after the floods of 1956, because reinvasions had taken place. Largemouth bass were introduced in 1957. Velká Azimova was poisoned in 1953, and carp were introduced later in the same year. Bezednice, 2.67 times as large as Poltruba, and 12.6 times as large as Velká Azimova, was not treated. Hrbáček made qualitative observations on the compositions of the plankton of the three pools and related these observations to the fish populations. The cladoceran species were the large *Daphnia pulicaria* (2.0–2.3 mm in average length in different pools) and *D. longispina*

(1.4–1.8 mm) and the small species *D. cucullata* (0.68–0.76 mm), *Bosmina longirostris* (0.33–0.38 mm), *Ceriodaphnia quadrangula* (0.8 mm), *C. reticulata* (0.75 mm), and *C. pulchella* (0.43 mm). He found that where there were dense fish populations, only small species of zooplankton were present; large species appeared only where fish populations were low. Thus, in Poltruba, the dominant species in 1953–5 were *Bosmina* and *Daphnia cucullata*. In those two years, the fish populations were estimated as 34,000 and 69,000 fish per hectare, respectively, mostly small species. After the poisonings, the Cladocera populations were dominated by *D. longispina* in 1956. In Velká Azimova, the fish population was described as "overstocked" in 1953, but there were no observations on the plankton. In 1954, after the poisoning and introduction of carp, the dominant plankter was *D. longispina*. In Bezednice, where no management was involved, but the fish were said to be "overstocked," the dominant species were *Bosmina* and *D. cucullata*. Thus, there was an association between small cladoceran species and the presence of dense fish populations. Hrbáček estimated the biomasses (expressed as total nitrogen) of all trophic levels and found that the herbivorous zooplankton biomasses were not different, whether large or small cladocerans were dominant. It should be noted that "trophic level" was used by Hrbáček to mean the degree of eutrophy, rather than the conventional meaning as used in the preceding sentence. There was a difference in the abundances of nannoseston, with higher levels found in the presence of fish and small cladocerans. Where large species of Cladocera were dominant, the nannoseston was reduced to the point where the transparency was increased twofold to fourfold (Hrbáček 1958). In a separate report, Hrbáček et al. (1961) compared limnological events in Poltruba with those in a fourth pool, Procházka, 1,500 m² in area, in which the fish stock was not followed, but was said to be comparable to the overstocked condition of Poltruba before poisoning. The results were similar to those described for Poltruba.

Hrbáček (1962) also followed the limnological phenomena in two large ponds, originally oligotrophic, but raised to mesotrophy by human activity. Velký Pálenec, covering 31 ha, was fertilized with lime, superphosphate, potassium salt, and pig manure in each year, 1954–7. Smyslov, 21.5 ha in area, was fertilized with the same mixture in 1955 and 1956. Even with fertilization, the nutrient level was far below that in the eutrophic pools, and the fish stocks were correspondingly lower: 312–417 per hectare in four different years in Velký Pálenec, and 500–660 per hecatare in two different years in Smyslov. From 1954 until late summer 1957, the herbivorous plankton in Velký Pálenec was dominated by *Daphnia pulicaria*, but then *D. longispina* appeared and was followed by the small species of *Ceriodaphnia* and *Diaphanosoma*. In Smyslov, the dominant cladocerans were *D. longispina* in 1955 and *D. pulicaria* in 1956. Hrbáček could not understand the shift in Velký Pálenec until the pond was drained in the autumn of 1957, when it was discovered that perch had bred that year, and there were large numbers of fry present, not noticed previously. These small fish apparently had consumed the large zooplankton.

As interesting and as pioneering as these observations are, it is beyond reason to call them experiments. Moreover, the effect of a lack of any design can be understood from two standpoints: The first concerns Hrbáček's own data (1962, p. 64) on the relative amounts of nitrogen contained in two trophic levels under different conditions, which were reported to range from 113 percent of nannoseston N in zooplankton N to 250 percent (average 193%) in five ponds/years when *Bosmina longirostris* was dominant to a range from 42 percent to 200 percent (average 94%) in six ponds/years when large *Daphnia* were dominant. The second standpoint is in comparison with the carefully replicated experiments of Hall et al. (1970), who experienced so much variation between replicated ponds that they could not obtain statistical significance between most of the means tested, as described later in this chapter.

Brooks and Dodson (1965) observed that small lakes in southern Connecticut with populations of the planktivorous fish *Alosa pseudoharengus* had zooplankton assemblages markedly different from those in otherwise similar lakes without that species. In the presence of the fish, the dominant crustaceans were the small forms *Bosmina longirostris*, *Ceriodaphnia lacustris*, *Cyclops bicuspidatus*, and *Tropocyclops prasinus*. Where the fish were absent, the larger species *Daphnia galeata*, *D. catawba*, and *Diaptomus minutus* were most abundant. They also had data from the same lake before a related fish, *Alosa aestivalis*, had been introduced and after it had become abundant. The two surveys confirmed the same pattern of zooplankton as was expected from the comparative analysis. In 1942, the zooplankton was dominated by *Daphnia catawba* and *Diaptomus minutus;* in 1964, the dominant species were *Bosmina longispina*, *Cyclops bicuspidatus* and *Tropocyclops prasinus*. The size distributions of the individuals in the two collections overlapped by a very small amount. Brooks and Dodson realized that they had to account for the smaller size in the presence of the planktivore and the larger size in its absence. They argued that the fish selectively fed on the larger species, thus tending to eliminate them from the community, an explanation that would account for the small average size in the presence of fish, subsequently demonstrated in the laboratory experiments of Werner and Hall (1974). This has become known as the size-selective predation hypothesis. Its accuracy depends on the visual capability of the predator. Large bluegills (*Lepomis macrochirus*) have more acute vision than small ones and are better able to distinguish prey size. Small specimens are influenced more by the distance they are from the prey (Hairston, Li, & Easter 1982; Li, Wetterer, & Hairston 1985).

Brooks and Dodson (1965) also advanced the size-efficiency hypothesis, arguing that large herbivorous plankton could feed on phytoplankton and detritus of a large array of sizes, whereas smaller forms would be restricted to smaller algae, bacteria, and other particles of similar size. They also calculated that the filtering surface would be proportional to the square of a linear dimension, and because *Daphnia catawba* was four times as long as *Bosmina longirostris*, its filtering surface would be sixteen times as great, a figure that agrees with some known filtering rates. These differences would put the larger species at a competitive advantage and would account for their dominance where planktivorous fish were absent. Brooks (1968) conducted an experiment to test size-selective predation. He used a large tank, approximately 250 liters, through which he circulated water from the Connecticut River, whence he had obtained a school of sixty-five young *Alosa pseudoharengus* (mean length 4 cm). After one week of feeding only on the sparse plankton from the river, the fish were provided plankton netted in a nearby lake (one of the fish-free lakes in the first study). The zooplankton disappeared so rapidly that a second collection was added after two more days. Four one-liter plankton samples from the tank, taken each 15 min for 1 h, showed that the two largest species, *Daphnia catawba* and *Epishura nordenskioldi*, either were not present at the first sampling (*D. catawba*) or were too rare for analysis. *Diaptomus minutus* provided the best data, disappearing from the samples at rates inversely related to size, adults being taken first, followed by stage III and larger copepodids, then stage II, stage I, and finally the nauplii. A control, not otherwise described, indicated no nonpredatory mortality during the experiment.

Size-selective predation is widely accepted and has been the subject of a number of demonstration projects in which piscivorous fish were introduced into lakes formerly containing only planktivores (Benndorf et al. 1984; Shapiro & Wright 1984; Carpenter et al. 1987). In all three studies, the secondary effects have been release of the zooplankton from fish predation, an increase in the abundance of large forms (especially *Daphnia* species), and a decrease in the standing crop of phytoplankton, reflected in an increase in transparency. These were not experiments in the proper sense, as they lacked controls and replicates, but the repeatability of the results under different conditions makes the studies more convincing than any one would be alone. The results appear to apply to eutrophic and mesotrophic bodies of water, and the "top-down" regulation does not extend to the algae in deep oligotrophic lakes (Lehman 1988). It is also true that the studies were continued for two years at most, and evidence of a final equilibrium was not presented.

The size-selective predation hypothesis has been modified to incorporate differential visibility. Because many species of planktonic animals are transparent, their visibility to fish may depend on attributes other than size. Pigmentation is an important trait in the relationship. A number of laboratory experiments, reviewed by Zaret (1980), showed that Cladocera of the same size, but with larger eyes, were more heavily preyed on than those with smaller eyes. In a similar vein, Hairston (1976, 1979) investigated color differences in the copepod *Diaptomus nevadensis* in two saline lakes in the Grand Coulee, Washington State. In Soap Lake, where the salinity was 17 g liter^{-1}, the copepods were bright red in color; in Lake Lenore, where the salinity was one-tenth that in Soap Lake, the copepods were almost clear, being either blue or pale red. The high salinity in Soap Lake was associated with an impoverished fauna that included no vertebrate predators and a population of visually hunting damselflies that was only one-seventh as dense as a related species in Lake Lenore, which also supported a population of the predatory salamander *Ambystoma tigrinum*. Both lakes had populations of the hemipteran *Coenocorixa explecta* in shallow water.

Hairston proposed that the difference in color of the copepods was related to higher predation in Lake Lenore, where selection would be for lower visibility. He collected salamanders, damselfly nymphs, and corixids from Lake Lenore, and damselfly nymphs and corixids from

Soap Lake, for experiments on their ability to distinguish red and pale specimens of *D. nevadensis*. In the laboratory, he presented each predator with one pale copepod and one red copepod and recorded which was taken. Repeated trials gave the following results: salamanders took the red individual first 68 percent of the time; damselfly nymphs took the red individual first 65 percent of the time; both performances were significantly greater than the 50 percent expected from chance. The behavior of both of these predators showed that they oriented to the prey by sight. The corixids were never seen capturing a prey, but did not respond to their presence in the same way as the other two predators. Their performance could be tallied, however, and they took red copepods first in 48 percent of the trials (not significantly different from chance). They obviously were not visual predators.

The results of predation experiments established a basis for selection against red color in Lake Lenore, leaving the question of why the copepods in Soap Lake were red. Following a suggestion by Griffiths et al. (1955) that carotenoid pigment protects organisms from photooxidation of sensitive molecules, Hairston exposed *Diaptomus nevadensis* in plastic tissue culture flasks to approximately the intensity of blue light reaching the surface of a lake in midsummer (first experiment), or that reaching the surface on a sunny winter day (second experiment). For each experiment he placed twenty copepods from Lake Lenore in each of four flasks, and the same number from Soap Lake in each of four flasks. The eight flasks were exposed to the artificial light from the side, and daily survival was recorded. Eight similarly arranged flasks were placed in a dark box as controls. The results (Fig. 7.8) leave no doubt that red copepods survived better, thus establishing a basis in natural selection for the conspicuous color where visual predators were absent or uncommon.

A similar situation was investigated by Luecke and O'Brien (1981). In the Toolik Lake region of Alaska, the copepod *Heterocope septentrionalis* occurs in two forms, a dark red form living in shallow ponds with no fish, and a pale green form in deep lakes with fish, especially grayling, *Thymallus arcticus*. They showed, with small enclosures placed in a lake, that grayling preyed more heavily on the red morph, and they showed that in small plastic enclosures immersed in wading pools, some shaded and some exposed to direct sunlight, red individuals survived better than green ones under both conditions, but shaded specimens survived better than did those in the direct sunlight.

Thus extended to include any form of conspicuous appearance, the

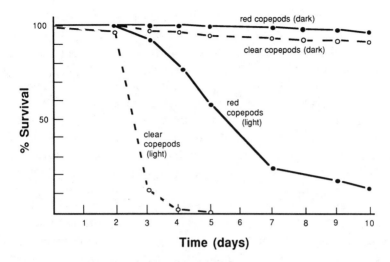

Figure 7.8. Survivorship of *Diaptomus nevadensis* with large (red copepods) and small (clear copepods) amounts of carotenoid pigment when exposed to visible blue light (450 nm) at peak summer intensity (1.6 mW cm^{-2}). (From Hairston 1976.)

size-selective predation part of the Brooks and Dodson theory has become well established. The size-efficiency part of the theory has met many difficulties. As already described in the work of Lynch (1978) and DeMott and Kerfoot (1982), larger species of Cladocera do not regularly win in competition with smaller ones, when put under more or less natural conditions. The experiments had different outcomes at different seasons (Lynch), or the species coexisted through food partitioning (DeMott & Kerfoot).

An alternative hypothesis, at least partly supported by experiments, is that small herbivorous zooplankton species are differentially eliminated from some lakes by invertebrate predators, especially *Chaoborus*, that have difficulty preying on large forms. Von Ende and Dempsey (1981) observed that among twenty-two lakes in northern Michigan, *Bosmina longirostris* was present in nearly all of the lakes supporting fish, but absent from those without fish. *Chaoborus americanus*, the third and fourth instars of which do not migrate to the sediments during the day, was absent from all lakes with fish. In those lakes, other species of *Chaoborus* were present. The fishless lakes had different plankton communities, but all had larger zooplankton species than did those with fish. Two kinds of experiments were conducted in small (0.95-liter) plastic containers suspended in a lake at a depth of 0.5 m. The first set tested for competition between the larger *Daphnia* and the smaller *Bosmina*. There were five replicates with both species present (initial density eight individuals each), four replicate controls starting with sixteen *Bosmina* alone, and three with sixteen *Daphnia* alone. After forty days, both species had achieved higher densities alone than in combination, but there was no evidence of competitive displacement. The second set of experiments tested for the effects of predation by *C. americanus* on *Bosmina*, *Daphnia*, and *Diaptomus*. For the first experiment, equal numbers (six) of *Bosmina* and *Daphnia* and two *Diaptomus* were exposed to three *Chaoborus* in each of four replicates for 48 h. The *Daphnia* and *Diaptomus* survived perfectly in both the experimental containers and in the four controls. *Bosmina* dropped to 0.5 per container in the experimentals, but survived perfectly in controls. The second experiment, run for 24 h, tested for the effects of size differences in *Daphnia* (three sizes) and *Diaptomus* (two sizes). Six individuals of each size, and six *Bosmina*, were exposed to three *Chaoborus* (five replicates). The results were similar to those in the first experiment. *Bosmina* were reduced to one-third the initial density; the remainder showed essentially no change. The third experiment exposed *Bosmina* and two sizes of *Diaptomus* to three *Chaoborus*, with results as before. The fourth experiment exposed *Bosmina* for nine days, while mimicking the migration of *Chaoborus* during the day to a location just below the lowest level at which *Bosmina* occurred naturally. Again, *Bosmina* was decimated in each of the three replicates while doubling in density in the controls. Von Ende and Dempsey considered that with sufficiently high densities of *Chaoborus*, *Bosmina* would be eliminated, regardless of any competitive effect of larger zooplankters. The experiments were properly replicated and controlled, and the results are convincing.

Experiments in ponds

There are several advantages associated with experimenting in ponds, as compared with lakes: It is possible in many cases to use the whole body of water, instead of having to attempt to isolate parts for manipulation; when isolation of parts is needed, ponds are more easily subdivided than are lakes; there have been several studies in which artificial ponds were constructed to be identical, providing for complex replicated experiments.

Density dependence in pond herbivores

Eisenberg (1966) is generally credited with the first properly designed field experiments in fresh water. He worked in a permanent pond near Ann Arbor, Michigan, and tested the hypothesis that the population of the pond snail *Lymnaea elodes* was regulated in a density-dependent manner. The species is an annual in the pond. It overwinters as immature individuals that grow to maturity (15–30 mm in length) by late spring. They reproduce during June and July; after hatching, they grow to a maximum length of about 4 mm before estivating as the pond decreases in depth and leaves their pond-edge habitat dry.

Eisenberg constructed a number of pens 0.91 by 4.57 m perpendicular to the shore and situated according to the results of a preliminary sampling program. In order to allow free access between the pens and the rest of the pond, the ends of the pens were not closed in until the start of manipulations. He used four replicates for each of these treatments: control, one-fifth the density in early June, and five times the early June density. The treatments were begun 10 June and completed 30 June, by which time the snails had matured and begun to reproduce. The populations in the pens were sampled with a coring device on four occasions: 7 July, 20 July, 27 July, and over a period in September and October. The results (Fig. 7.9) were conclusive. One week after the completion of the manipulations, there was already an inverse relationship between the number of adults introduced and the number of young snails in the pens, and this situation remained through the July samplings, although the differences among treatments were not significant at any sampling. Thus, reproduction and/or survival of young snails at least compensated for initial differences in density.

Eisenberg was surprised at the rapidity of response to manipulations in density, and he conducted an additional experiment on the effect of adding high-quality food. On 30 July, he distributed 283.3 g of frozen spinach over the still-inundated part of each of two of the pens that had not been used. The result was a dramatic increase (25-fold) in the number of eggs that could be found, and as Figure 7.9 shows, the numbers of young per pen were four to nine times those in the pens of the basic density manipulation, differences that were statistically significant. The conclusion was that it was the quality of the added food, rather than an initial absolute shortage, that brought about the result.

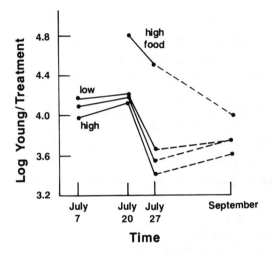

Figure 7.9. Relationships of numbers of young snails to treatments in the three sets in the basic design and the fed pens during July and in the fall. Numbers adjusted to a per-pen basis. The control set is unlabeled: high food = fed; low = reduced density; high = increased density. (From Eisenberg 1966.)

The population was food-limited in the classical density-dependent manner. The basic experiment had proper controls and adequate replication. In hindsight, it could have been improved by completing the manipulations before reproduction began. The food-addition experiment gave such dramatic results that complaints seem inappropriate, but, again, a start at the beginning of the season of reproduction would have been preferable.

Density dependence in predatory vertebrates

Competition among pond-dwelling vertebrates was investigated by Gill (1979) in a study of density dependence in the red-spotted newt, *Notophthalmus viridescens*. As part of a long-term study of these amphibians in a series of ponds in the mountains of Virginia, he removed nearly all of the newts from one pond and introduced them into a second pond, with the result that the first pond had a population only 1.26 percent as large as the original (16 of 1,274), and the second pond had a population 1.74 times the natural population (2,982 vs. 1,713). The populations in four additional ponds were kept as unmanipulated controls. The newts had been followed for several years prior to the experiment, and resident specimens were recognizable through

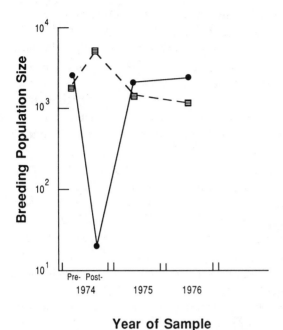

Figure 7.10. Total breeding population size for adult newts in a pond from which newts were removed (filled circles) and a pond to which the newts were added (squares) during and after the experimental perturbation in 1974. (From Gill 1979.)

individually different markings. Toe clips and foot removals were carried out for quick identification of the animals that were moved. Gill assessed the effects of the manipulations by changes in the populations in both ponds, by the survival of both sexes, and by changes in mean body weight in the two experimental ponds as well as in the control ponds. The results were dramatic. In the summer after the experiment, both ponds returned to near their original densities (Fig. 7.10). No such changes occurred in the control ponds. The changes were brought about by different processes for the two sexes. After remaining during the summer in the pond where they had been introduced, 348 of the 536 males that were recaptured the following year had returned to the pond from which they had been removed. This amounted to 32.3 percent of the 1,081 that had been transplanted, and 65 percent of the surviving transplanted males. Females survived poorly, but the survivors tended to return to their home pond with the same fidelity. Only 32 of the 695 (4.6%) that had been transplanted ever returned to their pond of origin, whereas 20 remained in the new location. Total survival was thus 7.5 percent. The low survival was observed for resident females in the overstocked pond. Only 11.9 percent returned from migration, compared with 46 percent in the control ponds. The return of the population in the depleted pond was brought about by increased recruitment. Nearly 96 percent of the breeding females in the following year were breeding for the first time, compared with 65 percent in the control ponds. The low survival in the crowded pond gave an opportunity to new females there also, as 80 percent of the breeding females in the second year were breeding for the first time.

Average changes in weight were mostly as expected. Females were especially sensitive to crowding. Normally, they lose weight during the summer, through deposition of eggs, whereas males gain weight in the same interval. Under normal conditions, this loss is made up in the autumn through oogenesis, which is apparently the first priority for food obtained then. Fat is apparently stored in the spring, after demands of oogenesis are met, and it is this fat that provides for survival during the next winter. Gill's interpretation of the low survival of females was that the crowding lowered the food supply during the period when fat would be deposited, bringing about an inadequate reserve for the next winter. Males, by contrast, gain during the summer period, and even the crowded ones obtained enough food to store some fat for the following winter.

This experiment provided good evidence that the newt populations were near the carrying capacity of each of the two ponds, and a plausible mechanism for the observed results was presented. As in so many experiments, however, treatments and ponds were confounded, and the elaborate statistical analyses should be viewed with caution, as far as the probability estimates are concerned.

Competition among pond-living predators

A series of experiments was conducted by Werner and Hall (1976, 1977, 1979) on the effects of competition among sunfishes of the genus *Lepomis* in southern Michigan. The propensity of sport fishermen to introduce species into habitats where they do not occur is well known and has resulted in a group of species that no longer have natural distributions. Thus, the experiments cannot be considered to relate to any initial conditions, but the results are interesting as a rare example of an experimental test of niche partitioning. Three species were used: *L. macrochirus*, the bluegill, *L. cyanellus*, the green sunfish, and *L. gibbosus*, the pumpkinseed. Michigan State University had con-

Table 7.4. *Percentage contributions of prey categories to the diets of the bluegill* (L. macrochirus), *pumpkinseed* (L. gibbosus), *and green sunfish* (L. cyanellus)

Prey	L. macrochirus	L. gibbosus	L. cyanellus
Species alone			
Vegetation dwellers	61	41	43
Benthic in- and epifauna	10	12	23
Open-water zooplankton	8	1	1
Other	21	47	33
Species together			
Vegetation dwellers	15	5	40
Benthic in- and epifauna	15	34	12
Open-water zooplankton	33	6	4
Other	37	55	44

Note: Based on dry weight and computed for the entire experimental period.
From Werner and Hall (1976), *Science* 191:404–6. Copyright © 1976 by the AAAS.

structed a number of circular ponds 29 m in diameter, with a maximum depth of 1.8 m. Nine hundred individuals of each species were introduced into separate ponds, and a fourth pond received 900 individuals of all three species, or 2,700 in all. Thus, the total crowding was three times as great in the fourth pond as in the other three. The fish were matched for size and introduced into the ponds in June. Samples of fifteen specimens of each species were taken a number of times from the ponds for determining stomach contents and growth rate. In October, the ponds were drained, and the fish were counted and weighed. Survival was not affected by crowding, but growth was reduced for all three species. Only *L. macrochirus* had its growth reduced in proportion to the crowding, however.

The most interesting result was the effect of the manipulation on where the different species foraged. The prey organisms could be assigned to one of four categories: those that were typical of the zone of emergent vegetation around the edge of the pond, those that lived on the bottom of the pond, those that were planktonic in the open water, and those that could be found in two or more habitats. Werner and Hall argued that the last category could be subdivided by the habitats of the more restricted species in a given stomach, although they reported them separately (Table 7.4). When alone in a pond, all three species took more prey from the zone of vegetation than elsewhere.

When crowded together, only *L. cyanellus* was able to forage effectively there; *L. gibbosus* altered its foraging to bottom fauna, and *L. macrochirus* took plankton more than species from other habitats.

The competitive superiority of *L. cyanellus* in the vegetation was shown in a second experiment in which the vegetation zone was fenced and subdivided into three equal parts of about 50 m², one of which was stocked with 500 *cyanellus*, one with 500 *macrochirus*, and one with 250 of each species (Werner & Hall 1977). For both species, survival was 5 percent better in the presence of the other species than with the same number of conspecifics; *cyanellus* had a higher survival under both conditions. *Lepomis cyanellus* grew 24 percent larger than *L. macrochirus* when each was alone and 44 percent better when they were together.

Two further experiments (Werner & Hall 1979) extended and confirmed the shifts to separate parts of the habitat when the species were crowded together.

These experiments can be criticized on one or more grounds. First, in all of them, replicates were omitted, again confounding the effect of treatment with interpond differences. Second, in two of the experiments the interspecific effect was confounded with general crowding. Finally, in the last experiment, in which macrophytes were removed, there was no control. Despite these shortcomings, the body of work does present a convincing case for niche partitioning in the presence of crowding competitors. In most treatments of the subject, niche partitioning is considered to be an evolutionary response to interspecific competition (Lawlor & Maynard Smith 1976; Roughgarden 1976). The present example makes the response a flexible one.

Predation in ponds

The use of initial conditions in assigning treatments to experimental ponds by Hurlbert and Mulla (1981) has been described in Chapter 2. They were interested in the effect of mosquitofish (*Gambusia affinis*) on the plankton community in small (4 × 6 m) artificial ponds in southern California. Twelve ponds, supplied from a common source, were used in an unbalanced design: five fishless controls, four with 50 fish added, and three with 450 fish. Zooplankton were monitored for nine months, August to May, and phytoplankton from October to May. After the introduction of fish, the only manipulations were the regular removal of macrophytes and the replacement of fish in two ponds after a mass kill, presumably from eucalyptus bark blown in. The fish reproduced so rapidly that the ponds became indistinguishable, and the authors presented their data as with fish present or absent.

There was an important effect on all elements of the plankton, except for cyclopoid copepods and the rotifer *Keratella quadrata*. The large crustaceans *Diaptomus pallidus*, *Ceriodaphnia* sp., and *Daphnia pulex* had significantly lower populations in the ponds with fish at nearly every sampling. In contrast, phytoplankton and the rotifers *Keratella cochlearis*, *Polyarthra* sp., *Synchaeta* sp., and *Trichocera* sp. were significantly more abundant in the presence of fish. The convergence of the fish populations, despite a ninefold initial difference, demonstrates density dependence (although this was not mentioned by the authors). If that had been appreciated initially, the unbalanced design might have been avoided. Otherwise, the separate statistical analyses for different dates are praiseworthy, especially as the results were clear without the need to use all of the data at once, as is possible with the statistical analysis known as the repeated-measures design (Freund & Littell 1981). The difference between five and three replicates for statistical analysis is dramatic, as shown by a comparison of this study with that of Hall et al. (1970), described later. Hurlbert and Mulla presented data for their individual ponds, thereby calling attention to the large amount of variation among replicates with the same treatment.

Interactions among the benthic animals of ponds apparently are more intricate than is the case with plankton. Gilinsky (1984) investigated the relationships among the level of predation by the sunfish *Lepomis macrochirus*, the complexity of the habitat, represented by artificial plastic "rope plants," and the trophic level of the prey organisms. She placed fiberglass window-screen cages, 2 by 3 m in dimension, in a shallow permanent pond near Chapel Hill, North Carolina. Half of the eighteen cages were provided with sixty artificial plants each, so as to represent heterogeneous environments. Each plant consisted of fifty lengths of polypropylene rope attached to a mesh base that was weighted with a small stone. Three cages were left without either fish or plants; three without plants had twenty fish added, and three had sixty fish added. The same numbers of replicates for the different fish treatments were applied to the cages with plants. All fish were seined from the same pond, and those introduced were chosen from the 40–60-mm size class. The experiment continued for twelve months after a six-week period of acclimation. At four-week intervals, a bottom sample was taken with an Ekman dredge from a randomly chosen location in each cage without plants. In each cage with high heterogeneity, a randomly chosen plant was lifted carefully, and the organisms were removed. The sediment below it was sampled with the dredge, and the plant was replaced.

As might have been anticipated, either from the increased heterogeneity or from the increased surface area, the species diversity was always greater in the cages with artificial plants, regardless of the presence or number of fish.

The remaining results would have been difficult to predict. During the fall and winter, the presence of fish had a significant positive effect on the mean density of the total of all macroinvertebrates in the bottom sediment. That was not true in spring or summer. A possible explanation came from the effect of fish on the predaceous Chironomidae. *Clinotanypus pinguis*, the dominant species, was strongly negatively affected by the presence of fish in all seasons, as were *Procladius* spp. during the fall and the rope-plant-dwelling predaceous chironomids during the summer. Herbaceous Chironomidae were positively affected by the presence of fish during fall and winter, but the situation was reversed during the summer. These data are for numerical abundance; the possibility that shifts in size classes were involved was not investigated. The remaining groups of macroinvertebrates were not influenced by fish in any coherent way, nearly all of the differences being nonsignificant. An obvious interpretation of these results, and the first offered by Gilinsky, is that by feeding on the dominant invertebrate predators, fish relieve their pressure on the herbivores, with the result that the total effect is to increase the numbers of macroinvertebrates taken as a group.

This experiment used a good, balanced design, with proper controls. The statistical analysis may have involved counts that were not strictly independent, because within a season there were some samples taken from the same cages, although care was taken not to repeat a location within a cage. Despite the potential shortcoming, the experiment revealed second-order interactions in an interesting way.

Combined effects of nutrients and predators

One of the first studies in replicated ponds was by Hall et al. (1970). Their ambitious plan was to investigate the effects of enrichment and manipulated levels of predation on both the characteristics of production and the structure of the zooplankton and benthos communities, thus uniquely combining two approaches to ecology that had been practiced in isolation. They made use of twenty square ponds on the grounds of Cornell University, Ithaca, New York. The ponds had been constructed to be as close to identical as possible. They were 1.3 m deep; each covered an area of 0.07 ha at the surface and 0.04 ha at the level bottom. They were supplied with water from a common source. Hall and associates used a randomized block design, with three levels of nutrient and two levels of predator density. For each combination of treatments, there were two replicates in each of three blocks, accounting for eighteen ponds. Two were left as unmanipulated controls. The highest nutrient level, 2.72 kg of commercial fertilizer per week (mid-June to late August), was set to be high enough to stimulate production, but not high enough to result in the anoxia that had characterized artificially fertilized fish ponds. The medium nutrient level was originally 0.23 kg per week, but measured concentrations could not be distinguished from those in the ponds without added nutrient, and the level was raised to 0.69 kg per week in the third year. During the first two years of work, invertebrate predators were seined from the low-predation ponds and added to the high-predation ponds. The predators were the hemipterans *Buenoa margaritacea, Notonecta undulata,* and *N. insulata* and several odonate species, including especially *Anax junius* and *Libellula* sp. All fed on both zooplankton and benthos. During the third year, the only predator used experimentally was the bluegill sunfish, *Lepomis macrochirus.* Half of the ponds were stocked with a controlled array of sizes of sunfishes at least 1 year old. The total amounted to about 3.3 kg per pond, an amount within the range of standing crops for ponds at comparable latitudes.

Chlorophyll *a* was measured weekly during the first season as an estimate of the standing crop of phytoplankton under the various treatments, and observations on primary production, measured as carbon assimilation using the ^{14}C technique, were carried out six times during the second season. For both measures, the high-nutrient ponds had levels approximately ten times those in the others, which were not significantly different from each other. Neither measure showed a significant difference between predation levels. The variability among ponds with the same treatment was surprisingly high: Standard errors ranged from one-seventh to more than one-third of the means.

Macroscopic plant abundance was determined in each of the first two years by series of seventeen transects out from the shore of each pond. In high-nutrient ponds, the dominant forms were the filamentous algae *Rhizoclonium* and *Spirogyra*; in low- and medium-nutrient ponds, *Chara* dominated, with *Eleocharis* a secondary dominant at the shore. Other species were of minor importance.

Inasmuch as the animal communities in the plankton and the benthos constituted the important response variables of the experiments, sampling of these elements was intensive. Two perpendicularly oriented sweeps with a plankton net, randomly chosen from nine possibilities, were made weekly in every pond. Each tow strained 1,870 liters. As the net was estimated to be only about 50 percent efficient, a doubling correction factor was used in comparing plankton values with those from the benthos. Seventeen species of Cladocera, ten species of Copepoda, and thirty-nine species of Rotifera were identified during the study. The size of each member of the first two groups was measured, and either direct dry weights or estimates from volumes were used in biomass analyses. Only the nine most important rotifer species were so treated.

Benthic organisms were sampled with an Ekman dredge. Three samples, the locations of which were chosen randomly, were taken weekly in each pond. In addition, emergent insects were collected twice weekly in emergence traps. Twenty-nine benthic invertebrate taxa were identified, with instars being recorded and dry weights determined. Eleven taxa of emergent insects were also recorded.

Despite the careful design and the replicate ponds constructed specifically to reduce variation of results, the data were too variable to yield statistically significant results in most cases. Hall and associates recognized the nonindependence of samples taken over the summer from a given pond and thus avoided temporal pseudoreplication. Much of the difference between replicate ponds came from the asynchronous histories of the populations. Thus, although similar events occurred, they could find no way to adjust the time scales so as to make legitimate statistical tests. An example of the variation within treatments is shown in Table 7.5, which gives the zooplankton production for the different treatments during the summer of the second year. It can be estimated that 95 percent confidence limits would include zero for at least some of the values. It is small wonder that differences were not statistically significant. They had been in the first year, but a change in sampling from day to night late in July apparently biased the data in favor of the high-nutrient treatment.

Even with the statistical problems in mind, it is difficult to resist the

Table 7.5. *Zooplankton production estimates[a] for summer 1966 and percentage contributions[b] of dominant species*

Pond[c]	Total production	*Ceriodaphnia*	Rotifers	*Simocephalus*
HN	4,756 ± 647	3,908 ± 525 (82)	349 ± 79 (7)	499 ± 251 (10)
MN	3,514 ± 578	2,972 ± 466 (85)	268 ± 83 (8)	274 ± 57 (8)
LN	3,925 ± 405	3,322 ± 427 (85)	146 ± 34 (4)	457 ± 60 (12)
HP	3,911 ± 343	3,283 ± 286 (84)	288 ± 67 (7)	340 ± 58 (9)
LP	4,218 ± 554	3,518 ± 483 (83)	220 ± 54 (5)	480 ± 164 (11)
HNHP	4,415 ± 680	3,658 ± 431 (83)	391 ± 114 (9)	366 ± 180 (8)
HNLP	5,097 ± 1,250	4,158 ± 1,062 (82)	306 ± 129 (6)	633 ± 514 (12)
MNHP	3,440 ± 462	2,857 ± 357 (83)	309 ± 154 (9)	274 ± 25 (8)
MNLP	3,586 ± 1,197	3,086 ± 961 (86)	227 ± 95 (6)	273 ± 126 (8)
LNHP	3,878 ± 705	3,334 ± 693 (86)	164 ± 61 (4)	380 ± 60 (10)
LNLP	3,970 ± 561	3,310 ± 657 (83)	127 ± 44 (3)	533 ± 92 (13)

[a]Mean ± s.e. (μg/l dry weight).
[b]Percentages shown in parentheses.
[c]H, high; M, medium; L, low; N, nutrients; P, predators.
From Hall et al. (1970).

impressions given by the graphic representations of the results. For example, the total zooplankton biomass was highest in both of the first two summers with the high-nutrient treatment (Fig. 7.11), as were the densities of the dominant planktonic crustacean, *Ceriodaphnia reticulata* (Fig. 7.12). For the same two statistics, levels were higher in the low-predator ponds than in the high-predator ponds (Fig. 7.13). Conversely, the rotifer *Keratella* had lower densities in high-nutrient and low-predator ponds. As already described for Neill's experiments, rotifers responded favorably to lowered densities of Cladocera, whether from the presence of predators on Cladocera or from the exclusion of *Daphnia*.

The change in type of predator from invertebrate to fish in the third year of the experiments gave much the same results, as far as the response of the plankton to nutrients was concerned. Fish predation, however, apparently had a much heavier impact on the population of *Ceriodaphnia* than was true of the invertebrate predators (Fig. 7.14). This resulted in a marked change in the plankton community, which was dominated by *Ceriodaphnia* under all other experimental conditions. With fish present, it became of almost negligible importance, and a large array of other species replaced it (Fig. 7.15). Thus, as far as the plankton was concerned, the fish acted as a classical keystone pred-

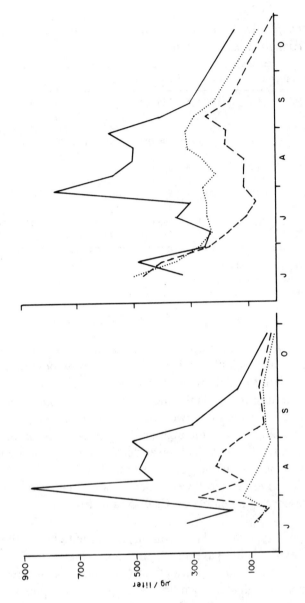

Figure 7.11. Mean zooplankton biomass at three nutrient levels in 1965 and 1966: high nutrient, solid line; medium nutrient, broken line; low nutrient, dotted line. (From Hall et al. 1970.)

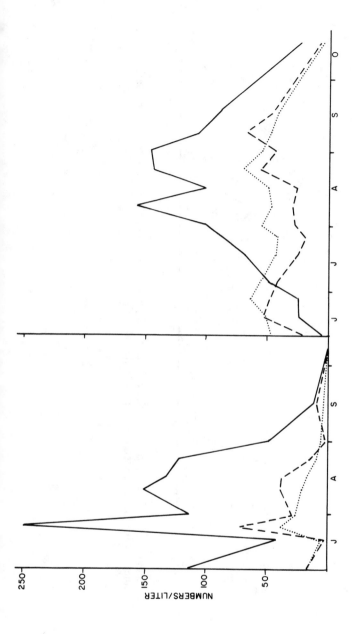

Figure 7.12. Mean densities of *Ceriodaphnia* at three nutrient levels in 1965 and 1966. Symbols as for Figure 7.11. (From Hall et al. 1970.)

241

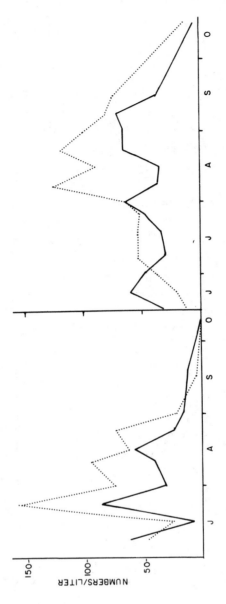

Figure 7.13. Mean densities of *Ceriodaphnia* at two predator levels in 1965 and 1966: high predation, solid line; low predation, dotted line. (From Hall et al. 1970.)

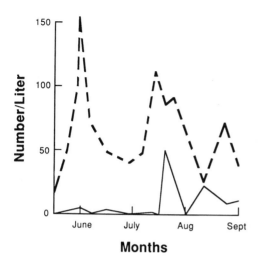

Figure 7.14. Mean densities of *Ceriodaphnia* in ponds with (solid line) and without (dashed line) fish in 1967. (From Hall et al. 1970.)

ator by drastically reducing the population of the competitive dominant. This result is in contrast to the effect of invertebrate predation on the plankton community. Although Figure 7.13 suggests an effect on the *Ceriodaphnia* population, the community composition changed relatively little compared with the effect of fish predation.

The benthos in ponds is relatively more important to the overall ecology than it is in lakes, and the effects of the experimental manipulations might have been expected to reveal at least as much about the benthic community as they did about the plankton. Unfortunately, two problems prevented the experiments from producing definitive results. The first, as with the plankton, was the variation among replicates, making interpretation of raw mean values hazardous (Table 7.6). The second was the inconsistent responses of the benthic organisms between the years. Over the first two years, this applied both to nutrient manipulations (Fig. 7.16) and to predator densities (Fig. 7.17). Hall and associates attributed this difference to continual changes in the macrophytes – an explanation that seems plausible, but being a posteriori, is exactly the questionable procedure that experiments are designed to avoid. Only further experimentation can determine the correctness of the explanation. Gilinsky (1984) has manipulated arti-

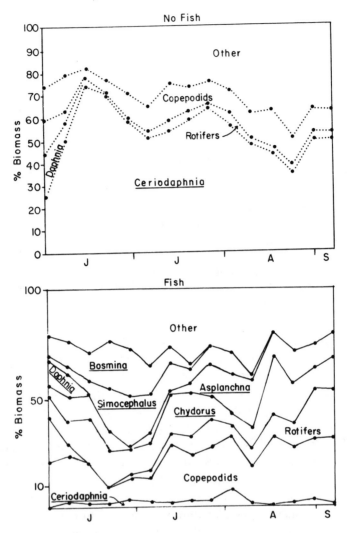

Figure 7.15. Mean percentage biomass contributions of dominant zooplankters in ponds with no fish (top) and ponds with fish (bottom). (From Hall et al. 1970.)

ficial macrophytes in an attempt to resolve some of the questions, as already described.

The third year yielded largely inconclusive results, as far as the benthos was concerned. The total production of benthic fauna was no more interpretable than it had been in the first two years, and fish pre-

Table 7.6. Chironomus tentans *production,*[a] *14 June–*
7 September 1967

Predation level	Block	Nutrient level		
		Low	Medium	High
Without fish	I	248.12	638.02	318.71
	II	141.08	88.91	144.16
	III	371.19	444.32	122.01
With fish	I	74.08	200.99	451.90
	II	46.50	85.96	91.59
	III	169.18	484.52	159.08
Average		175.02	323.79	214.58
Control: Pond 27, 55.88; Pond 34, 80.07				

[a] In milligrams dry weight per 232 cm^3.
From Hall et al. (1970).

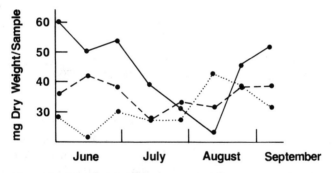

Figure 7.16. Mean biomass per sample of benthic fauna at three nutrient levels in 1966: high nutrient, solid line; medium nutrient, broken
line; low nutrient, dotted line. (From Hall et al. 1970.)

dation had no measurable effect. One of the most interesting results
was the clear and statistically significant relationship between the
growth of the introduced fishes and the nutrient level. This also produced a puzzle, as the authors were unable to relate the growth to production in individual ponds. Most of the stomach contents of the fish
were from the benthos, but as noted, the mean benthic biomass was
not affected by the presence of fish.

One must confess that these experiments did not produce results
commensurate with the careful planning and the large amount of effort
that went into their execution. The authors provided many plausible

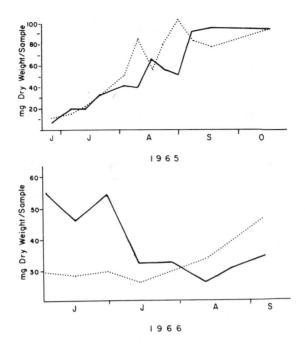

Figure 7.17. Mean total benthic biomass at two predation levels in 1965 (left) and 1966 (right). (From Hall et al. 1970.)

accounts, but the variation among replicates and the cumulative effects of the treatments, especially nutrient levels, largely defeated conclusive statements that could be supported statistically. Their experience has provided a wealth of cautionary information for anyone attempting experiments in ponds.

Experiments in large metal tanks

The most complex and sophisticated experiments that have been conducted out of doors are those of Wilbur and his students (Morin 1983a; Morin et al. 1983; Wilbur et al. 1983; Alford & Wilbur 1985; Wilbur & Alford 1985; Wilbur 1987). The experiments have tested for possible interspecific interactions among species of pond-dwelling amphibians and in some cases have involved species of planktonic crustaceans. Replicated pools were created in steel cattle tanks 1.52 m in diameter and 0.61 m deep. These were painted with epoxy to prevent leaching of toxic cations and were filled with about

1,000 liters of water. A nutrient base was provided each tank by the addition of 1 kg of air-dried litter from the margin of a natural pond, plus 50 g of commercial trout food and 20 stems of the macrophyte *Myriophyllum heterophyllum*. Carefully randomized collections of plankton were also added. Great care was taken to randomize the assignment of treatments to tanks. In most of the experiments, the tanks were placed in a hexagonal array and assigned to blocks, within which each treatment was represented at least once, thus eliminating differences between parts of the field in which the tanks were placed as a source of complication in the experiments.

The experiments were conducted on anuran tadpoles from temporary pond communities in the Sand Hills region of the coastal plain of North Carolina. Depending on the hypotheses being tested, three, four, or six species were chosen from the following array: *Rana utricularia* (= *R. sphenocephala*), *Scaphiopus holbrooki*, *Bufo terrestris*, *B. americanus*, *B. woodhousei fowleri*, *Hyla crucifer*, *H. chrysoscelis*, and *H. gratiosa*. When predation was one of the interactions investigated, the newt *Notophthalmus viridescens* was used, with or without larvae of the tiger salamander, *Ambystoma tigrinum*. The number of hatchling tadpoles introduced into each tank was stated to be realistic, as based on field surveys. In experiments where the strength of competition was being measured, the total number of tadpoles was varied over a factor of four. Not all species of frogs breed at the same time, and each species was introduced as it became available. The number of predators was varied according to the design of the particular experiment. They were introduced at the start of each experiment in which they were used.

The complexity of interactions in this community has been revealed in an elegant manner in these experiments. All of the hypothesized factors were shown to be statistically significant, although their relative importance varied considerably. In the first published study, Morin (1981, 1983a) used six species of tadpoles and four densities of newts, each newt density (0, 2, 4, and 8) being replicated four times. Without newts, *Scaphiopus* dominated the composition of metamorphs leaving the tanks, with *Bufo terrestris*, *Hyla chrysoscelis*, *Rana sphenocephala*, *Hyla crucifer*, and *H. gratiosa* following in declining order. Newt predation had a significant effect on the total number of tadpoles that were able to metamorphose (or to survive to overwinter as tadpoles in the case of *Rana*). There were two further results that were even more interesting. Predation had a highly significant effect on the relative

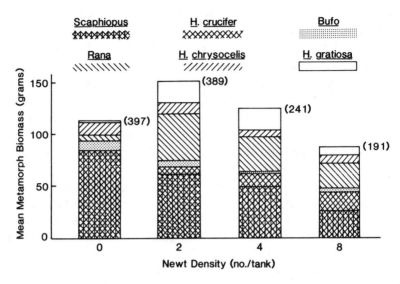

Figure 7.18. Mean biomass of metamorphs of each species censused from four replicates of each *Notophthalmus* density treatment. The biomass of each species is stacked to reflect the sequence of metamorphosis in each treatment (species metamorphosing first at the base). Numbers in parentheses indicate mean numbers of metamorphs contributing to total guild biomass in each treatment. (From Morin 1983b.)

abundances of the frog species at the end of the experiment. As the number of newts was increased, *Scaphiopus*, *Bufo*, *Hyla chrysoscelis*, and *Rana* declined in relative importance, and *Hyla crucifer* came to dominate the community at the highest newt density. *Hyla gratiosa* was never as successful as the other species, but performed best with intermediate densities of newts. Equally interesting was the interaction between competition and predation. Without predation, all species except *Scaphiopus* had, on the average, smaller individuals at the end of the experiment than they did in the presence of newts. Predation released the surviving tadpoles from the effects of competition, with the result that the extra growth by the survivors meant that the total biomass of metamorphs was greater at intermediate densities of newts than without them or with the highest density (Fig. 7.18). The observed changes in relative biomass were highly significant statistically.

In a separate experiment using *Ambystoma tigrinum* larvae, with and without newts, Morin found that only 13 tadpoles survived to metamorphosis out of a total of 7,200 introduced into six tanks. The experiment also revealed intraspecific density effects among newts.

The limits of repeatability were tested inadvertently in subsequent experiments. Wilbur (1987) showed that *Scaphiopus holbrooki* was again the competitive dominant in a four-species community of tadpoles and was selectively consumed by predatory newts. A spring drought during another experiment delayed anuran breeding, and the tanks developed a bloom of filamentous algae before the tadpoles could be introduced. *Scaphiopus* was unable to feed on that resource and did not compete well with *Rana sphenocephala, Bufo woodhousei fowleri*, or *B. terrestris* (Wilbur et al. 1983). Thus, initial conditions were important in these seminatural ponds. In this experiment, three densities of tadpoles (550, 800, and 1,300) were crossed with three densities of adult newts (0, 4, and 8). Competition was demonstrated in the tanks without newts. None of the responses, in terms of survival, was linear with density. Newt predation overwhelmed the system, and for quantitative assessment of its importance, lower densities would have to be used.

Despite the controllable conditions in these tanks, detection of effects was not always possible. Alford and Wilbur (1985) and Wilbur and Alford (1985) tested for "priority effects" in a system of three species of tadpoles (*Rana sphenocephala, Bufo americanus*, and *Hyla chrysoscelis*). The advantages of early establishment had been demonstrated in other systems, and the sequence of breeding by anurans in natural ponds suggested that similar effects took place there. *Bufo* and *Rana*, both early breeding species, were placed in the tanks reciprocally, each being present six days before the other, and each being placed alone at the beginning and six days later. All conditions were replicated three times. Mean mass at metamorphosis and duration of the larval period of each species were tested simultaneously by multivariate analysis of variance (MANOVA). The combined effect of the experimental manipulations on these two responses was assessed by principal components analysis. Survival to metamorphosis was assessed by standard analysis of variance (ANOVA). There were five statistically significant results among the sixteen reported. In both MANOVA and ANOVA, the performance of *Bufo* was affected by the time of its own introduction into the tanks, later introduction giving better results. The MANOVA for *Rana* was significant for the interaction between the time of its introduction and that of *Bufo*, as it did poorly when both species were introduced late. None of the statistical analyses of principal component 1 for *Bufo* revealed significance; two did so for *Rana*: It was affected by competition from *Bufo*, having a better performance where the latter was absent, and also performed better when it was put into the tanks after *Bufo* than before.

Hyla chrysoscelis breeds much later than the other two species. It was introduced into the tanks either sixty-eight or seventy-four days later than the other two, and after nearly all of the *Bufo* tadpoles had metamorphosed and been removed. The most interesting results of this experiment involved significant differences in the effects of both competitors between having been introduced sixty-eight versus seventy-four days before *Hyla*. Thus, very small differences in the timing of the introductions of *Rana* and *Bufo* were detectable through the impact on the performance of *Hyla* introduced more than two months later. The interpretation was naturally that there is a delicate relationship involving the timing of breeding by different species, and the mutual effects among them. These two papers suffer from what can only be called wishful thinking. In several places, effects are discussed as though they were real, when they were not significant statistically. The most obvious example: "In all blocks, size at metamorphosis was consistently larger and larval period was consistently shorter in the new than in the old communities, although these results were not statistically significant with the conservative test used" (Wilbur & Alford, 1985, p. 1109). The probability of the result being due to chance was .30, and most authors probably would not have reported it.

In all of the foregoing experiments, the tanks continued to hold water until the experiment was terminated. For most of the species, that was a questionable procedure, as they are temporary pond species. The problem was at least partly overcome by Wilbur (1987), who arranged an experiment in which some tanks held water continually, some were drained on a schedule that left them dry after 50 days, and some were dry after 100 days. The experiment also tested the effect of predation by newts and the effects of different densities of tadpoles. The initial introductions on 23 March were four newts or none, and 50 or 200 *Rana*. On 4 April, 65 or 260 *Scaphiopus* were added, and on 19 April, 200 or 800 *Bufo americanus*. The 50-day tanks had been drained and refilled by the time for the addition of 125 or 500 *Hyla chrysoscelis* (31 May).

All of the main factors (drying, newts, and density) and the two-way interactions between them had highly significant effects on the composition of the tadpole community. In the low-density tanks, newts virtually eliminated *Rana* and *Scaphiopus*, but their impact on the high-density tanks was negligible, indicating that they had been satiated early in the experiment, when the tadpoles were small enough to be eaten. *Scaphiopus* was the competitive dominant in the tanks without newts, especially at high density, where an average of 80.9 percent were recovered as metamorphs, versus maxima of 14 percent of *Bufo*, 10.7 percent of *Rana*, and 0.9 percent of *Hyla*. *Rana* was unable to complete development in any of the 50-day tanks, whether newts were present or not. It normally requires more time to metamorphosis than the other species, and the result is not surprising. The unexpected result was that correlation analysis showed that *Rana* had a strong positive effect on the performance of *Scaphiopus*. Wilbur suggested that in scraping periphyton from the sides of the tanks, *Rana* increased nutrients for the phytoplankton, on which *Scaphiopus* grows much better than on the periphyton. Inasmuch as *Scaphiopus* had a strong negative effect on all of the other species, *Rana* had a secondary effect in the same direction, over and above its direct effect, which was also negative.

These cattle tank ("mesocosm," according to Wilbur) experiments have revealed a wealth of information on the kind and strength of interactions in the amphibian assemblages introduced into them. The results point to possibilities of what can happen in nature, and to the degree that they incorporate a sufficient degree of realism, they suggest what does happen. A number of the interactions would have been difficult or impossible to demonstrate without the sophisticated experimental designs used, and moving from the seminatural tanks to natural ponds will require careful choices among less complex designs. Such work is needed in order to discover the effect of using samples of the natural frog communities (at most 6 of 17 species that have been heard calling on the same night at the same pond), the effect of a sample of the array of predators, and the importance of the vertical sides of the tanks.

Experiments in streams

Streams are perhaps as difficult habitats for experimenters as any that exist. The large array of substrates make one kind of challenge, and the huge variations in rates of flow constitute irregular disturbances that may easily destroy the best-planned experiment. Yet competition and predation are to be expected among the organisms in streams, and their relative importance should be known for an understanding of the ecology of stream communities, as they are for other kinds of habitats. Two parts of streams have received special attention by experimental ecologists: the community of animals living among the rocks in riffles, and one set of animals living partly on stream banks, but with larvae in the water, as are the adults of some species.

Insects in riffles

A straightforward test for density dependence among the insects in the interstices between stones in streambeds was conducted by Peckarsky (1979). She used cages of 0.81-cm wire mesh, except at the end, where the mesh could be set by changing a baffle set into a slot. The mesh used was set to allow colonization of the cages by the sizes of insects used in the experiments. Preliminary observations revealed the normal density of insects. Then, clean rocks were placed in the cages, and densities of insects were added to approximate the following: none, half the normal density, normal density, twice normal density, and three times the normal density. The cages with each condition were replicated three times, and the experiment was repeated three or four times in each different location or year. Each cage was buried in a riffle 10 cm under the surface, with the wide-mesh end placed facing either upstream or downstream, to test for colonization from the two directions. After an appropriate colonization period (three days in the first experiment), each cage was closed by a solid baffle and taken from the streambed. The insects were collected and preserved for laboratory analysis. Initial densities were subtracted from final densities to yield a net change. The median net change per cage, plotted against initial density, is shown in Figure 7.19. The results are clear. There was a significant negative relationship between the change in abundance and the initial density. The insects were able to detect and respond to the number already present in the cages. In the legend, "upstream" and "downstream" refers to the direction of movement of the colonists. For those moving downstream into the cages, Peckarsky believed that some were carried passively, because the cages also contained debris. The analysis has been criticized by Sell (1981), and corrected by Peckarsky (1981), but the qualitative conclusions remain unchanged.

Reice (1984, 1985) addressed the question of the effect of disturbance, as by spates, on the same kind of community. He sank thirty-

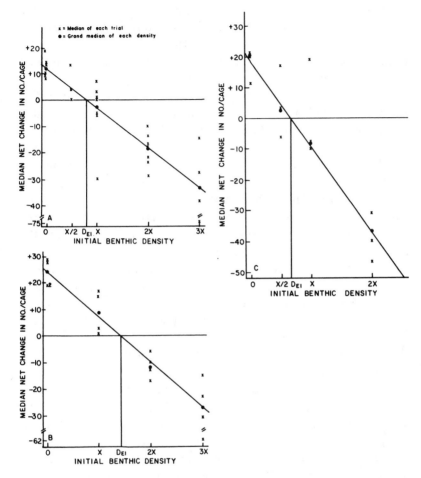

Figure 7.19. Median net change in numbers per cage versus initial benthic density: D_{EI}, equilibrium density; A, Otter Creek, upstream direction; B, Otter Creek, downstream direction; C, East River, upstream direction. (From Peckarsky 1979.)

two hardware cloth baskets (0.63-cm mesh) containing clean cobbles into the beds of riffles in a stream in Piedmont North Carolina. Three treatments were carried out. One set of twelve baskets ("D_1") was shaken for thirty seconds, and four of them were removed for tabulation of the fauna; another set of eight ("D_2") was shaken and not otherwise disturbed, and of the remaining set of twelve ("D_0"), four were removed for tabulation as controls. After two more weeks had elapsed, the sets of D_0 and D_1 were again sampled, the set of D_2 was again shaken for thirty seconds, four of were them removed for analysis, and a fresh set of eight clean controls ("C_1") was sunk in the streambed as further controls for the single- and double-disturbance treatments. The remaining baskets were removed after two more weeks, and the experiment was terminated.

As might have been expected, disturbance resulted in an immediate decrease in the fauna. This amounted to more than 60 percent, relative to the controls, for both the once-disturbed and twice-disturbed baskets. The proportional decrease was greater for the number of individuals than for the number of taxa, and the recovery of the number of taxa was complete in two weeks, whereas it was only after four weeks that the number of individuals had recovered to control levels. Reice pointed out that indexes of community similarity did not show a pattern over time between disturbed and undisturbed samples and that there was no indication of a distinct set of colonizing species. That seems to be a consequence of the necessity for all species in the riffle substrate to be adapted to unpredictable disturbances. The design of this experiment was adequate to show the effect claimed, and the sequential introduction of control baskets was an ingenious addition to allow for seasonal changes.

Even in such a disturbance-adapted community, interspecific interactions have been demonstrated experimentally. McAuliffe (1984) used experimental bricks to test for competition among grazers of periphyton in a stream in Montana. He took advantage of the fact that the numerically dominant grazer, the caddis fly *Glossosoma* sp., built heavy cases of sand and gravel and hence were unlikely to colonize new surfaces except by crawling, whereas other grazers could colonize the surfaces by drifting in the current. In a well-replicated design, he used rubber bands coated with Vaseline as barriers to crawling colonists for some bricks, and he placed those bricks and others randomly in rows in an unshaded riffle. Quantitative collections of periphyton after twenty-three days showed significantly greater densities on bricks that had been protected by the Vaseline barriers. Three other sets of bricks were treated as follows: "A" bricks had the rubber bands removed, and all insects removed without disturbing the periphyton; "B" bricks, which never had Vaseline barriers, had all insects removed; "C" bricks, also without Vaseline barriers, had all insects except *Glossosoma* removed. These three sets of bricks were returned to the stream within a few minutes, and colonization was allowed to proceed for 24 h, after which they were removed from the stream, and all insects were preserved for counting. The design allowed clear

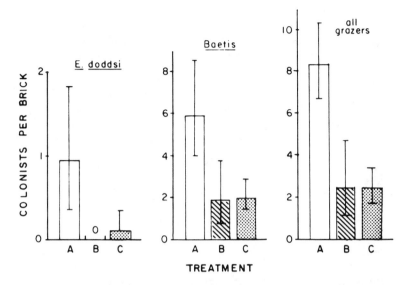

Figure 7.20. Short-term colonization responses to (A) high resource levels and absence of potential interference, (B) low resource levels and absence of potential interference, and (C) low resource levels and presence of potential interference from high *Glossosoma* densities. Vertical lines are derived confidence limits. (From McAuliffe 1984.)

choices among these possibilities: *Glossosoma* has no competitive effect on the other grazers (A = B = C); *Glossosoma* has only an exploitative competitive effect (A > B = C); *Glossosoma* has both exploitative and interference effects (A > B > C); interference is the sole competitive effect of *Glossosoma* (A = B > C). The results were unequivocal (Fig. 7.20). The A bricks, which had higher densities of periphyton and no competing grazers of any kind, had been colonized significantly more than the other two, which were statistically indistinguishable. Clearly, exploitation of the food resource by *Glossosoma* had a strong competitive effect on the other grazers, and interference was not detected. This result was at variance from those of Reice, but a consideration of the resource bases in the two streams helps explain the difference. Reice worked in a woodland stream, where the resource is almost exclusively allochthonous material from the surrounding forest. This arrives mostly in a short period in the autumn and doubtless is present in excess of demand by the (largely) shredding insects. McAuliffe's experiment was conducted in a sunny riffle, where the resource was periphyton, and the dynamics of the system could be expected to be different.

Streambank salamanders

Most aquatic faunas are thought of as ideally delimited by the edge of the water, in contrast to terrestrial systems, where the limits of communities and guilds frequently are arbitrary in practice. An exception to the neat separation of aquatic organisms concerns those that live at the edges of streams and use both streambed and terrestrial habitats, as well as aquatic ones. The example chosen is described here, rather than in Chapter 4 (forests), in order to emphasize the distinction between important forces in stream and forest ecology.

The salamander genus *Desmognathus* provides a good example of a group of species occupying the gradient from aquatic to terrestrial beside streams. The different but overlapping distributions of the species, in combination with other ecological differences in food and in size, have been interpreted as reflecting selection for reduced competition (Hairston 1949, 1973; Krzysik 1979). The alternative interpretation that increased terrestrialism reflects selection to avoid intrageneric predation has also been offered (Tilley 1968; Hairston 1980c). In the latter publication, I proposed an experiment to test the two hypotheses. The species involved were *D. quadramaculatus*, the largest and most aquatic (80–85% found in daytime refuges in the water), *D. monticola*, the next largest (41% in water, 48% within 1.5 m of the water, 11% farther away), *D. ochrophaeus*, smaller than *monticola* (11% in the water, 33% less than 0.3 m away, 46% 0.3–3 m away, and 10% 3–7 m away), and *D. aeneus*, the smallest species (9% between 0.3 and 1.5 m away from water, 13.6% 1.5–3 m away, and 77.4% more than 3 m away). If the larger ones preyed on the smaller ones, the hypotheses could be tested by removing *ochrophaeus* from some replicated plots, and *monticola* from others. If competition were the important interaction, removing *ochrophaeus* should benefit *monticola*; if predation were important, the experiment should not help *monticola*, and might cause the population to decrease, if *ochrophaeus* were an important food item. The same might also be true of the effect on *quadramaculatus*. Removing *monticola* should result in an increase in *ochrophaeus* under either hypothesis, but should help *quadramaculatus* only if the interaction were competition.

The experiment was conducted at the Coweeta Hydrologic Laboratory, an experimental forest in the Nantahala Mountains of North Carolina (Hairston 1986). Three small streams were selected as blocks, and one plot of each treatment (*ochrophaeus* removal, *monticola* removal, and control) was established on each stream. Each plot consisted of 10 m of stream, plus a strip 7 m wide on each side of the stream (see also Chapter 2). All plots were visited nine times in each active season, and each plot was searched three times on each visit during the last three years of the experiment. *Desmognathus ochrophaeus* and *D. monticola* were removed from the appropriate plots on each search, and all individuals of all species were recorded, with their locations on the plots.

The results of the experiment confirmed predation as the most important interspecific interaction in the guild. *Desmognathus monticola* started the experiment more abundant on plots from which *ochrophaeus* was to be removed than on the control plots. The difference was highly significant on a routine statistical test (ANOVA), and also on a much more conservative test. After the removals had gone on for four years, the difference was not distinguishable statistically. Thus, *monticola* definitely was not helped by the removal, and apparently declined in abundance. On the plots from which *monticola* was removed, *ochrophaeus* started slightly less abundant than on the controls. In both of the last two years, it was significantly more abundant than on the controls by ANOVA, and in the last year it was significantly more abundant on the *monticola*-removal plots by the more conservative test as well. This result was, of course, necessary for the success of the test, whatever its result. The effect of the removals on *quadramaculatus* was less clear, as the significance was confirmed only by ANOVA. In the last year, mean density on *ochrophaeus*-removal plots was lower than on the controls, and in the last two years, mean density was higher on the *monticola*-removal plots than on the controls. This last result was the only indication that competition was detectable in the guild.

Of almost equal interest was the failure of *D. aeneus* to respond to the removal of either *ochrophaeus* or *monticola*. The interpretation given was that its observed secretive behavior was an adaptation to predation by its larger congeners in the past.

The behavioral and physiological effects of the species of *Desmognathus* on one another were investigated by Southerland (1986a,b). He constructed enclosures of two types. The first were twelve circular arenas 0.5 m in diameter with screen lids. Each arena was provided with three kinds of substrate: large rocks (50 cm^2 surface), small rocks (10 cm^2), and small pieces of wood (10 cm^2), covering equal areas in random compass directions for the different arenas. He placed individual salamanders of each of four species (*D. quadramaculatus, D. monticola, D. fuscus,* and *D. ochrophaeus*) and each of three sex or age classes (adult male, adult female, and juvenile) into the arenas and replicated the observations twelve times, randomizing the assignments to arenas for each replication. The observations established the significance of differences of substrate choice. *Desmognathus quadramaculatus* was found associated with large rocks 67 percent of the time at night and 75 percent of the time during the day; *monticola* chose large rocks 47 percent of the time at night and 63 percent of the time during the day; *fuscus* chose wood 69 percent of the time at night and 61 percent of the time during the day; *ochrophaeus* chose wood 67 percent of the time at night and 83 percent of the time during the day. The figures are for all sex/age classes combined. Southerland then concentrated on *monticola*, which is intermediate both in ecological distribution and in size, in two experiments. Juveniles were paired in the arenas with a second juvenile *monticola*, with a *fuscus* of equal size, with an *ochrophaeus* of equal size, and with a *quadramaculatus* at least twice as long. Alone, juvenile *monticola* had chosen large rocks 58 percent of the time, and wood 25 percent. When with another juvenile *monticola*, the distribution was virtually uniform, 33 percent being associated with large rocks. With *fuscus*, the distribution shifted away from wood entirely, mostly to large rocks; when with *ochrophaeus*, the shift was toward small rocks, as it was with *quadramaculatus*, where only 25 percent of the juvenile *monticola* chose large rocks. Of the other species, only *fuscus* shifted away from its solitary distribution in these tests; it became more uniform than when alone. In a separate set of trials, adult *monticola* shifted toward a slightly more uniform distribution when paired together, and markedly away from large rocks when paired with *quadramaculatus*. For the second experiment, Southerland constructed four pens 3 m long and 1.7 m wide, oriented with one end in the stream and the other in the forest, so that each contained 1 m of water, 0.5 m of bank, and 1.5 m of forest floor. He placed five *monticola* in each pen and monitored the distributions within the pens for two weeks, then added five more and continued the monitoring for another two weeks. The average location, counting the stream end as 0 m, was 1.37 m in daylight and 1.65 m at night for five individuals, and 1.38 m and 1.62 m, respectively, for ten – virtually identical, and not different from the distribution of local unenclosed specimens. Southerland then added ten *quadramaculatus* to two of the pens and ten *ochrophaeus* to the other two. The presence of *quadramaculatus* caused a statistically significant shift to 1.60 m in daylight and 1.29 m at night; there was also a significant reduction of the number of *monticola* seen above the surface at night. There was no behavioral response to the presence of *ochrophaeus*. During these manipulations, each salamander was weighed, and whereas *monticola* alone gained 2.6–3.7 percent per week, comparable to free-ranging marked individuals, in the presence of *quadramaculatus* there was an average loss of 9.2 percent, and a loss of 7.0 percent when penned with *ochrophaeus*.

These ingenious experiments were well replicated and carefully controlled. They have added the dimensions of behavior and physiology to our understanding of this group of species.

Summary

Lakes, ponds, and streams are natural divisions in which to consider freshwater communities. Experiments in lakes make sense if the lakes are divided into those with low nutrient levels (oligotrophic) and those richer in nutrients (mesotrophic or eutrophic). Oligotrophic lakes are sensitive to the addition of nutrients, and the algae are so limited by the nutrient supply that they do not respond to the depletion of herbivorous zooplankton, which are in strong competition for food. Above that level, the composition of the community depends on the number of trophic levels present, with piscivorous fish having the effect of removing planktivores, to the advantage of the zooplankton. In eutrophic lakes, manipulation of the nutrient level is less effective, and the "top-down" system extends to the algae, which respond to the addition of piscivorous fish by decreasing, as a result of the increase of herbivorous plankton brought on by the decrease in planktivores.

In ponds, competition has been demonstrated almost universally among both herbivores and predators, as has the effect of predators on the composition of both plankton and benthos. It has been difficult to demonstrate an effect of adding nutrients. Large amounts are necessary, perhaps because much of the addition becomes bound to clay sediments.

Biological interactions have been demonstrated in streams, but generalizations about the stream community have not been successful, possibly because the sources of food differ in different streams, coming from allochthonous sources (leaf fall) in some and from photosynthesis by algae in streams in open country.

8

Experiments in marine environments

Introduction

Unlike experiments undertaken in terrestrial situations, or in lakes or ponds, the logical orientation in marine locations deals less with trophic position than with exposure to wave action and the nature of the substrate. Herbivory and predation do indeed play important roles in some marine locations, but producers, filter feeders, and sessile predators have been found to compete for space in various combinations, making the classical trophic level organization less basic to understanding the ecology of marine shores, where nearly all of these experiments have taken place.

The nature of the substrate has provided the most convenient basis for dividing experiments into groups, rocky shores and areas with soft sediments (either sand or mud) being the two principal types. All experiments on soft bottoms have taken place in protected bays or marshes, because it is not feasible to conduct experiments on wave-swept beaches.

Rocky shores

The favorite environment in which experiments have been conducted has been the rocky coast. For readers not familiar with rocky shores, such as those living south of New York on the Atlantic Coast of the United States, there are many books describing the habitats, such as Rickets and Calvin (1968) and the beautiful volume by Wertheim (1985). Here, there are vertical levels that may determine the possible array of species. At the highest level, the rock may become wet only because of breaking waves – not actually covered by the tide at all. Downward is the intertidal zone, which is covered by water part of the time; it can be subdivided on the basis of how high the location is with respect to the high or low spring tide, and by whether or not the spot is a vertical face or is more or less horizontal. In the latter case, it may contain tide pools that do not dry out, but are affected by waves at high tide. Some experiments have been conducted in the subtidal zone. Of necessity, they have been in protected areas such as bays or estuaries. An additional dimension is the latitudinal gradient. Intertidal rocks in the Temperate Zone tend to be covered with sessile species, either animals or plants, but in the tropics, rocks not covered with coral are much less richly supplied with obvious organisms. These dimensions really mean that the rocky intertidal is a complex of ecotones, and it is not surprising that "It depends" is a common answer to a request for an explanation of events.

Some experiments on rocky shores: competition for space

For many years it was axiomatic among ecologists that experiments were of necessity confined to the unrealistic domain of the laboratory. (It was traditional to ignore the work of foresters and other applied scientists who had been conducting field experiments throughout the twentieth century.) Thus, it was an exciting experience to read the early papers of Connell (1961a,b) and to realize that definitive results could be obtained from ecological experiments carried out in the field. It is true that Hatton had published his experiments on barnacles well before Connell, but they did not attract attention, and Connell is generally acknowledged to have demonstrated the feasibility of field experiments to ecologists. His work has been described in many textbooks and compendia. It is repeated here to show that good field experimentation is not solely a product of the last quarter of the century.

Connell worked with two species of barnacles, *Chthamalus stellatus* and *Balanus balanoides*, and a predatory snail, *Thais lapillus*, on an island in the estuary of the River Clyde in Scotland. *Chthamalus* adults were found between 0.95 m and 1.49 m above mean tide level (MTL); *Balanus* adults occupied the region from 1.56 m below MTL up to where they overlapped slightly with *Chthamalus*. As for nearly all sessile organisms in this kind of habitat, reproduction is by releasing reproductive products into the water. The larvae lead a free-swimming existence for varying amounts of time before they settle permanently on hard surfaces. *Chthamalus* larvae settle irregularly in autumn and may then be found from MTL to just above 1.49 m higher. Few if any of those settling below +0.95 m survive to adulthood. *Balanus* larvae settle in spring throughout the region between

−1.56 m and +1.49 m, and they tend to occur more regularly and in larger numbers than *Chthamalus*. The predatory snail *Thais* was present up to a line 0.67 m above MTL. Starfish were present, but only up to 0.76 m below MTL.

Connell's experiments were designed to test for competitive effects of *Balanus* on *Chthamalus* and for the effect of predation by *Thais*. He wanted to know why *Chthamalus* did not reach maturity in the lower half of the zone over which the larvae settled. Starting at 1.07 m above MTL, he searched for "patches" of *Chthamalus* and selected those whose density was at least fifty per 0.1 m². He could not find any such patches below +0.7 m, and to find out what happened down to −0.76 m, he used pieces of stone from higher levels with barnacles attached and screwed them to the rocks at appropriate levels. At each of nine levels, he marked two or four areas 10.7 by 8.2 cm by drilling holes at the corners. The position of each barnacle was recorded. He selected half of the marked areas by chance and removed all *Balanus* that were touching or "immediately surrounding" a *Chthamalus*. The remaining marked areas were left as controls. In the six locations where four areas were marked, one of each kind (with and without *Balanus*) was covered with 3.8-mm stainless-steel mesh screwed to the rock. This excluded *Thais* and was effective in keeping out predators, except at the lowest level, where starfish got into the cage.

From the standpoint of experimental design, the work had an excellent study of initial conditions (sixteen months of observations before the experiment) and controls at all tidal levels of both *Balanus*-removal and *Thais*-exclusion treatments. It was deficient only in replicates at all except one position, and in hindsight the overall results were so consistent that the lack of replicates does not prevent the results from being convincing.

At all levels below the zone where the adults of the two species overlapped (+0.95 m), removing *Balanus* improved the survival of *Chthamalus*, in most locations dramatically so (Fig. 8.1). In the area of overlap of adults, however, survival of *Chthamalus* was not affected by the removal of *Balanus*. In contrast, the exclusion of *Thais* had no effect. Connell's explanation was that the predator preferred large barnacles, and *Balanus* was the larger of the two species. Caging without removal of *Balanus* gave lower survival of *Chthamalus* than no caging. How, then, does the population of *Chthamalus* persist? Connell found, by following the survival of both species, that it resists desiccation better than *Balanus*, especially in calm, warm weather when there is no

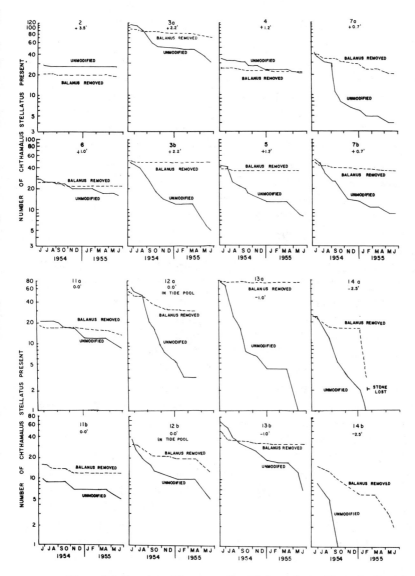

Figure 8.1. Survivorship curves for *Chthamalus stellatus* that had settled naturally (upper two rows) and on stones transplanted from high
levels (lower two rows). Areas designated "a" were protected from
predation by cages. (From Connell 1961b.)

spray from breaking waves. *Chthamalus* is thus able to occupy the higher levels in the intertidal, despite its weak competitive ability. The situation is reminiscent of the salamanders *Plethodon cinereus* and *P. shenandoah*, described in Chapter 4.

On the Atlantic coast of the northeastern United States, Menge (1976) investigated the effects of height on the shore, exposure to wave action, and slope on the outcomes of interspecific interactions (competition and predation) on two of the same species, *Balanus* and *Thais*. His objective measure of exposure to waves was the rate of loss of predator-exclusion cages. At Pemaquid Point, Maine, he lost 7.43 cages per 100 cage-months of exposure. At Little Brewster Point, the loss was 2.44; at Chamberlain, 1.58; at Little Brewster Cove, 1.20; at Grindstone Neck, 0.56; and at Canoe Beach Cove, none. Menge's design was somewhat different from that of Connell. He set up transects through the high and middle intertidal at each of the six locations. His measure of the natural distributions of the different species, and the natural changes in those distributions, was to count all organisms in each of ten randomly placed quadrats, 0.5 m square, at both high and middle intertidal levels. In the high intertidal, the barnacle *Balanus balanoides* occupied more than three-fourths of the area, except in the protected locations, where half or more of the area was bare. At the midintertidal levels, the mussel *Mytilus edulis* occupied most of the space on exposed sites and was replaced by bare rock in protected sites. Except for encrusting algae and lichens, no other species held an appreciable amount of primary space.

Menge's technique was to clear experimental areas with a scraper and wire brush. Within each area, he placed one stainless-steel mesh cage 10 by 10 by 3 cm to exclude the predatory snail *Thais* and one 10 by 10 cm "roof" to control for the effect of shading. In some experimental areas he added cages in which all *Mytilus* or all *Balanus* were removed as they appeared. He left one equal area bare as a control. He thus had two kinds of controls – the transects, where the natural situation was observed, and the cleared controls, where the return to the natural state could be compared with the results of the other manipulations. In each location he had more than one experimental area. His results were reported as typical examples of these areas, rather than incorporating statistical measures of variability.

In the high intertidal on exposed sites, the results of all manipulations were the same as for the controls: Barnacles came to occupy all of the space (Fig. 8.2). In the midintertidal on exposed sites, *Balanus*

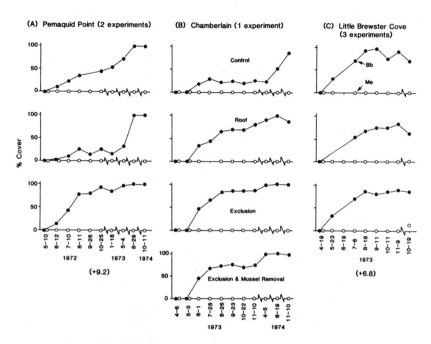

Figure 8.2. Three long-term (>1 yr) high intertidal experiments on horizontal or inclined substrata. Results in this and Figures 8.3 and 8.4 are typical examples selected from all experiments done at an area. The number of experiments of each type at each area is given in each figure. Results on horizontal and inclined substrata were similar. No mussel-removal cages were included in experiments initiated in 1972. Intertidal levels are given in feet above mean low water to conform with conventional treatment of tidal levels. To convert to meters, multiply by 0.3048. Species codes are Bb = *Balanus balanoides* and Me = *Mytilus edulis* in this and Figures 8.3 and 8.4. Breaks in abscissa indicate periods over which little change in barnacle or mussel abundance occurred. (From Menge 1976.)

first colonized the areas, but eventually it was replaced by *Mytilus*, except where that species was removed systematically (Fig. 8.3). Predation was shown to be important in the most protected areas at the midintertidal level. In the predator-exclusion cages, events were much the same as on exposed sites – *Balanus* was the first colonist, but was replaced by *Mytilus*. On control plots and under roofs, *Balanus* colonized the plots, but was eventually reduced to insignificance through predation by *Thais* (Fig. 8.4). Where predators were excluded and mussels were removed, the barnacles came to occupy all of the space.

Menge's experiments were well planned and executed, and there

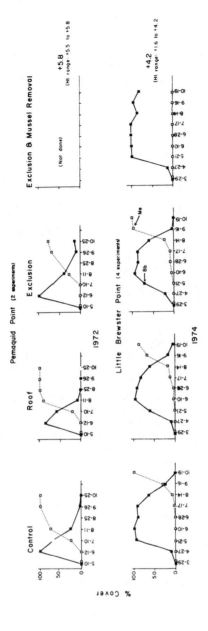

Figure 8.3. Examples of short-term (5–7-month) midintertidal experiments. Number of experiments of this type at each area is indicated in parentheses. (From Menge 1976.)

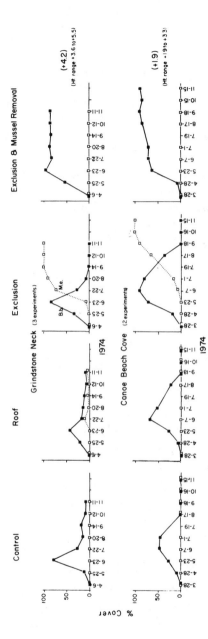

Figure 8.4. Examples of short-term (7-month) midintertidal experiments on horizontal or slightly inclined sub-strata at two relatively protected areas. Number of experiments at each area is shown in parentheses. Note that the time scales vary. (From Menge 1976.)

were excellent controls. Although replicate experiments were conducted, the selection of some as "typical" examples introduced an unnecessary element of subjectivity into the reporting of results. The experiments gave convincing results in revealing the conditions under which competition or predation was important in determining the species composition and degree of cover.

Many experiments on animals and plants of rocky shores have involved removals of one or more species – either singly or by scraping replicated areas (e.g., for interspecific competition) (Dayton 1971; Black 1979; Taylor & Littler 1982). Harger (1972) took a different approach in his experiments on competition between two species of mussels, *Mytilus edulis* and *M. californianus*, on the coast of southern California. The two species have different distributions, *M. californianus* being typical of the outer coast, exposed to maximum wave action, and *M. edulis* being typical of quieter water. They overlap along the exposure gradient.

The location of Harger's experiments was a large pier near Santa Barbara, California. The pier was supported by 340 H-beam steel pilings, 23 cm on a side. Clumps of mussels were present on the pilings over a vertical range of 2.1–2.75 m, and ranging in size from a few individuals up to 5.2 m in circumference. The largest clumps consisted of a thickness fourteen or more mussels deep. One-third of the pilings supported pure *M. californianus*; one-third had a mixture, with 10–50 percent being *M. edulis*; and one-third had no mussels. Dissection of the clumps revealed that on the inside there were many empty shells of *M. edulis*, and a number of specimens with heavy, twisted shells. There were no empty shells of *M. californianus* inside the clumps, although some showed evidence of being forced against each other. The observations suggested that *M. edulis* settled on the outside of clumps and became covered and crushed by subsequently settling *M. californianus*.

Harger's experiments were carried out in cylindrical hardware cloth cages 21.6 cm long by 17.8 cm in diameter, with five replicates for each condition. He used the same size distribution of ninety specimens in each cage. Each species was established separately, as well as being in equal mixture. Originally, some had each species on the outside and the other on the inside of the mixture, but he found that small *M. edulis* moved to the outside in all cases, and the mixtures became identical. The cages were hung from the pier at high and low intertidal levels, the single-species cages being also placed at the midintertidal level.

The experiment was partly repeated by suspending cages from floats in Santa Barbara harbor: mixed populations, and each species alone.

Responses to the competitive situation were assessed as growth and survival. As far as growth was concerned, both species grew better at the pier than in the harbor; both grew better at the low intertidal level than at the high; and both grew better on the outside of clumps than inside. *Mytilus edulis* grew better in mixed clumps than did *californianus*, and better than in pure *edulis* clumps. *Mytilus californianus* suffered more from self-crowding than from *edulis*. *Mytilus edulis* suffered more from crowding by *californianus* than from self-crowding within the clumps.

As far as survival was concerned, *californianus* survived much better than *edulis* at the pier; *edulis* survived much better than *californianus* in the harbor, where the latter inside clumps became smothered by silt (remember that *edulis* crawls to the outside of clumps). *Mytilus californianus* survived better in mixed clumps at the pier; *edulis* survived better in pure clumps at the pier; and *californianus* survived better in pure clumps in the harbor.

Harger's conclusion was that the traits that made for success in competition were adaptations to the physical environment (heavy shells of *californianus*, crawling to the outside of clumps by *edulis*), not adaptations to the presence of the other species. He argued that the environment provided a sufficient variety of conditions to permit coexistence at the area level, but not in all cases at the local level. The experiments were ingenious and were well controlled and replicated. It can be argued that the use of cages introduced an element of unrealism, but the events in the cages were easily reconciled to the observations made in dissecting the clumps of mussels. Perhaps the weakest part of the study was the initial evidence that the two species competed, inasmuch as one-third of the pilings at the pier were unoccupied, showing that space was not limiting, unless there was some unidentified feature of the exact space where the mussel clumps occurred.

An extensive set of experiments on competition among species of macroalgae was conducted by Sousa (1979). He incorporated a test of some theories of how succession works. Sousa's experiments were carried out in a boulder field west of Santa Barbara, California. The boulders, which were of various sizes, supported a thick growth of macroalgae: the green alga *Ulva* and a number of species of red algae, the most important ones being *Gigartina canaliculata*, *G. leptorhynchos*, *Geli-*

dium coulteri, and *Rhodoglossum affine*. Storms overturned some of the boulders, depending inversely on their sizes, and created either bare patches or, if the boulder remained upended, a completely clear surface. Sousa's first problem was to discover the natural sequence in the recolonization of the bare surfaces. He was unable to locate enough similar boulders for properly replicated experiments, and he substituted concrete blocks. He started with six replicates per set, but some were washed away, leaving a minimum of four per set.

The results (Fig. 8.5) show the importance of knowing initial conditions. The green alga *Ulva* was the first to occupy the surfaces of the blocks, but the length of time that it remained dominant depended on when the observations were started. The only early competition was from the barnacle *Chthamalus fissus*, which disappeared within six months. Eventually, the red algae appeared on the blocks. Unlike *Ulva*, which reproduced year-round, these species produced settling sporelings only in the fall and winter, and even so, success was irregular, being better in 1974–5 than in the next year. *Ulva* lost ground when winter conditions caused it to become defoliated, permitting the red algae to become established. The final outcome was apparent only on the blocks exposed first in September. *Gigartina canaliculata* came to occupy more than half of the space by the end of the observations in March 1977. *Ulva* had virtually disappeared from those blocks a year previously. On the blocks exposed in January 1975 or May 1975 it experienced a crash between August and October 1976. To summarize these observations, the sequence was *Ulva* first, followed by *Gelidium*, *Gigartina leptorhynchos*, and *Rhodoglossum*, these three being replaced by *Gigartina canaliculata*.

Sousa conducted several experiments to discover the mechanism of the sequence. He pointed out three theories that might account for succession. The first was what he called the facilitation theory, early colonists making the area suitable for colonization by other species, which are then better able to hold the space than were the pioneers. A second theory was that later-arriving species grew up through the canopy of the pioneers and displaced them through shading or some other competitive mechanism. The third theory was that the pioneers were better at colonizing, but less able to withstand external sources of mortality than were later-arriving (and less successful colonizing) species.

Superior competitive ability by *Gigartina* was denied by an experiment in which he removed *Ulva*. *Gigartina* (both species combined, because they were not distinguishable as small sporelings) was much

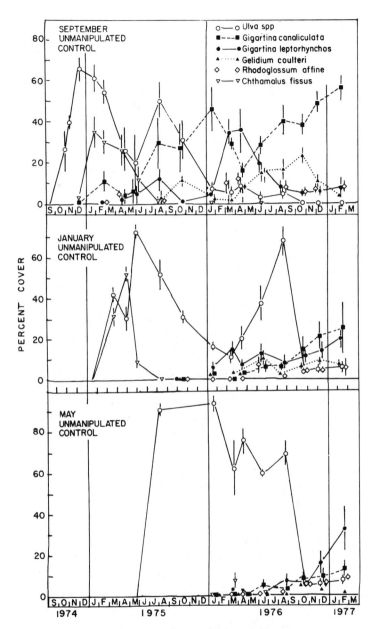

Figure 8.5. Mean percentage cover of algae and barnacles that colonized unmanipulated concrete blocks. Sets of blocks were established in September 1974, January 1975, and May 1975. The mean (±s.e. of the mean) for four to six blocks in each set is indicated. Only species that held an average of at least 5% cover at some sampling date are included. (From Sousa 1979.)

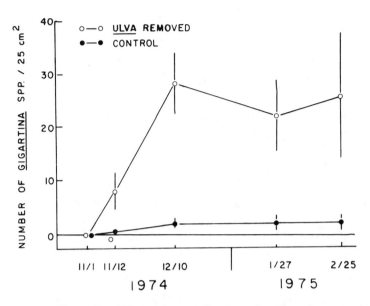

Figure 8.6. Effects of manually removing the early successional species, *Ulva*, on the recruitment of *Gigartina* spp. over a 4-month period from 15 October 1974 to 25 February 1975. Data are mean numbers of *Gigartina leptorhynchos* and *G. canaliculata* sporelings that recruited to four 25-cm² plots on concrete blocks from which *Ulva* was removed and four on which it was left undisturbed. The two species of *Gigartina* are indistinguishable to the unaided eye when less than 0.5 cm tall. The mean (±1 s.e. of the mean) is indicated. (From Sousa 1979.)

more successful than on uncleared plots on concrete blocks (Fig. 8.6). In the reverse experiment (Fig. 8.7), overhanging canopy of *Gigartina canaliculata* inhibited colonization by *Ulva* or anything else until severe conditions in the winter of 1975–6 caused defoliation of *G. canaliculata*. Removal of the "middle successional species" from areas where they were temporarily dominant resulted first in a spurt by *Ulva*, followed by an increase in cover by *G. canaliculata*. Sousa concluded that the facilitation model of succession did not apply in this case, because each stage inhibited recruitment by the next. He also pointed out a lack of evidence that later-arriving species grew up through the existing canopy and outcompeted the pioneers.

To test the third theory, he marked thirty individuals of each of five species (*Ulva, G. leptorhynchos, Gelidium, Rhodoglossum,* and *G. canaliculata*) and followed their survival through the physically harsh

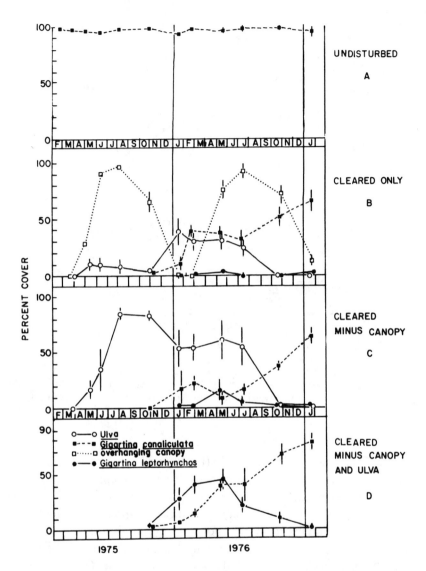

Figure 8.7. Effects of various manipulations on the recruitment and growth of algae in 100-cm² plots cleared in solid beds of *Gigartina canaliculata*. Sixteen plots were cleared in February 1975, and five others were left undisturbed. Eight of the cleared plots were not further manipulated. In four others the overhanging canopy of surrounding adult *G. canaliculata* plants was kept cut back, and in the remaining four, both this canopy and the *Ulva* that recruited into the plots were removed. Data are mean percentage covers of algae in the plots and of the overhanging canopy. The mean (±1 s.e. of the mean) is indicated. All limpets and chitons that recruited into the plots were removed at each sampling date. (From Sousa 1979.)

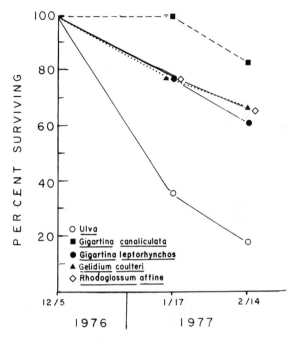

Figure 8.8. Survival curves for five species of algae over a 2-month period from 5 December 1976 to 14 February 1977, when low tides occurred in the afternoon, creating harsh physical conditions. Thirty plants of each species were tagged on the initial date. (From Sousa 1979.)

period starting in December 1976 (Fig. 8.8). *Ulva* had much the highest loss rate. Three middle successional species were approximately alike and died faster than *G. canaliculata*. This last species forms low-lying perennial turfs and, moreover, reproduces by spreading vegetatively. Thus, once established, it does not need to wait until sporulating season to take space where another plant has died. Figure 8.7 shows that neither keeping the canopy cut back nor removing the *Ulva* that settled made any difference in the rate at which *canaliculata* recovered the plots.

Sousa concluded that succession is a matter of ability to survive better and retain space against a superior colonizer that survives poorly, either in adverse weather or in the face of grazing. He was not alone in tending to extrapolate his conclusions beyond his system. It should be noted that in Menge's experiments, as described earlier, the facilitation model was at work in the midtidal zone, where barnacles had to settle first before mussels could attach satisfactorily. The mussels then supplant the barnacles (Figs. 8.3 and 8.4).

Some experiments on rocky shores: herbivory

Both microalgae and macroalgae are grazed on rocky shores, and two experiments on these effects were reported at the same time as Connell's papers – one of them, by Castenholz (1961), in the same issue of *Ecology*. The second was by Kitching and Ebling (1961); it is described later in conjunction with other experiments on macroalgae.

Castenholz acknowledged Connell's help in designing his experiments; so he obviously conceded the priority. The work was conducted on the coast of Oregon and was stimulated by the observation that the rock in the high intertidal was coated with diatoms during winter, but was mostly bare in summer. Removal of all organisms from an area in summer resulted quickly in the development of a diatom "slick." The experiments were carried out in two situations: a bench into which Castenholz chiseled six square basins 24 by 24 by 4.5 cm to serve as uniform tide pools, and a vertical rock face on which he fixed two rows of four hardware cloth cages 15 by 15 cm. In the most carefully conducted experiments, snails of the genus *Littorina* were collected in nearby natural tide pools and caged under hardware cloth in some pools; other pools were similarly caged without snails. The series of experiments involved different densities of snails, which he recorded as total volume. His results, shown in Figure 8.9, showed that a snail volume of $0.2–0.25$ cm^3 dm^{-2} was sufficient to keep the pools clear of any diatom mat, whereas the control pools developed thick mats. Lower densities gave an approximately linear effect on the diatom cover. The natural density of snails usually was two to three times as great as that necessary to keep the pools clear. On the vertical rock face, similar experiments with limpets of the genus *Acmaea* gave similar results. The designs of these experiments were not always perfectly balanced, but there were adequate controls and replicates. There is little room for debate over the results.

The demonstration that diatoms are kept at very low densities by gastropods suggested that the latter are limited by the food supply and that where two or more species cooccur, they should be in competition. That hypothesis was tested by Haven (1973), who worked with two

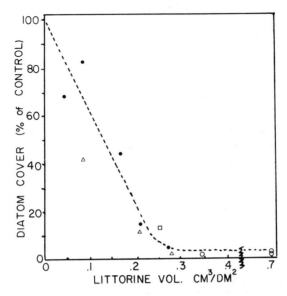

Figure 8.9. Relationship between total littorine volume (not individual volumes) and the amount of diatom cover developed. In all cases, littorines were introduced into bare, sterilized pools. The dashed line is for guidance. Different symbols represent separate experiments. (From Castenholz 1961.)

species of limpets, *Acmaea digitalis* and *A. scabra*, on the coast of northern California. They overlap in distribution on the rocks, but there are differences: *A. digitalis* is more abundant on vertical surfaces, *scabra* on horizontal ones; *digitalis* occurs higher in the intertidal zone than does *scabra*; and *digitalis* increases in relative abundance with greater wave action.

Haven's experiments involved setting up fenced plots 20 by 40 cm, one for each of these conditions: *A. digitalis* removed, *A. scabra* removed, and both species removed. He also marked many individuals that were outside the experimental areas to serve as completely unmanipulated controls. The design is given in Table 8.1. Experiments 1 and 2 are straightforward, but experiment 3 requires some explanation and illustrates the kind of problem that can arise in field experimentation. The difficulty involved the spontaneous reduction in numbers of *A. digitalis* in plot C, where *A. scabra* was removed. The second start of plots C and D was inspired by this decrease.

Table 8.1. *Experimental procedures and limpet numbers in plots*

Exp. no.	Plot	Dates	Treatment	Species	No. of limpets per plot		
					Initial	Avg.[a]	Final
1	A	Oct 63–	A. scabra	scabra	32	—	—
		May 64	removed	digitalis	15	16	18
	B	Oct 63–	A. digitalis	scabra	28	33	36
		May 64	removed	digitalis	21	—	—
	C	Oct 63–	Control, both	scabra	50	52	52
		May 64	present	digitalis	20	24	26
2	A	Jan 64–	Control, both	scabra	11	11	9
		May 65	present	digitalis	11	11	11
	B	Jan 64–	A. digitalis	scabra	13	12	12
		May 65	removed	digitalis	5	—	—
	C	Jan 64–	A. scabra	scabra	9	—	—
		Aug 65	removed	digitalis	5	5	5
3	B	Aug 64–	A. digitalis	scabra	12	11	10
		Jan 66	removed	digitalis	31	—	—
	C	Aug 64–	A. scabra	scabra	16	—	—
		Jan 65	removed	digitalis	25	23	16
	D	Aug 65–	Control, both	scabra	14	13	13
		Jan 65	present	digitalis	19	23	23
	C	Jan 65–	A. digitalis	digitalis	11	10	9
		Jan 66	reduced				
	D	Jan 64–	Both reduced	scabra	6	5	5
		Jan 66		digitalis	6	6	6

[a] Average of all counts during the experiment.
From Haven (1973).

Haven measured the results of competition as growth of limpets in the fenced plots. In experiment 1, *A. scabra* came to have an average size that was larger on the plot from which *digitalis* had been removed than on the control plot, apparently significantly so. *Acmaea digitalis* increased in size on the *scabra*-removal plot relative to the control, but to a lesser degree. Experiment 2, in which the control and *scabra*-removal treatments were reversed, showed the difficulty arising from not having replicates. *Acmaea scabra* then showed a much smaller increase in size relative to the control than it did in experiment 1, and *digitalis* began larger on the *scabra*-removal plot than on the control, a condition that remained unchanged throughout the experiment, which thus failed to repeat the results. Trying a third time only made matters worse. In that case, *digitalis* grew faster on the control plot than it did on the *scabra*-removal plot, a result that Haven attributed to the already noted spontaneous decline on the experimental plot. To compensate for this, he removed some specimens of both species from the "control" plot – "control" now in quotes because it had been manipulated. There was a slight increase in size relative to the control, but intraspecific crowding is an equally plausible explanation.

My conclusion from this work is that *A. scabra* is probably influenced by *digitalis* in interspecific competition, but more work needs to be done before the relationship between the two species can be stated with confidence. Replication and, above all, better understanding of the natural history of *A. digitalis* would have improved matters. Differences (explained after the fact) between the homing tendencies of the two species would have led to more convincing results (*A. digitalis* has a home range much larger than the experimental plots). The assessment of competition involved pseudoreplication, because using the sizes of individual limpets to establish within-treatment variation involved between-location differences as well.

Competition for algae suggests the possibility of another common adaptation – the phenomenon of territoriality. Stimson (1970, 1973) carried out experiments in California to explore the possibility. *Lottia gigantea*, the owl limpet, reaches 8 cm in length – huge for a North American limpet. Where it is found in the high to midintertidal zone, its presence is obvious from areas densely covered with algae, where the rest of the rock surface is bare or nearly so. In Stimson's experience, such areas always had a *Lottia* present. When he removed the limpet, the algae-covered area quickly lost its character and approached the condition of the rest of the rock surface. He could distinguish the marks of the radulas (scraping mouth parts) of *Lottia* from the smaller ones of other limpets, and he observed that the algal mats showed only the former type unless he removed the resident.

Stimson counted the numbers of *Acmaea* (smaller limpets) in quadrats that did and did not contain the algal mats. The results are shown in Table 8.2. He also tried removing all limpets from caged areas, and he found that algal mats formed quickly. An experiment on the effect of the presence of *Lottia* on the number of *Acmaea* involved the removal of *Lottia* from three replicates, the addition of *Lottia* to three apparently suitable areas where there had been none, and three control areas where the resident *Lottia* were left in place. The results were as

Table 8.2. *Comparison of quadrat counts of* Acmaea/930 *cm² inside and outside territories on 12 April 1965 (three different reefs)*

Area	No. of quadrats	Avg. no. of *Acmaea*	s.d.	Welch's *t* stat.	Signif. (*p*)
Reef 5					
Inside	6	3.17	1.72	6.50	<.01
Outside	12	17.83	7.39		
Reef 8					
Inside	6	4.17	4.40	5.19	<.01
Outside	12	21.00	9.33		
Reef 11					
Inside	6	3.00	2.61	7.97	<.01
Outside	12	19.50	6.15		

From Stimson (1970).

expected. *Acmaea* quickly became abundant in all three areas where *Lottia* had been removed, but disappeared from the areas where *Lottia* had been added. The controls had virtually none.

The most interesting aspect of this work was the direct behavioral experiments. When Stimson put an *Acmaea* in a position where it was touching a *Lottia*, the latter went into a highly specific behavior pattern, the result of which was the dislodging of the *Acmaea*, which was washed away with the next wave, or, if it was not washed away, the attack was continued until the *Acmaea* was pushed out of the algal mat. Stimson also experimented with other potential competitors for space (the anemone *Anthopleura* and the mussel *Mytilus*). In both cases, he observed the same pushing behavior. He also watched intra-specific encounters, which had the same result. This was an apparently genuine case of territoriality.

Macroalgae have a role in the marine environment very different from that of the microalgae, herbivory on which has just been described. Some of the macroalgae, as seen from the work of Sousa, are long-lived organisms, capable of holding primary space for a long time. By creating two conditions, they have a strong influence on the ability of other species to colonize adjacent space or to hold it if they do colonize it. The two conditions are shading, the effect of which is obvious, and whiplashing, in which the long, tough algae are whipped around by waves and denude the rock of other plants and sessile animals in the immediate vicinity. The animals that are capable of affecting the abundance of macroalgae by feeding on them are mollusks and, to a much greater extent, sea urchins. Experiments on the effects of grazing on macroalgae have been conducted on both sides of the Atlantic and on the Pacific Coast of the United States.

Among marine environments, the most intensively studied small location is Lough Ine, a rocky inlet on the south coast of Ireland. The rectangular inlet, less than 1 km² in area, is connected with the sea by a narrow rocky channel, through which the water rushes with each change of tide. The ecology of this body of water was studied for at least fifteen years by Kitching, Ebling, and their colleagues, as summarized by Kitching and Ebling (1967). Although their publications began a number of years before Connell's first papers, they have attracted less attention than the detailed observations and ingenious experiments deserve. In the present context of herbivory on macroalgae, they describe the effect of manipulating sea urchins (*Paracentrotus*) (Kitching & Ebling 1961). Along the shore of an island in Lough Ine, the distribution of *Paracentrotus* and that of the green alga *Enteromorpha* were almost mutually exclusive. The urchins were present in a large area from 0.2 m below the low water line to 0.8 m below. In shallower water and in deeper water there were dense stands of *Enteromorpha* (Fig. 8.10). The experiment consisted in removing the urchins from a strip 20 m wide across the area that they occupied and keeping them from immigrating from the sides. The first removal was on 7 July 1959. *Enteromorpha* responded promptly: By 23 July it covered 10 percent of the experimental area, by 10 August, 25 percent, and by 3 September, 50 percent. One year after the removal, the area cleared of *Paracentrotus* had a thick complete cover of algae, mostly *Enteromorpha*. The urchins removed from the experimental area were not simply discarded. They were transferred to a bed of *Enteromorpha* near the parent population of urchins, at a depth of about 0.5 m. The dramatic result is shown in Figure 8.11.

From the standpoint of experimental design, this work leaves much to be desired. There was no replication, nor any predesignated equal-size areas. Were it not for the absolute results, an objective assessment of the success of the experiment would have been impossible. As it is, the results are most convincing.

An experiment on urchin removal with a good design was carried

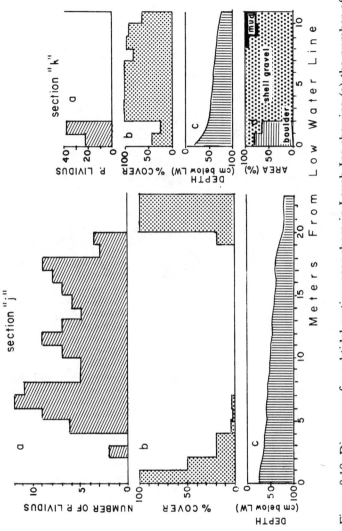

Figure 8.10. Diagrams of a subtidal section near shore in Lough Ine showing (a) the number of *Paracentrotus* per square meter, (b) the percentage coverage of the bottom with algae, (c) the bottom profile, and (d) the nature of the bottom expressed as the percentage area covered with boulders, gravel, or mud. (From Kitching & Ebling 1961.)

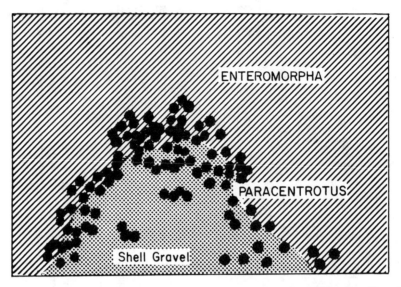

Figure 8.11. Distribution of *Paracentrotus* at transfer station K on 10 August 1959. Only one end of the oval patch is represented. The positions of the *Paracentrotus* have been traced from a color photograph. (From Kitching & Ebling 1961.)

out by Paine and Vadas (1969) in tide pools on the semiprotected outer coast of Washington State. Six matched pairs of pools were selected, and one of each pair was designated to be cleared of all sea urchins (*Strongylocentrotus* sp.). The experiments were continued for one to three years. All experimental pools developed algal cover, some within three months. Paine and Vadas also followed the succession of algal species, which gradually became dominated by the brown alga *Hedophyllum sessile* (Fig. 8.12). Dayton (1975), also working on the coast of Washington State, obtained similar results from the removal of *Strongylocentrotus purpuratus* in a less well replicated experiment.

Most studies, including some with good experimental designs, have failed to show that grazing mollusks have a demonstrable impact on the abundance of macroalgae (e.g., Sousa 1979). Most commonly, the mollusks are unable to reach high enough densities unless protected from wave action or predators or both. There have been at least two experiments, however, showing an effect of mollusks – one on each coast of the United States.

Lubchenco (1978), working in high intertidal pools in Massachusetts, noticed a positive association between the abundance of the snail

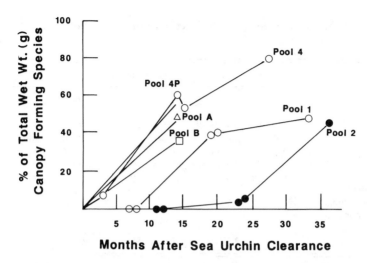

Figure 8.12. Tendency toward domination by *Hedophyllum* in urchin-free intertidal pools. (From Paine & Vadas 1969.)

Littorina littorea and the perennial red alga *Chondrus*, but a negative association between the abundance of the snail and the green alga *Enteromorpha*. She chose three tide pools as similar as she could find. One was dominated by *Enteromorpha* (95% cover), the other two by *Chondrus* (85% and 40% cover). The first pool contained *Littorina* at a concentration of 4 m^{-2}; the others, respectively, had 233 and 267 m^{-2}. Her hypothesis was that the abundances of algae were caused by the abundances of *Littorina*, because she knew that *Enteromorpha* was a highly favored food of the snail and that *Chondrus* was rarely, if ever, eaten.

Lubchenco removed all of the snails from one of the *Chondrus* pools and put them into the *Enteromorpha* pool. The second *Chondrus* pool was left as a control. The experiment was followed for sixteen months. *Chondrus* remained dominant in the control; *Enteromorpha* declined to insignificance in the pool where it had been dominant, and it quickly reversed roles with *Chondrus* in the pool from which snails had been removed. A second exchange was carried out five months later, with the aim of testing for seasonal differences. Presumably, the same unmanipulated pool was considered the control for this experiment as well. The only unexpected result was the failure of *Chondrus* to colonize the first pool to which snails had been added. Was that the reason for the second experiment?

Table 8.3. *Experimentally induced dominance of the alga* Alaria marginata

	Katharina present		Katharina absent				
	Control (all grazers present)	Minus all grazers except *Katharina*	Minus all grazers	Minus all grazers except *Collisella pelta*	Minus all grazers except *Acmaea mitra*	Minus all grazers	Minus all grazers
Mean percentage canopy cover by *Alaria marginata*	2.8	2.3	48.8	51.3	70.0	71.3	71.3

Note: Dominance shown either in the enforced absence of all grazers ($N = 3$ sites) or in the general absence of all grazers except the limpets *Collisella pelta* or *Acmaea mitra* ($N = 2$ sites). At experimental sites with the chiton *Katharina tunicata* ($N = 1$), or at controls with the normal complement of all grazers ($N = 1$), the brown alga *Hedophyllum* dominates. Estimates based on four 900-cm^2 quadrat samples within each treatment. Treatments within boxes are statistically indistinguishable from each other; the two groups are significantly different, $p < .05$, Student–Newman–Keuls test.
From Paine (1984).

There are three things wrong from the standpoint of design. The first is the failure to have replicates. The difference between the two pools to which snails were added demonstrates the need. The second is the absence of a control for the second experiment (Lubchenco mentions several pools observed but, "no data taken"). The third is the implication of statistical significance with 95 percent confidence limits within each pool. These were calculated from three or four permanent quadrats in each pool – a clear example of confounding treatment with place.

The second example of an effect of molluskan herbivory was reported by Paine (1984). The mollusk was the large chiton *Katharina tunicata*; the plant was the large alga *Alaria marginata*. Removal of *Katharina* resulted in a dramatic increase in the percentage cover by *Alaria* (Table 8.3). Removing the limpets *Collisella pelta* and *Acmaea mitra* had no effect in increasing the cover of *Alaria*. This experiment also revealed competition between *Alaria* and the brown alga *Hedophyllum sessile*. The latter species was the normal dominant, and following removal it promptly recovered its position, except where

Katharina was removed. Thus, its dominance depended on the preference of the chiton for the competitively superior *Alaria*.

As can be seen from the footnote to Table 8.3, the calculation of statistical significance on the basis of several quadrats within each treatment area was not justified. Consider the three columns headed "Minus all grazers." They represent the entire spread of mean values for all treatments without *Katharina*, and although there would be statistical significance in the difference between the means, that was not what was tested.

Some experiments on rocky shores: predation

Although others (e.g., Kitching, Sloane, & Ebling 1959; Connell 1961a) had studied the effects of predators, it was Paine's paper (1966) that caught the attention of ecologists, and although the paper was cited regularly, theoretical work on communities did not include predation. Paine reported that he had carried out experimental removal of the large predatory starfish *Pisaster ochraceus* on the coast of Washington State, and he subsequently coined the phrase "keystone predator" to describe its effect on the community, but he presented no experimental results until eight years later (Paine 1974). The favored prey of *Pisaster* is the mussel *Mytilus californianus*. At a site on the exposed outer coast, he established the constancy of the upper edge of the dense band of mussels by setting stainless screws permanently in the rock and making measurements to the upper edge on eleven occasions over a two-year period. Among screws, the range of measured distances was from 12 to 35 cm per screw, with an average coefficient of variation of 6.9 percent. The constancy of the lower edge of the mussel band in the presence of *Pisaster* was established by repeatedly photographing the area from the same spot, showing tracings of the successive positions of the lower edge of the mussel band. *Pisaster* is unable to remain out of the water, and its upward distribution is more limited than is that of *Mytilus*. Its effect on the mussel would therefore be expected to be greatest at the lower edge of the mussel band. *Mytilus* settles in the autumn of some years. In Paine's experiment at a semi-protected site on the outer coast, good settlement occurred in five of the ten or eleven years of observation. After good years, small (newly settled) *Mytilus* composed at least 25 percent of the diet of *Pisaster*. After poor settlement, the mussels fell to as low as 2 percent of the diet of the predator. At that site, he chose a flat platform, accompanied in part by a vertical wall. The platform was interrupted by a "small projection" into two subequal parts. The part next to the wall and the wall itself were subjected to monthly (winter) and twice monthly (summer) removals of *Pisaster* every year for five years. During that period, the first two years were good settlement years, and the mussel band extended its vertical distribution downward by at least 79 cm. After the cessation of removal of *Pisaster*, the lower edge became higher over the next five years, reaching a level only 13–14 cm below its original position. At the site on the exposed outer coast, the downward extension of the mussel zone after the removal of *Pisaster* was even more pronounced, amounting to as much as 193 cm.

The most spectacular result of these experiments was the change in species composition on the flat area at the semiprotected site. The removal of *Pisaster* resulted in the disappearance of twenty-eight species of animals and plants, until only *Mytilus californianus* remained. It was both the prime food for *Pisaster* and the winner in competition for space. When the starfish was removed, *Mytilus* took over the area, and after the experiment ended, *Pisaster* could not recover the space for the other species, because in five years *Mytilus* had become so large that the starfish could no longer prey on it.

These experiments have the primary problem of lacking local replication. Moreover, there is a problem in temporal replication, because of the irregular settling pattern of *Mytilus*. Dayton (1971) was unable to repeat Paine's results, apparently because of the failure of the mussels to settle large numbers of young in 1968–9 as they did for Paine in 1962–4. Both of the replication problems were acknowledged by Paine. They are mentioned here to call them to the attention of others.

The experiments of Connell (1970) are described briefly in Chapter 3. In a protected site (San Juan Island in Puget Sound), he found in replicated caging experiments that the predatory snail *Thais emarginata* apparently consumed all of the regularly settling young of the barnacle *Balanus glandula* below the highest tide level. He was concerned with balancing the disappearance of the barnacles with the rate of consumption by *Thais*. He enclosed one or two *Thais* at middle and lower tide levels in each of a number of cages in two different years and recorded the number of barnacles eaten. He also recorded the settling density of *Balanus* and the population density of *Thais emarginata* in the same location. His calculation showed that the rate of predation was sufficient to remove the entire population of *Balanus glandula* at those levels each year, and there were other predators present (R. T.

Paine pers. commun.), a fact that would only reinforce the conclusion that predation determined the distribution of *Balanus glandula*. These well-replicated and well-controlled experiments were unusual in demonstrating the effects of predation by mollusks on populations of their prey.

The work of Kitching et al. (1959) involved a different kind of experiment. Instead of protecting the prey organisms (mussels, in this case) from predators, they moved groups of mussels attached to rocks into apparently suitable areas that did not have populations. They then followed survival at each level in each location. Mussels were moved from the outer coast (Carrigathorna), where they were small (up to 2.5 cm long), and from the north end of Lough Ine (away from the inlet), where they were 3–7 cm long, to several locations at the south end of the lough. Nearly all of the small mussels had disappeared within one week, but the large ones survived well at some levels (Fig. 8.13). They set up two observation sites to find out what the predators were, and they made direct observations every forty minutes for fifty-three hours. "Thousands" of mussels were used to avoid diminution of the supply. The animals seen actively engaged in predation were largely two species of crabs. Starfish, though present, were uncommon, and the prawns and shrimps seen could not harm intact mussels.

As an experimental design, this was not elegant. There was one control on moving mussels from one part of the outer coast to the other, and they survived well. The different sites in the lough could be considered replicates, but there was no replication of the control. It is worth noting that the crabs also acted as secondary predators. The primary predator on the outer coast (*Thais lapillus*) could not be established in the lough because of predation by the crabs.

Interspecific competition between predators in rocky marine environments has been the subject of experiments by Menge (1972). He worked in the San Juan Islands (Washington State). His interest was in the possibility of competition for food between the large starfish *Pisaster* and a much smaller one, *Leptasterias*. He first established that the mean weight of *Leptasterias* was inversely related to the abundance of *Pisaster* at different locations, as were the weight of individual prey and the diversity of available prey that were eaten (Table 8.4). (Direct observation of starfish feeding is readily observed by lifting them, because they feed by everting their stomachs and engulfing their prey.) Menge found that the two species overlapped extensively (about 71%) in the compositions of their diets. He brought *Leptasterias* into the

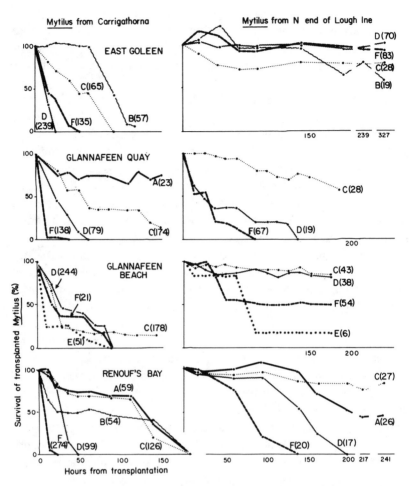

Figure 8.13. Percentage survival of mussels from Carrigathorna and from the north end of the lough transferred (with rock substratum) to positions in the lough. The letters A–F represent levels into which the mussels were transferred. The numbers of mussels transferred are given in parentheses. (From Kitching et al. 1959.)

laboratory and showed that given ample food they grew much faster than other members of the same population grew in the field.

He then conducted a field experiment, taking advantage of the fact that starfish do not descend far into the subtidal zone. That allowed him to use small rock islands (reefs) for his manipulations. He removed all *Pisaster* from one reef and used them to quintuple the

Table 8.4. *Mean Leptasterias wet weight, mean individual sizes of prey consumed and available, numbers of species eaten and available, and* Pisaster *density at four areas*

Area	Mean *Leptasterias* wet wt. (g)	Dry wt. of avg. individual prey size eaten (mg)	Dry wt. of avg. prey length available (mg)	No. prey sp. eaten	No. potential prey sp.	Density of *Pisaster* (no./m²)
Lonesome Cove Resort area	3.2 ± 0.1 (1,262)	4.2 ± 1.5 (381)	3.3 ± 2.0 (2,481)	13	18	0.3
Far point	3.6 ± 0.1 (1,470)	7.7 ± 3.1 (275)	24.2 ± 9.2 (388)	12	18	0.1
Deadman's Bay	7.7 ± 0.3 (1,191)	26.6 ± 11.1 (438)	81.2 ± 31.6 (211)	19	20	0.01
Cattle Point	8.4 ± 0.4 (956)	70.3 ± 18.8 (134)	34.1 ± 16.7 (384)	18	20	0.01

Note: Means are followed by 95% confidence intervals; *N* is in parentheses. Dry weight of each prey consumed was estimated with length–weight regressions. The data are summarized over 2–2.5 years. From Menge (1972).

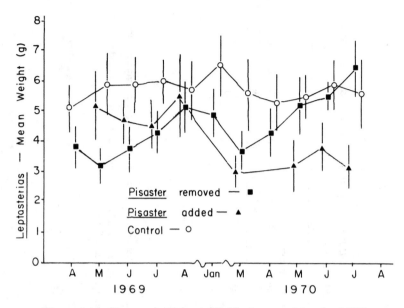

Figure 8.14. Changes in mean individual wet weights (and 95% confidence intervals) of *Leptasterias* at Gull (*Pisaster* removed), Davis Point (*Pisaster* added), and Buoy Reefs (control) from April 1969 to July 1970. The decrease in mean size observed from August 1969 or January 1970 to March 1970 indicates weight lost during reproduction. (From Menge 1972.)

abundance of that species on another reef. A third was kept as a control. All *Leptasterias* on all three reefs were weighed eleven times over the next fifteen months (Fig. 8.14). On the *Pisaster*-removal reef, *Leptasterias* was initially significantly smaller than on the control; by the end of the experiment, it was slightly larger in average weight, although not significantly so. Initially, on the *Pisaster*-addition reef, *Leptasterias* was as large as it was on the control reef; by the end of the experiment, it was significantly smaller. The experiment gave evidence of a strong negative effect of *Pisaster* on *Leptasterias*, but there was pseudoreplication in the analysis of the data, because there was no replication of treatments, and it was possible (though not likely) that the changes in sizes were dependent on the respective locations.

Experiments on consumers in a tropical setting

In contrast to the luxuriant biota on temperate rocky coasts, the shore of Taboguilla Island in the Bay of Panama is superficially barren, with bare rock in the high intertidal, and rock covered with algal crusts in the middle and low zones (Lubchenco et al. 1984; Menge, Lubchenco, & Ashkenas 1985; Menge et al. 1986a,b). Closer examination reveals that the species diversity is high when the organisms found in cracks or holes are included. Among these are mobile but slow-moving animals (mostly gastropods), both herbivores and carnivores. The sessile forms are primarily solitary filter-feeding animals (barnacles and oysters), but there are some colonial animals (hydroids and tunicates), and fleshy algae and a few anemones are present. The other organisms present are faster-moving consumers – fish and crabs, many of which are omnivores.

In the low intertidal zone, Menge, Lubchenco, and their associates conducted a three-year experiment on the effects of four distinct groups of consumers on the community. They chose four different areas: one for the removal of slow-moving predators, one for the removal of slow-moving herbivores, one for the removal of all slow-moving consumers, and one with no such manipulation. Within each of those areas they had three treatments: four square plots 0.5 m on a side, two plots of the same size, but caged to exclude highly mobile consumers of two classes (large fishes and small fishes plus crabs), and two plots with the roof of the cage only – excluding large fishes but not the other highly mobile consumers. The design (Table 8.5) permitted them to compare the control areas and the areas from which the following had been removed:

1. all mobile consumers
2. all except small fishes and crabs
3. all except slow-moving predators
4. all except slow-moving herbivores

They were also able to compare the effects of all combinations of removing one or two groups, with one exception: They were unable to exclude small fishes and crabs without also excluding large fishes. There were thus twelve different treatments, including the completely unmanipulated controls.

This is undoubtedly the most complex experiment that has been conducted in any marine habitat, involving as it did all elements of all trophic levels. The vagile nature of some of the members of the community meant that in order to keep them excluded, large areas had to be cleared to prevent immigration from being a factor. Thus, the caging experiments were within the larger control areas and those cleared of slow-moving herbivores and slow-moving carnivores. This involved an unavoidable element of pseudoreplication, as Menge et al.

Table 8.5. *Design of consumer-deletion experiments*

Treatments

Slow-moving consumer manipulations (removals)	Fast-moving consumer manipulations (exclusions)	Code[a]
No manipulation (site 6)	No exclusion (4)[b]	+H + P + LF + SFC
	2-sided cage (2)	+H + P − LF + SFC
	Complete cage (2)	+H + P − LF − SFC
Predator removal (site 1)	No exclusion (4)	+H − P + LF + SFC
	2-sided cage (2)	+H − P − LF + SFC
	Complete cage (2)	+H − P − LF − SFC
Herbivore removal (site 4)	No exclusion (4)	−H + P + LF + SFC
	2-sided cage (2)	−H + P − LF + SFC
	Complete cage (2)	−H + P − LF − SFC
Predator and herbivore removal (site 2)	No exclusion (4)	−H − P + LF + SFC
	2-sided cage (2)	−H − P − LF + SFC
	Complete cage (2)	−H − P − LF − SFC

[a]Presence (+) or absence (−) of consumer groups: H, slow-moving herbivores; P, slow-moving predators; LF, large fishes; SFC, small fishes and crabs.
[b]Number of plots of each treatment given in parentheses.
From Menge et al. (1986a).

(1986b) freely acknowledged, but many of the effects were so impressive that the flaw appears to have been minor.

Sessile organisms, mainly algal crusts, retained large and nearly constant percentages of the unmanipulated areas (Fig. 8.15), and there were relatively small seasonal fluctuations in the numbers of mobile species (Fig. 8.16). Sessile animals changed equally in abundance, but with different patterns (Fig. 8.16). The results of the experiments were so numerous and complex that only a sample can be given here. In the plots from which all consumers were excluded, there was a slow but continuous decrease in the abundance of crustose algae and a corresponding increase in the solitary sessile animals. The data for two plots are given in Figure 8.17. Among the slow-moving mollusks, the predatory snails had a strong impact on the abundance of the herbivorous limpets and chitons (Fig. 8.18). The highly mobile consumer groups, consisting of large fishes in one group, and small fishes and crabs in the other, were important in reducing the density of the predaceous gastropods themselves. Table 8.6 gives the statistical details, which are typical of the statistics throughout the series of papers. The interac-

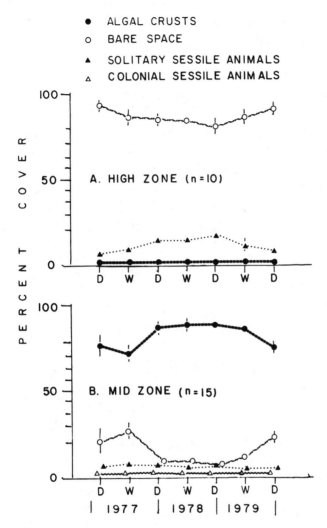

Figure 8.15. Temporal changes in percentage cover of major primary space-occupying groups in the high and middle zones on site 6: mean and s.e. are plotted for each date; when no s.e. bar is shown, the symbol is larger than the s.e.; number of quadrat samples is given in parentheses; the units of the ordinate are transformed with the arcsine transformation. (From Lubchenco et al. 1984.)

tions just described provide only a sampling of the strong direct effects, which are summarized in the interaction web (Fig. 8.19). This is doubtless the most completely documented figure of its kind among many in the literature. The situation is more complex than can be repre-

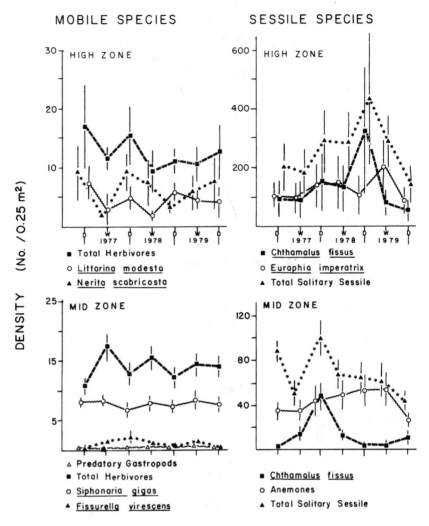

Figure 8.16. Temporal changes in densities of most abundant groups and species of mobile and solitary sessile animals in the high and middle zones on site 6. See legend to Figure 8.15 for further explanation. (From Lubchenco et al. 1984.)

sented in such a diagram, because of the many indirect and combined effects. The indirect beneficial effects included the removal of solitary sessile animals by slow consumers and large fishes, thus favoring the retention of space by the grazer-resistant algal crusts. An indirect neg-

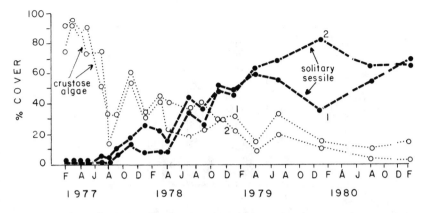

Figure 8.17. Changes in abundance of two dominant sessile organism groups, crustose algae and solitary sessile animals, in total-exclusion plots 1 and 2, 1977–80. (From Menge et al. 1985.)

ative effect was inhibition of the settling of the oyster *Chama echinata* through the removal of its favored settling surface on algal turf by herbivorous mollusks. The impact of the combined effects is best seen in the comparison between the summed effects of the four different consumer groups measured individually and their effect when all were excluded. The total effect in decreasing the cover of crustose algae was much greater than the summed effects (Fig. 8.20), and the effect of total exclusion in increasing the abundance of solitary sessile animals was much greater than the summed effects of excluding the four individual consumer groups (Fig. 8.21).

This study resulted in an excellent understanding of the effects of herbivory and predation in determining the nature of the community. Competition appears to have been important largely among the grazing-resistant algal crusts. The study emphasized the large number of qualifications that must be included in the description of initial conditions before any prediction can be made concerning rocky intertidal communities. The height in the intertidal zone, the slope and even the rugosity of the surface, the degree of exposure to waves, and the severity and kind of seasonal changes must all be specified. Even more frustrating for any generalizer is the necessity to know something about the life histories of the different species themselves, such as the regularity with which the dispersal phases settle.

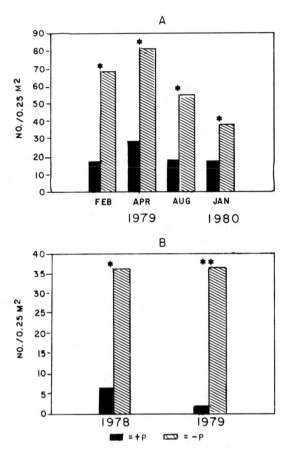

Figure 8.18. Effects of predatory gastropods on density of herbivorous mollusks. A: Effects on residents, February 1979 to January 1980. B: Effects on recruits, January 1978 and 1979; +P, predatory gastropods present; −P, predatory gastropods absent. Densities did not differ on other dates (sampled every 1 to 5 months from February 1977 to January 1980; $*p< .05$; $**p< .01$, tested using one-way ANOVA corrected with Bonferroni approximation for multiple comparisons. (From Menge et al. 1986a.)

Experiments on fouling communities

Substrates that become available at irregular times are colonized by assemblages of species different from those characteristic of rocky shores. This is especially true of the bottoms of boats, which are said to become fouled by barnacles, sponges, bryozoans, hydroids, and

Table 8.6. *Effects of LF and SFC on density (no./plot) of resident and recruited predaceous gastropods*

MANOVAs Response variable	Test	F	d.f.	Multiple comparisons 1977 D	1977 W	1978 D	1978 W	1979 D	1979 W	1980 D	d.f.
Resident density (+H sites)	Full model	3.04*	14, 14	NS	NS	NS	*	NS	*	NS	2, 26
	Roof effect (−LF + SFC)	2.16 (NS)	7, 7	—	—	—	NS	—	NS	—	1, 13
	Cage effect (−LF − SFC)	4.47*	7, 7	—	—	—	**	—	**	—	1, 13
Number of recruits (−H sites)	Full model	3.92**	14, 14	NS	NS	*	**	NS	NS	*	2, 26
	Roof effect (−LF + SFC)	4.88*	7, 7	—	—	NS	**	—	—	NS	1, 13
	Cage effect (−LF − SFC)	9.96**	7, 7	—	—	**	**	—	—	*	1, 13

Note: D, dry season; W, wet season. Significance levels: $*p < 0.05$; $**p < 0.01$; NS = $p > 0.05$; — = no test necessary because full model was not significant on that date. See Table 8.5 for explanation of other symbols and abbreviations. From Menge et al. (1986b).

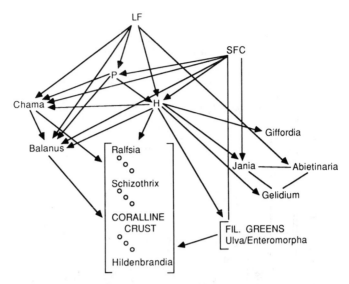

Figure 8.19. Interaction web at Taboguilla Island, Panama. LF, large fishes; SFC, small fishes and crabs; P, predaceous gastropods; H, herbivorous mollusks. Strong (i.e., statistically significant) consumer–prey interactions are indicated by solid lines; arrow points to prey. Open-dot lines indicate competition for space occurring in consumer-exclusion experiments. Dotted lines without arrowheads indicate that no clear competitive dominant was apparent in the interaction. Numerous indirect interactions also occur in this web. (From Menge et al. 1986b.)

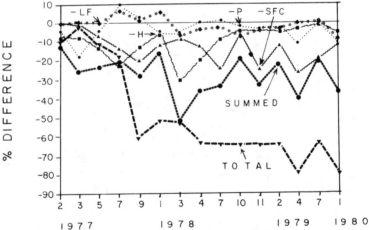

Figure 8.20. Effects of consumers on space availability as estimated by the differences between abundances of crustose algae in consumer-deletion treatments and controls: TOTAL is the total effect of consumers as estimated by the difference between percentage cover of

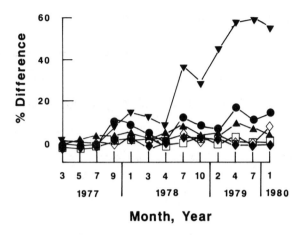

Figure 8.21. Effects of consumers on solitary sessile animals. Symbols coded as in Figure 8.20. (From Menge et al. 1986a.)

tunicates. Many of the same species are typical of wooden wharf piles in protected locations. Sutherland (1974, 1978) and Sutherland and Carlson (1977) were interested in the great variety of species occurring in the vicinity of Beaufort, North Carolina. By hanging sets of ceramic tiles underneath a dock at monthly intervals from April to November, exposure to different colonists was provided, and the effect of periodic browsing by sea urchins was mimicked. The hanging plates were not accessible to the urchins. The composition of the community developing on the plates depended on the month of exposure. Three exposed in May 1971 were first dominated by the hydroid *Tubularia*, which was quickly displaced by the tunicate *Styela*. The latter species, being heavy, dropped off the plates in the fall, to be replaced by *Tub-*

Caption to Figure 8.20 (*cont.*)
crusts in total consumer deletions and controls (i.e., TOTALS − CO); SUMMED is the total effect of consumers as estimated by the sum of the effects of each of the four consumer groups as separately estimated by the differences between percentage cover of crusts in deletions of single consumer groups and controls; i.e., (H − CO) + (P − CO) + (LF − CO) + (SFC − LF) = SUMMED effect; −H, −P, −LF, and −SFC indicate the separate effects of the single consumer groups that when added yield the SUMMED line in the figure; the negative initial values (i.e., for 2/77) indicate that the average abundance of crusts in treatments was initially slightly less than in controls; this was regarded as within the range of normal variation. (From Menge et al. 1986a.)

Table 8.7. *Effects of resident species on recruitment and/or growth of new recruits*[a]

Resident species	New recruits						
	Tubularia	Pennaria	Bugula	Schizoporella	Styela	Ascidia	Balanus
Hydractinia	0	0	0	0	0	0	0
	18	30	50	60	14	31	62[b]
Schizoporella	13	0	16		6 (NS)	8	0
	43	30	50		14	31	38
Styela		6		0		1	0
		70		43		72	77
Ascidia				4			0
				42			77
Balanus	4			3			
	44			42			

[a]In each pairwise comparison, the top number is the mean (on 3 or 4 plates) percentage cover for the recruit after 90 days on plates dominated by the resident during that period. The bottom number is the mean percentage cover for the recruit on newly submerged plates after the same 90-day period. Mann–Whitney U-tests were conducted on all comparisons except those with the *Hydractinia*-dominated plate. All were significant at $p <$ .05, except for the one marked NS.
[b]After one month.
From Sutherland & Carlson (1977).

ularia until the following spring, when *Styela* regained dominance. Other species were of minor importance until the second summer, when a diverse assemblage developed. Three plates first exposed in August gradually became dominated by the bryozoan *Schizoporella*, which retained its dominance through seventeen months, although *Tubularia* managed to occupy 25 percent of the surface during the winter, and several other forms became fairly common during the second summer and fall. There were clear priority effects (Table 8.7), and Sutherland and Carlson recognized five different assemblages, each dominated by different species, usually a single species.

Sutherland (1978) conducted two sets of experiments designed to elucidate the interactions. In the first, he excluded fishes from four plates by the use of fine nets, exposing them and four control plates in April 1972. The plates inside the nets devloped a nearly complete cover of *Styela*, whereas those outside were quickly dominated by *Schizoporella*, and *Styela* was not able to cover more than 5 percent of

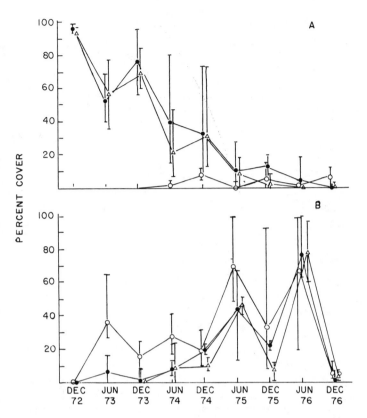

Figure 8.22. October 1972 experiment. Arithmetic means (*n* = 4) and ranges of percentage cover of *Schizoporella* (A) and *Styela* (B) on the three experimental groups. Filled circles, control group; open circles, *Schizoporella*-removal group; triangles, *Styela*-removal group. (From Sutherland 1978.)

the area through the rest of the year. The control plates might be considered an attempt to repeat the observation starting in May of the previous year, in which case it would be a failure, as there was a different dominant species. Perhaps there were fewer fishes in 1971, thus permitting *Styela* to cover the plates, or perhaps there was some other disturbing factor.

Sutherland's second kind of experiment involved selective removal of *Styela* from one set of four plates, and *Schizoporella* from another set. A third set was kept as a control. The results (Fig. 8.22) were not impressive, although there were significant effects on some of the minor constituents of the community (Table 8.8).

Table 8.8. *Density comparisons of common species between experimental groups*

Taxa	Control	*Schizoporella* removed	*Styela* removed
October 1972 experiment			
December 1972			
Balanus	1	27	0
June 1973			
Balanus	1	10	0
Hydroides	6	3	7
Styela	7	37	—
December 1973			
Styela	2	16	—
Halichondria	0	12	1
October 1973 experiment			
December 1973			
—			
June 1974			
Schizoporella	19	—	45
Styela	42	26	—
December 1974			
Haliclona	6	19	3

Note: Values are arithmetic means of untransformed estimates of percentage cover ($N = 4$ for each group). Differences evaluated with one-way ANOVA after applying the angular transformation to percentage cover estimates on each plate. Only significant differences ($p < .05$) are reported. From Sutherland (1978).

The experiments were carefully conducted, with adequate replication and appropriate controls. Predictability was very low in this community, and Sutherland claimed that was the effect of having a number of different "stable states." Some conditions depend on which species colonize the plates first; others depend on competitive dominance, and still others are influenced by predatory browsing. Among experiments in marine environments, only those of Sale (1977) have revealed less predictability.

Experiments in areas dominated by coral

Corals constitute a kind of habitat markedly different from any of the marine situations thus far considered. The experiment of Sale (1977) involved introducing numerous blocks of coral, some living, some dead, into an open area within a shallow lagoon on the Australian Great Barrier Reef. His purpose was to discover any pattern in the colonization and development of community structure among the many species of fishes that characterize coral reefs. He was unable to make any general statements, and he concluded that the communities formed from fortuitous arrival of larval individuals, rather than from any ecological interaction among the species after they reached the coral blocks.

Another experiment of a different type was carried out on the north coast of Jamaica by Williams (1981). The habitat was a back-reef lagoon 3–5 m deep, with a floor of coral rubble. Colonies of staghorn coral formed loose clumps of various sizes. Williams was interested in the behavior of the three-spot damselfish (*Eupomacentrus planifrons*). She observed it picking up sea urchins of two species, *Echinometra viridis* and *Diadema antillarum*, and removing them from the coral clumps. Inasmuch as the territorial fish and both urchins feed on algae growing on the surface of the coral, she hypothesized that there was competition among them. The fish maintain an algal "lawn" on the upper and outer branches. The urchins browse mostly in the center of the clump (*Echinometra*) or on lower levels (*Diadema*). Using scuba, Williams surveyed a large area and selected fifty-three patches of coral that met the following criteria: small enough for urchin manipulation (0.6–1.6 m diameter), presence of at least one three-spot damselfish, and discrete patch boundaries. She marked each patch with a numbered aluminum tag and counted the fishes and urchins on each. The populations changed only slightly over the five-month period of her work.

Her first experiment tested the effects of the two urchin species on each other. The treatments were as follows: removal of each species, adding twice the mean number of each species, and unmanipulated controls. These were completely crossed, making a nine-unit matrix, which was replicated three times. She chose twenty-seven patches randomly from the fifty-three available. Manipulations were maintained daily for two weeks. *Diadema* is much more motile than *Echinometra* and is more vulnerable to attack by damselfish. Even daily additions achieved only moderate elevations in its density. *Echinometra*, however, tended to accumulate where it was added. The anticipated interference of each species with the other was demonstrated (Table 8.9). Because the repeated counts on the same patches were not independent, the estimates of probability should be viewed with caution.

A major experiment with predator-exclusion cages and appropriate

Table 8.9. *Three-way ANOVA table on the effects of* Diadema–Echinometra *manipulations on* Echinometra *and* Diadema *mean densities*

	Echinometra				Diadema			
Source of variation	d.f.	Sums of squares	Mean square	F	d.f.	Sums of squares	Mean square	F
Main effects								
Diadema manipulations	2	164.89	82.44	13.80***	2	40.10	20.05	17.53***
Echinometra manipulations	2	1,009.74	504.87	84.49***	2	7.83	3.91	3.42*
Time	10	63.85	6.39	1.07	10	9.56	.96	.84
First-order interactions								
Diadema × Echinometra	4	70.33	17.58	2.94*	4	49.07	12.27	10.73***
Diadema × time	20	18.19	.91	.15	20	6.90	.35	.30
Echinometra × time	20	314.81	15.74	2.63***	20	8.57	.43	.38
Second-order interactions								
Diadema × Echinometra × time	40	44.15	1.10	.19	40	27.49	.69	.60
Error	198	1,183.20	5.98		198	226.48	1.14	
Total	296				296			

Note: Statistics computed on data transformed with $\sqrt{x + 0.5}$ transformation; *p* < .05; ***p* < .001.
From Williams (1981).

Table 8.10. *Effects of three-spot damselfish removals on urchin mean density compared with densities on control patches*[a]

Day[b]	Diadema mean density (no./m^3 ± s.e.)		Echinometra mean density (no./m^3 ± s.e.)	
	Experimental	Control	Experimental	Control
0	13.76 ± 2.3	15.22 ± 2.7	19.35 ± 3.1	14.53 ± 2.6
1	21.63 ± 3.6	11.36 ± 1.9	19.23 ± 2.8	17.06 ± 3.3
2	23.51 ± 4.3	12.31 ± 2.8	19.59 ± 3.8	13.55 ± 4.7
3	24.89 ± 5.2	9.38 ± 4.0	28.90 ± 5.3	14.74 ± 5.2

[a]Experimental patches had damselfish removed; control patches were not manipulated.
[b]Day 0 = day of removal; days 1–3 = observational period following removals.
From Williams (1981).

controls for cage effects gave essentially negative results. The experiment should not be regarded as a failure, because the potential of predators for affecting the outcome of competition could not be ignored a priori.

The final experiment consisted of removing three-spot damselfish from seventeen coral patches and retaining seventeen as controls. Both species of urchins responded positively to the removal of the fish (Table 8.10). As in the earlier experiment, *Diadema*, being much more mobile than *Echinometra*, responded more quickly to the manipulation. Almost its whole response took place in the first day after the removal of the damselfish. *Echinometra* did not show a significant response until the third day.

This was a well-designed study, with ample baseline information and adequate replication and controls. It demonstrated a complex set of interactions among competitors that composed, a priori, an unlikely set.

The experiments of Jackson and Buss (1975) revealed one of the most interesting sets of relationships in any marine environment. They were interested in the nearly complete coverage of the undersides of foliose corals by a variety of colonial and solitary animals, including sponges, ectoprocts, ascidians, serpulids, brachiopods, and bivalves. The virtual absence of unoccupied space (1–5%) suggested intense competition, and Jackson and Buss devised an experimental test for interference mechanisms. Interference was suggested by a band of dead ectoproct zooids around the growing edges of some sponges. They prepared homogenates of the tissues of nine different species of sponges by scraping them from the corals, grinding them in filtered sea water, and diluting with more sea water. A small amount (2–5 ml) of each homogenate was added to a 1-liter aquarium containing small pieces of coral, with a colony of a single species of the target ectoproct. The result was observed on five replicate colonies daily for five to eight days, and the target was classified in one of four ways: dead, zooids deteriorating, no movement or feeding, or normal. Four different species of ectoprocts were used, although only two species were tested against all nine species of sponges. The homogenates of five species of sponges had detectable effects. Three affected a single species each, one affected two species, and one affected three. None of the five affected all species of ectoprocts adversely. Conversely, of the two species of ectoprocts tested against all nine sponge homogenates, one was damaged by only three species, and the other by two species. Appropriate controls were maintained, and none suffered any ill effects.

The experiments demonstrated the existence of toxic material in the tissues of the sponges, and at the concentrations employed there was a highly selective action of the allelochemicals. As Jackson and Buss pointed out, the employment of such chemicals as competitive interference mechanisms was not demonstrated, but the potential is certainly there. The selective nature of the action of the homogenates may have been related to an interesting set of observations on these organisms (Buss & Jackson 1979). By examining the edges of adjacent colonies, they were able to determine if one was overgrowing the other, and by observing all combinations of pairs of species in their system, they determined that not all combinations of three or four species showed transitivity of effect. Some combinations were "networks," in which, for example, species *A* overgrew *B*, *B* overgrew *C*, but *C* overgrew *A*. Such combinations can be explained by the differential effects of interference mechanisms, but it is also true that the dominant ectoproct grows directionally, rather than radially (R. T. Paine pers. commun.), meaning that its flanks are vulnerable, because it cannot overgrow the other species in those directions. Among the current examples there were four species of sponges and four species of ectoprocts. Three species in each group had been used in the earlier experiments, and it seems likely that the differential effects of the sponge homogenates on ectoproct species were involved in the many networks observed.

Subdivisions of marine soft sediments

The nature of the bottom of any aquatic habitat is determined largely by the sizes of the particles that compose it, ranging from stones and pebbles through sand of various degrees of coarseness to silt and mud. The kind of bottom is determined, in turn, by the amount of action of the water, whether by currents or waves. Where waves or currents are strong, the particles are large; where the water is calm, the bottom is composed of silt. In hydraulically active areas, where coarse sand is present, the presence of organisms is rarely obvious from inspection, but as finer particles become more prominent, small mounds made by burrowers, or the tops of worm tubes frequently are abundant. In the quieter locations, submerged plants may be present. Where the bottom is fine silt, and the water is shallow, emergent grasses, mostly *Spartina*, make prominent salt marshes. In the most active water, experiments have not been possible, but where there are moderate currents or small waves, there have been some notable ecological experiments. Those to be described are taken in order of increasing particle size.

The experiment of Stiven and Kuenzler (1979), described in Chapter 3, revealed that superficially similar salt marshes were quite different in the abundance of two species of mollusks, one a filter feeder and the other a scraper, and showed the effects of density on growth and survival of the two species under some conditions. They also showed that despite the seemingly uniform nature of the habitat, the distribution of salt-marsh invertebrates is so heterogeneous that inadequate replication may be a serious problem in experiments conducted there.

Salt-marsh animals do not all live on the *Spartina*. Some live in the mud and are known as infauna; others swim in with the tide, feed, and depart as the water level falls; some small swimming forms remain in puddles when the tide is out. The small fish *Fundulus heteroclitus* is a major predator in this community, taking many species of invertebrates (Kneib 1986); adults spend low tides in the creeks draining the marsh; young remain in puddles. Kneib and Stiven (1982) conducted an experiment near Beaufort, North Carolina, to test for the effects of fish of three sizes on the invertebrate populations. They constructed square cages of 1.5-mm-mesh window screening, with the bottom sunk in the marsh. These were arranged in a randomized block design, each block consisting of eleven treatments: three sizes of fish crossed with three densities, plus a control cage with no fish and another control area that was not enclosed. The experiment was started in June 1978. Invertebrates were sampled by taking three cylindrical cores from the substrate of each cage (or uncaged plot), starting in July. Sampling was repeated in October and in April of the following year. The cores were washed through seives and the invertebrates were sorted by hand.

The results were surprising, if an effect of fish predation was expected, but they were consistent internally. There were statistically significant *positive* effects of fish size on three species of polychaetes, on oligochaetes treated as a group, on the tanaid crustacean *Leptochelia rapax*, on ostrocods, and on both gastropod and bivalve mollusks. The density of fish had much less effect, but there were significant positive effects of interactions between size and density of fish on most of the same taxa. The significant *negative* effect of excluding fish from control cages was consistent with the other experimental results. Kneib and Stiven presented evidence that their results showed that *Fundulus* is a second-order predator. Of 484 fish stomachs examined, 44 contained the remains of the grass shrimp *Palaeomonites pugio*. This species is a prominent predator on salt-marsh invertebrates, and reduction of its density by *Fundulus* apparently released them from that predation. Thus, the presence of a large array of invertebrate species in the guts of *Fundulus* could easily have been interpreted as showing a negative effect of the fish. Only through the experiment could it have been concluded that the opposite was the case. These gut analyses were done after the fact, but Kneib (1987) subsequently showed in enclosure experiments in a salt marsh in Georgia that the presence of large *Fundulus* decreased survival of the shrimp from 73.7–88.5 percent without fish to 3.4–9.2 percent in their presence.

An excellent set of experiments was conducted by Woodin (1978, 1981) in a shallow-water tidal sandflat in a protected bay on the coast of Virginia. She was interested in the positive association between a large polychaete annelid, *Diopatra cuprea*, and other members of the infauna (mostly subsurface polychaetes). *Diopatra* is conspicuous by its size (30 cm long) and the length of its heavy, membranous tube (1 m). Woodin constructed sampling devices that gave concentric cores 14 cm deep. The inner core had a diameter of 11.3 cm and covered an area of 0.01 m^2; the outer core added 0.01 m^2 to the inner core. By centering the cores over one or a group of *Diopatra*, she could count the animals in each of the two cores and thus measure the density next

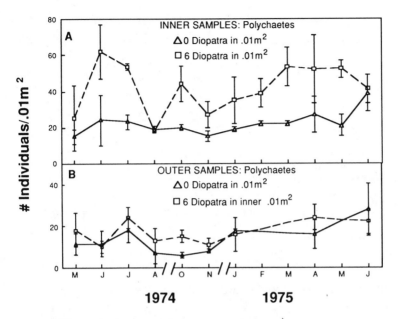

Figure 8.23. Abundances of polychaetes in inner samples (A) and outer samples (B) from May 1974 to June 1975. Means and standard deviations for zero *Diopatra* samples (triangles) and six *Diopatra* samples (open squares) shown. (From Woodin 1978.)

to the tube(s), then contrast that with the density in a sample covering the same area at a slightly greater distance.

She centered the inner core over areas with zero, one, or six *Diopatra* tubes and was able to quantify their association with the remaining species of infauna. The association was confirmed over the sampling period of one year (Fig. 8.23). The abundance of polychaetes near six *Diopatra* was greater than that where there were none for nine of the twelve sets of cores, a difference that was not observed in the outer cores. The number of individuals increased as the number of *Diopatra* tubes increased from one to six, and the number of species was greater where there was one tube than where there was none. These relationships were significant statistically. Apparently, the tubes interfered with any disturbance of the sediment and in that way protected the infauna.

Two hypotheses were available to explain the observations. The first was that the *Diopatra* tubes somehow protected the infauna from pre-

Table 8.11. *Summary of one-way ANOVA for the effects of the densities of artificial and natural* Diopatra *tubes on the infauna*

Parameter	0D vs. 6D	6D vs. 6p vs. 1D + 5p	0D vs. 6D and 6p and 1D + 5p
No. of species	*	NS	*
No. of individuals	*	NS	**
No. of polychaete individuals	*	NS	**

Note: Inter samples from areas with 0 *Diopatra* (0D), 6 *Diopatra* (6D), 6 plastic straws (6p), and 1 *Diopatra* plus 5 plastic straws (1D + 5p). Asterisks give conventional probability levels.
From Woodin (1978).

dation, and the second was that the tubes enhanced settling of the larvae of the infaunal species by impeding water flow in their vicinity. Before these hypotheses could be tested, it was necessary to ask whether the protection was entirely physical, or was due to the presence of the living *Diopatra*. Woodin answered this question by using plastic drinking straws of the same diameter as the tubes. She inserted dowels into the straws, pushed them into the sediment to the appropriate depth, and arranged them so that either six of them were located where there were no *Diopatra*, or five were placed around a single individual of that species. The experiment was begun in May. In October, she sampled it in the routine way. That the replication was adequate is shown by the results (Table 8.11). The presence of a living worm was not necessary to achieve the effect of an increased density of infauna where either tubes or plastic straws, or combinations of them were present.

The most prominent disturbance to the sediment came from the activity of two large animal species that were present in the habitat in numbers from May to September or October. They were the blue crab, *Callinectes sapidus*, and the horseshoe crab, *Limulus polyphemus*. Both species make shallow pits in the sediment by stirring it, and they feed on the small infaunal elements thus disturbed. Samples taken in the pits showed marked reductions in both numbers of species and numbers of individuals, relative to undisturbed areas. It thus seemed probable that it was through inhibiting this activity that *Diopatra* tubes permitted the existence of a more abundant fauna in their immediate vicinity.

To test the two stated hypotheses, Woodin used exclosures consisting of 0.625-cm-mesh cages, 0.5 m on a side, and the following partial cages as controls on the cage effect: cages without tops, to control for shading; cages without sides, to control for the restriction of water flow by complete and topless cages; cages confined to that part below the surface of the sediment, to control for possible effects of the complete cages in restricting mechanical shifting of the sediment. The general control consisted of unmanipulated sites. Locations for the different treatments were chosen at random along a transect parallel to the shore. Initially, there were three replicates for each treatment. As three densities of *Diopatra* were used, there were nine cages of each kind. Not all of the cages survived the experimental period (one of the recognized hazards of conducting experiments out-of-doors), but enough remained for most of the statistical calculations to be satisfactory. Both hypotheses predicted a higher abundance of polychaetes in complete cages than elsewhere; the refuge hypothesis predicted that this would be the only difference; the larval settlement hypothesis predicted that sideless cages would have smaller numbers than topless cages. The results supported the predation hypothesis.

Woodin next devised an experiment to determine whether blue crabs or horseshoe crabs were more important as predators on the infauna. Blue crabs dig pits up to 6 cm deep, but smaller in diameter than those of the horseshoe crabs, which are only about 3 cm deep. Early in spring, before the crabs arrived on the sandflat, she drove stakes into the sediment at intervals of 10–12 cm around areas 3 by 3 m. Inasmuch as horseshoe crabs were at least 19 cm in diameter, and blue crabs presumably could pass between the stakes, the arrangement excluded only horseshoe crabs. The differential exclusion was carried out only in 1976, the total exclusions having been conducted in 1974 and 1975 as well. The results of all predator exclusions are given in Table 8.12. Blue crabs clearly were more important predators on polychaetes; horseshoe crabs had a significant effect on the small clam *Gemma*. These were well-planned, ingenious experiments. The use of plastic straws was original, and the use of experimental design to distinguish between competing hypotheses was excellent.

A community of mobile, filter-feeding species was the subject of experiments by Peterson and Andre (1980). The location was Mugu Lagoon in southern California – a tidal lagoon with bottom areas con-

Table 8.12. *Summary of one-way ANOVA tests and* t *test (1976b) for abundance effects associated with exclusion of predators on the infauna*

Comparison	1974 (May–Oct.)	1975 (Aug.–Oct.)	1976a (Apr.–July)	1976b (Apr.–July)
No. of individuals	*** (+)	*** (+)	** (+)	* (+)
No. of polychaete individuals	*** (+)	*** (+)	** (+)	NS
Abundance of:				
Streblospio	*** (+)	*** (+)	** (+)	* (+)
Spiochaetopterus	*** (+)	*** (+)	NS	NS
Nereis	*** (+)	*** (+)	NS	NS
Tharyx	*** (+)	NS	* (+)	NS
Gemma	NS	NS	NS	* (+)

Note: All epifauna > 0.625 cm excluded in 1974, 1975, and 1976a. Only *Limulus* excluded in 1976b. Direction of change relative to controls noted. Asterisks indicate conventional probability levels.
From Woodin (1981).

sisting of coarse sand, fine sand, silt, or a combination. The experiment was conducted in an area of mixed sediment types. Four filter-feeding bivalve mollusks were involved in the experiments, of which three were normally present in the area. They were *Protothaca straminea*, living at a depth of 2–8 cm in the sediment, *Saxidomus nuttalli*, at a depth of 23–51 cm, and *Tresus nuttallii*, at a depth of 30–60 cm. The fourth species, *Sanguinolaria nuttallii*, was not present at the location of the experiment, but was common in areas of coarse sand. Two other species of macrofauna were present: the sand dollar *Dendraster* sp. and the bivalve *Apolymetis biangulata*. Neither is a filter feeder. *Dendraster* lives in the top 2 cm, and *Apolymetis* at a depth of 8–16 cm.

It seemed unlikely that the filter feeders were competing for the food that flowed past with the tide, and the vertical stratification suggested that competition for space by the two deep-dwelling species prevented *Sanguinolaria* from being present. The design of the experiment was to have two blocks of square enclosures 50 by 50 cm. The enclosures were sunk in the substrate to a depth of 17 cm in the first year and 21–23 cm in the second year. There was no replication within blocks, and fortunately subsequent analysis revealed no significant differences between them.

Within each enclosure, the sediment was removed by hand and sieved, and the clams were identified and counted. At deeper depths

Table 8.13. *Densities and average lengths of clams used in each block (A, B) during summer 1975 and 1976*

Manipulated species	Density per 0.25 m² in single treatment		Average shell length (cm)	
	A	B	A	B
Summer 1975 (15 June–9 Aug.)				
Tresus + Saxidomus	6	11	10.8	8.8
Protothaca	15	15	1.8	2.2
Sanguinolaria	7	7	3.8	5.2
Summer 1976 (17/18 May–15/16 July)				
Tresus + Saxidomus	10	13	10.2	9.5
Protothaca	23	23	2.5	2.7
Sanguinolaria	15	15	4.6	4.8
Dead *Tresus + Saxidomus*	10	10	10.2	10.2

From Peterson and Andre (1980).

in the sediment, macrofauna were removed by groping in the remaining sediment. It was stated to be easy, but the total depth to which the animals were removed was not given. *Tresus* and *Saxidomus*, the local deep-dwelling species, were then reintroduced in their normal positions according to the experimental design, and the 15 cm of sediment was returned. Fixed numbers of *Sanguinolaria* and *Protothaca* were then placed on the surface of the sediment, into which they burrowed within 30 min. Other macrofauna were introduced at average densities into each enclosure. The experiment consisted of introducing *Sanguinolaria* into all enclosures and having different combinations of other species present: none, *Protothaca*, *Tresus* plus *Saxidomus*, and *Protothaca* plus *Tresus* plus *Saxidomus*. An additional enclosure had *Protothaca* alone. The effects on *Sanguinolaria* and *Protothaca* were measured by growth over the summer (15 June–9 August 1975; and 17 May–16 July 1976). In 1976, the effect of the physical presence of *Tresus* and *Saxidomus*, as compared with the living animals, was assessed by using shells of dead clams, packed with sand and equipped with wooden dowels to simulate siphons. The initial conditions are given in Table 8.13, and the results are in Table 8.14. Because of the absence of block effects, data for the two blocks were pooled in both years. In both years, there was a significant depression of growth by *Sanguinolaria* in the presence of living *Tresus* and *Saxidomus*, but there was no

Table 8.14. *Effects of* Tresus + Saxidomus *(T),* Protothaca *(P), and dead shells of* Tresus + Saxidomus *(DT) on* Sanguinolaria *(S)*

1975 experiment	S only	S + P	S + T	S + P + T
Density of S (pooling both replicates)				
Initial number	14	14	14	14
Final number (after 55 d)	14	13	8	7
Average growth (mm) of all S < 60 mm[a]	1.63	1.31	0.30	0.18

1976 experiment	S + P	S only	S + DT	S + T	S + P + T
Density of S (pooling both replicates)					
Initial number	30	30	30	30	30
Final number (after 60 d)	30	26	26	28	28
Percentage below 15-cm depth	83	92	88	86	79
Average growth (mm) of all S < 46.5 mm[b]	0.73	0.61	0.41	0.21	0.12

Note: Means that do not differ significantly ($p > .05$) in Scheffé post hoc comparisons are connected by (overlapping) boxes. In growth analysis, $N = 35$ in 1975, and $N = 55$ in 1976.
[a]Treatment effect highly significant at $.001 < p < .005$ for two-way ANOVA: Scheffé post hoc comparisons show *Sanguinolaria* growth significantly affected by *Tresus* + *Saxidomus* ($.005 < p < .01$ for $X_S - X_{S+T} + X_{S+P} - X_{S+P+T}$), but not significantly affected by *Protothaca*.
[b]Treatment effect highly significant at $p < .001$ for two-way ANOVA: Scheffé post hoc comparisons show *Sanguinolaria* growth significantly affected by *Tresus* + *Saxidomus* ($p < .001$), but not significantly affected by *Protothaca*.
From Peterson and Andre (1980).

measurable effect of dead shells, nor of *Protothaca*. They also found no effect of the other species on growth of *Protothaca*. They concluded that there was competition for space at deeper levels, because there was no effect on the filter-feeding *Protothaca*, which does not overlap in vertical distribution with the other three species.

Although technically there was pseudoreplication in that individuals within enclosures were assumed to be independent, the absence of block effects virtually eliminated any problem of confounding location with treatment in determining the result.

Summary

Like those in terrestrial and freshwater environments, marine experiments are best considered in subgroups. They are divided according to the substrate: rocky, soft, "fouling," and coral. The ecological interactions are quite different in these situations. The rocky intertidal habitats have attracted the most attention, and there have been many successful experiments there. Explanations of the results in general terms require many qualifications about exposure to wave action, height in the intertidal, and even, apparently, latitude, as each of these factors has been shown to affect the results. Predation and competition are common, and indirect effects have been demonstrated. In nearly all cases, competition has involved interference, mostly in competition for attachment space. Interference has also been demonstrated among clams in soft sediments and among encrusting colonial animals beneath coral fronds. In the same kind of habitat, fish have been shown to carry away competing sea urchins. In fouling communities, preemption of space is the rule. This means that priority effects are common, any of several species being able to hold off the others until it is removed physically. The difficulty of reaching general conclusions about marine communities may be related to the fact that much of the food supply comes from external sources, that is, the water coming in with each tide. A full understanding may have to await integration of this pelagic contribution to the intertidal communities.

9

Conclusions to be drawn from field experiments

Introduction

The numbers of ecological field experiments have grown at an increasing rate over the past two decades, and because the theme of this book is that experimentation is necessary for progress in ecology, it is fair to ask what the experiments have revealed about ecological processes. Obviously, observations of field situations and spontaneous occurrences have provided insight throughout the history of ecology, but the present discussion is restricted to intentional manipulations and their contributions to understanding ecological processes.

The most important conclusion to be drawn from the whole group of experiments is that each kind of environment should be considered separately, because there are few, if any, specific statements about ecological processes that will be true across all environments. As stated in the Preface, that is the reason for arranging the experiments by kind of environment in which they were conducted, instead of by kind of interaction, for example. Thus, simultaneous consideration of all experiments on competition, or predation, would not permit as clear statements about ecological processes as does the arrangement adopted.

Forests

The ecological phenomena that have been revealed or confirmed for forests can be assembled into a more coherent analysis than can the results in any other kind of habitat. The experiments in each trophic level have given internally consistent results, and the relationships between trophic levels are consistent with those within each. Those are the reasons for beginning the descriptions and critiques with the forest environment and for beginning this chapter with an interpretation of the forest ecosystem, as revealed by the outcome of the experiments.

316

Decomposers in forests have been tested for density dependence within species, as well as for competition between species. Although not all experiments tested for these interactions directly, the most obvious interpretation of the indirect ones is that interspecific competition was involved in the outcome. Negative interactions among decomposer species have been found in nearly all systems tested, and most of the experimenters have interpreted their results as showing interference competition.

The competitive effects of forest trees have been thoroughly documented, whether by testing for competition among the roots or among the crowns.

Forest herbs have been the objects of several excellent studies. The competitive influence of tree roots in trenching experiments is well documented, but there have been convincing experiments showing that within woodlands, the ecological distribution of herb species is determined by the distribution of nutrients or toxic ions. The small fraction of forest production that is consumed by folivores and sapsuckers has received three different interpretations: the effect of weather in keeping herbivore populations in check (Andrewartha & Birch 1954), the effect of predators in regulating herbivore populations below the level at which they can consume a large fraction of the plant production (Hairston et al. 1960), and the possession of defensive chemicals by the dominant plants (Murdoch 1966; Rosenthal & Janzen 1979).

The adaptations of trees to herbivore damage have been well documented, but the adaptational responses of the herbivores to plant defenses have also been shown experimentally to be ubiquitous and effective. The inedibility of the dominant trees is a myth.

Only one experiment has demonstrated unequivocally that competition was limiting forest herbivore populations: that of McClure. His clear demonstration of competition between two species of herbivores on hemlocks confirms the observation that nearly all examples of forest defoliation, and the implied competition among herbivores, were by introduced pests, the most famous example being of the gypsy moth, *Lymantria dispar*.

The effects of predators and parasites on forest herbivores have been demonstrated in a number of experiments. These have involved excluding birds or ants or all predators and parasitoids from certain plants and not from others. In all cases, the survival of the herbivores was greatly enhanced, and although a density-dependent relationship was not looked for, the results provided a highly necessary condition for the regulation of herbivore populations by their enemies.

Although one could wish for better experimental design in some cases, competition among granivores and among predators has been shown in a substantial majority of experiments.

Finally, it should be noted that except for the trenching experiments on competition among forest trees, nearly all of the experiments described for that habitat were conducted after the publication of Hairston, Smith, and Slobodkin (HSS) (1960), and after the subsequent exchange of comments (Murdoch 1966; Ehrlich & Birch 1967; Slobodkin et al. 1967). Many of the investigators noted the implications of their work for our hypotheses. The publication has been sustained well in the temperate forests where the basic observations are easily verified: We are not making coal, and the world is green.

Successional communities

In habitats that are undergoing succession, relationships in and between most trophic levels are less consistent than they are in forests. Decomposers are an exception in that all experiments have shown these organisms to be in competition, just as they are in forests. That result shows that the accumulation of organic matter in most terrestrial situations is too slow to be of importance in preventing competition among the fungi and bacteria. The universality of competition in that group suggests that the animals feeding on them are not themselves food-limited. This principle of alternating limitation of trophic levels was expressed in Varley's presidential address (1957). These animals, sometimes called decomposers, obtain part of their nutrition from the dead plant material directly, part through ingested microbial enzymes, and part from the digestion of the bacteria and fungi that are present (Martin 1987). In the process of chewing the dead plant matter, the detritus feeders create smaller particles and thus larger surface areas for the true decomposers to colonize. To some extent, there is thus a mutualistic relationship. The line of reasoning suggests that the populations of detritus feeders themselves are limited by a factor other than competition. I have found few references relevant to the suggestion, but Sunderland and Sutton (1980) obtained impressive evidence that woodlice (the Isopoda *Philoscia muscorum* and *Armadillidium vulgare*) are important components in the diet of a number of invertebrate predators and scavengers. They estimated that predation could have reduced the prebreeding population by at least 24 percent and that juvenile mortality due to predation was as much as 51 percent. No evidence was presented on the possible density-dependent relationships of this predation, but the data are consistent with the hypothesis that detritus feeders are predator-limited. As with other ecolgical interactions, introduced species are exceptional. Paris (1963) found no evidence that predation affected the population of *Armadillidium vulgare* that he studied in California.

Among successional plants, competition has been demonstrated experimentally in several studies, but some have failed to show it, and among those that have shown it, interspecific effects were weak and diffuse in at least two studies, in marked contrast to competition among forest trees. The picture is consistent with a number of studies showing that herbivores have an important impact on successional plants, as well as a few studies showing at least minimal competition among the herbivores. Many of these plants are known to produce chemicals that protect them from at least some of their herbivores, but other herbivores have evolved specific mechanisms to detoxify, sequester, or rapidly excrete these chemicals. Predation has been shown to have a significant effect on the populations of some herbivores, but competition among the predators has been difficult to demonstrate.

The experiments that have been conducted in successional communities confirm the existence of much weaker links among the producer–herbivore–predator trophic levels than is apparently true in forest ecosystems. I suggest that the weaker links contribute to the continuation of the successional process. As the process goes on, these interspecific interactions become stronger, and the processes within and between trophic levels become more consistent. Eventually, a condition is reached where instability is so infrequent that the whole ecosystem has become impossible for another to replace. Of course, deliberate interference by humans or their domestic animals can halt the process. These interpretations are compatible with the views recently expressed by Oksanen (1988).

Arid environments

The experiments in desert ecosystems have shown that there are three more or less independent sets of interrelationships. These are the perennial plants and the food chains depending on them, the annual plant–granivore set, and the insectivores plus their prey and predators. There have not been enough experiments for us to conclude firmly that these ecological groups have so few connections that complete independence can be assumed in constructing theories, which would thereby be simpler, but it is possible to understand what still needs to be done.

The relationships that most resemble those in more humid regions are the ones involving the perennial plants. As is pointed out in Chapter 6, the desert world is green for only a small part of the time, and over less than one-third of its area, but the shrubs and perennial grasses occupy all of the space through their widespread roots. Competition among these producers is strong, and the best experimental evidence for folivore damage concerns a successional species, with the folivore hastening the replacement of its food by later successional species.

Two sources of evidence affirm that the distribution and abundance of these plants are governed by interspecific interactions, rather than by specific adaptation to local conditions: the experience of ranching, where shrubs (sagebrush, creosote bush, or mesquite) have increased as the grasses have been consumed, and the experiment of Gurevitch (1986) in demonstrating the suitability of physical conditions where a species was not found, provided that competitors were removed.

Following the reasoning of HSS, it should be rewarding to devise experiments testing the hypothesis that predation is responsible for preventing the folivores from becoming numerous enough to damage the perennial vegetation. Three groups of insectivorous predators have been investigated: scorpions, lizards, and spiders. Scorpion populations appear to be controlled by cannibalism, and the evidence for competition among lizards is equivocal, the implications of which are discussed later. One spider species, however, has been shown to occupy territories of a fixed size when in harsh environments, with good evidence against compressibility. Territory size appears to be selectively adjusted to lows in the fluctuations of their prey, which suggests strongly that the supply of prey frequently is below predator demand in the desert grassland habitat. Most of the prey were either folivores or sapsuckers, but their food plants were not listed, and it is not known that they were primarily perennials.

Some experiments have demonstrated competitive effects of perennials on annuals, and between annuals, but the interactions between granivores and annuals, and between different groups of granivores, appear to dominate this ecologically separate group of desert organisms. Experiments have left little doubt that granivores compete with each other and that they have a powerful influence on the abundance and species composition of the annual plants. Competition, however, is not purely exploitative. The species benefiting from the removal of competitors do not fully compensate for the extra food made available, and only one species, the competitive dominant, increases in abundance when supplementary food is provided. A most interesting question remains: Is there no impact of predators on these competing granivores? Experiments along that line would give interesting results, no matter what their outcome.

The third ecologically distinct group, the insectivores, might be expected to be tied to the annual plant–granivore group through predation on ants by lizards, and the potential impact of this predation on the ant population has been reported (Whitford & Bryant 1979; Munger 1984), but not actual effects. The generally low level of interspecific competition among desert lizards, if it occurs at all, suggests that population sizes are determined by factors other than the availability of their prey or competition for territory. Predation on the lizards is a possibility, and because most of their predators are also reptiles, removal experiments might be both feasible and rewarding.

Clearly, the desert ecosystem has been the location of a number of revealing experiments and might eventually become the best understood.

Fresh water

Despite good individual experiments, the stream community, if it exists as an interacting group of species, is less well understood than are lake and pond communities. Perhaps that is because there is so much disturbance in many streams that net interactions are weak, or perhaps the difficulty is related to the divergent sources of nutrients, a difference that apparently caused opposing results in experiemnts testing for competition.

In lakes, two factors appear to be of greatest importance in determining community structure and dynamics: nutrients and the number of trophic levels. The sensitivities of the communities in oligotrophic lakes to manipulations of the nutrient level have been successfully analyzed through a number of experiments, spanning the size range from small containers through large bag enclosures to whole lakes. The results for different trophic levels are determined largely by the presence of an immediately higher trophic level, which in many examples prevents expansion of the next lower level to the benefit of the second trophic level down. In mesotrophic and eutrophic lakes, those with planktivores and no piscivores have increased densities of phytoplankton; those with piscivores have abundant large zooplankton and clearer water. Thus, an effect of planktivorous fish on the species composition of the plankton is well established, but the reasons for the decrease in phytoplankton with an increase in abundance of large zooplankton are not clear, because there is competition, apparently for food, within both kinds of zooplankton communities. Top–down control of successive trophic levels does not hold for phytoplankton in deep oligotrophic lakes.

Where predation is lessened, interspecific competition among prey species has been demonstrated experimentally for the prey of both invertebrate and vertebrate predators.

Some of the relationships in eutrophic and mesotrophic lakes have been found to be less obvious than those in oligotrophic lakes. The findings that cyanophytes (blue-greens) fixed nitrogen and that their abundance was correlated with a low N–P ratio (e.g., Hutchinson 1944) led to the suggestion that blooms of blue-greens could be suppressed by the addition of ammonium nitrate, because the other algae presumably could win in competition under that condition. The experiment was not successful. The bloom developed independent of the experimental conditions. The inedibility of blue-greens by many zooplankters has also upset a logical analysis through the trophic level approach. The reverse experiment of adding nitrate and phosphate to an oligotrophic lake produced a bloom of the blue-green *Anabaena spiroides* (Schindler 1974), as described in Chapter 7. No such result was obtained by adding nitrate alone. The addition of ammonium nitrate to a eutrophic lake did not prevent a bloom of blue-greens.

Ecologists working on ponds have been concerned primarily with direct biotic interactions, and only the observations of Hrbáček (1962) and the classic experiments of Hall et al. (1970) tested the effects of adding nutrients. In the latter example, the addition of 0.23 kg of commercial fertilizer (N : P : K = 10 : 1 : 1) per week to about 7,150 m^3 of water gave no detectable increase in the concentrations; more than ten times that amount had to be used to obtain convincing results. Presumably, the clay sediments bound the lesser amounts. The two large ponds studied by Hrbáček were both fertilized, but that could not be considered an experiment (Chapter 7).

Biotic interactions have been demonstrated experimentally in practically all cases where they have been sought. They include density dependence in both herbivores and predators, competition among both herbivores and predators, and the effects of predators on the compositions of communities of plankton and benthos. There is a difficulty in understanding coevolution in ponds, because almost universal introduction of exotic species of fish by sportsmen or government agencies has made the original compositions of pond communities unknowable. The same is true of many, if not most, lake communities.

Despite the difficulties, experimentation in freshwater habitats has greatly expanded our understanding of ecological processes there.

Marine environments

Experimentation in marine environments has revealed an array of biological interactions as extensive as those on land, but it is difficult to find common themes because of the great importance of the nature of the substrate and the nature of physical forces under different conditions.

From the many successful experiments that have been carried out there, it should be possible to produce at least verbal theories of the complex of ecological processes in marine communities. That is probably true, if sufficient subdivisions of the environment are made. The first division must be made on the basis of the substrate, and the rocky intertidal is the one in which the interactions are most completely known. There, distinctions must be made according to two more dimensions: height in the intertidal zone and amount of exposure to waves. Both dimensions involve relative resistance to physical factors: resistance to desiccation and resistance to being swept away. These factors determine the species that can be present, at least potentially. Competition and predation sort among those species and determine which will be present, and in what abundance. Lower in the intertidal, where the physical environment is less severe, the biotic interactions are more important, and the compositions of the communities are more interesting. Perhaps theories could start at the physical extremes, where the interactions are few and simple, and work toward calmer water and lower levels, where the complexity will require deep knowledge and great ingenuity. A good theory will have to be able predict changes with the gradients; otherwise, we shall be left in our present state of having experiments that resolve questions about highly specific localities, without the results being capable of being extrapolated.

In considering the array of experiments that have demonstrated the existence of interspecific competition, one is struck by the universal finding that the competition is based on some form of interference. Examples are the crushing or undermining of one species of barnacle by another, the smothering of some species by others, the unknown reasons for crowding in some soft sediments, the allelochemical effects among colonial animals on the undersides of corals, the results of whiplashing by large algae, and the physical removal of sea urchins by a fish. These mechanisms demonstrate the importance of space as the overwhelmingly important resource in all kinds of marine environments.

Except for areas exposed to extreme physical disturbance, it is only where herbivory or predation keeps surfaces clean of sessile forms that there is open space. The factors that permit these consumers to dominate a situation are known for some rocky locations: protection from wave action; occupying a low level in the intertidal region. That these do not account for all cases is shown by the striking differences between rocky shores in temperate and tropical locations. The former normally are covered with an abundance of sessile animals or macrophytes, whereas the latter appear superficially to support only algal crusts. The difference appears to be related to the abundance of fishes and other motile consumers in the tropics, but that does not explain their absence off temperate shores. Much of the attraction of these marine environments for experimenters lies in the densely crowded populations of sessile organisms, readily available in ample numbers of specimens that can be followed individually, sometimes for years. Such situations have led to much ingenious experimentation. The great shortcoming in most marine locations lies in the fact that the larval or spore stages occur in the inaccessible open water, with poorly understood great variations in abundance from season to season or from year to year. That these fluctuations can make a great difference in the outcomes of experiments on the sessile adults, and on their interpretation, is well documented (Underwood & Denley 1984; Gaines & Roughgarden 1987). Perhaps when someone is ingenious enough to discover the basis of the fluctuations, the reasons for the lack of a generalization about the ecology of rocky marine shores will be understood, and the many experiments will be brought together in a theoretical framework.

In marine habitats with soft sediments as the substrate, there is less obvious local heterogeneity than in rocky habitats, but there have been fewer experiments, and generalizations have been difficult. The demonstration of the importance of secondary predation is only one complication that shows the need for more work in these habitats.

Experiments needed for further understanding

In several places in the text, I have mentioned experiments that would promote an understanding of the complete set of interspecific interactions in particular situations. To emphasize the incompleteness of the ecology of all environments and the need for more experimentation, suggestions for experiments on the interactions whose detection and measurement would especially promote an understanding of their ecosystems are assembled in this final section.

As far as forests generally are concerned, there is a great need for an understanding of the effects of parasitoid insects on populations of their hosts in natural situations. There is also a need for knowledge of possible competition among them, and between them and other secondary consumers, such as birds, in forest ecosystems. It will not be easy to exclude parasitoids without having unwanted cage effects, and it will not be possible to exclude parasitoids and permit access by birds, but the exclusion of both and the separate exclusion of birds should help. Controls for cage effects have been devised regularly by marine ecologists, and similar ingenuity could prevail on land. At another level, the widely confirmed existence of competition among decomposers suggests that the animals that consume them do not have a large quantitative effect on the populations of bacteria and fungi. Experiments testing for predation on these detritus feeders are needed, as are experiments testing for competition among them. Their nutrition comes through three different routes: the bodies of decomposers, the cellulytic enzymes captured from the decomposers, and, for some of them at least, their own cellulases. The determination of the abundance of the detritivores is largely unknown.

As a special case, the *Eucalyptus* forests of Australia require a number of experiments because of the much greater proportion of primary production that is consumed by herbivores there than in other Temperate Zone forests: Is the proportion sufficient to reduce or eliminate competition among the trees? Is there competition among the herbivores, as might be expected from the reduction in their food supply? A few experiments that have been conducted on competition between predators and on their effects on herbivores suggest that the general relationships are much like those in North America, but such a conclusion is still premature.

In successional communities, the few experiments that have been conducted suggest that competition among predators is weak to the point of being undetectable, although some of the same kinds of predators (spiders, for example) have been shown experimentally to compete in other kinds of habitats, such as a salt marsh (Spiller 1984). The generality of the absence of competition among successional predators needs testing with more experiments, using other kinds of predators. Flying insects and birds are prime candidates for such experiments, although admittedly a high level of ingenuity will be required to devise satisfactory designs. In the process, however, it should be possible to test for the effects of predation in those communities.

Desert communities appear to consist of three sets of species that interact within these sets, but have little impact on each other. Is this impression correct, or does it depend on the absence of certain critical experiments? Experiments are needed on competition among desert folivores and on the effects of predation on three classes of prey: folivores, granivores, and insectivores. Experiments on lizards have yielded inconclusive results. What determines their abundance, which is considerable, especially in North American deserts? Are birds important predators in desert communities? Many of them are granivores, but they have received no experimental attention. That birds are difficult experimental subjects is well known, but in other habitats successful experiments have been carried out. Effective predation on desert insectivores would help explain the lack of trophic links between these apparently independent series: perennial plants and their dependent consumers, annual plants and their consumers, and the insectivorous lizards and their predators and prey.

In freshwater communities, a number of experiments would improve matters. The hypothesis that the systems are most strongly influenced by predation (in its widest sense), as opposed to control by nutrient supply, is controversial, and experiments permitting elucidation of the relationship between these two factors are needed. These would include replicated experiments of long duration in lakes on the "trophic cascade." The effect of adding piscivorous fish, observed in several cases, should be followed long enough to establish whether or not the system was in equilibrium. The kind of planktivorous fish involved in such experiments is important – just any fish would not constitute an adequate test. These experiments need to be conducted in both oligotrophic and eutrophic lakes, and it is most important to monitor all trophic levels. They might well solve the question, raised in Chapter 7, of why the algae, so conspicuous in Schindler's whole-lake experiment (1974), were not consumed by the herbivorous zooplankton, although further experiments excluding either planktivores piscivores or both might still be needed.

Subsidiary experiments that would be helpful would include competition among species of algae, with and without the presence of each of two kinds of herbivorous plankton, a large *Daphnia* and *Bosmina*, for example. Experiments are needed that will test for the effect of predaceous zooplankton within the context of the addition of piscivorous fish.

It is surprising that more experiments on the effects of nutrient levels in ponds have not been conducted. Perhaps that is related to the difficulties experienced by Hall et al. (1970), but adequate replication could overcome most problems, especially in artificial ponds. Long-term experiments would be important here, as elsewhere.

In streams, the most pressing problem appears to be an understanding of the full importance of the source of nutrients for the communities for all interspecific interactions. Perhaps manipulation of light for streams where allochthonous material is important, or the addition of allochthonous material into streams where producers are important, would elucidate matters. Streams are difficult because of the unpredictable disturbances that may wreck the experiments.

The greatest need in many marine habitats is more knowledge of the life history stages occurring in the open water. In most cases, the abundance of larvae is known only after they have settled, and from that information, some correlations can be made about seasonal and other fluctuations, but the causes of many of these fluctuations have so far been deduced through weak inference.

Experiments are needed to establish whether failure to settle is caused by a failure of larvae to be produced or by the vagaries of currents keeping them away from appropriate sites. It is not clear in many cases how far the larvae drift before settling, nor does it appear to be known how much spatial variation exists in their production. With a thorough knowledge of local distributions, an ingenious ecologist might be able to answer some of these questions experimentally. Some species are unable to settle where the surface is not completely acceptable. What are the necessary conditions?

Another set of determinants concerns the effects of predators on the free-swimming larvae. Gaines and Roughgarden (1987) presented evidence that fish fry influence the number of barnacles available for settling, and it is possible that sessile predators could be effective as well. Clearly, a theory of the ecology of any marine environment must eventually incorporate statements about the larval stages of the organisms concerned.

Marine communities where the substrate is not rocky are less well known than are those on the rocks, because the organisms are for the most part concealed within the sand or silt and hence are less tempting to inquisitive ecologists. Competition and predation have been demonstrated, but their importance to the dynamics of the communities is not well understood. Experiments yielding quantitative estimates are needed. The demonstration of secondary predation by an abundant predator (*Fundulus*) in the salt-marsh habitat is most interesting, especially in view of the fact that it is also a primary predator. Further experiments in that habitat, elucidating the potential impact of the exclusively primary predator, *Palaemonetes*, on competition among the prey, would improve our understanding of the community interactions.

Perhaps the greatest need resulting from the ecological experiments that have been conducted is for a comprehensive theory for each kind of environment, taking the experimental results into account in realistic ways. These theories could then be used in making predictions that could be tested by further experiments. The next major advances will come from experiments testing hypotheses that incorporate a higher level of complexity than has been used in the first wave of experimentation. Several authors, most recently Yodzis (1988), have called attention to the many indirect effects that must operate in natural communities, and how such effects can alter the outcomes of experiments designed to test for simple interactions. When the direction and magnitude of indirect effects can be predicted sufficiently well to permit the conduct of experiments testing the validity of the predictions, ecology will have arrived at a new level of scientific precision.

References

Adams, D. H., & L. F. Roth. 1969. Intraspecific competition among genotypes of Fomes cajanderi decaying young-growth Douglas-fir. *Forest Science* 15:327–31.

Addicott, J. F. 1986. On the population consequences of mutualism. In: *Community Ecology*, J. Diamond & T. J. Case, eds., pp. 425–36. New York, Harper & Row.

Alford, R. A., & H. M. Wilbur. 1985. Priority effects in experimental pond communities: competition between *Bufo* and *Rana*. *Ecology* 66:1097–105.

Al-Naib, F. A.-G., & E. L. Rice. 1971. Allelopathic effects of *Platanus occidentalis*. *Bulletin of the Torrey Botanical Club* 98:75–82.

Anderson, R. M., & R. M. May. 1979. Population biology of infectious diseases: I & II. *Nature* 280:361–7, 455–61.

– 1981. The population dynamics of microparasites and their invertebrate hosts. *Philosophical Transactions of the Royal Society* 291:451–524.

Andrewartha, H. G. 1958. The use of conceptual models in population biology. *Cold Spring Harbor Symposia on Quantitative Biology* 22:219–36.

– 1963. Density-dependence in the Australian thrips. *Ecology* 44:218–20.

Andrewartha, H. G., & L. C. Birch. 1954. *The Distribution and Abundance of Animals*. Chicago, University of Chicago Press.

Askenmo, C., A. von Bromssen, J. Ekman, & C. Jansson. 1977. Impact of some wintering birds on spider abundance in spruce. *Oikos* 28:90–4.

Bailey, J. R. 1937. Notes on plethodont salamanders of the southeastern United States. *Occasional Papers of the Museum of Zoology, University of Michigan* 364:1–10.

Barica, J., H. Kling, & J. Gibson. 1980. Experimental manipulation of algal bloom composition by nitrogen addition. *Canadian Journal of Fisheries and Aquatic Science* 37:1175–83.

Belovsky, G. E. 1984. Moose and snowshoe hare competition and a mechanistic explanation from foraging theory. *Oecologia (Berlin)* 61:150–9.

Bender, E. A., T. J. Case, & M. E. Gilpin. 1984. Perturbation experiments in community ecology: theory and practice. *Ecology* 65:1–13.

Benndorf, J., H. Kneschke, K. Kossatz, & E. Penz. 1984. Manipulation of the pelagic food web by stocking with predacious fishes. *Internationale Revue der gesamten Hydrobiologie* 69:407–28.

Berendse, F. 1983. Interspecific competition and niche differentiation between *Plantago lanceolata* and *Anthoxanthum odoratum* in a natural hayfield. *Journal of Ecology* 71:379–90.

329

Birch, L. C. 1953. Experimental background to the study of the distribution and abundance of insects. I. The influence of temperature, moisture and food on the innate capacity for increase of three grain beetles. *Ecology* 34:698–711.

− 1958. The role of weather in determining the distribution and abundance of animals. *Cold Spring Harbor Symposia on Quantitative Biology* 22:203–18.

Black, R. 1979. Competition between intertidal limpets: an intrusive niche on a steep resource gradient. *Journal of Animal Ecology* 48:401–11.

Blanchette, R. A., & C. G. Shaw. 1978. Associations among bacteria, yeasts, and basidiomycetes during wood decay. *Phytopathology* 68:631–7.

Brand, C. J., L. B. Keith, & C. A. Fischer. 1976. Lynx responses to changing snowshoe hare densities in central Alberta. *Journal of Wildlife Management* 40:416–28.

Brian, P. W. 1957. The ecological significance of antibiotic production. In: *Microbial Ecology. Seventh Symposium of the Society for General Microbiology*, pp. 168–88. Cambridge University Press.

Brooks, J. L. 1968. The effects of prey size selection by lake planktivores. *Systematic Zoology* 17:273–91.

Brooks, J. L., & S. I. Dodson. 1965. Predation, body size, and composition of plankton. *Science* 150:28–35.

Brown, J. H., & D. W. Davidson. 1986. Reply to Galindo. *Ecology* 67:1423–5.

Brown, J. H., D. W. Davidson, J. C. Munger, & R. S. Inouye. 1986. Experimental community ecology: the desert granivore system. In: *Community Ecology*, J. Diamond & T. J. Case, eds., pp. 41–61. New York, Harper & Row.

Brown, J. H., D. W. Davidson, & O. J. Reichman. 1979a. An experimental study of competition between seed-eating desert rodents and ants. *American Zoologist* 19:1129–43.

Brown, J. H., & J. C. Munger. 1985. Experimental manipulation of a desert rodent community: food addition and species removal. *Ecology* 66:1545–63.

Brown, J. H., O. J. Reichman, & D. W. Davidson. 1979b. Granivory in desert ecosystems. *Annual Review of Ecology and Systematics* 10:201–27.

Brown, V. K., A. C. Gange, I. M. Evans, & A. L. Storr. 1987a. The effect of insect herbivory on the growth and reproduction of two annual *Vicia* species at different stages in plant succession. *Journal of Ecology* 75:1173–89.

Brown, V. K., M. Leijn, & C. S. A. Stinson. 1987b. The experimental manipulation of insect herbivore load by the use of an insecticide (malathion): the effect of application on plant growth. *Oecologia (Berlin)* 72:377–81.

Bryant, J. P. 1981. Biochemical deterrence of snowshoe hare browsing by adventitious shoots of four Alaskan trees. *Science* 213:889–90.

Bryant, J. P., F. S. Chapin, & D. R. Klein. 1983. Carbon/nutrient balance of boreal plants in relation to vertebrate herbivory. *Oikos* 40:357–68.

Bryant, J. P., & P. J. Kuropat. 1980. Selection of winter forage by subarctic browsing vertebrates: the role of plant chemistry. *Annual Review of Ecology and Systematics* 11:261–85.

Bultman, T. L., & S. H. Faeth. 1986. Experimental evidence for intraspecific competition in a lepidopteran leaf miner. *Ecology* 67:442–8.

Bush, A. O., & J. C. Holmes. 1983. Niche separation and the broken-stick model: use with multiple assemblages. *American Naturalist* 122:849–55.

Buss, L., & J. Jackson. 1979. Competitive networks: nontransitive competitive relationships in cryptic coral reef environments. *American Naturalist* 113:223–34.

Cable, D. R. 1969. Competition in the semidesert grass-shrub type as influenced by root systems, growth habits, and soil moisture extraction. *Ecology* 50:27–38.

Cameron, G. N. 1977. Experimental species removal: demographic responses by *Sigmodon hispidus* and *Reithrodontomys fulvescens*. *Journal of Mammalogy* 58:488–506.

Cameron, G. N., & B. Kincaid. 1982. Species removal effects on movements of Sigmodon hispidus and Reithrodontomys fulvescens. *American Midland Naturalist* 108:60–7.

Carpenter, S. R., J. F. Kitchell, J. R. Hodgson, P. A. Cochran, J. J. Elser, M. M. Elser, D. M. Dodge, D. Kretchmer, S. He, & C. M. von Ende. 1987. Regulation of lake primary productivity by food web structure. *Ecology* 68:1863–76.

Castenholz, R. W. 1961. The effect of grazing on marine littoral diatom populations. *Ecology* 42:783–94.

Cates, R. G., & G. H. Orians. 1975. Successional status and the palatability of plants to generalized herbivores. *Ecology* 56:410–8.

Chappell, M. A. 1978. Behavioral factors in the altitudinal zonation of chipmunks (*Eutamias*). *Ecology* 59:565–79.

Clark, F. E., & E. A. Paul. 1970. The microflora of grassland. *Advances in Agronomy* 22:375–435.

Cohen, J. E. 1968. Alternate derivations of a species-abundance relation. *American Naturalist* 102:165–72.

– 1978. *Food Webs and Niche Space*. Princeton, N.J., Princeton University Press.

Connell, J. H. 1961a. Effects of competition, predation by *Thais lapillus*, and other factors on natural populations of the barnacle *Balanus balanoides*. *Ecological Monographs* 31:61–104.

– 1961b. The influence of interspecific competition and other factors on the distribution of the barnacle *Chthamalus stellatus*. *Ecology* 42:710–23.

– 1970. A predator-prey system in the marine intertidal region. I. *Balanus glandula* and several predatory species of *Thais*. *Ecological Monographs* 40:49–78.

– 1971. On the role of natural enemies in preventing competitive exclusion in some marine animals and in rain forest trees. In: *Dynamics of Populations*, P. J. den Boer & G. Gradwell, eds., pp. 298–312. Wageningen, Centre for Agricultural Publishing and Documentation.

– 1975. Some mechanisms producing structure in natural communities: a model and evidence from field experiments. In: *Ecology and Evolution of Communities*, M. L. Cody & J. M. Diamond, eds. pp. 460–90. Cambridge, Mass., Harvard University Press.

- 1980. Diversity and the coevolution of communities, or the ghost of competition past. *Oikos* 35:131–8.
- 1983. On the prevalence and relative importance of interspecific competition: evidence from field experiments. *American Naturalist* 122:661–98.
Connell, J. H., & R. O. Slatyer. 1977. Mechanisms of succession in natural communities and their role in community stability and organization. *American Naturalist* 111:1119–44.
Connor, E. F., & D. Simberloff. 1978. Species number and compositional similarity of the Galapagos flora and avifauna. *Ecological Monographs* 48:219–48.
- 1979. Assembly of species communities: chance or competition? *Ecology* 60:1132–40.
Crawley, M. J. 1983. *Herbivory. The Dynamics of Animal–Plant Interactions.* Oxford, Blackwell.
Crombie, A. C. 1945. On competition between different species of graminivorous insects. *Proceedings of the Royal Society of London, Biological Sciences* 132:362–95.
- 1946. Further experiments on insect competition. *Proceedings of the Royal Society of London, Biological Sciences* 133:76–109.
Davidson, D. W., R. S. Inouye, & J. H. Brown. 1984. Granivory in a desert ecosystem: experimental evidence for indirect facilitation of ants by rodents. *Ecology* 65:1780–6.
Davidson, D. W., D. A. Samson, & R. S. Inouye. 1985. Granivory in the Chihuahuan desert: interactions within and between trophic levels. *Ecology* 66:486–502.
Davidson J., & H. G. Andrewartha. 1948a. Annual trends in a natural population of *Thrips imaginis* (Thysanoptera). *Journal of Animal Ecology* 17:193–9.
- 1948b. The influence of rainfall, evaporation, and atmospheric temperature on fluctuations in the size of a natural population of *Thrips imaginis*. *Journal of Animal Ecology* 17:200–22.
Dayton, P. K. 1971. Competition, disturbance and community organization: the provision and subsequent utilization of space in a rocky intertidal community. *Ecological Monographs* 41:351–89.
- 1973. Two cases of resource partitioning in an intertidal community: making the right prediction for the wrong reason. *American Naturalist* 107:662–70.
- 1975. Experimental evaluation of ecological dominance in a rocky intertidal algal community. *Ecological Monographs* 45:137–59.
DeMott, W., & W. C. Kerfoot. 1982. Competition among cladocerans: nature of the interaction between *Bosmina* and *Daphnia*. *Ecology* 63:1949–66.
Denno, R. F., & M. S. McClure, eds. 1983. *Variable Plants and Herbivores in Natural and Managed Systems*, New York, Academic Press.
De Vita, J. 1979. Niche separation and the broken-stick model. *American Naturalist* 114:171–8.
de Vos, A. 1964. Food utilization of snowshoe hares on Manitoulin Island, Ontario. *Journal of Forestry* 62:238–44.

Dhondt, A. A., & R. Eyckerman. 1980. Competition between the great tit and the blue tit outside the breeding season in field experiments. *Ecology* 61:1291–6.

Dhondt, A. A., R. Eyckerman, & J. Huble. 1979. Will great tits become little tits? *Biological Journal of the Linnean Society* 11:289–94.

Diamond, J. 1986. Overview: laboratory experiments, field experiments, and natural experiments. In: *Community Ecology*, J. Diamond & T. J. Case, eds., pp. 3–22. New York, Harper & Row.

Dobbs, C. G., & W. H. Hinson. 1953. A widespread fungistasis in soils. *Nature* 172:197–9.

Dunham, A. E. 1980. An experimental study of interspecific competition between the iguanid lizards *Sceloporus merriami* and *Urosaurus ornatus*. *Ecological Monographs* 50:309–30.

Edmunds, G. F., & D. N. Alstad. 1978. Coevolution in insect herbivores and conifers. *Science* 199:941–5.

Edson, J. L. 1985. The influences of predation and resource subdivision on the coexistence of goldenrod aphids. *Ecology* 66:1736–43.

Ehrlich, P. R., & L. C. Birch. 1967. The "balance of nature" and "population control." *American Naturalist* 101:97–107.

Ehrlich, P. R., & J. Roughgarden. 1987. *The Science of Ecology*. New York, Macmillan.

Eickwort, K. R. 1977. Population dynamics of a relatively rare species of milkweed beetle (*Labidomera*). *Ecology* 58:527–38.

Eisenberg, R. M. 1966. The regulation of density in a natural population of the pond snail, *Lymnaea elodes*. *Ecology* 47:889–906.

Embree, D. G. 1971. The biological control of the winter moth in eastern Canada by introduced parasites. In: *Biological Control*, C. B. Huffaker, ed., pp. 217–26. New York, Plenum Press.

Endler, J. A. 1986. *Natural Selection in the Wild*. Princeton, N.J., Princeton University Press.

Engelmann, M. D. 1961. The role of soil arthropods in the energetics of an old field community. *Ecological Monographs* 31:221–38.

Fabricius, L. 1929. Neue Versuche zur Feststellung des Einflusses von Wurzelwettbewerbs und Lichtenzug des Schirmstandes auf den Jungwuchs. *Forstwissenschaftliches Centralblatt* 51:477–506.

Faeth, S. H. 1980. Invertebrate predation of leaf-miners at low densities. *Ecological Entomology* 5:111–4.

Feeny, P. 1970. Seasonal changes in oak leaf tannins and nutrients as a cause of spring feeding by winter moth caterpillars. *Ecology* 51:565–81.

Fetterolf, P. M. 1983. Effects of investigator activity on ring-billed gull behavior and reproductive performance. *Wilson Bulletin* 95:23–41.

Fisher, R. A. 1960. *The Design of Experiments*, 7th ed. New York, Hafner.

Fisher, R. A., A. S. Corbet, & C. B. Williams. 1943. The relation between the number of species and the number of individuals in a random sample of an animal population. *Journal of Animal Ecology* 12:42–57.

Fonteyn, P. J., & B. E. Mahall. 1981. An experimental analysis of structure in a desert plant community. *Journal of Ecology* 69:883–96.

Fowler, N. 1981. Competition and coexistence in a North Carolina grassland II. The effects of the experimental removal of species. *Journal of Ecology* 69:843–54.

– 1986. The role of competition in plant communities in arid and semiarid regions. *Annual Review of Ecology and Systematics* 17:89–110.

Fowler, N., & J. Antonovics. 1981. Competition and coexistence in a North Carolina grassland. I. Patterns in undisturbed vegetation. *Journal of Ecology* 69:825–41.

Fox, L. R., & B. J. Macauley. 1977. Insect grazing on *Eucalyptus* in response to variation in leaf tannins and nitrogen. *Oecologia (Berlin)* 29:145–62.

Frank, P. W. 1952. A laboratory study of intraspecies and interspecies competition in *Daphnia pulicharia* (Forbes) and *Simocephalus vetulus* (O. F. Müller). *Physiological Zoology* 25:173–204.

– 1957. Coactions in laboratory populations of two species of *Daphnia*. *Ecology* 38:510–19.

Frankland, J. C. 1966. Succession of fungi on decaying petioles of *Pteridium aquilinum*. *Journal of Ecology* 54:41–63.

– 1969. Fungal decomposition of bracken petioles. *Journal of Ecology* 57:25–36.

Frankland, J. C., J. N. Hedger, & M. J. Swift, eds. 1982. *Decomposer Basidiomycetes: Their Biology and Ecology*. Cambridge University Press.

Fretwell, S. D. 1977. The regulation of plant communities by the food chains exploiting them. *Perspectives in Biology and Medicine* 20:169–85.

– 1987. Food chain dynamics: the central theory of ecology? *Oikos* 50:291–301.

Freund, R. J., & R. C. Littell. 1981. *SAS for linear models: a guide to the ANOVA and GLM procedure*. Cary, N.C., SAS Institute.

Friedman, J. 1971. The effect of competition by adult *Zygophyllum dumosum* Bioss. on seedlings of *Artemisia herba-alba* Asso in the Negev desert of Israel. *Journal of Ecology* 59:775–82.

Friedman, J., G. Orshan, & Y. Ziger-Cfir. 1977. Suppression of annuals by *Artemisia herba-alba* in the Negev desert of Israel. *Journal of Ecology* 65:413–26.

Futuyma, D. J. 1976. Food plant specialization and environmental predictability in Lepidoptera. *American Naturalist* 110:285–92.

Gaines, S. D., & J. Roughgarden. 1987. Fish in offshore kelp forests affect recruitment to intertidal barnacle populations. *Science* 235:479–81.

Galindo, C. 1986. Do rodent populations increase when ants are removed? *Ecology* 67:1422–3.

Gause, G. F. 1934. *The Struggle for Existence*. Baltimore, Williams & Wilkins; reprinted 1964 by Hafner, New York.

Gibb, J. 1950. The breeding biology of the great and blue titmice. *Ibis* 92:507–39.

Gibson, C., & M. Visser. 1982. Interspecific competition between two field populations of grass-feeding bugs. *Ecological Entomology* 7:61–7.

Gilinsky, E. 1984. The role of fish predation and spatial heterogeneity in determining benthic community structure. *Ecology* 65:455–68.

Gill, D. E. 1979. Density dependence and homing behavior in adult red-spotted newts *Notophthalmus viridescens* (Rafinesque). *Ecology* 60:800–13.

– 1981. Parasites as model ecological and evolutionary organisms. *Evolution* 35:402–4.

Gilpin, M. E., M. P. Carpenter, & M. J. Pomerantz. 1986. The assembly of a laboratory community: multispecies competition in *Drosophila*. In: *Community Ecology*, J. Diamond & T. J. Case, eds., pp. 23–40. New York, Harper & Row.

Gottfried, B. M., & C. F. Thompson. 1978. Experimental analysis of nest predation in an old-field habitat. *Auk* 95:304–12.

Grant, P. R. 1969. Experimental studies of competitive interaction in a two-species system. I. *Microtus* and *Clethrionomys* species in enclosures. *Canadian Journal of Zoology* 47:1059–82.

– 1972. Interspecific competition among rodents. *Annual Review of Ecology and Systematics* 3:79–106.

Griffin, G. J. 1962. Production of a fungistatic effect by soil microflora in autoclaved soil. *Phytopathology* 52:90–1.

Griffiths, M., W. R. Sistrom, G. Cohen-Bazier, & R. Stanier. 1955. Function of carotenoids in photosynthesis. *Nature* 176:1211–15.

Grubb, P. J. 1982. Control of relative abundance in roadside *Arrhenatheretum*: results of a long-term garden experiment. *Journal of Ecology* 70:845–61.

Gunnarsson, B. 1983. Winter mortality of spruce-living spiders: effect of spider interactions and bird predation. *Oikos* 40:226–33.

Gurevitch, J. 1986. Competition and the local distribution of the grass *Stipa neomexicana*. *Ecology* 67:46–57.

Hairston, N. G. 1949. The local distribution and ecology of the plethodontid salamanders of the southern Appalachians. *Ecological Monographs* 19:47–73.

– 1951. Interspecies competition and its probable influence upon the vertical distribution of Appalachian salamanders of the genus *Plethodon*. *Ecology* 32:266–74.

– 1957. Comment. *Cold Spring Harbor Symposia on Quantitative Biology* 22:327.

– 1959. Species abundance and community organization. *Ecology* 40:404–16.

– 1964. Studies on the organization of animal communities. *Journal of Animal Ecology* [*Supplement*] 33:227–39.

– 1969. On the relative abundance of species. *Ecology* 50:1091–4.

– 1973. Ecology, selection and systematics. *Breviora* 414:1–21.

– 1980a. The experimental test of an analysis of field distributions: competition in terrestrial salamanders. *Ecology* 61:817–26.

– 1980b. Evolution under interspecific competition: field experiments on terrestrial salamanders. *Evolution* 34:409–20.

– 1980c. Species packing in the salamander genus *Desmognathus:* what are the interspecific interactions involved? *American Naturalist* 115:354–66.

– 1981. An experimental test of a guild: salamander competition. *Ecology* 62:65–72.

- 1983. Alpha selection in competing salamanders: experimental verification of an *a priori* hypothesis. *American Naturalist* 122:105–13.
- 1984. Inferences and experimental results in guild structure. In: *Ecological Communities: Conceptual Issues and the Evidence*, D. R. Strong, Jr., D. Simberloff, L. G. Abele & A. B. Thistle, eds., pp. 19–27. Princeton, N.J., Princeton University Press.
- 1986. Species packing in *Desmognathus* salamanders: experimental demonstration of predation and competition. *American Naturalist* 127:266–91.
- 1987. *Community Ecology and Salamander Guilds.* Cambridge University Press.
Hairston, N. G., J. D. Allan, R. K. Colwell, D. J. Futuyma, J. Howell, M. D. Lubin, J. Mathias, & J. H. Vandermeer. 1968. The relationship between species diversity and stability: an experimental approach with protozoa and bacteria. *Ecology* 49:1091–101.
Hairston, N. G., & G. W. Byers. 1954. A study in community ecology: the soil arthropods in a field in southern Michigan. *Contributions From the Laboratory of Vertebrate Biology, The University of Michigan* 64:1–37.
Hairston, N. G., & C. H. Pope. 1948. Geographic variation and speciation in Appalachian salamanders (*Plethodon jordani* group). *Evolution* 2:266–78.
Hairston, N. G., F. E. Smith & L. B. Slobodkin. 1960. Community structure, population control, and competition. *American Naturalist* 94:421–5.
Hairston, N. G., Jr., 1976. Photoprotection by carotenoid pigments in the copepod *Diaptomus nevadensis. Proceedings of the National Academy of Sciences U.S.A.* 73:971–4.
- 1979. The adaptive significance of color polymorphism in two species of *Diaptomus* (Copepoda). *Limnology and Oceanography* 24:15–37.
Hairston, N. G., Jr., K. T. Li, & S. S. Easter. 1982. Fish vision and the detection of planktonic prey. *Science* 218:1240–2.
Hall, D. J., W. E. Cooper, & E. E. Werner. 1970. An experimental approach to the production dynamics and structure of freshwater animal communities. *Limnology and Oceanography* 15:839–938.
Harger, R. J. 1972. Competitive coexistence: maintenance of interacting associations of the sea mussels *Mytilus edulis* and *Mytilus californianus. Veliger* 14:387–410.
Harper, J. E., & J. Webster. 1964. An experimental analysis of the coprophilous fungus succession. *Transactions of the British Mycological Society* 47:511–30.
Harper, J. L. 1969. The role of predation in vegetational diversity. *Brookhaven Symposium in Biology* 22:48–62.
- 1977. *Population Biology of Plants.* New York, Academic Press.
Hassell, M. P. 1980. Foraging strategies, population models and biological control: a case study. *Journal of Animal Ecology* 49:603–28.
Haukioja, E. & P. Niemela. 1979. Birch leaves as a resource for herbivores: seasonal occurrence of increased resistance in foliage after mechanical damage of adjacent leaves. *Oecologia (Berlin)* 39:151–9.
Haven, S. B. 1973. Competition for food between the intertidal gastropods *Acmaea scabra* and *Acmaea digitalis. Ecology* 54:143–51.

Heads, P. A., & J. H. Lawton. 1984. Bracken, ants and extrafloral nectaries. II. The effect of ants on the insect herbivores of bracken. *Journal of Animal Ecology* 53:1015–31.

Heisey, R. M., & C. C. Delwiche. 1985. Allelopathic effects of *Trichostema lanceolatum* (Labiatae) in the California annual grassland. *Journal of Ecology* 73:729–42.

Hering, T. F. 1965. Succession of fungi in the litter of a Lake District oakwood. *Transactions of the British Mycological Society* 48:391–403.

– 1967. Fungal decomposition of oak leaf litter. *Transactions of the British Mycological Society* 50:267–73.

Highton, R. 1972. Distributional interactions among eastern North American salamanders of the genus *Plethodon*. In: *The Distributional History of the Biota of the Southern Appalachians*, P. C. Holt, ed., pp. 138–88. Research Division Monograph 4. Blacksburg, Virginia Polytechnic Institute and State University.

– 1983. A new species of woodland salamander of the *Plethodon glutinosus* group from the southern Appalachian Mountains. *Brimleyana* 9:1–20.

Hikino, H., Y. Ohizumi, & T. Takemoto. 1975. Detoxication mechanism of *Bombyx mori* against exogenous phytoecdysone ecdysterone. *Journal of Insect Physiology* 21:1953–63.

Hils, M. H., & J. L. Vankat. 1982. Species removals from a first-year old-field plant community. *Ecology* 63:705–11.

Högstedt, G. 1980. Prediction and test of the effects of interspecific competition. *Nature* 283:64–6.

Holmes, J. C., & P. W. Price. 1980. Parasite communities: the roles of phylogeny and ecology. *Systematic Zoology* 29:203–13.

Holmes, R. T., J. C. Schultz, & P. Nothnagle. 1979. Bird predation on forest insects: an exclosure experiment. *Science* 206:462–3.

Hora, F. B. 1959. Quantitative experiments on toadstool production in woods. *Transactions of the British Mycological Society* 42:1–14.

Horton, C. C., & D. H. Wise. 1983. The experimental analysis of competition between two syntopic species of orb-web spiders (Araneae: Araneidae). *Ecology* 64:929–44.

Hrbáček, J. 1958. Typologie und Produktivität der teichartigen Gewässer. *Verhandlungen Internationale Vereinigung für theoretische und angewandte Limnologie* 13:394–9.

– 1962. Species composition and the amount of zooplankton in relation to the fish stock. *Rozpravy Čzeskoslovenské Akademie Věd ăda matematických a řpridonich věd* 72:1–114.

Hrbáček, J., M. Dvořakova, V. Kořinek, & L. Procházkva. 1961. Demonstration of the effect of the fish stock on the species composition of zooplankton and the intensity of metabolism of the whole plankton association. *Verhandlungen Internationale Vereinigung für theoretische und angewandte Limnologie* 14:192–5.

Hunt, R., & C. J. Doyle. 1984. Modelling the partitioning of research effort in ecology. *Journal of Theoretical Biology* 111:451–61.

Hurd, L. E., & R. M. Eisenberg. 1984a. Experimental density manipulations of the predator *Tenodera sinensis* (Orthoptera: Mantidae) in an old-field community. I. Mortality, development and dispersal of juvenile mantids. *Journal of Animal Ecology* 53:269–81.

– 1984b. II. The influence of mantids on arthropod community structure. *Journal of Animal Ecology* 53:955–67.

Hurlbert, S. H. 1984. Pseudoreplication and the design of ecological field experiments. *Ecological Monographs* 54:187–211.

Hurlbert, S. H., & M. S. Mulla. 1981. Impacts of mosquitofish (*Gambusia affinis*) predation on plankton communities. *Hydrobiologia* 83:125–51.

Hutchinson, G. E. 1944. Limnological studies in Connecticut. VII. A critical examination of the supposed relationship between phytoplankton periodicity and chemical changes in lake waters. *Ecology* 25:3–26.

– 1957. Concluding remarks. *Cold Spring Harbor Symposia on Quantitative Biology* 22:415–27.

– 1959. Homage to Santa Rosalia *or* Why are there so many kinds of animals? *American Naturalist* 93:145–59.

Ikediugwu, F. E. O., & J. Webster. 1970. Antagonism between *Coprinus heptemerus* and other coprophilus fungi. *Transactions of the British Mycological Society* 54:181–204.

Inouye, R. S. 1980. Density-dependent germination response by seeds of desert annuals. *Oecologia (Berlin)* 46:235–8.

Inouye, R. S., G. S. Byers, & J. H. Brown. 1980. Effects of predation and competition on survivorship, fecundity, and community structure of desert annuals. *Ecology* 61:1344–51.

Jackson, J. B. C., & L. Buss. 1975. Allelopathy and spatial competition among coral reef invertebrates. *Proceedings of the National Academy of Sciences U.S.A.* 72:5160–3.

Jaeger, R. G. 1971a. Competitive exclusion as a factor influencing the distribution of two species of terrestrial salamanders. *Ecology* 52:632–7.

– 1971b. Moisture as a factor influencing the distributions of two species of terrestrial salamanders. *Oecologia (Berlin)* 6:191–207.

Janzen, D. H. 1969. Seed-eaters versus seed size, number, toxicity and dispersal. *Evolution* 23:1–27.

Jones, M., & J. L. Harper. 1987. The influence of neighbours on the growth of trees. I. The demography of buds in *Betula pendula*. II. The fate of buds on long and short shoots in *Betula pendula*. *Proceedings of the Royal Society of London, Biological Sciences* 232:1–33.

Jordan, P. A., D. B. Botkin, & M. L. Wolfe. 1971. Biomass dynamics in a moose population. *Ecology* 52:147–52.

Joule, J., & D. L. Jameson. 1972. Experimental manipulation of population density in three sympatric rodents. *Ecology* 53:651–60.

Juliano, S. J. 1986. A test for competition for food among adult *Brachinus* spp. (Coleoptera: Carabidae). *Ecology* 67:1655–64.

Kerfoot, W. C., & W. R. DeMott. 1980. Foundations for evaluating community interactions: the use of enclosures to investigate coexistence of *Daphnia* and *Bosmina*. In: *Evolution and Ecology of Zooplankton Communities*, W. C. Kerfoot, ed., pp. 725–41. Hanover, N.H., University Press of New England.

Kincaid, W. B., & G. N. Cameron. 1982. Effects of species removal on resource utilization in a Texas rodent community. *Journal of Mammalogy* 63:229–35.

Kitching, J. A., & F. J. Ebling. 1961. The ecology of Lough Ine. XI. The control of algae by *Paracentrotus lividus*. *Journal of Animal Ecology* 30:373–83.

– 1967. Ecological studies at Lough Ine. *Advances in Ecological Research* 4:197–291.

Kitching, J. A., J. F. Sloane, & F. J. Ebling. 1959. The ecology of Lough Ine. VIII. Mussels and their predators. *Journal of Animal Ecology* 28:331–41.

Kneib, R. T. 1986. The role of *Fundulus heteroclitus* in salt marsh trophic dynamics. *American Zoologist* 26:259–69.

– 1987. Predation risk and use of intertidal habitats by young fishes and shrimp. *Ecology* 68:379–86.

Kneib, R. T., & A. E. Stiven. 1982. Benthic invertebrate responses to size and density manipulations of the common mummichog, *Fundulus heteroclitus*, in an intertidal salt marsh. *Ecology* 63:1518–32.

Knipe, D., & C. H. Herbel. 1966. Germination and growth of some semidesert grassland species treated with aqueous extract from creosotebush. *Ecology* 47:775–81.

Korstian, C. F., & T. S. Coile. 1938. Plant competition in forest stands. *Duke University School of Forestry Bulletin* 3:1–125.

Krebs, J. R. 1971. Territory and breeding density in the great tit, *Parus major* L. *Ecology* 52:2–22.

Krieger, R. L., P. P. Feeny, & C. F. Wilkinson. 1971. Detoxication enzymes in the guts of caterpillars: an evolutionary answer to plant defenses? *Science* 172:579–81.

Krzysik, A. J. 1979. Resource allocation, coexistence, and the niche structure of a streamside salamander community. *Ecological Monographs* 49:173–94.

Kulman, H. M. 1971. Effects of insect defoliation on growth and mortality of trees. *Annual Review of Ecology and Systematics* 16:289–324.

Lack, D. 1966. *Population Studies of Birds*. Oxford University Press.

Landa, K., & D. Rabinowitz. 1983. Relative preference of *Arphia sulphurea* (Orthoptera: Acrididae) for sparse and common prairie grasses. *Ecology* 64:392–5.

Lawlor, L. R., & J. Maynard Smith. 1976. The coevolution and stability of competing species. *American Naturalist* 110:79–99.

Lawton, J. H., & D. R. Strong, Jr. 1981. Community patterns and competition in folivorous insects. *American Naturalist* 118:317–38.

Lehman, J. T. 1980. Nutrient recycling as an interface between algae and grazers in freshwater communities. In: *Evolution and Ecology of Zooplankton Communities*, W. C. Kerfoot, ed., pp. 251–62. Hanover, N.H. University Press of New England.

– 1986. Control of eutrophication in Lake Washington. In: *Ecological Knowledge and Problem-solving*, pp. 301–12. Washington, D.C., National Academy Press.

– 1988. Algal biomass unaltered by food-web changes in Lake Michigan. *Nature* 332:537–8.

Lehman, J. T., & C. D. Sandgren. 1978. Documenting a seasonal change from phosphorus to nitrogen limitation in a small temperate lake, and its impact on the population dynamics of *Asterionella*. *Verhandlungen Internationale Vereinigung für theoretische und angewandte Limnologie* 20:375–80.

Lenington, S. 1979. Predators and blackbirds: the "uncertainty principle" in field biology. *Auk* 96:190–2.

Lenski, R. E. 1982. Effects of forest cutting on two *Carabus* species: evidence for competition for food. *Ecology* 63:1211–17.

– 1984. Food limitation and competition: a field experiment with two *Carabus* species. *Journal of Animal Ecology* 53:203–16.

Levins, R. 1968. *Evolution in Changing Environments.* Princeton, N.J., Princeton University Press.

Levins, R., & D. Culver. 1971. Regional coexistence of species and competition between rare species. *Proceedings of the National Academy of Sciences U.S.A.* 68:1246–8.

Lewin, R. 1986. In ecology, change brings stability. *Science* 234:1071–3.

Li, K. T., J. K. Wetterer, & N. G. Hairston, Jr. 1985. Fish size, visual resolution, and prey selectivity. *Ecology* 66:1729–35.

Lockwood, J. L. 1977. Fungistasis in soils. *Biological Reviews of the Cambridge Philosophical Society* 52:1–43.

Löhrl, H. 1977. Nistökologische und ethologische Anspassungsscheinungen bei Höhlenbrütern. *Vogelwarte* Sonderheft:92–101.

Lowe, W. E., & T. R. G. Gray. 1972. Ecological studies on coccoid bacteria in a pine forest soil. I. Classification. *Soil Biology & Biochemistry* 4:459–68.

– 1973. Ecological studies on coccoid bacteria in a pine forest soil. III. Competitive interactions between bacterial strains in soil. *Soil Biology & Biochemistry* 5:463–72.

Loyn, R. H., R. G. Runnalls, G. Y. Forward, & J. Tyers. 1981. Territorial bell miners and other birds affecting populations of insect prey. *Science* 221:1411–3.

Lubchenco, J. 1978. Plant species diversity in a marine intertidal community: importance of herbivore food preference and algal competitive abilities. *American Naturalist* 112:23–39.

Lubchenco, J., B. A. Menge, S. D. Garrity, P. J. Lubchenco, L. R. Ashkenas, S. T. Gaines, R. Emlet, J. Lucas, & S. Strauss. 1984. Structure, persistence, and role of consumers in a rocky intertidal community (Taboguilla Island, Bay of Panama). *Journal of Experimental Marine Biology and Ecology* 78:23–73.

Luecke, C., & W. J. O'Brien. 1981. Phototoxicity and fish predation: selective factors in color morphs in *Heterocope*. *Limnology and Oceanography* 26:454–60.

Lynch, M. 1978. Complex interactions between natural coexploiters – *Daphnia* and *Ceriodaphnia*. *Ecology* 59:552–64.

MacArthur, R. H. 1955. Fluctuations of animal populations, and a measure of community stability. *Ecology* 36:533–6.

- 1957. On the relative abundance of bird species. *Proceedings of the National Academy of Sciences U.S.A.* 43:293–5.
- 1960. On the relative abundance of species. *American Naturalist* 94:25–36.
- 1962. Some generalized theorems of natural selection. *Proceedings of the National Academy of Sciences U.S.A.* 48:1893–7.
- 1966. Note on Mrs. Pielou's comments. *Ecology* 47:1074.
- 1968. The theory of the niche. In: *Population Biology and Evolution*, R. C. Lewontin, ed., pp. 159–76. Syracuse, N.Y., Syracuse University Press.
- 1969. Species packing and what competition minimizes. *Proceedings of the National Academy of Sciences U.S.A.* 64:1369–71.
- 1970. Species packing and competitive equilibrium for many species. *Theoretical Population Biology* 1:1–11.

MacArthur, R. H., & R. Levins. 1967. The limiting similarity, convergence and divergence of coexisting species. *American Naturalist* 101:377–85.

McAuliffe, J. R. 1984. Resource depression by a stream herbivore: effects on distributions and abundances of other grazers. *Oikos* 42:327–33.

McBrien, H., R. Harmsen, & A. Crowder. 1983. A case of insect grazing affecting plant succession. *Ecology* 64:1035–9.

McClure, M. S. 1980. Competition between exotic species: scale insects on hemlock. *Ecology* 61:1391–401.

- 1986. Population dynamics of Japanese hemlock scales: a comparison of endemic and exotic communities. *Ecology* 67:1411–21.

McClure, M. S., & Price, P. W. 1975. Competition and coexistence among sympatric *Erythroneura* leafhoppers (Homoptera: Cicadellidae) on American sycamore. *Ecology* 56:1388–97.

Martin, M. H. 1968. Conditions affecting the distribution of *Mercurialis perennis* L. in certain Cambridgeshire woodlands. *Journal of Ecology* 56:777–93.

Martin, M. M. 1987. *Invertebrate-Microbial Interactions: Ingested Fungal Enzymes in Arthropod Biology.* Ithaca, N.Y., Comstock.

May, R. M. 1972. Will a large complex system be stable? *Nature* 238:413–14.

- 1973. Stability in randomly fluctuating versus deterministic environments. *American Naturalist* 107:621–50.

- 1985. Regulation of populations with nonoverlapping generations by microparasites: a purely chaotic system. *American Naturalist* 125:573–84.

- 1986. The search for patterns in the balance of nature. *Ecology* 67:1115–26.

May, R. M., & W. J. Leonard. 1975. Nonlinear aspects of competition between three species. *Society for Industrial and Applied Mathematics. Journal of Applied Mathematics* 29:243–53.

May, R. M., & R. H. MacArthur. 1972. Niche overlap as a function of environmental variability. *Proceedings of the National Academy of Sciences U.S.A.* 69:1109–13.

Mech, L. D. 1966. The wolves of Isle Royale. *Fauna of the National Parks of the United States, Fauna Series* 7:xiv, 210.

- 1974. A new profile of the wolf. *Natural History* 83:26–31.

Menge, B. A. 1972. Competition for food between two intertidal starfish species and its effect on body size and feeding. *Ecology* 53:635–44.

- 1976. Organization of the New England rocky intertidal community: role of predation, competition, and environmental heterogeneity. *Ecological Monographs* 46:355–93.

Menge, B. A., J. Lubchenco, & L. R. Ashkenas. 1985. Diversity, heterogeneity and consumer pressure in a tropical rocky intertidal community. *Oecologia (Berlin)* 65:394–405.

Menge, B. A., J. Lubchenco, L. R. Ashkenas, & F. Ramsey. 1986a. Experimental separation of effects of consumers on sessile prey in the low zone of a rocky shore in the Bay of Panama: direct and indirect consequences of food web complexity. *Journal of Experimental Marine Biology and Ecology* 100:225–69.

Menge, B. A., J. Lubchenco, S. D. Gaines, & L. R. Ashkenas. 1986b. A test of the Menge-Sutherland model of community organization in a tropical rocky intertidal food web. *Oecologia (Berlin)* 71:75–89.

Miller, T. E., & P. A. Werner. 1987. Competitive effects and responses between plant species in a first-year old-field community. *Ecology* 68:1201–10.

Minot, E. O. 1981. Effects of interspecific competition for food in breeding blue and great tits. *Journal of Animal Ecology* 50:375–85.

Mitchley, J., & P. J. Grubb. 1986. Control of relative abundance of perennials in chalk grassland in southern England. I. Constancy of rank order and results of pot- and field-experiments on the role of inteference. *Journal of Ecology* 74:1139–66.

Montgomery, W. J. 1981. A removal experiment with sympatric populations of *Apodemus sylvaticus* (L.) and *A. flavicollis* (Melchior) (Rodentia: Muridae). *Oecologia (Berlin)* 51:123–32.

Morin, P. J. 1981. Predatory salamanders reverse the outcome of competition among three species of anuran tadpoles. *Science* 212:1284–6.

– 1983a. Predation, competition, and the composition of larval anuran guilds. *Ecological Monographs* 53:119–38.

– 1983b. Competitive and predatory interactions in natural and experimental populations of *Notophthalmus viridescens dorsalis* and *Ambystoma tigrinum*. *Copeia* 1983:628–39.

– 1987. Predation, breeding asynchrony, and the outcome of competition among treefrog tadpoles. *Ecology* 68:675–83.

Morin, P. J., H. M. Wilbur, & R. N. Harris. 1983. Salamander predation and the structure of experimental communities: responses of *Notophthalmus* and microcrustacea. *Ecology* 64:1430–6.

Morris, R. D. 1972. The effects of endrin on *Microtus* and *Peromyscus*. II. Enclosed field populations. *Canadian Journal of Zoology* 50:885–96.

Morris, R. D., & P. R. Grant. 1972. Experimental studies of competitive interaction in a two-species system. IV. *Microtus* and *Clethrionomys* species in a single enclosure. *Journal of Animal Ecology* 41:275–90.

Morrow, P. A., T. E. Bellas, & T. Eisner. 1976. *Eucalyptus* oils in the defensive oral discharge of Australian sawfly larvae (Hymenoptera: Pergidae). *Oecologia (Berlin)* 24:193–206.

Morrow, P. A., & V. C. LaMarche, Jr. 1978. Tree ring evidence for chronic insect suppression of productivity in subalpine *Eucalyptus*. *Science* 201:1244–6.

Muller, C. H., W. H. Muller, & B. L. Haines. 1964. Volatile growth inhibitors produced by aromatic shrubs. *Science* 143:471–3.

Munger, J. C. 1984. Long-term yield from harvester ant colonies: Implications for horned lizard foraging strategy. *Ecology* 65:1077–86.

Munger, J. C., & J. H. Brown. 1981. Competition in desert rodents: an experiment with semipermeable exclosures. *Science* 211:510–12.

Murdoch, W. W. 1966. "Community structure, population control, and competition" – a critique. *American Naturalist* 100:219–26.

Neill, W. E. 1981. Impact of *Chaoborus* predation upon the structure and dynamics of a crustacean zooplankton community. *Oecologia (Berlin)* 48:164–77.

– 1984. Regulation of rotifer densities by crustacean zooplankton in an oligotrophic montane lake in British Columbia. *Oecologia (Berlin)* 61:175–81.

Neill, W. E., & A. Peacock. 1980. Breaking the bottleneck: interactions of invertebrate predators and nutrients in oligotrophic lakes. In: *Evolution and Ecology of Zooplankton Communities*, W. C. Kerfoot, ed., pp. 715–24. Hanover, N.H., University Press of New England.

Nicholson, A. J. 1958. The self-adjustment of populations to change. *Cold Spring Harbor Symposia on Quantitative Biology* 22:153–73.

Nicholson, P. B., K. L. Bocock, & O. W. Heal. 1966. Studies on the decomposition of the faecal pellets of a millipede (*Glomeris marginata* [Villers]). *Journal of Ecology* 54:755–66.

Nolan, V. 1978. The ecology and behavior of the prairie warbler *Dendrioca discolor*. *Ornithological Monographs* 26:i–xxii, 1–595.

Oksanen, L. 1988. Ecosystem organization: mutualism and cybernetics or plain Darwinian struggle for existence? *American Naturalist* 131:424–44.

Otte, D. 1975. Plant preference and plant succession. A consideration of evolution and plant preference in *Schistocerca*. *Oecologia (Berlin)* 18:129–44.

Pacala, S., & J. Roughgarden. 1982. Resource partitioning and interspecific competition in two-species insular *Anolis* lizard communities. *Science* 217:444–6.

– 1985. Population experiments with the *Anolis* lizards of St. Maarten and St. Eustatius. *Ecology* 66:129–41.

Paine, R. T. 1966. Food web complexity and species diversity. *American Naturalist* 100:65–75.

– 1974. Intertidal community structure: experimental studies on the relationship between a dominant competitor and its principal predator. *Oecologia (Berlin)* 15:93–120.

– 1984. Ecological determinism in the competition for space. *Ecology* 65:1339–48.

– 1988. On food webs: road maps of interactions or the grist for theoretical development? *Ecology* 69:1648–54.

Paine, R. T., & R. L. Vadas. 1969. The effects of grazing by sea urchins, *Strongylocentrotus* spp. on benthic algal populations. *Limnology and Oceanography* 14:710–19.

Paris, O. H. 1963. The ecology of *Armadillidium vulgare* (Isopoda: Oniscoidea) in California grassland: food, enemies, and weather. *Ecological Monographs* 33:1–22.

Parker, M. A. 1985. Size-dependent herbivore attack and the demography of an arid grassland shrub. *Ecology* 66:850–60.

Parker, M. A., & R. B. Root. 1981. Insect herbivores limit habitat distribution of a native composite, *Machaeranthera canescens*. *Ecology* 62:1390–2.

Patten, B. C., & E. P. Odum. 1981. The cybernetic nature of ecosystems. *American Naturalist* 118:886–95.

Peckarsky, B. L. 1979. Biological interactions as determinants of distributions of benthic invertebrates within the substrate of stony streams. *Limnology and Oceanography* 24:59–68.

– 1981. Reply to comment by Sell. *Limnology and Oceanography* 26:982–7.

Perrins, C. M. 1965. Population fluctuations and clutch-size in the great tit, *Parus major* L. *Journal of Animal Ecology* 34:601–47.

Peters, R. H. 1976. Tautology in evolution and ecology. *American Naturalist* 110:1–12.

Peterson, C. H., & S. V. Andre. 1980. An experimental analysis of interspecific competition among marine filter feeders in a soft-sediment environment. *Ecology* 61:129–39.

Pianka, E. R. 1967. On lizard species diversity: North American flatland deserts. *Ecology* 48:333–51.

– 1971. Lizard species diversity in the Kalahari Desert. *Ecology* 52:1024–9.

– 1975. Niche relations of desert lizards. In: *Ecology and Evolution of Communities*, M. L. Cody & J. M. Diamond, eds., pp. 292–314. Cambridge, Mass., Harvard University Press.

Pianka, E. R., R. B. Huey, & L. R. Lawlor. 1978. Niche segregation in desert lizards. In: *Analysis of Ecological Systems*, D. J. Horn, G. R. Stairs, & R. D. J. Mitchell, eds., pp. 67–115. Columbus, Ohio State University Press.

Pielou, E. C., & A. N. Arnason. 1966. Correction to one of MacArthur's species-abundance formulas. *Science* 151:592.

Pigott, C. D. 1975. Experimental studies on the influence of climate on the geographical distribution of plants. *Weather* 30:82–90.

Pigott, C. D., & K. Taylor. 1964. The distribution of some woodland herbs in relation to the supply of nitrogen and phosphorus in the soil. *Journal of Ecology [Supplement]* 52:175–85.

Pimm, S. L. 1982. *Food Webs.* London, Chapman & Hall.

Platt, J. R. 1964. Strong inference. *Science* 146:347–53.

Polis, G. A., & S. J. McCormick. 1987. Intraguild predation and competition among desert scorpions. *Ecology* 68:332–43.

Pontin, A. J. 1961. Population stabilization and competition between the ants *Lasius flavus* (F.) and *L. niger* (L.). *Journal of Animal Ecology* 30:47–54.

– 1969. Experimental transplantation of nest-mounds of the ant *Lasius flavus* (F.) in a habitat containing also *L. niger* (L.) and *Myrmica scabrinodis* Nyl. *Journal of Animal Ecology* 38:747–54.

Pope, C. H. 1928. Some plethodontid salamanders from North Carolina and Kentucky with the description of a new race of *Leurognathus*. *American Museum Novitates* 306:1–19.

Preston, F. W. 1948. The commonness, and rarity, of species. *Ecology* 29:254–83.

Putwain, P. D., & J. L. Harper. 1970. Studies in the dynamics of plant populations. III. The influence of associated species on populations of *Rumex acetosa* L. and *R. acetosella* L. in grassland. *Journal of Ecology* 58:251–64.

Quinn, J. F., & G. R. Robinson. 1987. The effects of experimental subdivision on flowering plant diversity in a California annual grassland. *Journal of Ecology* 75:837–56.

Rausher, M. D. 1981. Host plant selection by *Battus philenor* butterflies: the roles of predation, nutrition, and plant chemistry. *Ecological Monographs* 51:1–20.

Rausher, M. D., & P. Feeny. 1980. Herbivory, plant density, and plant reproductive success: the effect of *Battus philenor* on *Aristolochia reticulata*. *Ecology* 61:905–17.

Reice, S. R. 1984. The impact of disturbance frequency on the structure of a lotic riffle community. *Verhandlungen Internationale Vereinigung für theoretische und angewandte Limnologie* 22:1906–10.

– 1985. Experimental disturbance and the maintenance of species diversity in a stream community. *Oecologia (Berlin)* 67:90–7.

Rickets, E. W., & J. Calvin. 1968. *Between Pacific Tides*, 4th ed., revised by J. W. Hedgepeth. Stanford University Press.

Riechert, S. E. 1981. The consequences of being territorial: spiders, a case study. *American Naturalist* 117:871–92.

Riechert, S. E., & C. R. Tracy. 1975. Thermal balance and prey availability: bases for a model relating web-site characteristics to spider reproductive success. *Ecology* 56:265–84.

Robertson, J. H. 1947. Responses of range grasses to different intensities of competition with sagebrush (*Artemisia tridentata* Nutt.). *Ecology* 28:1–16.

Root, R. B. 1967. The niche exploitation pattern of the blue-gray gnatcatcher. *Ecological Monographs* 37:317–50.

Rosenthal, G. A., & D. H. Janzen, eds. 1979. *Herbivores: Their Interaction with Secondary Plant Metabolites*. New York, Academic Press.

Rosenzweig, M. L., Z. Abramsky, B. Kotler, & W. Mitchell. 1985. Can interaction coefficients be determined from census data? *Oecologia (Berlin)* 66:194–8.

Roth, V. L. 1981. Constancy in the size ratios of sympatric species. *American Naturalist* 118:394–404.

Roughgarden, J. 1972. Evolution of niche width. *American Naturalist* 106:683–718.

– 1974. Species packing and the competition function with illustrations from coral reef fish. *Theoretical Population Biology* 5:163–86.

– 1976. Resource partitioning among competing species: a coevolutionary approach. *Theoretical Population Biology* 9:388–424.

– 1979. *Theory of Population Genetics and Evolutionary Ecology: An Introduction*. New York, Macmillan.

– 1986. A comparison of food-limited and space-limited communities. In:

Community Ecology, J. Diamond & T. J. Case, eds., pp. 492–516. New York, Harper & Row.

Roughgarden, J., D. Heckel, & E. R. Fuentes. 1983. Coevolutionary theory and the biogeography and community structure of *Anolis*. In: *Lizard Ecology: Studies of a Model Organism*, R. B. Huey, E. R. Pianka, & T. W. Schoener, eds., pp. 371–410. Cambridge, Mass., Harvard University Press.

Sale, P. 1977. Maintenance of high diversity in coral reef fish communities. *American Naturalist* 111:337–59.

Schindler, D. W. 1974. Eutrophication and recovery in experimental lakes: implications for lake management. *Science* 184:897–9.

Schoener, T. W. 1974. Resource partitioning in ecological communities. *Science* 185:27–39.

– 1976. Alternatives to Lotka–Volterra competition: models of intermediate complexity. *Theoretical Population Biology* 10:309–33.

– 1978. Effect of density-restricted food encounter on some single-level competition models. *Theoretical Population Biology* 13:365–81.

– 1982. The controversy over interspecific competition. *American Scientist* 70:586–95.

– 1983. Field experiments on interspecific competition. *American Naturalist* 122:240–85.

– 1985. Some comments on Connell's and my reviews of field experiments on interspecific competition. *American Naturalist* 125:730–40.

– 1986. Overview: kinds of ecological communities – ecology becomes pluralistic. In: *Community Ecology*, J. Diamond & T. J. Case, eds., pp. 467–79. New York, Harper & Row.

Schroder, G. D., & M. L. Rosenzweig. 1975. Perturbation analysis of competition and overlap in habitat utilization between *Dipodomys ordii* and *Dipodomys merriami*. *Oecologia (Berlin)* 19:9–28.

Scriber, J. M., & P. Feeny. 1979. Growth of herbviorous caterpillars in relation to feeding specialization and to the growth form of their food plants. *Ecology* 60:829–50.

Sell, D. W. 1981. Comment on "Biological interactions as determinants of distributions of benthic invertebrates within the substrate of stony streams" (Peckarsky). *Limnology and Oceanography* 26:981–2.

Shapiro, J., & D. I. Wright. 1984. Lake restoration by biomanipulation: Round Lake, Minnesota, the first two years. *Freshwater Biology* 14:371–83.

Shure, D. J. 1971. Insecticide effects on early succession in an old field ecosystem. *Ecology* 52:271–9.

Siegel, S. 1956. *Non-parametric Statistics for the Behavioral Sciences*. New York, McGraw-Hill.

Sih, A., P. Crowley, M. McPeek, J. Petranka, & K. Strohmeier. 1985. Predation, competition, and prey communities: a review of field experiments. *Annual Review of Ecology and Systematics* 16:269–311.

Simberloff, D. 1970. Taxonomic diversity of island biotas. *Evolution* 24:22–47.

– 1974. Equilibrium theory of island biogeography and ecology. *Annual Review of Ecology and Systematics* 5:161–82.

– 1980. A succession of paradigms in ecology: essentialism to materialism and probabilism. *Synthese* 43:3–39.

– 1983. Competition theory, hypothesis-testing, and other community ecological buzzwords. *American Naturalist* 122:626–35.

Simberloff, D., & W. Boecklen. 1981. Santa Rosalia reconsidered: size ratios and competition. *Evolution* 35:1206–28.

Simberloff, D., & E. F. Connor. 1981. Missing species combinations. *American Naturalist* 118:215–39.

Skinner, G. J., & J. B. Whittaker. 1981. An experimental investigation of interrelationships between the wood-ant (*Formica rufa*) and some tree-canopy herbivores. *Journal of Animal Ecology* 50:313–26.

Slobodkin, L. B. 1986. The role of minimalism in art and science. *American Naturalist* 127:257–65.

Slobodkin, L. B., F. E. Smith, & N. G. Hairston. 1967. Regulation in terrestrial ecosystems, and the implied balance of nature. *American Naturalist* 101:109–24.

Smith, D. C. 1981. Competitive interactions of the striped plateau lizard (*Sceloporus virgatus*) and the tree lizard (*Urosaurus ornatus*). *Ecology* 62:679–87.

– 1983. Factors controlling tadpole populations of the chorus frog (*Pseudacris triseriata*) on Isle Royale, Michigan. *Ecology* 64:501–10.

Smith, F. E. 1952. Experimental methods in population dynamics, a critique. *Ecology* 33:441–50.

– 1961. Density dependence in the Australian thrips. *Ecology* 42:403–07.

– 1963a. Density-dependence. *Ecology* 44:220.

– 1963b. Population dynamics in *Daphnia magna* and a new model for population growth. *Ecology* 44:651–63.

Sokal, R. R., & F. J. Rohlf. 1981. *Biometry*, 2nd ed. San Francisco, W. H. Freeman.

Sousa, W. P. 1979. Experimental investigations of disturbance and ecological succession in a rocky intertidal community. *Ecological Monographs* 49:227–54.

Southerland, M. T. 1986a. Behavioral interactions among four species of the salamander genus *Desmognathus*. *Ecology* 67:175–81.

– 1986b. Coexistence of three congeneric salamanders: the importance of habitat and body size. *Ecology* 67:721–8.

Spiller, D. A. 1984. Competition between two spider species: experimental field study. *Ecology* 65:909–19.

Stewart-Oaten, A., W. W. Murdoch, & K. R. Parker. 1986. Environmental impact assessment: "pseudoreplication" in time? *Ecology* 67:929–40.

Stiling, P. D. 1980. Competition and coexistence among *Eupteryx* leafhoppers (Hemiptera: Cicadellidae) occurring on stinging nettles (*Urtica dioica*). *Journal of Animal Ecology* 49:793–805.

Stimson, J. 1970. Territorial behavior of the owl limpet *Lottia gigantea*. *Ecology* 51:113–18.

– 1973. The role of territory in the ecology of the owl limpet *Lottia gigantea*. *Ecology* 54:1020–30.

Stiven, A. E., & E. J. Kuenzler. 1979. The response of two salt marsh molluscs, *Littorina irrorata* and *Geukensia demissa*, to field manipulations of density and *Spartina* litter. *Ecological Monographs* 49:151–71.

Strong, D. R., Jr. 1982. Harmonious coexistence of hispine beetles on *Heliconia* in experimental and natural communities. *Ecology* 63:1039–49.

– 1984. Exorcising the ghost of competition past from insect communities. In: *Ecological Communities: Conceptual Issues and the Evidence*, D. R. Strong, D. Simberloff, L. G. Abele, & A. B. Thistle, eds., pp. 28–41. Princeton, N.J., Princeton University Press.

Strong, D. R., J. H. Lawton, & Sir Richard Southwood. 1984a. *Insects on Plants. Community Patterns and Mechanisms*, Cambridge, Mass., Harvard University Press.

Strong, D. R., Jr., D. Simberloff, L. G. Abele, & A. B. Thistle, eds. 1984b. *Ecological Communities: Conceptual Issues and the Evidence*. Princeton, N.J., Princeton University Press.

Sugihara, G. 1980. Minimal community structure: an explanation of species abundance patterns. *American Naturalist* 116:770–87.

Sunderland, K. D., & S. L. Sutton. 1980. A serological study of arthropod predation on woodlice in a dune grassland ecosystem. *Journal of Animal Ecology* 49:987–1004.

Sutherland, J. P. 1974. Multiple stable points in natural communities. *American Naturalist* 108:859–73.

– 1978. Functional roles of *Schizoporella* and *Styela* in the fouling community at Beaufort, North Carolina. *Ecology* 59:257–64.

Sutherland, J. P., & R. H. Carlson. 1977. Development and stability of the fouling community at Beaufort, North Carolina. *Ecological Monographs* 47:425–46.

Tansley, A. G., & R. S. Adamson. 1925. Studies of the vegetation of the English chalk. III. The chalk grasslands of the Hampshire–Sussex border. *Journal of Ecology* 13:117–223.

– 1953. *The British Islands and Their Vegetation*. Cambridge University Press.

Tansley, A. G., & R. S. Adamson. 1925. Studies of the vegetation of the English chalk. III. The chalk grasslands of the Hampshire–Sussex border. *Journal of Ecology* 13:117–223.

Taylor, P. R., & M. M. Littler. 1982. The roles of compensatory mortality, physical disturbance, and substrate retention in the development and organization of a sand-influenced, rocky intertidal community. *Ecology* 63:135–46.

Tilley, S. G. 1968. Size–fecundity relationships and their evolutionary implications in five desmognathine salamanders. *Evolution* 22:806–16.

Tilman, G. D. 1984. Plant dominance along an experimental nutrient gradient. *Ecology* 65:1445–53.

Tinkle, D. W. 1982. Results of experimental density manipulation in an Arizona lizard community. *Ecology* 63:57–65.

Toft, C. A. 1986. Communities of species with parasitic life-styles. In: *Community Ecology*, J. Diamond & T. J. Case, eds., pp. 445–63. New York, Harper & Row.

Toumey, J. W., & R. Kienholz. 1931. Trenched plots under forest canopies. *Yale University School of Forestry Bulletin* 30:1–31.

Tribe, H. T. 1966. Interactions of soil fungi on cellulose film. *Transactions of the British Mycological Society* 49:457–66.

Tuomi, J., P. Niemela, E. Haukioja, S. Siren, & S. Neuvonen. 1984. Nutrient stress: an explanation for plant anti-herbivore responses to defoliation. *Oecologia (Berlin)* 61:208–10.

Turelli, M. 1978. A reexamination of stability in randomly varying versus deterministic environments with comments on the stochastic theory of limiting similarity. *Theoretical Population Biology* 13:244–67.

Underwood, A. J., & E. J. Denley 1984. Paradigms, explanations, and generalizations in models for the structure of intertidal communities on rocky shores. In: *Ecological Communities: Conceptual Issues and the Evidence*, D. S. Strong, Jr., D. Simberloff, L. G. Abele, & A. B. Thistle, eds., pp. 151–80. Princeton, N.J., Princeton University Press.

Vandermeer, J. H. 1969. The competitive structure of communities: an experimental approach with protozoa. *Ecology* 50:362–71.

Vandermeer, J. H., & R. H. MacArthur. 1966. A reformulation of alternative (b) of the broken-stick model of species abundance. *Ecology* 47:139–40.

Varley, G. C. 1957. Ecology as an experimental science. *Journal of Animal Ecology* 26:251–61.

Varley, G. C., G. R. Gradwell, & M. P. Hassell. 1974. *Insect Population Ecology. An Analytical Approach*. Berkeley, University of California Press.

Vaughan, G. L., & A. M. Jungreis. 1977. Insensitivity of lepidopteran tissues to ouabain: physiological mechanisms for protection from cardiac glycosides. *Journal of Insect Physiology* 23:585–9.

von Ende, C. N., & D. O. Dempsey. 1981. Apparent exclusion of the cladoceran *Bosmina longirostris* by invertebrate predator *Chaoborus americanus*. *American Midland Naturalist* 105:240–8.

Wallace, J. W., & R. L. Mansell, eds. 1976. *Biochemical Interaction Between Plants and Insects. Recent Advances in Phytochemistry*, vol. 10. New York, Plenum Press.

Wallner, W. E., & G. S. Walton. 1979. Host defoliation: a possible determinant of gypsy moth population quality. *Annals of the Entomological Society of America* 72:62–7.

Werner, E. E., & D. J. Hall. 1974. Optimal foraging and the size selection of prey by the bluegill sunfish (*Lepomis macrochirus*). *Ecology* 55:1042–52.

– 1976. Niche shifts in sunfishes: experimental evidence and significance. *Science* 191:404–6.

– 1977. Competition and habitat shift in two sunfishes (Centrarchidae). *Ecology* 58:869–76.

– 1979. Foraging efficiency and habitat switching in competing sunfishes. *Ecology* 60:256–64.

Wertheim, A. 1985. *The Intertidal Wilderness*. San Francisco, Sierra Club Books.

Westmoreland, D., & L. B. Best. 1985. The effect of disturbance on mourning dove nesting success. *Auk* 102:774–80.

Whitford, W. G., & M. Bryant. 1979. Behavior of a predator and its prey: the horned lizard (*Phrynosoma cornutum*) and harvester ants (*Pogonomyrmex* spp.). *Ecology* 60:686–94.

Whitford, W. G., S. Dick-Peddie, D. Walters, & J. A. Ludwig. 1978. Effects of shrub defoliation on grass cover and rodent species in a Chihuahuan desert ecosystem. *Journal of Arid Environments* 1:237–42.

Whittaker, J. B. 1982. The effect of grazing by a chrysomelid beetle, *Gastrophysa viridula*, on growth and survival of *Rumex crispus* on a shingle bank. *Journal of Ecology* 70:291–6.

Wicklow, D. T., & G. C. Carroll, eds. 1981. *The Fungal Community. Its Organization and Role in the Ecosystem.* New York, Marcel Dekker.

Wiens, J. A. 1977. On competition and variable environments. *American Scientist* 65:590–7.

Wilbur, H. M. 1987. Regulation of structure in complex systems: experimental temporary pond communities. *Ecology* 68:1437–52.

Wilbur, H. M., & R. A. Alford. 1985. Priority effects in experimental pond communities: responses of *Hyla* to *Bufo* and *Rana. Ecology* 66:1106–14.

Wilbur, H. M., P. J. Morin, & R. N. Harris. 1983. Salamander predation and the structure of experimental communities: anuran responses. *Ecology* 64:1423–9.

Williams, A. H. 1981. An analysis of competitive interactions in a patchy back-reef environment. *Ecology* 62:1107–20.

Williams, J. B., & G. O. Batzli. 1979a. Competition among bark-foraging birds in central Illinois: experimental evidence. *Condor* 81:122–32.

– 1979b. Interference competition and niche shifts in the bark-foraging guild in central Illinois. *Wilson Bulletin* 91:400–11.

Willis, E. O. 1973. Survival rates for visited and unvisited nests of bicolored antbirds. *Auk* 90:263–7.

Wilson, E. O. 1975. *Sociobiology. The New Synthesis.* Cambridge, Mass., Harvard University Press.

Wise, D. H. 1975. Food limitation of the spider *Linyphia marginata*: experimental field studies. *Ecology* 56:637–46.

– 1979. Effects of an experimental increase in prey abundance upon the reproductive rates of two orb-weaving spider species (Araneae: Araneidae). *Oecologia (Berlin)* 41:289–300.

– 1981. Inter- and intraspecific effects of density manipulations upon females of two orb-weaving spiders (Araneae: Araneidae). *Oecologia (Berlin)* 48:252–6.

Woodin, S. A. 1978. Refuges, disturbance, and community structure: a marine soft-bottom example. *Ecology* 59:274–84.

– 1981. Disturbance and community structure in a shallow water sand flat. *Ecology* 62:1052–66.

Woodward, F. I. 1975. The climatic control of the altitudinal distribution of *Sedum rosea* (L.) Scop. and *S. telephium* L. II. The analysis of plant growth in controlled environments. *New Phytologist* 74:335–48.

Woodward, F. I., & C. D. Pigott. 1975. The climatic control of the altitudinal distribution of *Sedum rosea* (L.) Scop. and *S. telephium* L. I. Field observations. *New Phytologist* 74:323–34.

Wright, J. M. 1956. Production of gliotoxin in soils. *Nature* 177:896.

Yodzis, P. 1986. Competition, mortality, and community structure. In: *Community Ecology*, J. Diamond & T. J. Case, eds., pp. 480–91. New York, Harper & Row.

– 1988. The indeterminacy of ecological interactions as perceived through perturbation experiments. *Ecology* 69:508–15.

Zaret, T. M. 1980. *Predation and Freshwater Communities.* New Haven, Yale University Press.

Name index

352

Subject index

355